Celebrate a New Tradition!

Relish 474 dishes sure to become heartwarming favorites in your home.

A trusted recipe exchange for decades, *Taste of Home* is synonymous with delicious home-cooked feasts, delightful desserts and everyday comfort food at its best. This is where good cooks gather to learn new secrets, create meal plans and share the dishes their own families love with one another.

As you page through this new edition of *Taste of Home Annual Recipes,* you'll discover 474 recipes in addition to personal notes describing what makes each dish unique.

This cookbook includes an entire year's worth of recipes from our magazine, plus hundreds of bonus dishes never before seen in *Taste of Home.* Featured chapters include:

- **Meal Planner**
  We show you how to get creative in the kitchen with smart ideas for leftovers, dinners that start with simple homemade sauces, and a master cookie mix you'll reach for time and again.
- **Holiday & Seasonal Celebrations**
  From Easter and Christmas menus to ideas for game nights and fireside gatherings, there's always a tasty way to celebrate.
- **Cook It Fast or Slow**
  Each of the recipes here includes cooking instructions for both the Instant Pot® and the slow cooker.

You'll also enjoy six icons that make the most of kitchen time:

= Finished in 30 minutes or less

= Lower in calories, fat and sodium

= Pressure-cooked recipe

= Made in a slow cooker

= Uses 5 or fewer ingredients (excluding water, salt, pepper and canola/olive oil)

= Includes freezing/reheating instructions

With the specialties found in *Taste of Home Annual Recipes,* serving hearty meals, gathering the family for memorable menus and creating new traditions have never been easier.

SAVOR THE FLAVORS

Discover wonderful takes on beloved classics when you cook with *Taste of Home Annual Recipes.* From just five ingredients, Rosemary Turkey Breast (top) is a lovely, good-for-you main dish perfect for potlucks and small holiday gatherings. Take a bite out of summer with luscious Huckleberry Cheese Pie (center). And meet your new favorite lunch for two—Colleen Delawder's Brown Sugar Bacon BLT Sandwiches (bottom). They're piled high with veggies and flavorful bacon on brioche buns!

CEYLON CHICKEN CURRY & RICE NOODLE SOUP PAGE 39

Taste of Home

1610 N. 2nd St., Suite 102,
Milwaukee WI 53212-3906

Executive Editor: Mark Hagen
Senior Art Director: Raeann Thompson
Senior Editor: Christine Rukavena
Art Director: Maggie Conners
Graphic Designer: Arielle Anttonen
Deputy Editor, Copy Desk: Dulcie Shoener

Cover Photographer: Dan Roberts
Set Stylist: Melissa Franco
Food Stylist: Shannon Norris

Pictured on front cover: Maple-Gingerroot Vegetables, p. 292; Spiral Ham with Cranberry Glaze, p. 288; Holiday Pretzel Salad, p. 211.
Pictured on back cover: Duo Tater Bake, p. 292; Pumpkin Egg Braid, p. 291.

International Standard Book Number:
D978-1-62145-767-1
U978-1-62145-768-8
International Standard Serial Number:
1094-3463

Component Number:
D 117400104H
U 117400106H

Printed in U.S.A.
1 3 5 7 9 10 8 6 4 2

Contents

Appetizers & Beverages............**4**

Salads & Dressings **20**

Soups & Sandwiches...............**34**

Quick Fixes..................................**48**

Main Dishes **62**

Meal Planner **90**

Cook It Fast or Slow..............**108**

Side Dishes & Condiments............................**124**

Breads, Rolls & Muffins........**144**

Breakfast & Brunch...............**158**

Cookies, Bars & Candies..... **174**

Cakes & Pies............................. **190**

Just Desserts **208**

Potluck Pleasers **228**

Holiday & Seasonal Celebrations......................... **244**

Cook's Quick Reference **304**

Indexes....................................... **306**

BLUE-RIBBON
BEEF NACHOS
PAGE 7

Appetizers & Beverages

Let's get this party started! Turn to this chapter for incredible dips, fruity and fun drinks, and hot snacks. You're sure to find a new favorite.

BEST OF THE BEST DISHES

Roasted Brussels Sprouts with Sriracha Aioli p. 9

Frozen Coconut Margarita p. 11

Hot Shrimp Dip p. 13

Samosas p. 17

Chili Queso Dip p. 18

ZUCCHINI PIZZA FRITTERS

These colorful fritters are the perfect after-school snack. Plus, they're freezer-friendly! Add a sauce—or several sauces.
—Marissa Allen, Frisco, TX

PREP: 20 min. • **COOK:** 15 min./batch
MAKES: 12 servings

- **2 medium zucchini**
- **1 medium potato, peeled**
- **½ small onion**
- **1 large egg, lightly beaten**
- **2 Tbsp. all-purpose flour**
- **½ cup shredded Parmesan cheese**
- **1 tsp. garlic powder**
- **1 tsp. onion powder**
- **½ tsp. dried parsley flakes**
- **½ tsp. salt**
- **1 tsp. pepper**
- **Optional: Marinara sauce, tzatziki sauce or ranch dressing**

1. Preheat air fryer to 400°. Coarsely grate zucchini, potato and onion. Place grated vegetables on a double thickness of cheesecloth or a clean tea towel; bring up corners and squeeze out any liquid. Transfer to a large bowl; stir in the egg, flour, Parmesan, garlic powder, onion powder, parsley, salt and pepper. Form mixture into ¼-cup patties.

2. In batches, place patties in a single layer onto greased tray in air-fryer basket. Cook until lightly browned, 15-20 minutes. Serve with sauce if desired.

Oven method: Preheat oven to 400°. Place fritters on a parchment-lined baking sheet. Bake until golden brown, 15-20 minutes.

1 FRITTER: *44 cal., 1g fat (1g sat. fat), 18mg chol., 164mg sod., 5g carb. (1g sugars, 1g fiber), 3g pro.*

ZUCCHINI PIZZA FRITTERS

POTATO LATKE FUNNEL CAKES

This savory funnel cake incorporates mashed potatoes and ranch seasoning into the dough. It's delicious. Just try it and you'll see!
—Chanie Apfelbaum, Brooklyn, NY

PREP: 30 min. • **COOK:** 5 min./batch
MAKES: 15 servings

- **1½ cups sour cream or plain Greek yogurt**
- **1 envelope ranch salad dressing mix (1 oz.), divided**
- **2 lbs. russet potatoes (about 3 large), peeled and cubed**
- **3 Tbsp. all-purpose flour**
- **1 large egg**
- **½ to 1 tsp. kosher salt**
- **½ to 1 tsp. pepper**
- **½ cup 2% milk, optional**
- **Oil for deep-fat frying**
- **Grated Parmesan cheese, optional**

1. Stir together sour cream and 1 Tbsp. ranch dressing mix; refrigerate, covered, until serving.

2. Place potatoes in a large saucepan; add water to cover. Bring to a boil. Reduce heat; cook, uncovered, until just tender, 15-20 minutes. Drain potatoes; return to pan and stir over low heat for 1 minute to dry. Mash potatoes; stir in flour, egg, salt, pepper, remaining ranch dressing mix and, if desired, milk until smooth.

3. In a deep cast-iron or electric skillet, heat oil to 350°. Transfer potato mixture to a pastry bag fitted with a small round pastry tip. Pipe batter in a spiral motion. Fry until golden brown, 1-2 minutes on each side. Drain on paper towels. Sprinkle with Parmesan cheese if desired; serve warm with dip.

1 CAKE: *165 cal., 11g fat (3g sat. fat), 18mg chol., 231mg sod., 14g carb. (1g sugars, 1g fiber), 3g pro.*

BLUE-RIBBON BEEF NACHOS

(SHOWN ON PAGE 4)

Chili powder and sassy salsa work together to season a mixture of ground beef and refried beans that's sprinkled with green onions, tomatoes and ripe olives.
—Diane Hixon, Niceville, FL

TAKES: 20 min. • **MAKES:** 6 servings

- **1 lb. ground beef**
- **1 small onion, chopped**
- **1 can (16 oz.) refried beans**
- **1 jar (16 oz.) salsa**
- **1 can (6 oz.) pitted ripe olives, chopped**
- **½ cup shredded cheddar cheese**
- **1 green onion, chopped**
- **2 Tbsp. chili powder**
- **1 tsp. salt**
- **Tortilla chips**
- **Optional: Sliced ripe olives, chopped green onions and diced tomatoes**

In a large skillet, cook the beef and onion over medium heat until meat is no longer pink; crumble the beef; drain. Stir in the next 7 ingredients; heat through. Serve over tortilla chips. If desired, top with olives, onions and tomatoes.

1 SERVING: *294 cal., 14g fat (6g sat. fat), 53mg chol., 1353mg sod., 19g carb. (5g sugars, 9g fiber), 20g pro.*

THE BEST HUMMUS

Hummus is my go-to appetizer when I need something quick, easy and impressive. Over the years I've picked up a number of tricks that make this the best hummus you'll ever have.
—James Schend, Pleasant Prairie, WI

PREP: 25 min. • **COOK:** 20 min. + chilling
MAKES: 1½ cups

- **1 can (15 oz.) garbanzo beans or chickpeas, rinsed and drained**
- **½ tsp. baking soda**
- **¼ cup fresh lemon juice**
- **1 Tbsp. minced garlic**
- **½ tsp. kosher salt**
- **½ tsp. ground cumin**
- **½ cup tahini**
- **2 Tbsp. extra virgin olive oil**
- **¼ cup cold water**
- **Optional: Olive oil, roasted garbanzo beans, toasted sesame seeds and ground sumac**

1. Place garbanzo beans in a large saucepan; add water to cover by 1 in. Gently rub beans together to loosen outer skins. Pour off water and any skins that are floating. Repeat 2-3 times until no skins float to the surface; drain. Return to saucepan; add baking soda and enough water to cover by 1 in. Bring to a boil; reduce heat. Simmer, uncovered, until beans are very tender and just starting to fall apart, 20-25 minutes.
2. Meanwhile, in a blender, process lemon juice, garlic and salt until almost a paste. Let stand 10 minutes; strain, discarding solids. Stir in cumin. In a small bowl, stir together tahini and olive oil.
3. Add beans to blender; add cold water. Loosely cover and process until completely smooth. Add lemon mixture and process. With blender running, slowly add tahini mixture, scraping sides as needed. Adjust seasoning with additional salt and cumin if desired.
4. Transfer mixture to a serving bowl; cover and refrigerate at least 30 minutes. If desired, top with additional olive oil and assorted toppings.

¼ CUP: *250 cal., 19g fat (3g sat. fat), 0 chol., 361mg sod., 15g carb. (2g sugars, 5g fiber), 7g pro.*

TEST KITCHEN TIP

This hummus recipe has a great thickness to it, but if you find the texture too thin, an easy fix is to pop it into the fridge to set. If the hummus is still not as thick as you like, blend in more chickpeas or tahini.

PHILLY CHEESESTEAK EGG ROLLS

PHILLY CHEESESTEAK EGG ROLLS

These cheesesteak-inspired egg rolls are dangerous. Served with chili sauce, they're absolutely swoonworthy.
—Marissa Allen, Frisco, TX

PREP: 35 min. • **COOK:** 5 min./batch • **MAKES:** 15 egg rolls

- **1 lb. beef ribeye steak, thinly sliced**
- **1 Tbsp. butter**
- **1 medium green pepper, seeded and thinly sliced**
- **1 medium onion, thinly sliced**
- **¾ cup 2% milk**
- **½ cup shredded provolone cheese**
- **1 oz. Velveeta**
- **1 tsp. Worcestershire sauce**
- **½ tsp. garlic powder**
- **½ tsp. salt**
- **½ tsp. pepper**
- **15 egg roll wrappers**
- **Oil for deep-fat frying**
- **⅓ cup sweet chili sauce**

1. In a large skillet, cook steak slices in butter over medium-high heat until browned, 4-6 minutes. Add pepper and onion; cook until tender, 3-4 minutes. Reduce heat to medium-low; stir in milk, provolone and Velveeta. Cook, stirring constantly, until cheese melts, about 3 minutes. Remove from heat; add Worcestershire, garlic powder, salt and pepper; cool.
2. Brush edges of an egg roll wrapper with water. Place 2 Tbsp. beef mixture in the center; fold bottom corner over filling. Fold sides over filling toward center; roll up tightly to seal. Repeat with remaining wrappers and filling.
3. In an electric skillet or deep-fat fryer, heat 1 in. canola oil to 375°. Fry egg rolls until golden brown, about 2 minutes on each side. Drain on paper towels. Serve hot with sweet chili sauce.
1 EGG ROLL: *259 cal., 13g fat (4g sat. fat), 28mg chol., 440mg sod., 24g carb. (4g sugars, 1g fiber), 10g pro.*

5i

LEMON, GINGER & TURMERIC INFUSED WATER

This flavored water is a fantastic pick-me-up when you feel a little under the weather or find yourself in need of a health boost. Studies indicate that turmeric is chock full of antioxidants. What a wonderful zero-calorie idea.
—Taste of Home *Test Kitchen*

PREP: 5 min. + chilling • **MAKES:** about 2 qt.

- **1 Tbsp. ground turmeric**
- **4 slices fresh gingerroot**
- **½ lemon, sliced**
- **2 qt. water**

Combine all ingredients in a large glass carafe or pitcher. Cover and refrigerate 12-24 hours.

LEMON, GINGER & TURMERIC INFUSED WATER

ROASTED BRUSSELS SPROUTS WITH SRIRACHA AIOLI

5i

ROASTED BRUSSELS SPROUTS WITH SRIRACHA AIOLI

This dish constantly surprises you—it's crispy, easy to eat and totally shareable and yet it's a vegetable! The recipe is also gluten-free, dairy-free and paleo, and can be vegan if you use vegan mayo.
—Molly Winsten, Medford, MA

PREP: 20 min. • **COOK:** 20 min. • **MAKES:** 8 servings

- **1 lb. fresh Brussels sprouts, trimmed and halved**
- **2 Tbsp. olive oil**
- **2 to 4 tsp. Sriracha chili sauce, divided**
- **½ tsp. salt, divided**
- **½ tsp. pepper, divided**
- **½ cup mayonnaise**
- **2 tsp. lime juice**
- **1 Tbsp. lemon juice**

1. Preheat oven to 425°. Place Brussels sprouts on a rimmed baking sheet. Drizzle with oil and 1 tsp. chili sauce; sprinkle with ¼ tsp. salt and ¼ tsp. pepper. Toss to coat. Roast until crispy, 20-25 minutes.
2. Meanwhile, mix mayonnaise, lime juice, and the remaining 1-3 tsp. chili sauce, ¼ tsp. salt and ¼ tsp. pepper. Drizzle lemon juice over Brussels sprouts before serving with the aioli.
4 HALVES WITH 1 TBSP. SAUCE: *146 cal., 14g fat (2g sat. fat), 1mg chol., 310mg sod., 6g carb. (2g sugars, 2g fiber), 2g pro.*

5i

PEPPER JELLY HOGS IN A BLANKET

We are addicted to these grown-up pigs in a blanket! There's so much flavor for bite-sized appetizers.
—Becky Hardin, St. Peters, MO

PREP: 20 min. • **BAKE:** 15 min. • **MAKES:** 2 dozen

- **1 tube (8 oz.) refrigerated crescent rolls**
- **1 pkg. (12 oz.) fully cooked spicy sausage links, cut into 1-in. slices**
- **¼ cup pepper jelly**
- **Stone-ground mustard**

1. Preheat oven to 375°. Coat 24 mini muffin cups with cooking spray.
2. Unroll crescent dough and separate into 2 rectangles; press perforations to seal. Cut dough lengthwise into ¾-in. strips. Wrap a strip of dough around a sausage slice, gently stretching dough as you roll. Place cut side up in a muffin cup; repeat with remaining dough and sausage. Spoon pepper jelly over each slice.
3. Bake until golden brown, 12-15 minutes. Let stand 5 minutes before removing to a serving plate. Serve warm with mustard.
1 APPETIZER: *65 cal., 3g fat (0 sat. fat), 11mg chol., 152mg sod., 7g carb. (3g sugars, 0 fiber), 3g pro.*

PEPPER JELLY HOGS IN A BLANKET

Margarita Mania

Whether you love 'em on the rocks or blended to perfection, these tart and tangy refreshers turn any smiley, sunny day into a fiesta.

To make salted rims, moisten rim of cocktail glass with lime wedge. Sprinkle salt onto a plate; dip rim into salt. Fill glass with ice.

SHAKEN MARGARITA

Pour ingredients into a cocktail shaker. Fill with ice; cover and shake until frost forms on outside of shaker, 15-20 seconds. Strain into prepared glass. Garnish if desired.

Classic Margarita
1½ oz. blanco tequila;
1 oz. Triple Sec;
½ oz. freshly squeezed lime juice.
Garnish: Lime wedge.

Melon Margarita
1½ oz. blanco tequila;
1½ oz. melon liqueur;
½ oz. freshly squeezed lime juice.
Garnish: Honeydew melon balls.

Caribbean Margarita
1½ oz. blanco tequila;
1 oz. blue curacao;
½ oz. freshly squeezed lime juice.
Garnish: Starfruit slice.

Amaretto Margarita
1½ oz. blanco tequila;
1 oz. Triple Sec;
½ oz. freshly squeezed lime juice;
½ oz. amaretto.
Garnish: Maraschino cherry.

Grapefruit Sunset Margarita
1½ oz. blanco tequila;
1 oz. Triple Sec;
1 oz. ruby red grapefruit juice.
Garnish: 1 tsp. grenadine syrup; grapefruit slice.

Blueberry-Mint Frozen Margarita
1 cup frozen unsweetened blueberries; 1½ oz. blanco tequila; 1 oz. Triple Sec; ½ oz. freshly squeezed lime juice; 4 fresh mint leaves.
Garnish: Sugared rim; mint sprig.

FROZEN MARGARITA

Prepare glass as desired. Pour ingredients into a blender; cover and process until smooth. Pour into glass. Garnish if desired.

Raspberry-Ginger Frozen Margarita
1 cup frozen unsweetened raspberries; 1½ oz. blanco tequila; 1 oz. ginger liqueur; 1 oz. raspberry liqueur; ½ oz. freshly squeezed lime juice.
Garnish: Sugared rim; strawberry; crystallized ginger slice.

Frozen Coconut Margarita
1 cup crushed ice; 2 oz. cream of coconut; 1½ oz. blanco tequila; 1 oz. Triple Sec; ½ oz. freshly squeezed lime juice.
Garnish: Chopped toasted shredded coconut on rim; toasted coconut slices.

Strawberry-Basil Frozen Margarita
1 cup frozen unsweetened sliced strawberries; 1½ oz. blanco tequila; 1 oz. Triple Sec; ½ oz. freshly squeezed lime juice; 4 fresh basil leaves.
Garnish: Sugared rim; strawberry; basil leaf.

Sriracha-Mango Frozen Margarita
1 cup frozen mango chunks; 1½ oz. blanco tequila; 1 oz. mango nectar; ½ oz. freshly squeezed lime juice; ½ tsp. Sriracha chili sauce.
Garnish: Sugared rim; mango slice.

TOMATO GALETTE WITH BASIL PESTO & FETA

TOMATO GALETTE WITH BASIL PESTO & FETA

This is a simple flaky butter pie crust filled with ripe heirloom or Roma tomatoes, pesto and feta cheese. The whole thing is baked as a rustic tart and is topped with Parmesan. It's a delicious way to use summer cherry tomatoes.
—Kate Wood, Selma, AL

PREP: 25 min. • **COOK:** 35 min. + cooling
MAKES: 6 servings

- **2 Roma tomatoes, sliced ⅛ in. thick**
- **1 pint grape tomatoes, halved**
- **¾ tsp. salt**
- **2 Tbsp. prepared pesto**
- **1 Tbsp. mayonnaise**
- **Dough for single-crust pie**
- **½ cup crumbled feta cheese, divided**
- **1 tsp. Italian seasoning**
- **½ tsp. pepper**
- **1 large egg**
- **1 Tbsp. water**
- **1 Tbsp. grated Parmesan cheese**
- **Fresh basil leaves, optional**

1. Place tomatoes on a double layer of paper towels; sprinkle with salt. Cover with additional paper towels. Meanwhile, in a small bowl, stir together pesto and mayonnaise. Preheat oven to 375°. On a floured sheet of parchment, roll dough into a 12-in. circle. Transfer to a baking sheet or pizza stone.
2. Spread pesto mixture over crust to within 2 in. of edge; top with ¼ cup feta. Arrange tomato slices over feta; arrange cherry tomatoes on top, cut sides up. Sprinkle with remaining ¼ cup feta, Italian seasoning and pepper. Fold crust edge over filling, pleating as you go and leaving center uncovered. In a small bowl, whisk egg and water; brush edge of crust with egg wash and sprinkle with Parmesan.
3. Bake until the crust is golden brown, 35-40 minutes. Cool for 10 minutes before slicing. If desired, top with basil before serving.

1 PIECE: *315 cal., 21g fat (12g sat. fat), 77mg chol., 693mg sod., 24g carb. (3g sugars, 2g fiber), 7g pro.*

DOUGH FOR SINGLE-CRUST PIE (9 IN.)
Combine 1¾ cups all-purpose flour, 1½ tsp. sugar and ¼ tsp. salt; cut in 6 Tbsp. cold butter and ⅓ cup shortening until crumbly. Gradually add 4-5 Tbsp. ice water, tossing with a fork until dough holds together when pressed. Wrap and refrigerate 1 hour.

5i

BLACKBERRY SHRUB

Making a shrub recipe is a creative way to use up extra fruit all the way through Labor Day. We were inspired by sampling the house-made shrubs at a restaurant in California. They are as colorful and refreshing as summer drinks should be.
—Gina Nistico, Denver, CO

PREP: 10 min. • **COOK:** 20 min. + chilling
MAKES: 2 cups

- **1½ cups fresh or frozen blackberries, crushed**
- **1 cinnamon stick (about 3 in.)**
- **1 cup cider vinegar**
- **1½ cups sugar**
- **½ cup water**

SERVING SUGGESTION
Optional: Ice cubes, sparkling water and fresh blackberries

1. Place blackberries and cinnamon stick in a sterilized pint jar. Bring vinegar just to a boil; pour over fruit, leaving ¼-in. headspace. Center lid on jar; screw on band until fingertip tight. Refrigerate for 1 week.
2. Strain vinegar mixture through a fine-mesh strainer into another sterilized pint jar. Press solids to extract juice; discard remaining fruit.
3. Bring sugar and water to a boil. Reduce heat; simmer until sugar is dissolved. Cool slightly. Stir into vinegar mixture; shake well. Store in the refrigerator up to 2 weeks.
4. To serve, drink 1-2 Tbsp. or add to a glass of ice, top with sparkling water and garnish with fresh blackberries.

2 TBSP. BLACKBERRY SHRUB SYRUP: *83 cal., 0 fat (0 sat. fat), 0 chol., 1mg sod., 20g carb. (20g sugars, 1g fiber), 0 pro.*

PEACHY-KEEN HALLOUMI FRITTERS

Use up the season's juicy, sun-ripened peaches in this corn fritter recipe filled with gooey Halloumi cheese and sweet onion. These fritters are decadent and slightly sweet, and homegrown herbs add a fresh taste. The addition of prosciutto makes this recipe feel fancy with little effort.
—Chainey Kuykendall, Richmond, VA

PREP: 25 min. + standing • **COOK:** 5 min./batch
MAKES: 2½ dozen

- **1¼ cups cornmeal**
- **2 Tbsp. minced fresh basil**
- **1 tsp. baking powder**
- **1 tsp. salt**
- **½ tsp. pepper**
- **1 large egg plus 1 large egg white**
- **¾ cup 2% milk**
- **2 Tbsp. honey**
- **1 cup finely chopped sweet onion**
- **½ cup diced Halloumi cheese**
- **Oil for deep-fat frying**
- **1 medium peach, chopped**
- **4 thin slices prosciutto, cut into thin strips**

1. In a large bowl, whisk the first 5 ingredients. In another bowl, whisk egg, egg white, milk and honey until blended. Add to dry ingredients, stirring just until moistened. Fold in onion and cheese; let stand 10 minutes.
2. In an electric skillet or deep fryer, heat oil to 375°. Stir batter. Drop batter by tablespoonfuls, a few at a time, into hot oil. Fry until golden brown, 2-3 minutes on each side. Drain on paper towels. (Keep cooked fritters warm on a baking sheet in a 200° oven until all fritters are made.)
3. Serve fritters with chopped peach and prosciutto; sprinkle with additional pepper.
1 FRITTER: *71 cal., 4g fat (1g sat. fat), 10mg chol., 159mg sod., 8g carb. (2g sugars, 0 fiber), 2g pro.*

HOT SHRIMP DIP

I came across a similar recipe that called for crawfish, and it sounded delicious. We don't have a lot of crawfish available in my area and I'm a big fan of shrimp, so I used that instead. This dip has become a family favorite, and I can guarantee no leftovers!
—Jill Burwell, Renton, WA

TAKES: 25 min. • **MAKES:** 4 cups

- **½ cup butter, cubed**
- **8 green onions, thinly sliced**
- **1 small green pepper, finely chopped**
- **1 lb. peeled and deveined cooked shrimp (61-70 per lb.)**
- **1 jar (4 oz.) diced pimientos, drained**
- **2 garlic cloves, minced**
- **2 tsp. Creole seasoning**
- **1 pkg. (8 oz.) cream cheese, cubed**
- **Chopped fresh parsley**
- **French bread baguette slices or assorted crackers**

1. In a Dutch oven, melt butter over medium heat. Add the green onions and green pepper; cook and stir until tender, 3-4 minutes. Add shrimp, pimientos, garlic and Creole seasoning. Cook and stir until heated through.
2. Stir in cream cheese until melted; sprinkle with parsley. Serve with baguette slices or crackers.
¼ CUP: *136 cal., 11g fat (7g sat. fat), 73mg chol., 217mg sod., 2g carb. (1g sugars, 0 fiber), 7g pro.*

HOT SHRIMP DIP

5i

TAJIN LIMEADE

Tajin is a blend of chile peppers, salt and lime. I sprinkle it on a lot of food, but I've found it's really delicious in limeade.
—Amanda Phillips, Portland, OR

PREP: 20 min. + freezing • **MAKES:** 8 servings

- **3 Tbsp. Tajin seasoning, divided**
- **1 cup plus 1 Tbsp. sugar, divided**
- **4 cups water, divided**
- **3 cups fresh lime juice**
- **Lime wedges, optional**

1. Sprinkle 2 Tbsp. Tajin seasoning evenly in the bottom of 2 ice cube trays (16 ice cubes each). Fill with water and freeze.
2. In a saucepan, stir together 1 cup sugar and 1 cup water over medium-high heat. Bring to a boil, stirring frequently, until sugar dissolves. Remove from heat and let cool to room temperature.
3. In a large pitcher or bowl, stir together lime juice, sugar mixture and remaining 3 cups water. On a small plate, combine remaining 1 Tbsp. Tajin seasoning and 1 Tbsp. sugar. Moisten rims of 8 tall glasses with lime wedges; dip rims in Tajin mixture. Place 3-4 ice cubes in each glass; fill with limeade. Garnish with lime wedges if desired.
1 CUP: *126 cal., 0 fat (0 sat. fat), 0 chol., 749mg sod., 34g carb. (28g sugars, 0 fiber), 0 pro.*

TAJIN LIMEADE

SPINACH PUFFS

SPINACH PUFFS

I love warm appetizers, and these bite-sized spinach puffs are full of cheese and creamy goodness.
—Marissa Allen, Frisco, TX

PREP: 20 min. • **COOK:** 20 min. • **MAKES:** 2 dozen

- **1 pkg. (17.3 oz.) frozen puff pastry, thawed**
- **1 pkg. (10 oz.) frozen chopped spinach, thawed and squeezed dry**
- **4 oz. cream cheese, softened**
- **½ cup shredded mozzarella cheese**
- **¼ cup crumbled feta cheese**
- **2 large eggs, divided use**
- **2 garlic cloves, minced**
- **½ tsp. pepper**
- **¼ tsp. salt**

1. Preheat oven to 400°. Unfold puff pastry; cut each sheet into 12 sections. Place in greased mini muffin cups, pressing gently onto bottoms and up sides, allowing corners to point up.
2. In a large bowl, stir together spinach, cream cheese, mozzarella, feta, 1 egg, garlic, pepper and salt. Spoon 1 Tbsp. into each cup. Bring pastry corners together and pinch to seal. In a small bowl, beat remaining egg. Brush over pastry edges. Bake until puffed and golden brown, about 20 minutes.
1 PUFF: *136 cal., 8g fat (3g sat. fat), 23mg chol., 147mg sod., 12g carb. (0 sugars, 2g fiber), 3g pro.*

BEST DEVILED EGGS

Herbs lend amazing flavor to these deviled eggs, which truly are the best you can make!
—Jesse and Anne Foust, Bluefield, WV

TAKES: 25 min. • **MAKES:** 2 dozen

- **½ cup mayonnaise**
- **2 Tbsp. 2% milk**
- **1 tsp. dried parsley flakes**
- **½ tsp. dill weed**
- **½ tsp. minced chives**
- **½ tsp. ground mustard**
- **¼ tsp. salt**
- **¼ tsp. paprika**
- **⅛ tsp. garlic powder**
- **⅛ tsp. pepper**
- **12 hard-boiled large eggs**
- **Minced fresh parsley and additional paprika**

In a small bowl, combine the first 10 ingredients. Cut the eggs lengthwise in half; remove yolks and set whites aside. In another bowl, mash yolks; add to mayonnaise mixture, mixing well. Spoon or pipe filling into egg whites. Sprinkle with parsley and additional paprika. Refrigerate until serving.

1 STUFFED EGG HALF: *73 cal., 6g fat (1g sat. fat), 108mg chol., 81mg sod., 0 carb. (0 sugars, 0 fiber), 3g pro.*

BEST DEVILED EGGS

MULLED WINE MARGARITAS

MULLED WINE MARGARITAS

These are so fun, festive and unique. This favorite holiday beverage has complex flavors and warms the soul. It's the ultimate Christmas cocktail!
—Becky Hardin, St. Peters, MO

PREP: 20 min. • **COOK:** 1 hour • **MAKES:** 8 servings (1½ qt.)

- **8 whole peppercorns**
- **8 whole allspice**
- **4 whole cloves**
- **3 cinnamon sticks (3 in.)**
- **1 bottle (750 ml) malbec or other dry red wine**
- **2 cups apple cider or juice**
- **½ cup packed dark brown sugar**
- **¼ cup agave nectar**
- **¼ cup tequila (preferably Exotico Reposado)**
- **¼ cup orange liqueur**
- **¼ cup orange juice**
- **1 large navel orange, sliced**
- **Optional: Orange slices, sea salt, sugar and orange zest**

1. In a Dutch oven, combine peppercorns, allspice, cloves and cinnamon sticks over medium heat until fragrant, about 2 minutes. Add wine, cider, brown sugar, agave, tequila, orange liqueur, orange juice and orange slices. Bring just to a simmer (do not boil). Reduce heat; simmer gently, covered, until flavors are blended, about 1 hour, stirring to dissolve sugar. Strain, discarding solids. Return mixture to pan; keep warm on low until serving.

2. If desired, using orange slices, moisten rims of glasses. Set aside orange slices for garnish. Combine salt, sugar and zest on a plate; hold each glass upside down and dip rim into salt. Pour warmed margaritas into prepared glasses. Garnish with orange slices. Serve immediately.

¾ CUP: *195 cal., 0 fat (0 sat. fat), 0 chol., 14mg sod., 32g carb. (29g sugars, 0 fiber), 0 pro.*

RED LENTIL HUMMUS WITH BRUSSELS SPROUT HASH

Instead of chickpeas, this spicy dip uses lentils to create a hearty, healthy appetizer. The Brussels sprout topping makes this feel more special than plain hummus, but you can serve it without the topping, too.
—Carolyn Manning, Seattle, WA

PREP: 20 min. • **COOK:** 15 min.
MAKES: 10 servings

- **1 cup dried red lentils, rinsed**
- **¼ cup tahini**
- **2 Tbsp. lemon juice**
- **1 Tbsp. olive oil**
- **3 garlic cloves, halved**
- **1 tsp. ground cumin**
- **1 tsp. curry powder**
- **½ tsp. salt**
- **½ tsp. ground ginger**
- **⅛ tsp. white pepper**
- **⅛ tsp. cayenne pepper**

BRUSSELS SPROUTS HASH

- **1 Tbsp. olive oil**
- **1 shallot, minced**
- **½ lb. fresh Brussels sprouts, thinly sliced**
- **1 cup canned diced tomatoes**
- **¼ tsp. salt**
- **¼ tsp. crushed red pepper flakes**
- **Assorted fresh vegetables**

1. Place lentils in a small saucepan; add water to cover. Bring to a boil; reduce heat. Simmer, covered, until lentils are tender, 12-15 minutes. Drain; cool 10 minutes. Transfer to a food processor. Add tahini, lemon juice, oil, garlic and seasonings. Process until smooth.
2. For hash, in a large skillet, heat oil over medium heat. Add shallot; cook and stir until tender, 3-4 minutes. Add Brussels sprouts and tomatoes; cook until sprouts are crisp-tender, 12-15 minutes longer. Remove from heat; stir in salt and pepper flakes. Spread hummus on a serving plate; top with hash. Serve with vegetables.

1 SERVING: *154 cal., 7g fat (1g sat. fat), 0 chol., 226mg sod., 18g carb. (2g sugars, 4g fiber), 7g pro.* **Diabetic exchanges:** *1½ fat, 1 starch.*

RED LENTIL HUMMUS WITH BRUSSELS SPROUT HASH

SALTY DOG SANGRIA

Mix up grapefruit vodka, ginger ale, grapefruit juice, a little wine and simple syrup and what do you get? A perfectly refreshing and beautiful sipper fit for any holiday or special gathering.
—Becky Hardin, St. Peters, MO

PREP: 30 min. + chilling
MAKES: 16 servings (3 qt.)

- **1 cup sugar**
- **1 cup water**
- **2 bottles (750 ml each) rose wine**
- **2 cups ruby red grapefruit juice**
- **1 can (12 oz.) ginger ale**
- **1 cup ruby red grapefruit-flavored vodka**
- **Grapefruit slices**
- **Coarse sea salt and grated grapefruit zest**

1. In a small saucepan, bring sugar and water to a boil. Reduce heat; simmer 10 minutes. Cool completely. Transfer to a large pitcher. Stir in the wine, juice, ginger ale, vodka and grapefruit slices. Refrigerate at least 2 hours.
2. Using water, moisten the rims of 16 wine glasses. Mix salt and grapefruit zest on a plate; hold each glass upside down and dip rim into salt mixture. Set aside. Discard remaining salt mixture on plate. Serve sangria over ice in prepared glasses.

¾ CUP: *186 cal., 0 fat (0 sat. fat), 0 chol., 2mg sod., 24g carb. (15g sugars, 0 fiber), 0 pro.*

WARM STRAWBERRY FONDUE

You need only a handful of ingredients to fix this spring fondue. Use grapes, bananas, strawberries, pineapple wedges and angel food cake cubes as dippers.
—Sharon Mensing, Greenfield, IA

TAKES: 15 min. • **MAKES:** 1½ cups

- 1 **pkg. (10 oz.) frozen sweetened sliced strawberries, thawed**
- ¼ **cup half-and-half cream**
- 1 **tsp. cornstarch**
- ½ **tsp. lemon juice**
- **Angel food cake cubes and fresh fruit**

1. In a food processor, combine the strawberries, cream, cornstarch and lemon juice; cover and process until smooth.
2. Pour into saucepan. Bring to a boil; cook and stir for 2 minutes or until slightly thickened. Transfer to a fondue pot or 1½-qt. slow cooker; keep warm. Serve with cake and fruit.
2 TBSP.: *30 cal., 1g fat (0 sat. fat), 3mg chol., 3mg sod., 7g carb. (6g sugars, 0 fiber), 0 pro.*

SAMOSAS

SAMOSAS

Samosas are one of my family's absolute favorites. These crispy dough pockets are stuffed with potatoes and peas, then air-fried to give them a healthier twist. They'd make a perfect starter, side dish or buffet food for your next party.
—Soniya Saluja, Chantilly, VA

PREP: 20 min. + rising • **COOK:** 15 min./batch
MAKES: 1 dozen

- 2 **cups all-purpose flour**
- 3 **Tbsp. ghee or canola oil**
- ½ **tsp. salt**
- ½ **tsp. caraway seeds**
- ¾ **cup cold water**

FILLING
- 5 **medium potatoes, peeled and chopped**
- 6 **Tbsp. canola oil, divided**
- 1 **cup fresh or frozen peas, thawed**
- 1 **tsp. minced fresh gingerroot**
- 1 **tsp. garam masala**
- ½ **tsp. cumin seeds**
- ½ **tsp. salt**
- **Optional: Fennel seed, crushed coriander seeds, caraway seeds or amchur (dried mango powder)**

1. In a large bowl, combine flour, ghee, salt and caraway seeds until mixture resembles bread crumbs. Gradually stir in enough water to form a firm dough. Turn onto a lightly floured surface; knead until smooth and elastic, 6-8 minutes. Cover and let rest for 1 hour.
2. Place potatoes in a large saucepan and cover with water. Bring to a boil. Reduce heat and cook until just tender, 8-10 minutes; drain. Set aside to cool slightly. In a large skillet, heat 3 Tbsp. oil over medium heat. Add potatoes and cook until potatoes start to cling to the skillet, about 5 minutes. Stir in peas, ginger, garam masala, cumin seeds and salt; cook until heated through, about 2 minutes. Stir in optional ingredients as desired. Set aside.
3. Divide dough into 6 pieces. Roll 1 piece of dough into a 10x6-in. oval. Cut dough in half. Moisten straight edge with water. Bring 1 corner of half moon up to meet the other corner of the half moon, forming a cone. Pinch seam to seal. Fill with 3-4 Tbsp. potato mixture. Moisten curved edge of dough with water; fold over top of filling and and press seam to seal. Gently press the bottom of the samosa to flatten slightly. Repeat with remaining dough and filling.
4. Preheat air fryer to 350°. Brush the samosas with the remaining 3 Tbsp. oil. In batches, arrange in a single layer without touching in the air-fryer basket. Cook until golden brown, about 15 minutes.
1 SAMOSA: *280 cal., 14g fat (3g sat. fat), 10mg chol., 203mg sod., 33g carb. (1g sugars, 3g fiber), 5g pro.*

TEST KITCHEN TIP

Samosas are savory fried pastries traditionally stuffed with spices, potatoes and other veggies. They're a common street food in the northern and western regions of India. Serve the samosas with a chutney for dipping.

GARLIC MOZZARELLA BREAD BITES

GARLIC MOZZARELLA BREAD BITES

These little balls of deliciousness are ridiculously easy to make and insanely tasty! They are the perfect low-carb, keto-friendly, gluten-free appetizer, snack or side dish. To make them extra cheesy, sprinkle the tops with more mozzarella cheese after taking them out of the oven the second time. Return them to the oven until the cheese is melted. Serve with your favorite low-carb dipping sauce.

—Anna Bowden, Littleton, CO

TAKES: 30 min. • **MAKES:** 1 dozen

- 1½ **cups shredded part-skim mozzarella cheese**
- 3 **oz. cream cheese, softened**
- 1 **large egg, room temperature**
- 1 **cup almond flour**
- ½ **tsp. onion powder**
- ½ **tsp. garlic powder**
- ½ **tsp. salt**
- ½ **tsp. pepper**

TOPPING

- 2 **Tbsp. unsalted butter, melted**
- 1½ **tsp. minced garlic**
- **Prepared pesto, optional**

1. Preheat oven to 400°. In a microwave-safe bowl, combine mozzarella cheese and cream cheese; microwave, covered, on high until melted, 30-60 seconds. Stir until smooth. Stir in egg. In another bowl, mix almond flour and seasonings; stir into cheese mixture until combined (mixture will be thick).

2. With wet hands, shape into 12 balls. Place 1 in. apart on a parchment-lined baking sheet. Bake for 12 minutes. Combine butter and garlic; brush over rolls. Bake until light brown, 2-4 minutes longer. Let cool 5 minutes before serving. If desired, serve with pesto.

1 APPETIZER: *144 cal., 12g fat (5g sat. fat), 37mg chol., 224mg sod., 4g carb. (1g sugars, 1g fiber), 6g pro.*

CHILI QUESO DIP

I've had this recipe for more than 42 years but I've updated it from time to time. This is an easy party favorite, and everyone loves the taquito dippers.

—Joan Hallford, North Richland Hills, TX

PREP: 20 min. • **COOK:** 2 hours
MAKES: 10 cups

- 1 **lb. ground beef**
- 1 **lb. bulk pork sausage**
- 1 **small onion, chopped**
- 2 **jalapeno peppers, seeded and finely chopped**
- 1 **garlic clove, minced**
- 1 **can (15 oz.) chili con carne (without beans)**
- 1 **can (10¾ oz.) reduced-fat reduced-sodium condensed cream of mushroom soup, undiluted**
- 1 **can (10 oz.) diced tomatoes and green chiles, drained**
- 1 **jar (4 oz.) diced pimientos, drained**
- 1 **pkg. (2 lbs.) Velveeta, cubed**
- **Prepared taquitos, tortilla chips or corn chips**

1. In a large skillet, cook beef and sausage with onion, jalapenos and garlic over medium-high heat until meat is no longer pink, 5-7 minutes, crumbling meat. Using a slotted spoon, transfer to a 5-qt. slow cooker. Stir in chili, soup, tomatoes, pimientos and cheese.

2. Cook, covered, on low until heated through, 2-3 hours, stirring halfway through cooking. Serve warm with taquitos.

NOTE: Wear disposable gloves when cutting hot peppers; the oils can burn skin. Avoid touching your face.

¼ CUP DIP: *147 cal., 11g fat (5g sat. fat), 39mg chol., 473mg sod., 4g carb. (2g sugars, 0 fiber), 8g pro.*

READER REVIEW

"This dip is outstanding! The only change I made was using my own homemade chili, since I had it on hand. Definite keeper!"

—CYNANDTOM, TASTEOFHOME.COM

SMASHED OLIVES

My best friend and I came up with this recipe to bring the wonderful tastes of Spain back with us. When you are finished with the olives, use the flavored olive oil for a chicken or shrimp marinade.
—Tiffani Warner, Fort Leavenworth, KS

PREP: 20 min. + marinating • **MAKES:** 2 cups

- **2 cups mixed pitted olives**
- **¾ to 1 cup olive oil**
- **½ small navel orange, cut in half**
- **½ medium onion, cut into wedges**
- **3 to 4 fresh rosemary sprigs**
- **6 to 8 fresh thyme sprigs**
- **5 garlic cloves, peeled**
- **2 bay leaves**
- **1 Tbsp. gin, optional**

1. In a large bowl, gently mash olives to break skins. Add the next 7 ingredients and, if desired, gin. Toss to coat; cover and refrigerate for up to 24 hours.
2. To serve, drain olives, reserving oil for another use; discard the bay leaves.

¼ CUP: *162 cal., 16g fat (2g sat. fat), 0 chol., 555mg sod., 5g carb. (1g sugars, 1g fiber), 1g pro.*

GREEN TOMATO SALSA

I dreamed up this fresh salsa so I could use all the green tomatoes from the garden when it started to get cold.
—Vanessa Moon, Tucson, AZ

PREP: 20 min. + standing • **COOK:** 10 min. **MAKES:** 6 cups

- **1 medium green pepper**
- **1 serrano pepper**
- **5 medium green tomatoes or 5 large tomatillos, husked**
- **1 medium onion, chopped**
- **2 garlic cloves, minced**
- **⅓ cup lime juice**
- **2 Tbsp. olive oil**
- **4 tsp. agave nectar**
- **1 tsp. coarsely ground pepper**
- **½ tsp. salt**
- **3 Tbsp. fresh cilantro leaves**
- **1 medium ripe avocado, peeled, pitted and quartered**
- **Tortilla chips**

1. Preheat broiler. Place peppers on a foil-lined baking sheet. Broil 3-4 in. from heat until skins blister, about 5 minutes. With tongs, rotate peppers a quarter turn. Broil and rotate until all sides are blistered and blackened. Immediately place in a bowl; let stand, covered, 20 minutes.
2. Using tongs, place tomatoes, a few at a time, in a pot of boiling water for 5 minutes. Remove tomatoes; cool slightly. Peel and finely chop tomatoes; place in a large bowl.
3. Remove skin, stems and seeds from charred peppers. Finely chop peppers; add to tomatoes. Stir in onion and garlic.
4. Place all remaining ingredients except chips in a blender; cover and process until smooth. Add to tomato mixture, stirring to combine. Serve with chips.

NOTE: Wear disposable gloves when cutting hot peppers; the oils can burn skin. Avoid touching your face.

¼ CUP SALSA: *27 cal., 2g fat (0 sat. fat), 0 chol., 50mg sod., 2g carb. (1g sugars, 1g fiber), 0 pro.* **Diabetic exchanges:** *Free food.*

WATERMELON "PIZZA",
PAGE 33

Salads & Dressings

Nothing rounds out menus like a refreshing salad. Turn here for entree salads, pasta salads, fruit salads, side salads and other garden-fresh specialties sure to brighten up your table.

OUR ALL-TIME FAVORITES

Shrimp & Scallops Tropical Salad p. 22

Grilled Romaine Salad p. 26

Special Fruit Salad p. 27

Chicken Strawberry Spinach Salad p. 29

Grandma's Classic Potato Salad p. 30

SHRIMP & SCALLOPS TROPICAL SALAD

SHRIMP & SCALLOPS TROPICAL SALAD

A fruity dressing makes this seafood salad shine. Served over greens, the scrumptious combination of grilled seafood, veggies and macadamia nuts is the perfect way to celebrate a special summer occasion.
—Jackie Pressinger, Stuart, WI

PREP: 35 min. • **COOK:** 5 min.
MAKES: 2 servings

- **2 Tbsp. diced peeled mango**
- **1 Tbsp. diced fresh pineapple**
- **1½ tsp. mango chutney**
- **1½ tsp. olive oil**
- **1 tsp. rice vinegar**
- **¾ tsp. lime juice**
- **Dash salt**
- **Dash crushed red pepper flakes**
- **3 cups torn Bibb or Boston lettuce**
- **1 cup chopped peeled cucumber**
- **½ medium ripe avocado, peeled and sliced**
- **2 Tbsp. coarsely chopped macadamia nuts, toasted**
- **1 Tbsp. finely chopped red onion**
- **1 Tbsp. minced fresh cilantro**
- **2 Tbsp. canola oil**
- **1½ tsp. Caribbean jerk seasoning**
- **6 uncooked large shrimp, peeled and deveined**
- **6 sea scallops, halved**

1. Place the first 8 ingredients in a blender. Cover and process until blended; set aside. Divide lettuce, cucumber, avocado, nuts, onion and cilantro between serving plates.
2. In a small bowl, combine oil and jerk seasoning. Thread shrimp and scallops onto 2 metal or soaked wooden skewers; brush with oil mixture.
3. Grill skewers, covered, over medium heat until shrimp turn pink and scallops are firm and opaque, 2-3 minutes on each side. Place on salads; drizzle with dressing.
1 SALAD: *413 cal., 32g fat (4g sat. fat), 96mg chol., 523mg sod., 16g carb. (6g sugars, 5g fiber), 19g pro.*

SPINACH SALAD WITH GOAT CHEESE & BEETS

Here's a super easy salad that looks and tastes festive. We love it for the holiday season. Vinaigrette dressing coats the greens very nicely.
—Nancy Latulippe, Simcoe, ON

PREP: 45 min. + cooling • **MAKES:** 10 servings

- **1¼ lbs. fresh beets**
- **1 Tbsp. balsamic vinegar**
- **1½ tsp. honey**
- **1½ tsp. Dijon mustard**
- **¼ tsp. salt**
- **¼ tsp. pepper**
- **¼ cup olive oil**
- **5 cups fresh baby spinach**
- **2 oz. fresh goat cheese, crumbled**
- **½ cup chopped walnuts, toasted**

1. Scrub beets and trim tops to 1 in. Place in a Dutch oven and cover with water. Bring to a boil. Reduce heat; cover and simmer until tender, 30-60 minutes. Remove from the water; cool. Peel the beets and cut into 1-in. pieces.
2. In a small bowl, whisk the vinegar, honey, mustard, salt and pepper. Slowly whisk in oil until blended.
3. Place spinach in salad bowl. Drizzle with dressing; toss to coat. Top with beets, goat cheese and walnuts. If desired, sprinkle with additional pepper.
¾ CUP: *113 cal., 10g fat (2g sat. fat), 4mg chol., 128mg sod., 5g carb. (3g sugars, 1g fiber), 2g pro.*

TEST KITCHEN TIP

Spinach is a great way to amp up the flavor, color and nutrients of just about any green salad. Available in bulk or in packages of prewashed leaves, spinach is a smart kitchen staple for today's home cooks.

SLOW-COOKER BUFFALO CHICKEN SALAD

My husband and sons love chicken with blue cheese, so I created this salad. You can even make the chicken the day before and reheat it when you're ready to serve.
—Shauna Havey, Roy, UT

PREP: 20 min. • **COOK:** 2½ hours
MAKES: 6 servings

- **1½ lbs. boneless skinless chicken breast halves**
- **¾ cup Buffalo wing sauce**
- **3 Tbsp. butter**
- **1 envelope ranch salad dressing mix**
- **1 pkg. (10 oz.) hearts of romaine salad mix**
- **1 cup julienned carrot**
- **1 medium ripe avocado, peeled and cubed**
- **½ cup crumbled blue cheese**
- **½ cup blue cheese salad dressing**

1. Place chicken in a 1½- or 3-qt. slow cooker. Top with wing sauce, butter and ranch dressing mix. Cook, covered, on low until thermometer inserted in the chicken reads 165°, 2½-3 hours.
2. Remove chicken; shred with 2 forks. Reserve ⅓ cup cooking juices; discard the remaining juices. Return chicken and the reserved juices to slow cooker; heat through.
3. Place romaine salad mix in a serving dish. Top with shredded chicken, carrots, avocado and blue cheese; drizzle with blue cheese dressing. Serve immediately.
1 SALAD: *385 cal., 26g fat (9g sat. fat), 93mg chol., 1693mg sod., 12g carb. (2g sugars, 4g fiber), 28g pro.*

CRANBERRY AMBROSIA SALAD

My paternal grandmother used to make this for Christmas dinner. I'm not sure how many batches she made, as there were nearly 50 aunts, uncles and cousins in our family. I still make the recipe in memory of her, and it's just as good as I remember.
—Janet Hurley, Shell Rock, IA

PREP: 20 min. + chilling • **MAKES:** 9 servings

- **1 lb. fresh or frozen cranberries**
- **1 can (20 oz.) crushed pineapple, drained**
- **1 cup sugar**
- **2 cups miniature marshmallows**
- **1 cup heavy whipping cream, whipped**
- **½ cup chopped pecans**

1. In a food processor, cover and process cranberries until coarsely chopped. Transfer to a large bowl; stir in pineapple and sugar. Cover and refrigerate overnight.
2. Just before serving, fold in marshmallows, whipped cream and pecans. If desired, top with additional chopped pecans.
¾ CUP: *331 cal., 15g fat (7g sat. fat), 36mg chol., 17mg sod., 52g carb. (43g sugars, 3g fiber), 2g pro.*

CRANBERRY AMBROSIA SALAD

MAC ATTACK

Noodling over what to bring to a cookout? Try a twist on classic mac salad and watch as guests elbow their way through to scoop it up!

START HERE

In a small bowl, combine 1 cup mayonnaise, 2 tsp. sugar, ¾ tsp. ground mustard, ¼ tsp. salt and ⅛ tsp. pepper. Place 4 cups cooked elbow macaroni in a large bowl. Stir in the dressing and additional ingredients; toss gently to coat. Refrigerate until serving.

5

3

4

1

2

3

4

5

1 GRECIAN MACARONI SALAD

Add 2 tsp. dried oregano; 2 tsp. grated lemon zest; ½ cup crumbled feta cheese; ½ cup chopped peeled cucumber; ½ cup sliced red onion; ½ cup cherry tomatoes, halved; and ¼ cup Greek olives, chopped.

Brigette Schroeder, Yorkville, IL

2 SCANDINAVIAN MACARONI SALAD

Add 2 tsp. snipped fresh dill; 1 cup peeled and deveined cooked shrimp; 1 small cucumber, chopped; and 1 small red onion, thinly sliced. Top with additional dill if desired.

Kallee Krong-McCreery, Escondido, CA

3 CAPRESE MACARONI SALAD

Add 1 Tbsp. Italian salad dressing mix; 1 pint cherry tomatoes, halved; and 1 cup fresh mozzarella cheese pearls. Top with minced fresh basil and grated Parmesan cheese.

Debbie Glasscock, Conway, AR

4 MIDDLE EASTERN MACARONI SALAD

Add ½ lb. cooked ground lamb; one 16-oz. can chickpeas, rinsed and drained; ¼ cup chopped onion; and 1 tsp. za'atar seasoning. Top with plain yogurt and grated lemon zest if desired.

Ruth Hartunian-Alumbaugh, Willimantic, CT

5 CHICKEN CAESAR MACARONI SALAD

Add 2 Tbsp. Italian salad dressing mix; 1 cup chopped cooked chicken; one 14-oz. can water-packed artichoke hearts, drained and chopped; ¼ cup grated Parmesan cheese; and 2 Tbsp. capers, drained. Top with croutons if desired.

Shawn Barto, Palmetto, FL

6 POLYNESIAN MACARONI SALAD

Add one 12-oz. can SPAM, cubed and cooked; one 8-oz. can water chestnuts, drained; 1 chopped red pepper; and one 8-oz. can unsweetened pineapple tidbits, drained. Top with chopped green onions if desired.

Susan Bickta, Kutztown, PA

7 CUBANO MACARONI SALAD

Add 1 cup shredded Swiss cheese, 1 cup cubed cooked pork, 1 cup cubed fully cooked ham, ½ cup chopped sweet pickles and ½ cup chopped onion.

Marina Castle Kelley, Canyon Country, CA

8 CHICKEN TACO MACARONI SALAD

Add 2 Tbsp. reduced-sodium taco seasoning; 2 cups cubed cooked chicken; 1 small sweet yellow or orange pepper, chopped; and 1 jalapeno pepper, seeded and chopped. Top with fresh cilantro leaves if desired.

Lisa Allen, Joppa, AL

9 BARBECUE MACARONI SALAD

Add 1 to 3 Tbsp. barbecue sauce; 1 Tbsp. ranch salad dressing mix; 2 hard-boiled eggs, chopped; and 2 Tbsp. sweet pickle relish. Drizzle with additional barbecue sauce if desired.

Andrea Bolden, Unionville, TN

10 SHRIMP & CRAB MACARONI SALAD

Add 2 tsp. Old Bay Seasoning; 1 tsp. garlic powder; 6 oz. imitation crabmeat; 1 small cucumber, chopped; and 1 cup peeled and deveined cooked shrimp. Top with chopped green onions if desired.

Darla Andrews, Boerne, TX

TABBOULEH

Tabbouleh is a classic Middle Eastern salad. The fresh veggies and mint leaves make it light and refreshing on a hot day.
—Michael and Mathil Chebat, Lake Ridge, VA

TAKES: 30 min. • **MAKES:** 8 servings

- ¼ cup bulgur
- 3 bunches fresh parsley, minced (about 2 cups)
- 3 large tomatoes, finely chopped
- 1 small onion, finely chopped
- ¼ cup lemon juice
- ¼ cup olive oil
- 5 fresh mint leaves, minced
- ½ tsp. salt
- ½ tsp. pepper
- ¼ tsp. cayenne pepper

Prepare bulgur according to package directions; cool. Transfer bulgur to a large bowl. Stir in remaining ingredients. If desired, chill before serving.

⅔ CUP: *100 cal., 7g fat (1g sat. fat), 0 chol., 164mg sod., 9g carb. (3g sugars, 2g fiber), 2g pro.* **Diabetic exchanges:** *1½ fat, ½ starch.*

TABBOULEH

GRILLED ROMAINE SALAD

GRILLED ROMAINE SALAD

For a great-tasting salad, try this recipe on the grill! It's equally good with any dressing of your choice.
—Susan Court, Pewaukee, WI

TAKES: 20 min. • **MAKES:** 12 servings

- ⅓ cup plus 3 Tbsp. olive oil, divided
- 2 Tbsp. white wine vinegar
- 1 Tbsp. dill weed
- ½ tsp. garlic powder
- ⅛ tsp. crushed red pepper flakes
- ⅛ tsp. salt
- 6 green onions
- 4 plum tomatoes, halved
- 1 large cucumber, peeled and halved lengthwise
- 2 romaine hearts

1. In a small bowl, whisk ⅓ cup oil, vinegar and seasonings. Set aside.

2. Brush the onions, tomatoes, cucumber and romaine with remaining oil. Grill onions, tomatoes and cucumber, uncovered, over medium heat for 4-5 minutes on each side or until onions are crisp-tender. Grill romaine for 30 seconds on each side or until heated through.

3. Chop the vegetables; place in a large bowl. Whisk dressing and pour over salad; toss to coat. Serve immediately.

¾ CUP: *98 cal., 10g fat (1g sat. fat), 0 chol., 30mg sod., 3g carb. (1g sugars, 1g fiber), 1g pro.*

ITALIAN DRESSING

This is a satisfying all-purpose vinaigrette. Use it on salad greens, in vegetable salads or even as a marinade for chicken.
—Taste of Home *Test Kitchen*

TAKES: 15 min. • **MAKES:** 1½ cups

- ¼ **cup lemon juice**
- ¼ **cup red wine vinegar**
- 2 **Tbsp. grated Parmesan cheese**
- 2 **garlic cloves, halved**
- 1 **tsp. sugar**
- ¾ **tsp. salt**
- ¾ **tsp. dried oregano**
- ½ **tsp. ground mustard**
- ½ **tsp. dried basil**
- ¼ **tsp. onion powder**
- 1 **cup olive oil**

Place the first 10 ingredients in a blender. Cover and process until pureed. While processing, gradually add oil in a steady stream. Refrigerate leftovers.

2 TBSP.: *167 cal., 18g fat (3g sat. fat), 1mg chol., 163mg sod., 1g carb. (0 sugars, 0 fiber), 0 pro.*

ITALIAN DRESSING

SPECIAL FRUIT SALAD

SPECIAL FRUIT SALAD

Dress up a sweet fruit salad with this drizzle of citrusy flavor. The creamy dressing sticks nicely to the fruit.
—Alice Orton, Big Bear Lake, CA

PREP: 10 min. + chilling • **MAKES:** 2 servings

- 1 **snack-sized cup (4 oz.) pineapple tidbits**
- ⅓ **cup chopped apple**
- ⅓ **cup cubed cantaloupe**
- 10 **green grapes, halved**
- 6 **fresh strawberries, quartered**
- 1 **medium kiwifruit, peeled and sliced**

DRESSING

- 2 **Tbsp. mayonnaise**
- 2 **Tbsp. sour cream**
- 1½ **tsp. sugar**
- 1 **tsp. orange juice**
- ¼ **tsp. lemon juice**
- ¼ **tsp. grated lemon or orange zest**

Drain pineapple, reserving 1 tsp. juice. In a salad bowl, combine the pineapple, apple, cantaloupe, grapes, strawberries and kiwi. In a small bowl, combine the dressing ingredients; add reserved pineapple juice and mix well. Refrigerate the fruit and dressing until chilled. Just before serving, pour the dressing over the fruit and toss to coat.

1 CUP: *136 cal., 2g fat (1g sat. fat), 7mg chol., 140mg sod., 28g carb. (22g sugars, 4g fiber), 3g pro.*

FRENCH DRESSING

FRENCH DRESSING

This dressing is a favorite of our family's. It's best shaken in a jar, not made in a blender. My mother made this recipe when I was a child, and we have been enjoying it for over 50 years!
—Gloria Rentmaster, De Pere, WI

PREP: 10 min. • **MAKES:** 3 cups

- **1 cup canola oil**
- **1 cup ketchup**
- **½ cup cider vinegar**
- **½ cup sugar**
- **1 Tbsp. steak sauce**
- **2 tsp. paprika**
- **1 tsp. salt**
- **1 small onion, minced (¼ cup)**

Place all ingredients in a jar with a tight-fitting lid; shake well. Refrigerate until serving. Shake dressing again just before serving.
2 TBSP.: *112 cal., 9g fat (1g sat. fat), 0 chol., 237mg sod., 7g carb. (7g sugars, 0 fiber), 0 pro.*

TARRAGON TUNA SALAD

It's surprising how a few herbs can brighten up tuna salad. Made with reduced-fat mayonnaise, this version gets its zip from mustard. It makes a terrific light lunch or Sunday brunch dish.
—Billie Moss, Walnut Creek, CA

TAKES: 10 min. • **MAKES:** 4 servings

- **2 cans (6 oz. each) light water-packed tuna, drained and flaked**
- **1 cup chopped celery**
- **¼ cup chopped sweet onion**
- **⅓ cup reduced-fat mayonnaise**
- **2 Tbsp. minced fresh parsley**
- **1 Tbsp. lemon juice**
- **1 tsp. minced fresh tarragon or ¼ tsp. dried tarragon**
- **½ tsp. Dijon mustard**
- **¼ tsp. white pepper**
- **Lettuce leaves, optional**

In a small bowl, combine the tuna, celery and onion. Combine the mayonnaise, parsley, lemon juice, tarragon, mustard and pepper. Stir into tuna mixture. If desired, serve on lettuce leaves.
⅔ CUP: *151 cal., 7g fat (1g sat. fat), 38mg chol., 373mg sod., 4g carb. (2g sugars, 1g fiber), 17g pro.* **Diabetic exchanges:** *2 lean meat, 1½ fat.*

TARRAGON TUNA SALAD

CHICKEN STRAWBERRY SPINACH SALAD

This pretty spinach salad topped with grilled chicken, strawberries and almonds features a delectably sweet poppy seed dressing. Ready in moments, it's a refreshing lunch or light supper for two.
—Ginger Ellsworth, Caldwell, ID

TAKES: 30 min. • **MAKES:** 2 servings

- ¾ **lb. boneless skinless chicken breasts, cut into strips**
- ¼ **cup reduced-sodium chicken broth**
- ¼ **cup poppy seed salad dressing, divided**
- 2 **cups fresh baby spinach**
- 1 **cup torn romaine**
- 1 **cup sliced fresh strawberries**
- ¼ **cup sliced almonds, toasted**

1. Place chicken on a double thickness of heavy-duty foil (about 18x15-in.). Combine broth and 1 Tbsp. poppy seed dressing; spoon over chicken. Fold edges of foil around chicken mixture, leaving center open. Grill, covered, over medium heat until chicken is no longer pink, roughly 10-12 minutes.
2. In a large salad bowl, combine the spinach, romaine and strawberries. Add chicken and the remaining poppy seed dressing; toss to coat. Sprinkle with almonds.
2 CUPS: *438 cal., 22g fat (3g sat. fat), 104mg chol., 386mg sod., 18g carb. (11g sugars, 5g fiber), 39g pro.*

SPICY THAI-INSPIRED NOODLE WATERMELON SALAD

SPICY THAI-INSPIRED NOODLE WATERMELON SALAD

Our county is famous for its fabulous Green River melons. While you won't find this unique and refreshing salad at the county fair, it's definitely our favorite way to eat watermelon all summer long!
—Carmell Childs, Orangeville, UT

PREP: 25 min. • **COOK:** 25 min.
MAKES: 10 servings

- 4½ **cups cubed watermelon, divided**
- ½ **cup sweet chili sauce**
- 3 **Tbsp. fish sauce or soy sauce**
- 2 **Tbsp. lime juice**
- ½ **tsp. minced fresh gingerroot**
- 7 **oz. uncooked stir-fry rice noodles**
- 1½ **cups julienned carrots**
- 1 **small red onion, halved and thinly sliced**
- ½ **cup fresh cilantro leaves, chopped**
- 3 **Tbsp. minced fresh mint**
- 1¼ **cups salted peanuts, chopped**
- **Lime wedges**

1. Place 2 cups watermelon in a blender; cover and puree until smooth. Press through a fine-mesh strainer into a bowl; discard pulp. Pour 1 cup juice into a small saucepan (save any remaining juice for another use). Add chili sauce, fish sauce, lime juice and ginger to saucepan. Bring to a boil; cook until liquid is slightly thickened, 20-25 minutes. Remove from the heat. Refrigerate until cooled.
2. Meanwhile, prepare noodles according to package directions; rinse with cold water and drain well. Place noodles in a large bowl. Add carrots, red onion, cilantro, mint and remaining 2½ cups watermelon. Drizzle with dressing; toss to coat. Serve with peanuts and lime wedges.
¾ CUP: *240 cal., 10g fat (2g sat. fat), 0 chol., 721mg sod., 34g carb. (14g sugars, 3g fiber), 7g pro.*

GRANDMA'S CLASSIC POTATO SALAD

FARRO SALAD WITH CHARRED SHISHITO PEPPERS & CORN

I am lucky that my mom has a really great garden every summer and gives me all kinds of vegetables to try. I've found most shishito peppers to be mild in heat. After discarding the stems, I add the remaining chopped pepper, including the seeds, to this dish. The salad can be enjoyed warm or can be refrigerated and served cold.
—Tracy Kaifesh, Laguna Niguel, CA

PREP: 25 min. • **COOK:** 25 min.
MAKES: 8 servings

- **1 cup farro, rinsed**
- **¼ cup plus 2 tsp. olive oil, divided**
- **¼ cup lime juice**
- **1 tsp. garlic powder**
- **½ tsp. ground cumin**
- **½ tsp. kosher salt**
- **4 oz. shishito peppers (about 20 peppers)**
- **2 medium ears sweet corn, husked**
- **1 cup chopped fresh tomatoes**
- **½ cup crumbled Cotija cheese**
- **½ cup sliced radishes**
- **½ cup chopped green onions**

1. Place farro in a large saucepan; add water to cover. Bring to a boil. Reduce heat; cook, covered, until tender, 25-30 minutes.
2. Meanwhile, for dressing, whisk together ¼ cup oil, lime juice, garlic powder, cumin and salt; set aside. Preheat a grill pan over medium-high heat. Toss peppers with 1 tsp. oil. Cook until all sides are blistered and blackened, 6-8 minutes, turning occasionally with tongs. Transfer to a cutting board. Chop peppers; discard stems. Transfer to a large bowl.
3. Brush corn with remaining 1 tsp. oil. Cook until lightly browned and tender, 10-12 minutes, turning occasionally. Cool slightly. Cut corn from cobs; add to peppers. Drain farro; add to corn mixture. Stir in tomatoes, cheese, radishes, green onions and dressing; toss to coat. Serve warm or chilled.

¾ CUP: *233 cal., 11g fat (2g sat. fat), 8mg chol., 240mg sod., 27g carb. (3g sugars, 5g fiber), 7g pro.* **Diabetic exchanges:** *2 starch, 2 fat.*

GRANDMA'S CLASSIC POTATO SALAD

When I asked my dear grandmother how old this classic potato salad recipe was, she told me that her mom used to make it when she was a little girl. It has definitely stood the test of time.
—Kimberly Wallace, Dennison, OH

PREP: 25 min. • **COOK:** 20 min. + chilling
MAKES: 10 servings

- **6 medium potatoes, peeled and cubed**
- **¼ cup all-purpose flour**
- **1 Tbsp. sugar**
- **1½ tsp. salt**
- **1 tsp. ground mustard**
- **1 tsp. pepper**
- **¾ cup water**
- **2 large eggs, beaten**
- **¼ cup white vinegar**
- **4 hard-boiled large eggs, divided use**
- **2 celery ribs, chopped**
- **1 medium onion, chopped**
- **Sliced green onions, optional**

1. Place potatoes in a large saucepan and cover with water. Bring to a boil. Reduce the heat; cover and cook until tender, 15-20 minutes. Drain potatoes and cool to room temperature.
2. Meanwhile, in a small heavy saucepan, combine flour, sugar, salt, mustard and pepper. Gradually stir in the water until smooth. Cook and stir over medium-high heat until thickened and bubbly. Reduce heat; cook and stir 2 minutes longer.
3. Remove from the heat. Stir a small amount of hot mixture into eggs; return all to the pan, stirring constantly. Bring to a gentle boil; cook and stir 2 minutes longer. Remove from the heat and cool completely. Gently stir in vinegar.
4. Chop and refrigerate 1 hard-boiled egg; chop the remaining 3 hard-boiled eggs. In a large bowl, combine the potatoes, celery, chopped onion and eggs; add dressing and stir until blended. Refrigerate until chilled. Garnish with reserved chopped egg and, if desired, sliced green onions.

¾ CUP: *144 cal., 3g fat (1g sat. fat), 112mg chol., 402mg sod., 23g carb. (3g sugars, 2g fiber), 6g pro.* **Diabetic exchanges:** *1½ starch, ½ fat.*

FARRO SALAD WITH CHARRED SHISHITO PEPPERS & CORN

APPLE MATCHSTICK SALAD

Cutting apples into matchstick-sized pieces for a salad makes them just a little more fun to eat, don't you think? Slice a few apples this way and toss them with chopped pecans (or any nuts), dried berries and raisins, plus some fresh cilantro. Dress them in a bit of olive oil, lemon and salt. Sweet, salty and savory!
—Erin Gleeson, Woodside, CA

TAKES: 15 min.
MAKES: 6 servings

- **2 Tbsp. olive oil**
- **2 tsp. fresh lemon juice**
- **⅛ tsp. salt**
- **4 medium apples, julienned**
- **¾ cup chopped pecans, toasted**
- **½ cup fresh cilantro leaves**
- **¼ cup dried cranberries**
- **¼ cup golden raisins**

In a large bowl, whisk together the olive oil, lemon juice and salt. Stir in the remaining ingredients.

1 SERVING: *225 cal., 15g fat (2g sat. fat), 0 chol., 52mg sod., 26g carb. (19g sugars, 4g fiber), 2g pro.* **Diabetic exchanges:** *3 fat, 1½ fruit.*

GRILLED TUNA SALAD

I love serving this tuna spinach salad! Tuna steaks are quick to cook and delicious, and although they're pretty inexpensive, they always seem a little more elegant than canned tuna. You can find them at most meat and seafood counters. Try this salad with fresh bread and tall glasses of lemonade.
—De'Lawrence Reed, Durham, NC

TAKES: 30 min.
MAKES: 2 servings

- **½ lb. tuna steaks**
- **1 tsp. olive oil**
- **⅛ tsp. salt**
- **⅛ tsp. pepper**
- **3 cups fresh baby spinach**
- **½ cup grape tomatoes**
- **⅓ cup frozen shelled edamame, thawed**
- **¼ cup frozen corn, thawed**

CITRUS VINAIGRETTE

- **1 Tbsp. olive oil**
- **1½ tsp. minced fresh basil**
- **1½ tsp. white wine vinegar**
- **1½ tsp. honey**
- **1½ tsp. lime juice**
- **1½ tsp. lemon juice**
- **1½ tsp. orange juice**
- **⅛ tsp. salt**
- **⅛ tsp. pepper**

1. Brush tuna with oil; sprinkle with salt and pepper. Grill, covered, over high heat on a greased grill rack or broil 3-4 in. from the heat for 3-4 minutes on each side for medium-rare or until slightly pink in the center. Let stand for 5 minutes.

2. Meanwhile, in a large bowl, combine the spinach, tomatoes, edamame and corn. In a bowl, whisk the vinaigrette ingredients; drizzle over salad and toss to coat. Divide salad between 2 plates; slice tuna and arrange over salads. Serve immediately.

2 CUPS SALAD WITH 3 OZ. COOKED TUNA: *290 cal., 12g fat (2g sat. fat), 51mg chol., 380mg sod., 16g carb., 3g fiber, 31g pro.* **Diabetic exchanges:** *4 lean meat, 2 fat, 1 vegetable, ½ starch.*

GRILLED TUNA SALAD

TEST KITCHEN TIP

Edamame

This popular Asian food is produced from soybeans that are harvested early, before the beans become hard. The young beans are parboiled and frozen to retain their freshness and can be found in the freezer of grocery and health food stores.

MINTED BEET SALAD

We have neighbors who share vegetables from their garden, and every year my husband and I look forward to their beets. My interest in Mediterranean food inspired this beet salad recipe—the vinegar and oil dressing with fresh mint tones down the sweetness of the beets, and the kalamata olives add a salty touch.
—Barbara Estabrook, Appleton, WI

PREP: 20 min. • **COOK:** 15 min. + chilling • **MAKES:** 6 servings

- **5 medium fresh beets (about 2 lbs.)**
- **2 Tbsp. water**
- **2 Tbsp. champagne vinegar or rice vinegar**
- **2 Tbsp. olive oil**
- **½ tsp. salt**
- **¼ tsp. coarsely ground pepper**
- **¼ cup pitted kalamata olives, quartered**
- **2 Tbsp. thinly sliced fresh mint, divided**

1. Scrub beets; trim tops to 1 in. Place in a single layer in a large microwave-safe dish. Drizzle with water. Microwave, covered, on high until easily pierced with a fork, turning once, 14-15 minutes; let stand 5 minutes.
2. When cool enough to handle, peel and cut the beets into ¾-in. pieces. In a bowl, whisk vinegar, oil, salt and pepper until blended. Add the olives, beets and 1 Tbsp. mint; toss to coat. Refrigerate, covered, until cold, at least 1 hour. Top with the remaining 1 Tbsp. mint.
½ CUP: *123 cal., 6g fat (1g sat. fat), 0 chol., 406mg sod., 16g carb. (12g sugars, 3g fiber), 3g pro.* **Diabetic exchanges:** *1 vegetable, 1 fat.*

MINTED BEET SALAD

WATERMELON "PIZZA"

WATERMELON "PIZZA"

Start with grilled melon slices and layer on tangy, salty and sweet toppings for a summer-fresh appetizer.
—Ellen Riley, Murfreesboro, TN

PREP: 25 min. • **GRILL:** 10 min. + chilling • **MAKES:** 8 servings

- **8 wedges seedless watermelon, about 1 in. thick**
- **1 cup heirloom cherry tomatoes, sliced**
- **1 cup fresh baby arugula**
- **½ cup fresh blueberries**
- **⅓ cup crumbled feta cheese**
- **⅓ cup pitted Greek olives, halved**
- **1 Tbsp. olive oil**
- **⅛ tsp. kosher salt**
- **⅛ tsp. coarsely ground pepper**
- **Balsamic glaze, optional**

1. Grill watermelon, covered, on a greased grill rack over medium-high direct heat until seared, 5-6 minutes on each side. Remove from heat; transfer to a platter. Chill.
2. To serve, top chilled watermelon with tomatoes, arugula, blueberries, feta and olives. Drizzle with olive oil; season with salt and pepper. If desired, drizzle with balsamic glaze.
1 WEDGE: *91 cal., 4g fat (1g sat. fat), 3mg chol., 169mg sod., 13g carb. (11g sugars, 1g fiber), 2g pro.* **Diabetic exchanges:** *1 fruit, 1 fat.*

HEARTY HOMEMADE CHICKEN NOODLE SOUP, PAGE 41

Soups & Sandwiches

Here's what comfort food is all about: steaming bowlfuls of wholesome soup, plus tasty handhelds for eating at home or on the go.

CHECK OUT THESE SPECIALTIES

Quick Tomato Soup p. 37

Grandma's French Tuna Salad Wraps p. 39

Hoisin Chicken Wraps p. 45

Irish Beef Stew p. 47

KILBOURN SANDWICH

This is a fun take on a Monte Cristo. The recipe makes a big batch so you can stock your freezer and cook them up whenever you need a quick meal.
—Dan Seering, Verona, WI

PREP: 30 min. + freezing
COOK: 10 min./batch • **MAKES:** 10 servings

- **1¼ lbs. sliced deli turkey**
- **1¼ lbs. sliced deli ham**
- **10 slices Swiss cheese**
- **20 slices white bread**
- **4 cups complete buttermilk pancake mix**
- **Oil for deep-fat frying**
- **Confectioners' sugar**
- **1 cup sour cream**
- **½ cup strawberry preserves**

1. Place turkey, ham and cheese on 10 bread slices; top with remaining bread. Cut each sandwich diagonally in half.
2. Prepare pancake mix according to package directions. Dip sandwiches in pancake batter, allowing excess to drip off. Freeze sandwiches on waxed paper-lined baking sheets until firm. Transfer to freezer containers; return to freezer.
3. To prepare, in an electric skillet or deep-fat fryer, heat oil to 375°. Fry frozen sandwiches, a few at a time, until golden brown, 3-4 minutes on each side. Drain on paper towels; sprinkle with confectioners' sugar. Combine sour cream and preserves; serve with sandwiches.

2 SANDWICH HALVES WITH ABOUT 2 TBSP. SAUCE: *844 cal., 44g fat (7g sat. fat), 61mg chol., 2020mg sod., 80g carb. (21g sugars, 3g fiber), 35g pro.*

KILBOURN SANDWICH

TRULY TEXAN CHILI

I am a native Texan, and this is the best chili recipe I've ever tasted. It's meaty and spicy. I'd make this whenever I was homesick during the years we spent away from Texas because of my husband's military career.
—Betty Brown, San Antonio, TX

PREP: 10 min. • **COOK:** 1¾ hours
MAKES: 8 servings

- **3 lbs. ground beef**
- **2 to 3 garlic cloves, minced**
- **¼ cup all-purpose flour**
- **2 to 3 Tbsp. chili powder**
- **1 Tbsp. dried oregano**
- **1 Tbsp. ground cumin**
- **2 cans (14½ oz. each) beef broth**
- **1 can (15 oz.) pinto beans, rinsed and drained, optional**
- **1 tsp. salt**
- **¼ tsp. pepper**
- **Optional garnishes: Shredded cheddar cheese, tortilla chips, sour cream and/or lime wedges**

1. In a Dutch oven, cook beef and garlic over medium heat until no longer pink; drain. Combine the flour, chili powder, oregano and cumin; sprinkle over meat, stirring until evenly coated. Add the broth, beans if desired, salt and pepper.
2. Bring to a boil. Reduce heat; cover and simmer for 1½-2 hours to allow flavors to blend, stirring occasionally. Sprinkle with cheese, tortilla chips, sour cream and/or lime wedges if desired.

1 SERVING: *343 cal., 21g fat (8g sat. fat), 105mg chol., 872mg sod., 5g carb. (0 sugars, 1g fiber), 32g pro.*

QUICK TOMATO SOUP

QUICK TOMATO SOUP

My family often requests my sweet homemade tomato soup on cold days. It's great with a sandwich and nearly as fast to make as canned soup.
—Jane Ward, Churchville, MD

TAKES: 15 min. • **MAKES:** 6 servings (1½ qt.)

- **¼ cup butter**
- **¼ cup all-purpose flour**
- **1 tsp. curry powder**
- **¼ tsp. onion powder**
- **1 can (46 oz.) tomato juice**
- **¼ cup sugar**
- **Optional: Oyster crackers or croutons**

In a large saucepan, melt butter. Stir in flour, curry powder and onion powder until smooth. Gradually add tomato juice and sugar. Cook, uncovered, until thickened and heated through, about 5 minutes. If desired, serve with crackers or croutons.
1 CUP: *156 cal., 8g fat (5g sat. fat), 20mg chol., 862mg sod., 22g carb. (15g sugars, 1g fiber), 2g pro.*

MY JUICY LUCY

Friends in Minnesota introduced me to the Juicy Lucy burger, a local favorite. Instead of putting the cheese on top, it gets stuffed inside, keeping the meat around the cheese nice and juicy. We love the meltiness of American cheese, but it works with any cheese you'd like.
—Brigette Kutschma, Lake Geneva, WI

TAKES: 30 min. • **MAKES:** 4 servings

- **1 lb. ground beef**
- **8 Tbsp. shredded American or cheddar cheese**
- **½ tsp. salt**
- **½ tsp. pepper**
- **4 hamburger buns, split and toasted**
- **Optional: Tomato slices, onion slices, lettuce**

1. Shape beef into 8 thin patties. Divide cheese among 4 patties; top with remaining patties and press edges firmly to seal. Sprinkle with salt and pepper.
2. Grill burgers, covered, over medium heat or broil 4 in. from heat until a thermometer reads 160° and juices run clear, 6-8 minutes on each side. Serve on buns with toppings of your choice.
1 BURGER: *376 cal., 19g fat (8g sat. fat), 84mg chol., 756mg sod., 23g carb. (4g sugars, 1g fiber), 27g pro.*

MY JUICY LUCY

RUSTIC FISH CHOWDER

RUSTIC FISH CHOWDER

For my version of this classic, I use halibut that my brother-in-law, a commercial fisherman, catches in Kodiak, Alaska. Top each serving with some grated Parmesan and minced green onions.
—Diana Lassen, Eugene, OR

PREP: 15 min. • **COOK:** 30 min. • **MAKES:** 12 servings (3 qt.)

- **¼ cup butter, cubed**
- **1 small onion, finely chopped**
- **1 garlic clove, minced**
- **3 lbs. potatoes (about 6 medium), cut into ½-in. cubes**
- **1½ cups fresh or frozen corn**
- **5 cups chicken broth**
- **1½ tsp. salt**
- **¾ tsp. celery salt**
- **¾ tsp. pepper**
- **½ tsp. dried thyme**
- **1 lb. cod or halibut fillets, cut into ¾-in. pieces**
- **1 cup heavy whipping cream**

1. In a 6-qt. stockpot, heat butter over medium heat. Add onion; cook and stir until tender, 3-4 minutes. Add garlic; cook 1 minute longer. Add potatoes, corn, broth, salt, celery salt, pepper and thyme; bring to a boil. Reduce heat; simmer, covered, until potatoes are tender, 10-15 minutes. Mash potatoes slightly.
2. Stir in cod and cream; bring to a boil. Reduce heat; simmer, covered, until the fish just begins to flake easily with a fork, 6-8 minutes.
1 CUP: *242 cal., 12g fat (7g sat. fat), 49mg chol., 842mg sod., 25g carb. (3g sugars, 3g fiber), 10g pro.*

BROWN SUGAR BACON BLT SANDWICHES

Simple BLT sandwiches are quite amazing, but when you add dill mayonnaise, avocado and brown sugar bacon, they become something spectacular! Any lettuce will do for this recipe, but I love the texture and flavor of butter lettuce. Try mixing fresh herbs into the mayo, too—chives, dill or basil would all be lovely.
—Colleen Delawder, Herndon, VA

PREP: 15 min. • **BAKE:** 35 min. • **MAKES:** 2 servings

- **6 thick-sliced bacon strips**
- **¼ cup packed brown sugar**
- **¼ tsp. cayenne pepper**
- **¼ cup mayonnaise**
- **½ tsp. dill weed**
- **¼ tsp. garlic powder**
- **¼ tsp. freshly ground pepper**
- **⅛ tsp. kosher salt**
- **2 brioche hamburger buns, split**
- **4 Bibb or Boston lettuce leaves**
- **1 medium ripe avocado, peeled and thinly sliced**
- **1 medium tomato, thinly sliced**

1. Place bacon on a rack in a foil-lined 15x10x1-in. baking pan. Place in a cold oven. Set oven to 350°. Bake for 20 minutes. Sprinkle bacon with brown sugar and cayenne pepper. Bake until sugar is melted and bacon is browned, 15-20 minutes longer.
2. Meanwhile, combine mayonnaise, dill, garlic powder, pepper and salt; spread over cut sides of buns. Layer bun bottoms with lettuce leaves, avocado, bacon and tomato; replace bun tops.
1 SANDWICH: *757 cal., 50g fat (10g sat. fat), 62mg chol., 1269mg sod., 63g carb. (35g sugars, 8g fiber), 19g pro.*

BROWN SUGAR BACON BLT SANDWICHES

GRANDMA'S FRENCH TUNA SALAD WRAPS

My French Canadian grandmother always made tuna salad with chopped egg in it. I've made my own version, adding veggies for complete nutrition and turning it into a wrap. It's fun and we get the memory of my grandmother with each bite.
—Jennifer Magrey, Sterling, CT

TAKES: 15 min. • **MAKES:** 2 servings

- **1 can (5 oz.) light water-packed tuna, drained and flaked**
- **1 celery rib, finely chopped**
- **¼ cup fat-free mayonnaise**
- **¼ tsp. pepper**
- **2 whole wheat tortillas (8 in.), room temperature**
- **½ cup shredded lettuce**
- **1 small carrot, shredded**
- **4 slices tomato**
- **2 slices red onion, separated into rings**
- **1 hard-boiled large egg, sliced**

In a small bowl, combine the tuna, celery, mayonnaise and pepper. Spoon the tuna mixture down the center of each tortilla. Top with lettuce, carrot, tomato, onion and egg. Roll up tightly.

1 SERVING: *328 cal., 7g fat (1g sat. fat), 135mg chol., 770mg sod., 32g carb. (7g sugars, 4g fiber), 30g pro.* **Diabetic exchanges:** *3 lean meat, 2 starch, 1 vegetable.*

CEYLON CHICKEN CURRY & RICE NOODLE SOUP

CEYLON CHICKEN CURRY & RICE NOODLE SOUP

Whenever cold or flu season hit, my mom always made a curried chicken rice noodle soup that was comforting and cozy. This turmeric lemongrass version is a take on that childhood favorite, loaded with ingredients to boost immunity. It can easily be made vegan or vegetarian.
—Sarita Gelner, Waunakee, WI

PREP: 25 min. • **COOK:** 25 min.
MAKES: 8 servings (2½ qt.)

- **6 oz. uncooked wide rice noodles**
- **2 Tbsp. ghee or olive oil, divided**
- **1 lb. boneless chicken breasts, thinly sliced and cut into ½-in. pieces**
- **1 medium onion, chopped**
- **⅔ cup sliced fresh carrots**
- **3 bay leaves**
- **2 Tbsp. minced fresh gingerroot**
- **1 lemongrass stalk**
- **1 whole star anise**
- **1 Tbsp. curry powder**
- **2 tsp. ground turmeric**
- **1 garlic clove, minced**
- **½ tsp. salt**
- **¼ tsp. cayenne pepper**
- **2 anchovy fillets, minced, optional**
- **2 Tbsp. white wine vinegar**
- **1 carton (32 oz.) chicken broth**
- **1 can (13.66 oz.) coconut milk**
- **2 Tbsp. jaggery or dark brown sugar**
- **1½ cups chopped fresh kale**
- **½ cup cherry tomatoes, halved**

1. Cook noodles according to package directions for al dente. Meanwhile, in a Dutch oven, heat 1 Tbsp. ghee over medium-high heat. Add chicken; cook and stir until no longer pink, 4-5 minutes. Remove from pan. Cook and stir onion and carrots in remaining 1 Tbsp. ghee until tender, 12-15 minutes. Add bay leaves, ginger, lemongrass, star anise, curry powder, turmeric, garlic, salt, cayenne and, if desired, minced anchovy fillets; cook 1 minute longer.

2. Add vinegar to pan; cook 30 seconds, stirring to loosen browned bits from pan. Add broth, coconut milk and jaggery. Bring to a boil; reduce heat. Add kale and tomatoes; simmer until tender, 6-8 minutes. Remove and discard bay leaves, lemongrass and star anise. Drain noodles; stir into soup. Add the chicken; heat through.

1¼ CUPS: *316 cal., 16g fat (11g sat. fat), 46mg chol., 758mg sod., 26g carb. (6g sugars, 2g fiber), 15g pro.*

SWISS POTATO SOUP

SWISS POTATO SOUP

You have a few options when it comes to fixing this soup—it can also be made in the microwave or started in a slow cooker in the morning.
—Krista Musser, Orrville, OH

TAKES: 30 min. • **MAKES:** 4 servings (1 qt.)

- **5 bacon strips, diced**
- **1 medium onion, chopped**
- **2 cups water**
- **4 medium potatoes, peeled and cubed**
- **1½ tsp. salt**
- **⅛ tsp. pepper**
- **⅓ cup all-purpose flour**
- **2 cups 2% milk**
- **1 cup shredded Swiss cheese**

1. In a large saucepan, cook the bacon until crisp; remove to paper towels with a slotted spoon. Drain, reserving 1 Tbsp. drippings.
2. Saute onion in drippings until tender. Add water, potatoes, salt and pepper. Bring to a boil. Reduce heat; simmer, uncovered, until potatoes are tender, about 12 minutes.
3. Combine flour and milk until smooth; gradually stir into potato mixture. Bring to a boil; cook and stir until thickened and bubbly, about 2 minutes. Remove from the heat; stir in cheese until melted. Sprinkle with bacon.
1 CUP: *455 cal., 17g fat (9g sat. fat), 46mg chol., 1218mg sod., 57g carb. (12g sugars, 4g fiber), 21g pro.*

HOW-TO

No-Stick Grated Cheese

A quick spritz of cooking spray will keep cheese from sticking to the grater. Cleanup is a lot easier.

BLACK BEAN RICE BURGERS

A salsa and sour cream sauce helps dress up these hearty vegetarian burgers. My fiance, who's a confirmed meat-and-potatoes man, loves these burgers and asks for them often.
—Laura Wimbrow, Ocean City, MD

TAKES: 20 min. • **MAKES:** 4 burgers

- **1 small onion, very finely chopped**
- **2 Tbsp. vegetable oil, divided**
- **1 can (15 oz.) black beans, rinsed and drained**
- **1 cup cooked brown rice**
- **¼ cup dry bread crumbs**
- **2 large egg yolks, lightly beaten**
- **2 Tbsp. plus ¼ cup salsa, divided**
- **½ tsp. salt**
- **¼ tsp. pepper**
- **¼ cup reduced-fat sour cream**
- **4 lettuce leaves**
- **4 slices reduced-fat cheddar cheese (1 oz. each)**
- **4 hamburger buns, split**
- **Optional: Sliced tomato and sliced red onion**

1. In a large nonstick skillet, cook chopped onions in 1 Tbsp. oil over medium heat until translucent but not browned, 2-4 minutes; remove from heat and set aside. In bowl of a food processor fitted with blade attachment, pulse half the beans and rice until mixture forms a thick paste. In a large bowl, add the processed bean mixture, remaining black beans and rice, cooked onion, bread crumbs, egg yolks, 2 Tbsp. salsa, salt and pepper; mix well with hands, squeezing until mixture holds together. Form bean mixture into 4 patties. Cook burgers over medium heat in remaining 1 Tbsp. oil until firm and browned, 4-5 minutes on each side.
2. In a small bowl, combine sour cream and remaining salsa. Layer a lettuce leaf, burger, cheese and sour cream mixture on each bun bottom, adding tomato and red onion as desired. Replace bun tops.
1 BURGER: *482 cal., 18g fat (6g sat. fat), 101mg chol., 1070mg sod., 55g carb. (7g sugars, 6g fiber), 21g pro.*

HEARTY HOMEMADE CHICKEN NOODLE SOUP

(*SHOWN ON PAGE 34*)

This satisfying homemade soup with a hint of cayenne is brimming with vegetables, chicken and noodles. The recipe came from my father-in-law, but I made some adjustments to give it my own spin.
—Norma Reynolds, Overland Park, KS

PREP: 20 min. • **COOK:** 5½ hours
MAKES: 12 servings (3 qt.)

- **12 fresh baby carrots, cut into ½-in. pieces**
- **4 celery ribs, cut into ½-in. pieces**
- **¾ cup finely chopped onion**
- **1 Tbsp. minced fresh parsley**
- **½ tsp. pepper**
- **¼ tsp. cayenne pepper**
- **1½ tsp. mustard seed**
- **2 garlic cloves, peeled and halved**
- **1¼ lbs. boneless skinless chicken breast halves**
- **1¼ lbs. boneless skinless chicken thighs**
- **4 cans (14½ oz. each) chicken broth**
- **1 pkg. (9 oz.) refrigerated linguine**
- **Optional: Coarsely ground pepper and additional minced fresh parsley**

1. In a 5-qt. slow cooker, combine the first 6 ingredients. Place the mustard seed and garlic on a double thickness of cheesecloth; bring up corners of cloth and tie with kitchen string to form a bag. Place in slow cooker. Add chicken and broth. Cover and cook on low for 5-6 hours or until chicken is tender.
2. Discard spice bag. Remove the chicken; cool slightly. Stir linguine into soup; cover and cook on high 30 minutes or until tender. Cut chicken into pieces and return to soup; heat through. Sprinkle with coarsely ground pepper and additional minced parsley if desired.
1 CUP: *199 cal., 6g fat (2g sat. fat), 73mg chol., 663mg sod., 14g carb. (2g sugars, 1g fiber), 22g pro.* **Diabetic exchanges:** *3 lean meat, 1 starch.*

LEBANESE STREET SANDWICHES

Arayes are grilled Lebanese-style pitas that are stuffed with a seasoned meat mixture. They're commonly found throughout the food stalls that line the streets of Beirut. If you'd rather not use a grill, they can be baked in the oven or made in a panini press, too.
—Nikki Haddad, Germantown, MD

PREP: 30 min. • **GRILL:** 10 min.
MAKES: 6 servings

- **2 large onions, coarsely chopped**
- **1½ cups packed fresh parsley sprigs**
- **1½ lbs. ground beef**
- **1 large egg, lightly beaten**
- **1 tsp. salt**
- **6 whole pita breads**
- **2 Tbsp. olive oil**

TAHINI SAUCE

- **⅓ cup tahini**
- **2 garlic cloves, minced**
- **¼ cup lemon juice**
- **2 Tbsp. water**
- **⅛ tsp. salt**

1. Place onions in a food processor; pulse until finely chopped. Remove and pat dry; transfer to a large bowl. Add parsley to processor; pulse until minced. Stir into onions. Add beef, egg and salt; mix lightly but thoroughly.
2. Slice pitas horizontally in half. Spread bottoms with meat mixture to edge. Replace pita tops; press lightly to adhere. Brush outsides of sandwiches with oil. Grill sandwiches, uncovered, over medium heat until a thermometer inserted into meat mixture reads 160°, 10-12 minutes, turning every 2 minutes. Cool slightly before cutting into quarters.
3. Combine sauce ingredients; serve with sandwiches.
1 SERVING: *545 cal., 28g fat (7g sat. fat), 101mg chol., 852mg sod., 42g carb. (3g sugars, 4g fiber), 30g pro.*

LEBANESE STREET SANDWICHES

GENERAL TSO'S CHICKEN SANDWICH WITH BROCCOLI SLAW

GENERAL TSO'S CHICKEN SANDWICH WITH BROCCOLI SLAW

I turned a classic takeout dinner into a sandwich that's simple to make at home. The air fryer keeps it lighter but still crunchy, and the recipe can be on the table in under 30 minutes, which is a must for our active family. We like spicy foods at our house, so this sauce has a good amount of heat.
—Julie Peterson, Crofton, MD

PREP: 30 min. • **COOK:** 10 min./batch
MAKES: 4 servings

- **½ cup reduced-fat mayonnaise**
- **2 Tbsp. honey**
- **1 Tbsp. rice vinegar**
- **2 tsp. hoisin sauce**
- **3 cups broccoli coleslaw mix**
- **½ cup sliced almonds**
- **1 lb. boneless skinless chicken thighs, cut into ½-in. strips**
- **4 Tbsp. cornstarch**
- **½ tsp. salt**
- **¼ tsp. pepper**

SAUCE

- **¼ cup hoisin sauce**
- **3 Tbsp. reduced-sodium soy sauce**
- **3 Tbsp. honey**
- **1 Tbsp. minced fresh gingerroot**
- **2 garlic cloves, minced**
- **½ to 1 tsp. crushed red pepper flakes**
- **Sesame seeds**
- **4 brioche hamburger buns, split**

1. In a large bowl, combine mayonnaise, honey, vinegar and hoisin sauce. Stir in coleslaw mix and almonds; refrigerate until serving.
2. Preheat air fryer to 400°. Toss chicken with cornstarch, salt and pepper. In batches, arrange chicken in a single layer on greased tray in air-fryer basket. Cook until lightly browned and chicken is no longer pink, 4-5 minutes on each side.
3. Meanwhile, in a small saucepan, combine hoisin sauce, soy sauce, honey, ginger, garlic and pepper flakes; bring to a boil. Reduce heat; simmer, uncovered, until sauce thickens, about 5 minutes. Add cooked chicken; toss to coat.
4. Spoon chicken on bun bottoms; top with the coleslaw mix and sprinkle with sesame seeds. Replace tops.

1 SANDWICH: *678 cal., 29g fat (5g sat. fat), 117mg chol., 1587mg sod., 75g carb. (37g sugars, 6g fiber), 32g pro.*

MEXICAN STREET CORN CHOWDER

Summer corn is one of my favorite vegetables, so when it's in season I always make this super easy soup in the slow cooker.
—Rashanda Cobbins, Milwaukee, WI

PREP: 35 min. • **COOK:** 3½ hours
MAKES: 8 servings (2 qt.)

- **10 ears fresh corn (about 5½ cups)**
- **1¼ to 2 cups water**
- **6 bacon strips, chopped**
- **2 small onions, chopped**
- **2 small green peppers, chopped**
- **1 jalapeno pepper, seeded and finely chopped**
- **1 tsp. ground chipotle pepper**
- **2 tsp. salt**
- **¾ tsp. ground cumin**
- **¼ tsp. pepper**
- **1 cup heavy whipping cream**
- **1 medium lime, zested and juiced**
- **Optional toppings: Fresh cilantro, lime wedges, sliced jalapeno, chopped bell pepper and crumbled cotija cheese**

1. Cut corn off cobs. Rub the edge of a knife over each cob to milk it; add enough water to cob juice to equal 2 cups. Add corn and liquid to a 5-qt. slow cooker.
2. In a large skillet, cook bacon over medium heat until crisp, 5-7 minutes. Remove with a slotted spoon; drain on paper towels. Discard drippings, reserving 2 Tbsp. in pan. Add the onions, green peppers and jalapeno to skillet; cook and stir over medium-high heat until soft, 3-4 minutes. Add seasonings and cook 1 minute longer; transfer to slow cooker. Cook on low 3½-4 hours or until corn is tender and mixture has thickened slightly.
3. Stir in cream and lime zest and juice. If desired, puree mixture with an immersion blender to desired consistency. Garnish with reserved bacon. Sprinkle with optional toppings as desired.

NOTE: Wear disposable gloves when cutting hot peppers; the oils can burn skin. Avoid touching your face.

1 CUP: *287 cal., 18g fat (9g sat. fat), 43mg chol., 743mg sod., 29g carb. (10g sugars, 4g fiber), 8g pro.*

MEXICAN STREET CORN CHOWDER

GRILLED PIMIENTO CHEESE SANDWICHES

Rich and creamy pimiento cheese is a southern favorite. It makes a tasty grilled cheese sandwich, especially with sweet hot pepper jelly. Serve this with a crisp salad for a fantastic lunch.
—Amy Freeze, Avon Park, FL

TAKES: 20 min. • **MAKES:** 2 servings

- **4 slices sourdough bread**
- **¼ cup butter, softened**
- **½ cup pimiento cheese spread**
- **2 Tbsp. pepper jelly**
- **6 cooked thick-sliced bacon strips**

1. Spread both sides of bread slices with butter. In a large skillet, toast bread on 1 side over medium heat until golden brown, 3-4 minutes.
2. Remove from heat; place toasted side up. Spread cheese over toasted bread slices. Top 2 slices with jelly, then with bacon. Top with remaining bread slices, cheese facing inward. Cook until bread is golden brown and cheese is melted, 3-4 minutes on each side. If desired, serve with additional jelly.
1 SANDWICH: *869 cal., 52g fat (28g sat. fat), 105mg chol., 1856mg sod., 70g carb. (19g sugars, 2g fiber), 27g pro.*

GRILLED PIMIENTO CHEESE SANDWICHES

SALMON SWEET POTATO SOUP

SALMON SWEET POTATO SOUP

I created this recipe as a healthier alternative to whitefish chowder, which is a traditional favorite in the area where I grew up. The salmon and sweet potatoes boost the nutrition and the slow cooker makes it more convenient to prepare. It's especially comforting on a cold fall or winter day!
—Matthew Hass, Ellison Bay, WI

PREP: 20 min. • **COOK:** 5½ hours • **MAKES:** 8 servings (3 qt.)

- **1 Tbsp. olive oil**
- **1 medium onion, chopped**
- **1 medium carrot, chopped**
- **1 celery rib, chopped**
- **3 garlic cloves, minced**
- **2 medium sweet potatoes, peeled and cut into ½-in. cubes**
- **1½ cups frozen corn, thawed**
- **6 cups reduced-sodium chicken broth**
- **1 tsp. celery salt**
- **1 tsp. dill weed**
- **½ tsp. salt**
- **¾ tsp. pepper**
- **1½ lbs. salmon fillets, skin removed and cut into ¾-in. pieces**
- **1 can (12 oz.) fat-free evaporated milk**
- **2 Tbsp. minced fresh parsley**

1. In a large skillet, heat oil over medium heat. Add onion, carrot and celery; cook and stir until tender, 4-5 minutes. Add garlic; cook 1 minute longer. Transfer to a 5-qt. slow cooker. Add the next 7 ingredients. Cook, covered, on low 5-6 hours, until sweet potatoes are tender.
2. Stir in salmon, milk and parsley. Cook, covered, 30-40 minutes longer, until fish just begins to flake easily with a fork.
1½ CUPS: *279 cal., 10g fat (2g sat. fat), 45mg chol., 834mg sod., 26g carb. (13g sugars, 3g fiber), 22g pro.* **Diabetic exchanges:** *3 lean meat, 1½ starch, ½ fat.*

PUMPKIN CLAM CHOWDER

When autumn arrives, I'm eager to celebrate with warm and cozy comfort food like this classic clam chowder, with pumpkin added. Use fresh clams if they are available. —Renee Murby, Johnston, RI

PREP: 30 min. • **COOK:** 30 min.
MAKES: 10 servings (2½ qt.)

- **6 bacon strips, chopped**
- **1 medium fennel bulb, chopped, fronds reserved**
- **1 medium onion, chopped**
- **½ cup chardonnay or clam juice**
- **5 bottles (8 oz. each) clam juice, divided**
- **4 cups cubed fresh pumpkin or butternut squash (½-in. cubes)**
- **2 medium potatoes, peeled and cut into ½-in. cubes**
- **⅓ cup all-purpose flour**
- **2 cans (10 oz. each) whole baby clams, drained**
- **1½ cups heavy whipping cream**
- **1 Tbsp. minced fresh tarragon or 1 tsp. dried tarragon**
- **½ tsp. salt**
- **½ tsp. pepper**

1. In a Dutch oven, cook bacon over medium heat until crisp, stirring occasionally. Remove with a slotted spoon; drain on paper towels. Cook and stir chopped fennel and onion in bacon drippings over medium heat until tender, 8-10 minutes. Add chardonnay to pan; increase heat to medium-high. Cook for 1-2 minutes, stirring to loosen browned bits from pan.

2. Add 4½ cups clam juice, pumpkin and potatoes. Bring to a boil; reduce heat. Simmer, uncovered, until pumpkin and potatoes are tender, 15-20 minutes, stirring occasionally.

3. Whisk flour and remaining ½ cup clam juice; stir into pan. Bring to a boil, stirring constantly; cook and stir until thickened, 2-3 minutes. Stir in clams, cream, tarragon, salt and pepper; heat through (do not boil). To serve, top soup with reserved chopped fennel fronds and cooked bacon.

1 CUP: *289 cal., 20g fat (11g sat. fat), 76mg chol., 661mg sod., 17g carb. (4g sugars, 2g fiber), 10g pro.*

HOISIN CHICKEN WRAPS

My recipe was inspired by Vietnamese pork banh mi, particularly the fresh carrot, cucumber and radish topping. It adds so much fresh flavor, color and crunch! —Debbie Glasscock, Conway, AR

PREP: 25 min. + marinating • **COOK:** 10 min.
MAKES: 6 servings

- **⅓ cup hoisin sauce**
- **¼ cup reduced-sodium soy sauce**
- **3 Tbsp. brown sugar, divided**
- **2 Tbsp. lime juice**
- **2 garlic cloves, minced**
- **6 chicken tenderloins (about ¾ lb.)**
- **2 Tbsp. rice vinegar**
- **¼ tsp. Sriracha chili sauce, divided**
- **1 cup julienned carrots**
- **1 cup julienned radishes**
- **1 Tbsp. canola oil**
- **½ cup mayonnaise**
- **1 tsp. honey**
- **6 flour tortillas (10 in.), room temperature**
- **4 miniature cucumbers, cut into thin ribbons**
- **Fresh mint or basil leaves**

1. In a small bowl or shallow dish, combine hoisin sauce, soy sauce, 2 Tbsp. brown sugar, lime juice and garlic. Add chicken; turn to coat. Refrigerate 30 minutes.

2. Meanwhile, in a large bowl, whisk rice vinegar, ⅛ tsp. Sriracha and remaining 1 Tbsp. brown sugar. Add carrots and radishes; toss to coat. Set aside.

3. Drain chicken, discarding marinade. In a large skillet, heat oil over medium heat. Add chicken; cook until a thermometer reads 165°, 4-5 minutes on each side. Remove to a cutting board; cool slightly. Slice into ½-in. pieces. Combine mayonnaise, honey and remaining ⅛ tsp. Sriracha; spread over tortillas. Layer with chicken, carrot mixture, cucumber and mint. Fold bottom and sides of tortilla over filling and roll up.

1 WRAP: *460 cal., 22g fat (4g sat. fat), 29mg chol., 828mg sod., 46g carb. (11g sugars, 4g fiber), 20g pro.*

DID YOU KNOW?

Hoisin sauce is a thick, sweet and somewhat spicy condiment popular in Chinese cooking. It's often made with fermented soybeans (miso), garlic, spices and sweet ingredients such as plums or sweet potatoes.

HOISIN CHICKEN WRAPS

STEAK SANDWICHES WITH CRISPY ONIONS

I created this recipe for my husband. He loves a good steak sandwich, but I wanted to do something a little different. The fried crispy onions are a family favorite and I thought it would be great to put them right on the sandwich. The chimichurri-inspired mayo gives it great freshness and flavor.
—Renee Seaman, Green Township, NJ

PREP: 45 min. + marinating • **GRILL:** 15 min.
MAKES: 6 servings

- **1 large sweet onion**
- **3 cups buttermilk**
- **2 cups minced fresh cilantro**
- **1 cup minced fresh parsley**
- **2 garlic cloves, minced**
- **½ tsp. plus 2 tsp. salt, divided**
- **¼ tsp. pepper**
- **½ cup mayonnaise**
- **½ cup plus 3 Tbsp. olive oil, divided**
- **1 beef flat iron steak or top sirloin steak (1½ lbs.)**
- **1½ cups all-purpose flour**
- **3 Tbsp. taco seasoning**
- **Oil for deep-fat frying**
- **12 slices Italian bread (½ in. thick)**
- **Optional: Fresh arugula and sliced tomato**

1. Cut onion into ¼-in. slices; separate into rings. Place in a large bowl or shallow dish. Add buttermilk; turn to coat. Refrigerate at least 4 hours or overnight.
2. In a small bowl, combine cilantro, parsley, garlic, ½ tsp. salt and pepper. Remove 2 Tbsp. herb mixture; stir into mayonnaise. Refrigerate until serving. Stir ½ cup olive oil into remaining herb mixture. Reserve 2 Tbsp. oil mixture for serving. Place the remaining oil mixture in a large bowl or shallow dish. Add beef; turn to coat. Refrigerate at least 4 hours or overnight.
3. Drain beef, discarding marinade. Grill beef, covered, over medium heat or broil 4 in. from heat until meat reaches desired doneness, 7-9 minutes on each side (for medium-rare, a thermometer should read 135°; medium, 140°; medium-well, 145°).
4. Meanwhile, drain onion rings, discarding marinade. In a shallow dish, combine flour, taco seasoning and remaining 2 tsp. salt. Roll onion rings in flour mixture. In an electric skillet or deep-fat fryer, heat 1 in. of oil to 375°. Fry onion rings, a few at a time, until golden brown, 1-1½ minutes on each side. Drain onion rings on paper towels; keep warm.
5. Remove steak to a cutting board; brush with reserved 2 Tbsp. oil mixture. Brush bread with remaining 3 Tbsp. olive oil. Grill bread over medium heat until toasted, 30-60 seconds on each side.
6. Spread the mayonnaise mixture over 1 side of each toast. Thinly slice steak. Top 6 slices of toast with steak, fried onions and, if desired, arugula and tomato slices. Top with remaining toast.

1 SANDWICH: *930 cal., 58g fat (10g sat. fat), 75mg chol., 1719mg sod., 68g carb. (6g sugars, 4g fiber), 32g pro.*

STEAK SANDWICHES WITH CRISPY ONIONS

TURKEY RANCH WRAPS

Here's a cool idea that's ready to gobble up in no time. It's a terrific use for deli turkey. Just add lettuce, tomato, green pepper, shredded cheese and ranch dressing for a flavorful blend.
—Taste of Home Test Kitchen

TAKES: 10 min. • **MAKES:** 4 servings

- **8 thin slices cooked turkey**
- **4 flour tortillas (6 in.), room temperature**
- **1 large tomato, thinly sliced**
- **1 medium green pepper, cut into thin strips**
- **1 cup shredded lettuce**
- **1 cup shredded cheddar cheese**
- **⅓ cup ranch salad dressing**

Place 2 slices of turkey on each tortilla. Layer with tomato, green pepper, lettuce and cheese. Drizzle with salad dressing. Roll up tightly.

1 SERVING: *403 cal., 25g fat (9g sat. fat), 76mg chol., 601mg sod., 19g carb. (3g sugars, 1g fiber), 26g pro.*

TOASTED CHICKEN SALAD SANDWICHES

I love chicken salad sandwiches. In this recipe, I use rotisserie chicken from the supermarket and toss it with avocado oil mayonnaise, capers and dill relish, then layer it on crusty bread with sliced radishes and butter lettuce. You can vary the flavor by adding herbs or some finely diced roasted red peppers.
—David Ross, Spokane Valley, WA

TAKES: 30 min. • **MAKES:** 10 servings

- **4 cups cubed rotisserie chicken**
- **¾ cup chopped celery**
- **½ cup chopped green onions**
- **½ cup reduced-fat mayonnaise or avocado oil mayonnaise**
- **2 Tbsp. capers, drained and chopped**
- **2 Tbsp. caper juice**
- **2 Tbsp. dill pickle relish**
- **½ tsp. salt**
- **½ tsp. pepper**
- **20 slices French bread (½ in. thick)**
- **3 Tbsp. butter, softened**
- **10 Bibb or Boston lettuce leaves**
- **1 cup thinly sliced radishes**

1. Place chicken in a food processor; pulse until finely chopped. Transfer to a large bowl; stir in the celery, green onions, mayonnaise, capers and juice, pickle relish, salt and pepper.
2. Brush 1 side of each bread slice with butter. In a large skillet, toast bread, buttered side down, in batches, over medium heat until golden brown. To assemble sandwiches, place 10 slices of bread toasted side down. Layer with lettuce, radishes and chicken salad; top with remaining toast slices.
1 SANDWICH: *249 cal., 12g fat (4g sat. fat), 63mg chol., 507mg sod., 15g carb. (1g sugars, 1g fiber), 19g pro.*

IRISH BEEF STEW

Rich and hearty, this stew is my husband's favorite. The beef is incredibly tender. Served with crusty bread, it's an ideal cool-weather meal and perfect for any Irish holiday.
—Carrie Karleen, Saint-Nicolas, QC

PREP: 40 min. • **COOK:** 3¼ hours
MAKES: 15 servings (3¾ qt.)

IRISH BEEF STEW

- **8 bacon strips, diced**
- **⅓ cup all-purpose flour**
- **1 tsp. salt**
- **½ tsp. pepper**
- **3 lbs. beef stew meat, cut into 1-in. cubes**
- **1 lb. whole fresh mushrooms, quartered**
- **3 medium leeks (white portion only), chopped**
- **2 medium carrots, chopped**
- **¼ cup chopped celery**
- **1 Tbsp. canola oil**
- **4 garlic cloves, minced**
- **1 Tbsp. tomato paste**
- **4 cups reduced-sodium beef broth**
- **1 cup dark stout beer or additional reduced-sodium beef broth**
- **2 bay leaves**
- **1 tsp. dried thyme**
- **1 tsp. dried parsley flakes**
- **1 tsp. dried rosemary, crushed**
- **2 lbs. Yukon Gold potatoes, cut into 1-in. cubes**
- **2 Tbsp. cornstarch**
- **2 Tbsp. cold water**
- **1 cup frozen peas**

1. In a stockpot, cook bacon over medium heat until crisp. Using a slotted spoon, remove to paper towels. In a large shallow dish, combine flour, salt and pepper. Add beef, a few pieces at a time, and turn to coat. Brown beef in the bacon drippings. Remove and set aside.
2. In the same pot, saute the mushrooms, leeks, carrots and celery in oil until tender. Add garlic; cook 1 minute longer. Stir in tomato paste until blended. Add the broth, beer, bay leaves, thyme, parsley and rosemary. Return beef and bacon to pot. Bring to a boil. Reduce heat; cover and simmer until beef is tender, about 2 hours.
3. Add potatoes. Return to a boil. Reduce heat; cover and simmer until potatoes are tender, about 1 hour longer. Combine cornstarch and water until smooth; stir into the stew. Bring to a boil; cook and stir until thickened, about 2 minutes. Add peas; heat through. Discard bay leaves.
1 CUP: *301 cal., 13g fat (4g sat. fat), 66mg chol., 441mg sod., 21g carb. (3g sugars, 2g fiber), 23g pro.*

READER REVIEW

"Hearty and robust stew with great complexity of flavors! Amazing!"
—GOOCH621, TASTEOFHOME.COM

SHRIMP TOSTADAS WITH AVOCADO SALSA
PAGE 53

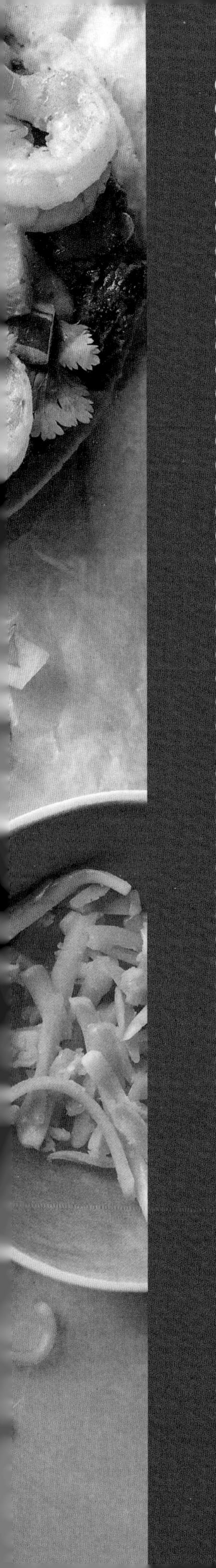

Quick Fixes

Turn here for dinners ready in just 30 minutes or less. You'll love adding these picks to your meal rotation.

MOST-REQUESTED RECIPES

One-Skillet Lasagna p. 50

Chicken Biscuit Skillet p. 52

Caribbean Shrimp Bowl p. 57

Mexican Steak Fajitas p. 60

CHICKEN BREASTS WITH MELON RELISH

CHICKEN BREASTS WITH MELON RELISH

This tropical-tasting melon relish is sweet and very flavorful. It tastes so good with the tender chicken breasts and is perfect for summer.
—*Roxanne Chan, Albany, CA*

TAKES: 30 min. • **MAKES:** 4 servings

- ¼ **tsp. salt**
- ¼ **tsp. ground ginger**
- ¼ **tsp. ground nutmeg**
- ¼ **tsp. pepper**
- 4 **boneless skinless chicken breast halves (6 oz. each)**
- 1 **Tbsp. canola oil**

RELISH

- 1 **cup diced cantaloupe**
- ¼ **cup finely chopped celery**
- 1 **green onion, chopped**
- 2 **Tbsp. minced fresh mint**
- 1 **Tbsp. chopped crystallized ginger**
- 1 **Tbsp. lime juice**
- 1 **Tbsp. honey**
- ½ **tsp. grated lime zest**

In a small bowl, combine the salt, ginger, nutmeg and pepper. Rub over both sides of chicken. In a large skillet, cook chicken in oil over medium heat 6-8 minutes on each side, until a thermometer inserted into chicken reads 165°. Meanwhile, in a small bowl, combine the relish ingredients. Serve with chicken.

1 CHICKEN BREAST HALF WITH ¼ CUP RELISH: *260 cal., 8g fat (2g sat. fat), 94mg chol., 243mg sod., 12g carb. (9g sugars, 1g fiber), 35g pro.* **Diabetic exchanges:** *4 lean meat, 1 starch, ½ fat.*

ONE-SKILLET LASAGNA

This is hands down one of the best skillet lasagna recipes our testing panel has ever tasted. With classic flavors and cheesy layers, it's definitely kid-friendly.
—Taste of Home *Test Kitchen*

TAKES: 30 min. • **MAKES:** 6 servings

- ¾ **lb. ground beef**
- 2 **garlic cloves, minced**
- 1 **can (14½ oz.) diced tomatoes with basil, oregano and garlic, undrained**
- 2 **jars (14 oz. each) spaghetti sauce**
- ⅔ **cup condensed cream of onion soup, undiluted**
- 2 **large eggs, lightly beaten**
- 1¼ **cups 1% cottage cheese**
- ¾ **tsp. Italian seasoning**
- 9 **no-cook lasagna noodles**
- ½ **cup shredded Colby-Monterey Jack cheese**
- ½ **cup shredded part-skim mozzarella cheese**

1. In a large skillet, cook beef and garlic over medium heat until meat is no longer pink; drain. Stir in tomatoes and spaghetti sauce and heat through. Transfer to a large bowl.
2. In a small bowl, combine the soup, eggs, cottage cheese and Italian seasoning.
3. Return 1 cup meat sauce to the skillet; spread evenly. Layer with 1 cup cottage cheese mixture, 1½ cups meat sauce and half the noodles, breaking to fit. Repeat layers of cottage cheese mixture, meat sauce and noodles. Top with remaining meat sauce. Bring to a boil. Reduce heat; cover and simmer for 15-17 minutes or until noodles are tender.
4. Remove from the heat. Sprinkle with shredded cheeses; cover and let stand for 2 minutes or until melted.

1 SERVING: *478 cal., 20g fat (8g sat. fat), 128mg chol., 1552mg sod., 43g carb. (15g sugars, 4g fiber), 31g pro.*

RAMEN NOODLE STIR-FRY

RAMEN NOODLE STIR-FRY

This mildly flavored stir-fry combines tender strips of chicken with vegetables and popular ramen noodles. I came up with this recipe when I wanted a quick-fix meal for myself. Sometimes I change the vegetables or substitute ground turkey for the chicken.
—Dawn Boothe, Lynn Haven, FL

TAKES: 15 min. • **MAKES:** 2 servings

1 pkg. (3 oz.) ramen noodles
1½ cups hot water
8 oz. boneless skinless chicken breasts, cut into 2-in. strips
2 tsp. canola oil, divided
1 large green pepper, cubed
⅔ cup chopped onion
1 garlic clove, minced
½ cup reduced-sodium chicken broth
2 tsp. reduced-sodium soy sauce
1 tsp. salt-free seasoning blend
1 small tomato, cut into wedges

In a bowl, place noodles in hot water for 2 minutes; drain and set aside. Discard seasoning package or save for another use. In a large nonstick skillet, stir-fry chicken in 1 tsp. oil until no longer pink. Remove and keep warm. Stir-fry the green pepper, onion and garlic in remaining 1 tsp. oil until crisp-tender. Add the chicken, broth, soy sauce, seasoning blend and noodles; toss gently. Add tomato; heat through.

2 CUPS: *410 cal., 15g fat (5g sat. fat), 63mg chol., 548mg sod., 38g carb. (6g sugars, 3g fiber), 30g pro.* **Diabetic exchanges:** *3 lean meat, 3 vegetable, 1½ starch, 1 fat.*

CRUMB-TOPPED SOLE

Looking for a low-carb supper that's ready in a pinch? These buttery sole fillets have just a dab of rich sauce topped with toasted bread crumbs.
—Taste of Home *Test Kitchen*

TAKES: 15 min. • **MAKES:** 4 servings

3 Tbsp. reduced-fat mayonnaise
3 Tbsp. grated Parmesan cheese, divided
2 tsp. mustard seed
¼ tsp. pepper
4 sole fillets (6 oz. each)
1 cup soft bread crumbs
1 green onion, finely chopped
½ tsp. ground mustard
2 tsp. butter, melted
Thinly sliced green onions, optional

1. Combine the mayonnaise, 2 Tbsp. cheese, mustard seed and pepper; spread over tops of fillets. Place on a broiler pan coated with cooking spray. Broil 4 in. from the heat until fish flakes easily with a fork, 3-5 minutes.
2. Meanwhile, in a small bowl, combine the bread crumbs, onion, ground mustard and remaining cheese; stir in butter. Spoon over fillets; spritz topping with cooking spray. Broil until golden brown, 1-2 minutes longer. Sprinkle with green onions if desired.

1 FILLET: *267 cal., 10g fat (3g sat. fat), 94mg chol., 378mg sod., 8g carb. (1g sugars, 1g fiber), 35g pro.* **Diabetic exchanges:** *5 lean meat, 1 fat, ½ starch.*

CRUMB-TOPPED SOLE

HAMBURGER STROGANOFF

This easy ground beef stroganoff makes a quick weeknight dinner. I like to serve it with a side salad for a complete meal.
—Deb Helmer, Lynden, WA

TAKES: 30 min. • **MAKES:** 6 servings

- **1½ lbs. ground beef**
- **½ cup chopped onion**
- **Dash garlic salt**
- **2 Tbsp. all-purpose flour**
- **1 cup water or beef broth**
- **1 can (10¾ oz.) condensed cream of mushroom soup, undiluted**
- **1 can (4½ oz.) mushrooms, drained**
- **1 cup sour cream**
- **Salt and pepper to taste**
- **Cooked noodles or rice**
- **Chopped fresh parsley, optional**

1. In a skillet, cook beef over medium heat, breaking into crumbles, until no longer pink, 5-7 minutes; drain. Add onion and garlic salt to beef; continue to cook until onion is soft. Stir in the flour; cook and stir 2-3 minutes. Add water or beef broth, condensed soup and mushrooms; bring to a simmer. Reduce heat; cook, stirring occasionally, 8-10 minutes.
2. Gently fold in sour cream; heat only until warm. Add salt and pepper. Serve over noodles or rice and, if desired, top with parsley.
1 SERVING: *318 cal., 19g fat (10g sat. fat), 84mg chol., 561mg sod., 10g carb. (3g sugars, 1g fiber), 23g pro.*

HAMBURGER STROGANOFF

CHICKEN BISCUIT SKILLET

CHICKEN BISCUIT SKILLET

My mother always made this when we were growing up. Now I make it for my own husband and kids. I use the small biscuits because they brown so nicely on top. I also add mushrooms sometimes because my family loves 'em.
—Keri Boffeli, Monticello, IA

TAKES: 30 min. • **MAKES:** 6 servings

- **1 Tbsp. butter**
- **⅓ cup chopped onion**
- **¼ cup all-purpose flour**
- **1 can (10½ oz.) condensed chicken broth, undiluted**
- **¼ cup 2% milk**
- **⅛ tsp. pepper**
- **2 cups shredded cooked chicken breast**
- **2 cups frozen peas and carrots (about 10 oz.), thawed**
- **1 tube (12 oz.) refrigerated buttermilk biscuits, quartered**

1. Preheat oven to 400°. Melt butter in a 10-in. cast-iron or other ovenproof skillet over medium-high heat. Add onion; cook and stir until tender, 2-3 minutes.
2. In a small bowl, mix flour, broth, milk and pepper until smooth; stir into pan. Bring to a boil, stirring constantly; cook and stir until thickened, 1-2 minutes. Add the chicken and peas and carrots; heat through. Arrange quartered biscuits over stew. Bake until biscuits are golden brown, 15-20 minutes.
1 SERVING: *320 cal., 11g fat (4g sat. fat), 42mg chol., 861mg sod., 36g carb. (4g sugars, 2g fiber), 22g pro.*

SHRIMP TOSTADAS WITH AVOCADO SALSA

(SHOWN ON PAGE 48)

Try this quick and easy entree for a fun, different Southwest meal idea. A splash of lime in the black beans balances the rich avocado salsa and shrimp.
—Karen Gulkin, Greeley, CO

TAKES: 30 min. • **MAKES:** 6 servings

- 1 **medium ripe avocado, peeled and chopped, divided**
- 1 **Tbsp. water**
- 3 **tsp. lime juice, divided**
- 2 **tsp. blackened seasoning, divided**
- 1 **tsp. ground cumin**
- 1 **can (15 oz.) black beans, rinsed and drained**
- 1 **small navel orange, peeled and chopped**
- ¼ **cup chopped red onion**
- 1 **jalapeno pepper, seeded and chopped**
- 1 **Tbsp. minced fresh cilantro**
- 6 **tostada shells**
- 1 **cup shredded reduced-fat Mexican cheese blend**
- 1 **Tbsp. canola oil**
- 1 **lb. uncooked large shrimp, peeled and deveined**

1. Preheat oven to 350°. In a small bowl, combine 2 Tbsp. avocado, water, 1 tsp. lime juice, 1 tsp. blackened seasoning and cumin. Set aside ¼ cup beans; add remaining beans to avocado mixture and mash with a fork. Stir in reserved whole beans. Set aside.
2. For salsa, in a small bowl, combine orange, onion, jalapeno, cilantro, and the remaining avocado and 2 tsp. lime juice. Cover and refrigerate until serving.
3. Place tostada shells on ungreased baking sheets; spread with bean mixture. Sprinkle with cheese. Bake until hot and cheese is melted, 4-6 minutes.
4. Meanwhile, in a large nonstick skillet, heat oil over medium-high heat. Add shrimp and remaining blackened seasoning. Cook and stir until shrimp turn pink, 4-6 minutes. Place on tostadas; serve with salsa.
NOTE: Wear disposable gloves when cutting hot peppers; the oils can burn skin. Avoid touching your face.
1 TOSTADA: *297 cal., 13g fat (4g sat. fat), 102mg chol., 446mg sod., 23g carb. (3g sugars, 5g fiber), 22g pro.* **Diabetic exchanges:** *3 lean meat, 2 fat, 1½ starch.*

WAFFLE-IRON PIZZAS

These little pizza pockets are a fun mashup using the waffle iron. Try your favorite toppings or even breakfast fillings like ham and eggs.
—Amy Lents, Grand Forks, ND

TAKES: 30 min. • **MAKES:** 4 servings

- 1 **pkg. (16.3 oz.) large refrigerated buttermilk biscuits**
- 1 **cup shredded part-skim mozzarella cheese**
- 24 **slices turkey pepperoni (about 1½ oz.)**
- 2 **ready-to-serve fully cooked bacon strips, chopped**
- **Pizza sauce, warmed**

1. Roll or press biscuits to fit waffle iron. On 1 biscuit, place ¼ cup cheese, 6 slices pepperoni and 1 scant Tbsp. chopped bacon to within ½ in. of edges. Top with a second biscuit, folding bottom edge over top edge and pressing to seal completely.
2. Bake in a preheated waffle iron according to manufacturer's directions until golden brown, 4-5 minutes. Repeat with remaining ingredients. Serve with pizza sauce.
1 PIZZA: *461 cal., 21g fat (8g sat. fat), 28mg chol., 1650mg sod., 50g carb. (5g sugars, 2g fiber), 19g pro.*

WAFFLE-IRON PIZZAS

SAUSAGE POTATO SKILLET

SAUSAGE POTATO SKILLET

During my childhood, I lived in an Italian neighborhood in New Jersey. Because both my parents were working, I went home for lunch with my Italian girlfriend. Lunch was always the same—sausage, fried potatoes, green peppers and onions—but I could never get enough of my favorite meal.
—Amelia Bordas, Springfield, VA

TAKES: 30 min. • **MAKES:** 2 servings

- **2 fresh Italian sausage links**
- **1 Tbsp. canola oil**
- **1 small onion, sliced**
- **¼ cup each sliced green and sweet red pepper**
- **2 small potatoes, sliced**
- **Salt and pepper to taste**

In a large skillet, brown sausage in oil until a thermometer reads 160°. Add onion and peppers; saute until vegetables are tender. Add potatoes and 2 cups water; bring to a boil. Reduce heat; cover and simmer for 15 minutes or until potatoes are tender. Drain; add salt and pepper.

1 SERVING: *416 cal., 22g fat (6g sat. fat), 45mg chol., 544mg sod., 40g carb. (6g sugars, 4g fiber), 15g pro.*

READER REVIEW

"I've been making this recipe regularly for years. The only difference is that I quadruple the batch...and I never have any leftovers!"

—KELLYS1061, TASTEOFHOME.COM

CRUNCHY BURGER QUESADILLAS

We love burgers—all kinds! We also love quesadillas and tacos. So I combined all of the above to make a great and very filling burger that my whole family loved.
—Ann Marie Eberhart, Gig Harbor, WA

TAKES: 30 min. • **MAKES:** 4 servings

- **1 lb. ground beef**
- **2 tsp. canola oil**
- **1 cup mayonnaise**
- **⅓ cup salsa**
- **4 flour tortillas (12 in.)**
- **4 slices pepper jack or cheddar cheese**
- **4 tostada shells**

1. Gently shape beef into 4 balls, shaping just enough to keep together (do not compact). In a large skillet, heat oil over medium heat. Working in batches, add beef. With a heavy metal spatula, flatten to ¼- to ½-in. thickness. Cook until edges start to brown, about 1½ minutes. Turn burgers; cook until well browned and a thermometer reads at least 160°, about 1 minute. Repeat with remaining beef. Remove from skillet; wipe skillet clean.

2. Combine mayonnaise and salsa; reserve half for serving. Spread remaining mixture over tortillas. On the center of each tortilla, place 1 slice cheese, 1 burger and 1 tostada shell. Fold sides of tortilla over burger; fold top and bottom to close, pleating as you go.

3. In batches, place wraps in skillet, seam side down. Cook over medium heat 1-2 minutes on each side or until golden brown. Serve with remaining sauce.

1 WRAP: *912 cal., 69g fat (17g sat. fat), 93mg chol., 1144mg sod., 41g carb. (2g sugars, 5g fiber), 31g pro.*

CRUNCHY BURGER QUESADILLAS

INDIAN-SPICED BEEFY LETTUCE WRAPS

Because I love Indian flavors, I almost always have coconut milk, a jar of mango chutney and garam masala seasoning in my pantry. This recipe is one of my go-tos when I am short on time but want something that tastes spectacular. If you'd like to give this a different style of Asian flair, use hoisin sauce in place of chutney and Chinese five-spice powder instead of the garam masala.
—Noelle Myers, Grand Forks, ND

TAKES: 30 min. • **MAKES:** 4 servings

- 1 **lb. ground beef**
- 1 **medium onion, finely chopped**
- 2 **garlic cloves, minced**
- ⅓ **cup mango chutney**
- 2 **Tbsp. soy sauce**
- 1 **tsp. garam masala**
- 1 **pkg. (12.7 oz.) Asian crunch salad mix**
- ¼ **cup canned coconut milk**
- 12 **Bibb or Boston lettuce leaves**
- 1 **medium mango, peeled and sliced**

1. In a large skillet, cook beef, onion and garlic over medium heat until beef is no longer pink and onion is tender, 6-8 minutes, breaking up beef into crumbles; drain. Stir in chutney, soy sauce and garam masala; heat through. Add salad mix (reserve packets); cook and stir until slightly wilted, about 5 minutes.

2. Combine coconut milk and reserved dressing packet until smooth. Spoon beef mixture into lettuce leaves; sprinkle with contents from reserved toppings packet. Drizzle with coconut milk mixture and top with mango.

3 FILLED LETTUCE WRAPS: *493 cal., 22g fat (8g sat. fat), 74mg chol., 957mg sod., 48g carb. (33g sugars, 5g fiber), 24g pro.*

INDIAN-SPICED BEEFY LETTUCE WRAPS

CHICKEN SCAMPI

This recipe is so delectable that I'm often asked to double it when family members visit over the holidays. I suggest preparing it with shrimp for a quick, convenient alternative that's also delicious.
—Janet Lebar, Centennial, CO

TAKES: 25 min. • **MAKES:** 2 servings

- 4 **oz. uncooked linguine**
- 3 **Tbsp. butter**
- 2 **Tbsp. olive oil**
- 2 **green onions, thinly sliced**
- 2 **garlic cloves, minced**
- 2 **boneless skinless chicken breast halves (4 oz. each)**
- ½ **tsp. salt**
- ¼ **tsp. coarsely ground pepper**
- ½ **cup chopped seeded tomatoes**
- 2 **Tbsp. lemon juice**
- 1 **Tbsp. minced fresh parsley**
- **Grated Parmesan cheese**

1. Cook linguine according to package directions. Meanwhile, heat a large skillet over medium heat. Add the butter and olive oil; cook the onions and garlic until tender. Sprinkle chicken with salt and pepper; add to skillet. Cook until a thermometer reaches 165°, 3-4 minutes on each side. Remove chicken and keep warm.

2. In the same skillet, combine the tomatoes, lemon juice and parsley; heat through. Drain linguine; toss with tomato mixture. Top with chicken and sprinkle with Parmesan cheese.

1 SERVING: *619 cal., 35g fat (14g sat. fat), 108mg chol., 791mg sod., 46g carb. (4g sugars, 3g fiber), 32g pro.*

CARIBBEAN SHRIMP BOWL

CARIBBEAN SHRIMP BOWL

After switching to a paleo diet a few years ago, we have started eating tons of veggies for almost every meal—yes, even breakfast. We've gotten used to swapping in cauliflower, broccoli and kale in place of carbs like rice or potatoes. This bowl is literally chock-full of veggies and has tons of Caribbean-inspired flavor! Plus, it is so simple to make and uses one skillet!
—Courtney Stultz, Weir, KS

TAKES: 30 min. • **MAKES:** 4 servings

- **2 Tbsp. olive oil or coconut oil, divided**
- **1 lb. uncooked shrimp (26-30 per lb.), peeled and deveined**
- **2 cups frozen riced cauliflower**
- **1 pkg. (12 oz.) broccoli coleslaw mix**
- **1 large sweet red pepper, chopped**
- **1 medium onion, chopped**
- **1 Tbsp. adobo seasoning**
- **¼ tsp. pepper**
- **¼ to ½ tsp. crushed red pepper flakes**
- **⅛ tsp. sea salt**
- **1 cup cubed fresh pineapple or unsweetened pineapple chunks, drained**
- **1 cup chopped peeled mango**
- **¼ cup minced fresh cilantro**

1. In a large skillet, heat 1 Tbsp. oil over medium-high heat. Add shrimp; cook and stir until shrimp turn pink, 3-4 minutes. Remove and keep warm.
2. In the same skillet, heat remaining 1 Tbsp. oil. Add cauliflower rice, broccoli slaw, red pepper, onion, adobo, pepper, pepper flakes and salt. Cook, covered, over medium heat until vegetables are crisp-tender, 8-10 minutes. Add pineapple, mango, cilantro and shrimp; heat through. Serve with additional cilantro if desired.
2¼ CUPS: *267 cal., 9g fat (1g sat. fat), 138mg chol., 1240mg sod., 26g carb. (16g sugars, 6g fiber), 23g pro.*

ANGEL HAIR PASTA WITH SAUSAGE & SPINACH

You won't miss the marinara once you taste this pasta dish flavored with chicken broth and Italian sausage. The sauce simmers away without much work on your part. My husband likes it so much that I make it twice a week.
—Daphine Smith, Baytown, TX

TAKES: 30 min. • **MAKES:** 4 servings

- **4 Italian sausage links (4 oz. each), sliced**
- **1 medium onion, chopped**
- **2 garlic cloves, minced**
- **2 tsp. olive oil**
- **2 cans (14½ oz. each) chicken broth**
- **8 oz. uncooked angel hair pasta, broken in half**
- **2 pkg. (9 oz. each) fresh spinach, trimmed and coarsely chopped**
- **2 Tbsp. all-purpose flour**
- **¼ tsp. pepper**
- **⅓ cup heavy whipping cream**

1. In a Dutch oven, cook the sausage, onion and garlic in oil over medium heat until meat is no longer pink; drain. Add broth; bring to a boil. Add pasta; cook for 3 minutes, stirring frequently.
2. Gradually add spinach. Cook and stir until pasta is tender and spinach is wilted, 2-3 minutes. In a small bowl, combine the flour, pepper and cream until smooth; gradually stir into pasta mixture. Bring to a boil; cook and stir until thickened, 1-2 minutes.
1½ CUPS: *563 cal., 26g fat (10g sat. fat), 77mg chol., 1546mg sod., 57g carb. (6g sugars, 6g fiber), 25g pro.*

ANGEL HAIR PASTA WITH SAUSAGE & SPINACH

SALMON GRILLED IN FOIL

SALMON GRILLED IN FOIL

Steamed in its own juices, this salmon is incredibly tender. Curry adds a punch of flavor that's perfectly balanced by onion and tomato.
—Merideth Berkovich, The Dalles, OR

TAKES: 20 min. • **MAKES:** 4 servings

- **4 salmon fillets (4 oz. each)**
- **1 tsp. garlic powder**
- **1 tsp. lemon-pepper seasoning**
- **1 tsp. curry powder**
- **½ tsp. salt**
- **1 small onion, cut into rings**
- **2 medium tomatoes, seeded and chopped**

1. Place salmon, skin side down, on a double thickness of heavy-duty foil (about 18x12 in.). Combine the garlic powder, lemon pepper, curry and salt; sprinkle over salmon. Top with onion and tomatoes. Fold foil over fish and seal tightly.
2. Grill, covered, over medium heat for 10-15 minutes or until fish flakes easily with a fork. Open foil carefully to allow steam to escape.
1 SERVING: *232 cal., 13g fat (3g sat. fat), 67mg chol., 482mg sod., 5g carb. (3g sugars, 1g fiber), 24g pro.*

AIR-FRYER ALMOND CHICKEN

My husband bought an air fryer oven about six months ago, after seeing it on television. We have used it at least twice a week and love how delicious the food has been. The chicken recipes are especially good because of how moist the chicken remains. We started a low-carb diet and did not want to use bread crumbs, so we tried the chicken with almonds and it is a favorite now.
—Pamela Shank, Parkersburg, WV

TAKES: 30 min. • **MAKES:** 2 servings

- **1 large egg**
- **¼ cup buttermilk**
- **1 tsp. garlic salt**
- **½ tsp. pepper**
- **1 cup slivered almonds, finely chopped**
- **2 boneless skinless chicken breast halves (6 oz. each)**
- **Optional: Ranch salad dressing, barbecue sauce or honey mustard**

1. Preheat air fryer to 350°. In a shallow bowl, whisk egg, buttermilk, garlic salt and pepper. Place almonds in another shallow bowl. Dip chicken into egg mixture, then into almonds, patting to help coating adhere.
2. Place chicken in a single layer on greased tray in air-fryer basket; spritz with cooking spray. Cook until a thermometer inserted in chicken reads at least 165°, 15-18 minutes. If desired, serve with ranch dressing, barbecue sauce or mustard.
1 CHICKEN BREAST HALF: *353 cal., 18g fat (2g sat. fat), 123mg chol., 230mg sod., 6g carb. (2g sugars, 3g fiber), 41g pro.*

AIR-FRYER ALMOND CHICKEN

PORK CHOPS WITH NECTARINE SALSA

My special pork dish has so much flavor and is a snap to prepare. A sweet, fruity salsa perfectly balances the spicy rub coating the pan-fried chops.
—Bonnie Bufford, Nicholson, PA

TAKES: 20 min. • **MAKES:** 4 servings

- 2 **tsp. chili powder**
- 1 **tsp. ground coriander**
- ½ **tsp. ground cumin**
- ½ **tsp. paprika**
- ¼ **tsp. salt**
- ¼ **tsp. pepper**
- 4 **boneless pork loin chops (4 oz. each and ½ in. thick)**
- 1 **Tbsp. olive oil**
- ¼ **cup salsa**
- 2 **Tbsp. apricot spreadable fruit**
- 2 **cups sliced peeled nectarines or peaches**
- 2 **Tbsp. minced fresh cilantro**
- 1 **Tbsp. minced fresh oregano or 1 tsp. dried oregano**

1. In a small bowl, combine the first 6 ingredients. Rub over both sides of pork chops. In a large nonstick skillet, cook pork chops in oil over medium-high heat until juices run clear, 5-6 minutes on each side. Remove to a serving platter and keep warm.
2. In the same skillet, combine salsa and spreadable fruit. Bring to a boil. Reduce heat; cook and stir over medium heat for 1 minute. Stir in nectarines, cilantro and oregano; cook until heated through, 2-3 minutes. Serve with pork.

1 PORK CHOP WITH ½ CUP SALSA: *246 cal., 10g fat (3g sat. fat), 55mg chol., 279mg sod., 15g carb. (10g sugars, 2g fiber), 23g pro.* **Diabetic exchanges:** *3 lean meat, 1 fruit.*

CHIMICHANGAS

CHIMICHANGAS

Though this is still debated, Tucson is generally credited as the original home of the chimichanga (fried burro, as we call them, stuffed with meat, onions and chiles). I've combined several recipes into this one, and it's fairly authentic.
—Laura Towns, Glendale, AZ

TAKES: 30 min. • **MAKES:** 12 servings

- ¼ **cup bacon grease**
- 2 **cups chopped or shredded cooked beef, pork or chicken**
- 1 **medium onion, diced**
- 2 **garlic cloves, minced**
- 2 **medium tomatoes, chopped**
- 2 **cans (4 oz. each) chopped green chiles**
- 1 **large peeled boiled potato, diced**
- 1 **tsp. salt**
- 1½ **tsp. dried oregano**
- 1 **to 2 tsp. chili powder or to taste**
- 2 **Tbsp. minced fresh cilantro**
- 12 **flour tortillas (12 in.), warmed**
- **Vegetable oil**
- **Optional toppings: Shredded cheddar cheese, sour cream, guacamole, salsa, shredded lettuce, chopped tomatoes, sliced ripe olives**

1. In a skillet, melt bacon grease over medium heat. Saute meat, onion, garlic, tomatoes, chiles and potato until the onion softens. Add salt, oregano, chili powder and cilantro; simmer 2-3 minutes.
2. Place a scant ½ cup meat filling on each tortilla. Fold, envelope-style, like a burrito. Fry, seam side down, in ½ in. of hot oil (360°-375°) until crispy and brown. Turn and brown other side. Drain briefly on a paper towel. Top as desired; serve immediately.

1 CHIMICHANGA: *343 cal., 13g fat (4g sat. fat), 25mg chol., 862mg sod., 41g carb. (2g sugars, 7g fiber), 16g pro.*

MEXICAN STEAK FAJITAS

CHICKEN-FRIED STEAKS

These crispy steaks will have people gushing about how good they are when you serve them for dinner. My husband asks me to prepare this recipe regularly. I like it because it's so easy to make.
—Denice Louk, Garnett, KS

TAKES: 25 min. • **MAKES:** 4 servings

- **2 cups all-purpose flour, divided**
- **2 tsp. baking powder**
- **¾ tsp. each salt, onion powder, garlic powder, chili powder and pepper**
- **1 large egg, lightly beaten**
- **1¼ cups buttermilk, divided**
- **4 beef cubed steaks (4 oz. each)**
- **Oil for frying**
- **1½ cups 2% milk**

1. In a shallow bowl, combine 1¾ cups flour, baking powder and seasonings. In another shallow bowl, combine egg and ¾ cup buttermilk. Dip each cube steak in buttermilk mixture, then roll in flour mixture. Let stand for 5 minutes.
2. In a large skillet, heat ½ in. of oil over medium-high heat. Fry steaks 5-7 minutes. Turn carefully; cook until coating is crisp and meat is no longer pink, about 5 minutes longer. Remove steaks and keep warm.
3. Drain, reserving ⅓ cup drippings; stir remaining flour into drippings until smooth. Cook and stir over medium heat for 2 minutes. Gradually whisk in milk and remaining buttermilk. Bring to a boil; cook and stir for 2 minutes or until thickened. Serve with steaks.

NOTE: To substitute for each cup of buttermilk, use 1 Tbsp. white vinegar or lemon juice plus enough milk to measure 1 cup. Stir, then let stand 5 min. Or, use 1 cup plain yogurt or 1¾ tsp. cream of tartar plus 1 cup milk.

1 STEAK WITH ½ CUP GRAVY: *537 cal., 11g fat (5g sat. fat), 186mg chol., 865mg sod., 64g carb. (11g sugars, 2g fiber), 43g pro.*

TEST KITCHEN TIP

Baking powder in the dredging mixture adds an airy texture to the crispy coating.

MEXICAN STEAK FAJITAS

Strips of sirloin pick up plenty of spicy flavor from a marinade seasoned with cayenne pepper and cumin. These colorful fajitas are speedy and satisfying.
—Shirley Hilger, Lincoln, NE

TAKES: 30 min. • **MAKES:** 6 servings

- **¼ cup orange juice**
- **¼ cup white vinegar**
- **4 garlic cloves, minced**
- **1 tsp. seasoned salt**
- **1 tsp. dried oregano**
- **1 tsp. ground cumin**
- **¼ tsp. cayenne pepper**
- **1 lb. beef top sirloin steak, cut into ¼-in. strips**
- **1 medium onion, thinly sliced**
- **1 medium green pepper, thinly sliced**
- **1 medium sweet red pepper, thinly sliced**
- **2 Tbsp. canola oil, divided**
- **6 flour tortillas (10 in.)**
- **Optional: Shredded cheddar cheese, picante sauce and sour cream**

1. In a large bowl, combine the orange juice, vinegar, garlic and seasonings; add the beef. Turn to coat; set aside. In a skillet, saute onion and peppers in 1 Tbsp. oil until crisp-tender; remove and set aside.
2. Drain and discard marinade. In the same skillet, cook beef in remaining 1 Tbsp. oil until it reaches desired doneness, 2-4 minutes. Return vegetables to pan; heat through. Spoon meat and vegetables onto tortillas. If desired, top with cheese and serve with picante sauce and sour cream.

1 FAJITA: *304 cal., 11g fat (2g sat. fat), 31mg chol., 425mg sod., 26g carb. (3g sugars, 5g fiber), 21g pro.*

PORTUGUESE SHRIMP

I received this recipe nearly 40 years ago from a co-worker who was raised in Portugal. She made it for an office potluck luncheon and everyone wanted the recipe! It is easy to make, impressive to serve, and delicious. The sauce is also good on fish fillets.
—Kristine Chayes, Smithtown, NY

TAKES: 30 min. • **MAKES:** 6 servings

- **2 Tbsp. olive oil**
- **1 medium onion, sliced**
- **½ cup chopped green pepper**
- **1 cup tomato sauce**
- **½ cup orange juice**
- **¼ cup diced pimientos, drained**
- **½ tsp. grated orange zest**
- **½ tsp. salt**
- **¼ tsp. pepper**
- **2 lbs. uncooked shrimp (16-20 per lb.), peeled and deveined**
- **4 cups hot cooked rice**
- **Minced fresh parsley, optional**

In a large skillet, heat oil over medium-high heat. Add onion and green pepper; cook until onion starts to turn brown, about 10 minutes. Stir in tomato sauce, orange juice, pimientos, zest, salt and pepper. Bring mixture to a boil, reduce heat and simmer 5 minutes. Add shrimp; simmer, covered, until shrimp turn pink, 4-5 minutes. Serve with rice. Sprinkle with parsley if desired.
1 SERVING: *336 cal., 7g fat (1g sat. fat), 184mg chol., 566mg sod., 38g carb. (4g sugars, 2g fiber), 29g pro.* **Diabetic exchanges:** *4 lean meat, 2½ starch, 1 fat.*

PORTUGUESE SHRIMP

STIR-FRIED SCALLOPS

STIR-FRIED SCALLOPS

Scallops meet mild tomato in this sublime stovetop supper. Try serving the saucy mixture over rice or angel hair pasta, and garnish with cilantro if you like.
—Stephany Gocobachi, San Rafael, CA

TAKES: 15 min. • **MAKES:** 2 servings

- **1 small onion, chopped**
- **3 garlic cloves, minced**
- **1 Tbsp. olive oil**
- **¾ lb. sea scallops, halved**
- **2 medium plum tomatoes, chopped**
- **2 Tbsp. lemon juice**
- **⅛ tsp. pepper**
- **Hot cooked rice or pasta, optional**

1. In a nonstick skillet or wok, stir-fry onion and garlic in hot oil until tender. Add scallops; stir-fry until scallops turn opaque. Add tomatoes; cook and stir until heated through, 1-2 minutes longer.
2. Stir in lemon juice and pepper. Serve with rice if desired.
1 CUP: *213 cal., 8g fat (1g sat. fat), 41mg chol., 672mg sod., 14g carb. (4g sugars, 2g fiber), 22g pro.* **Diabetic exchanges:** *3 lean meat, 2 vegetable, 1½ fat.*

CHIPOTLE PUMPKIN CHICKEN PIZZA, PAGE 71

Main Dishes

With this handy chapter, you'll find more than three dozen delicious options for Sunday dinners, party buffets and cozy weeknights. These family-favorite entrees will surely become staples in your home, too.

DISHES WE LOVE

Grilled Shrimp with Cilantro Dipping Sauce p. 65

Baked Chicken & Zucchini p. 69

Hearty Chicken Enchiladas p. 74

Mom's Oven-Barbecued Ribs p. 75

Herbed Roast Turkey Breast p. 84

Beer & Bacon Macaroni & Cheese p. 89

CHICKEN WITH PUMPKIN ALFREDO

CHICKEN WITH PUMPKIN ALFREDO

I love pumpkin and my kids love pasta, so this was a match made in heaven for us. Plus, it's an extra way to get some veggies into their diet. Use dairy-free or gluten-free ingredients if needed.
—Courtney Stultz, Weir, KS

PREP: 15 min. • **COOK:** 30 min. • **MAKES:** 4 servings

- **1 Tbsp. olive oil**
- **2 boneless skinless chicken breast halves (6 oz. each)**
- **1 Tbsp. Italian seasoning**
- **¾ tsp. salt**
- **½ tsp. pepper**
- **8 oz. uncooked spiral pasta**
- **2 cups fresh broccoli florets**
- **¼ cup butter, cubed**
- **3 garlic cloves, minced**
- **1 cup half-and-half cream**
- **1 cup canned pumpkin**
- **½ cup shredded Parmesan cheese**
- **4 bacon strips, cooked and crumbled**
- **⅛ tsp. ground nutmeg**
- **Minced fresh parsley**

1. In a large skillet, heat oil over medium heat. Sprinkle chicken with Italian seasoning, salt and pepper. Add to skillet; cook until a thermometer reads 165°, 6-8 minutes on each side. Remove and keep warm.
2. Meanwhile, in a large saucepan, cook pasta according to package directions, adding broccoli during the last 5 minutes of cooking. In the same skillet used to cook chicken, heat butter over medium heat. Add garlic; cook 1 minute. Stir in cream, pumpkin, Parmesan cheese and nutmeg until combined.
3. Drain pasta and broccoli; stir into sauce. Slice chicken; serve with pasta mixture. Sprinkle with bacon, parsley and if desired, additional Parmesan cheese.
1 SERVING: *631 cal., 30g fat (15g sat. fat), 123mg chol., 936mg sod., 53g carb. (6g sugars, 5g fiber), 35g pro.*

SLOW-COOKER ASIAN SHORT RIBS

My slow cooker is my best friend. I use it at least three times a week. This recipe is one of my favorites. The sauce can be used for other cuts of meat, too.
—Carole Resnick, Cleveland, OH

PREP: 15 min. • **COOK:** 6 hours • **MAKES:** 6 servings

- **¾ cup sugar**
- **¾ cup ketchup**
- **¾ cup reduced-sodium soy sauce**
- **⅓ cup honey**
- **¼ cup lemon juice**
- **3 Tbsp. hoisin sauce**
- **1 Tbsp. ground ginger**
- **2 garlic cloves, minced**
- **4 lbs. bone-in beef short ribs**
- **Optional: Hot cooked ramen noodles, sesame seeds, julienned green onions and carrots, sliced cucumber, radish, mushrooms and red chili pepper**

In a greased 4- or 5-qt. slow cooker, whisk together the first 8 ingredients. Add short ribs and turn to coat; cook, covered, on low 6-7 hours or until meat is tender. If desired, serve with ramen noodles and optional toppings.
1 SERVING: *460 cal., 15g fat (6g sat. fat), 73mg chol., 1706mg sod., 56g carb. (51g sugars, 0 fiber), 27g pro.*

SLOW-COOKER ASIAN SHORT RIBS

GRILLED SHRIMP WITH CILANTRO DIPPING SAUCE

I came up with this recipe when my daughter grew a beautiful jalapeno plant last summer. I already had some cilantro in the garden, so it seemed like a great combination for a sauce.
—Elizabeth Lubin, Huntington Beach, CA

PREP: 25 min. + marinating • **GRILL:** 5 min.
MAKES: 4 servings

- **2 Tbsp. minced fresh cilantro**
- **2 Tbsp. olive oil**
- **1 Tbsp. minced fresh chives**
- **1 garlic clove, minced**
- **1 lb. uncooked medium shrimp, peeled and deveined**

DIPPING SAUCE
- **1 cup fresh cilantro leaves**
- **1 cup fat-free mayonnaise**
- **1 jalapeno pepper, seeded**
- **1 garlic clove, peeled**
- **1 Tbsp. white vinegar**
- **1 tsp. sugar**
- **Dash cayenne pepper**

1. In a large bowl, combine the cilantro, oil, chives and garlic. Add the shrimp and turn to coat. Cover and refrigerate for 1 hour.
2. In a blender, combine sauce ingredients; cover and process until blended. Chill sauce until serving.
3. Thread the shrimp onto 4 metal or soaked wooden skewers. Grill, covered, over medium heat until shrimp turn pink, 2-3 minutes on each side. Serve with the dipping sauce.
NOTE: Wear disposable gloves when cutting hot peppers; the oils can burn skin. Avoid touching your face.
1 SERVING: *208 cal., 10g fat (2g sat. fat), 144mg chol., 615mg sod., 11g carb. (6g sugars, 1g fiber), 19g pro.*

READER REVIEW

"I made this for a get-together with neighbors and it was a hit! I'm using the extra dipping sauce on fish tacos this week."
—SAMMYMOM1, TASTEOFHOME.COM

GROUND BEEF WELLINGTONS

GROUND BEEF WELLINGTONS

Trying new recipes is one of my favorite hobbies. It's also the most gratifying. What could beat the smiles and compliments of the ones you love? This recipe is easy enough for weeknights yet fancy enough to serve for special occasions.
—Julie Frankamp, Nicollet, MN

PREP: 30 min. • **BAKE:** 25 min.
MAKES: 2 servings

- **½ cup chopped fresh mushrooms**
- **1 Tbsp. butter**
- **2 tsp. all-purpose flour**
- **¼ tsp. pepper, divided**
- **½ cup half-and-half cream**
- **1 large egg yolk**
- **2 Tbsp. finely chopped onion**
- **¼ tsp. salt**
- **½ lb. ground beef**
- **1 tube (4 oz.) refrigerated crescent rolls**
- **Large egg, lightly beaten, optional**
- **1 tsp. dried parsley flakes**

1. In a saucepan, saute mushrooms in butter until softened. Stir in flour and ⅛ tsp. pepper until blended. Gradually add the cream. Bring to a boil; cook and stir until thickened, about 2 minutes. Remove from the heat and set aside.
2. In a bowl, combine the egg yolk, onion, 2 Tbsp. mushroom sauce, salt and remaining ⅛ tsp. pepper. Crumble beef over mixture and mix well. Shape into 2 loaves. Separate crescent dough into 2 rectangles on a baking sheet. Seal perforations. Place a meat loaf on each rectangle. Bring dough edges together and pinch to seal. If desired, brush with egg wash. Bake at 350° until golden brown and a thermometer inserted into meat loaf reads 160°, 24-28 minutes.
3. Meanwhile, warm the remaining sauce over low heat; stir in parsley. Serve sauce with Wellingtons.
1 SERVING: *578 cal., 37g fat (16g sat. fat), 207mg chol., 909mg sod., 28g carb. (7g sugars, 1g fiber), 28g pro.*

FETA-STUFFED KIBBEH WITH HARISSA

FETA-STUFFED KIBBEH WITH HARISSA

There are countless versions of kibbeh recipes throughout the Middle East. This is our adaptation of this delicious dish. You can even substitute ground beef for lamb.
—Chris Bugher, Fairview, NC

PREP: 30 min. • **BAKE:** 15 min.
MAKES: 6 servings

- **1 cup bulgur (fine grind)**
- **¼ cup finely chopped red onion**
- **3 garlic cloves, minced**
- **2 tsp. ground allspice**
- **1 tsp. ground cumin**
- **½ tsp. salt**
- **½ tsp. ground cinnamon**
- **¼ tsp. pepper**
- **1 lb. ground lamb**
- **1 cup crumbled feta cheese**
- **¼ cup pine nuts**
- **2 Tbsp. harissa chili paste**
- **Refrigerated tzatziki sauce**

1. Preheat oven to 375°. Soak bulgur according to package directions. Drain and transfer to a large bowl. Add onion, garlic and seasonings. Add lamb; mix lightly but thoroughly. Divide meat mixture into 18 portions. In another bowl, combine feta, nuts and harissa. Shape each portion of meat mixture around 2 tsp. feta mixture to cover completely; form a football shape.
2. Place on parchment-lined baking sheets. Bake until cooked through, 15-20 minutes. Serve with tzatziki.

3 KIBBEH: *324 cal., 17g fat (7g sat. fat), 60mg chol., 474mg sod., 21g carb. (1g sugars, 4g fiber), 20g pro.*

TEST KITCHEN TIPS

- Try different fillings such as kalamatas, pepperoncini, or other cheeses.
- If you don't have tzatziki sauce, mix equal parts yogurt or sour cream with mayo. Then season with garlic, cumin, turmeric and lemon juice.

BAKED PASTA PUTTANESCA

This is a fancy version of my grandchildren's favorite baked spaghetti. It feels like such a special dinner, and it's so cozy for winter.
—Louise Miller, Westminster, MD

PREP: 25 min. • **BAKE:** 1 hour + standing
MAKES: 10 servings

- **1 pkg. (16 oz.) spaghetti**
- **1 lb. ground beef**
- **1 medium onion, chopped**
- **1 Tbsp. minced garlic**
- **1 jar (24 oz.) pasta sauce**
- **1 cup pitted ripe olives**
- **3 Tbsp. capers, drained**
- **3 anchovy fillets, minced**
- **½ to ¾ tsp. crushed red pepper flakes**
- **½ tsp. seasoned salt**
- **2 large eggs**
- **⅓ cup grated Parmesan cheese**
- **5 Tbsp. butter, melted**
- **2 cups 4% cottage cheese**
- **4 cups shredded part-skim mozzarella cheese**
- **Optional: Minced fresh basil, sliced olives and capers**

1. Preheat oven to 350°. Cook spaghetti according to package directions for al dente. Meanwhile, in a large skillet, cook beef, onion and garlic over medium heat until beef is no longer pink and onion is tender, 6-8 minutes, breaking up beef into crumbles; drain. Stir in pasta sauce, olives, capers, anchovies, red pepper flakes and seasoned salt; set aside.
2. In a large bowl, whisk the eggs, Parmesan cheese and butter. Drain spaghetti; add to egg mixture and toss to coat.
3. Place half of the spaghetti mixture in a greased 13x9-in. or 3-qt. baking dish. Top with half of the cottage cheese, meat sauce and mozzarella cheese. Repeat layers. Place baking dish on a rimmed baking sheet.
4. Cover and bake for 40 minutes. Uncover; bake until heated through, 20-25 minutes longer. Let stand 15 minutes before serving. If desired, sprinkle with fresh basil, olives and capers.

1¼ CUPS: *563 cal., 27g fat (13g sat. fat), 116mg chol., 1104mg sod., 48g carb. (10g sugars, 4g fiber), 33g pro.*

BAKED PASTA PUTTANESCA

MAIN DISHES

LEBANESE STUFFED CABBAGES

Malfouf, also known as Lebanese cabbage rolls, is a delicacy in the Middle East. Not only are cabbage rolls delicious, but they dress up any table with their beautiful presentation.
—Michael & Mathil Chebat, Lake Ridge, VA

PREP: 30 min. • **COOK:** 10 min.
MAKES: 6 servings

- **12 cabbage leaves**
- **1 cup canned garbanzo beans or chickpeas, rinsed and drained**
- **1 small onion, chopped**
- **½ cup cooked rice**
- **½ bunch fresh parsley, minced**
- **¼ cup butter, melted**
- **¼ cup olive oil**
- **¼ cup tomato paste**
- **1 tsp. Lebanese seven-spice blend**
- **1 tsp. ground allspice**
- **½ tsp. pepper**
- **½ lb. ground beef**
- **4 cups water**
- **½ cup lemon juice**
- **4 garlic cloves, minced**
- **Lemon slices, optional**

1. In batches, cook cabbage in boiling water until crisp-tender, 3-5 minutes. Drain; cool slightly. Trim thick vein from bottom of each cabbage leaf, making a V-shaped cut.
2. In a large bowl, combine garbanzo beans, onion, rice, parsley, butter, olive oil, tomato paste and seasonings. Add beef; mix lightly but thoroughly. Place about ¼ cup beef mixture on each cabbage leaf. Pull together cut edges of leaf to overlap; fold over filling. Fold in sides and roll up.
3. Place rolls in a Dutch oven, seam side down. Add water, lemon juice and garlic. Bring to a boil; reduce heat. Simmer, covered, until a thermometer inserted in beef reads 160° and cabbage is tender, 10-12 minutes. If desired, serve with lemon.
NOTE: Also known as baharat, Lebanese seven-spice blend is typically made with black pepper, allspice, nutmeg, cinnamon, coriander, cloves and ginger.
2 CABBAGE ROLLS: *311 cal., 22g fat (8g sat. fat), 44mg chol., 157mg sod., 19g carb. (5g sugars, 4g fiber), 11g pro.*

LEBANESE STUFFED CABBAGES

BROCCOLI TURKEY CASSEROLE

Whenever I serve this hearty, cheesy casserole at a gathering, people ask for the recipe. Sometimes I've given it out to everyone who was there!
—Muriel Shand, Isanti, MN

PREP: 20 min. • **BAKE:** 25 min.
MAKES: 8 servings

- **¼ cup chopped onion**
- **¼ cup chopped celery**
- **¼ cup butter, cubed**
- **4 cups cubed cooked turkey breast**
- **1 pkg. (16 oz.) frozen broccoli florets, thawed**
- **1 can (10¾ oz.) condensed cream of mushroom soup, undiluted**
- **1 can (10¾ oz.) condensed cream of chicken soup, undiluted**
- **1 cup cooked rice**
- **½ cup shredded part-skim mozzarella cheese**
- **1 can (2.8 oz.) french-fried onions**

1. In a large skillet, saute onion and celery in butter until tender. Stir in the turkey, broccoli, soups and rice; transfer to a greased shallow 2½-qt. baking dish.
2. Bake, uncovered, at 350° until bubbly, 25-30 minutes. Sprinkle with cheese and french-fried onions; bake until cheese is melted, about 5 minutes longer.
FREEZE OPTION: Sprinkle the cheese and french-fried onions over unbaked casserole. Cover and freeze. To use, partially thaw in the refrigerator overnight. Remove from refrigerator 30 minutes before baking. Preheat oven to 350°. Bake casserole as directed, increasing time as necessary to heat through and for a thermometer inserted in center to read 165°.
1 CUP: *344 cal., 17g fat (7g sat. fat), 84mg chol., 758mg sod., 20g carb. (2g sugars, 2g fiber), 26g pro.*

BAKED CHICKEN & ZUCCHINI

BAKED CHICKEN & ZUCCHINI

I love zucchini, so this colorful dish is one of my favorites, and I make it often in summer. It's especially good with garden-fresh tomatoes.
—Sheryl Goodnough, Eliot, ME

PREP: 20 min. • **BAKE:** 35 min. • **MAKES:** 4 servings

- **1 large egg**
- **1 Tbsp. water**
- **¾ tsp. salt, divided**
- **⅛ tsp. pepper**
- **1 cup dry bread crumbs**
- **4 boneless skinless chicken breast halves (6 oz. each)**
- **4 Tbsp. olive oil, divided**
- **5 medium zucchini, sliced**
- **4 medium tomatoes, sliced**
- **1 cup shredded part-skim mozzarella cheese, divided**
- **2 tsp. minced fresh basil**

1. In a shallow bowl, beat egg, water, ½ tsp. salt and pepper. Set aside 2 Tbsp. bread crumbs. Place the remaining crumbs in a large shallow dish. Dip chicken into egg mixture, then place in crumbs and turn to coat.
2. In a large skillet, cook chicken in 2 Tbsp. oil until golden brown, 2-3 minutes on each side; remove and set aside. In the same skillet, saute zucchini in remaining oil until crisp-tender; drain. Transfer to a greased 13x9-in. baking dish.
3. Sprinkle the reserved bread crumbs over the zucchini. Top with tomato slices; sprinkle with ⅔ cup mozzarella cheese, basil and remaining salt. Top with chicken. Cover and bake at 400° until a thermometer reads 170°, about 25 minutes. Uncover; sprinkle with remaining cheese. Bake until cheese is melted, about 10 minutes longer.
1 SERVING: *572 cal., 27g fat (7g sat. fat), 169mg chol., 898mg sod., 34g carb. (9g sugars, 5g fiber), 49g pro.*

SHEET-PAN JAMBALAYA WITH CAULIFLOWER RICE

Sheet-pan dinners are a busy cook's dream with quick prep and easy cleanup. This Cajun-inspired recipe is a healthy twist on a classic that uses cauliflower rice for a lower-carb supper.
—Julie Peterson, Crofton, MD

PREP: 20 min. • **BAKE:** 15 min. • **MAKES:** 4 servings

- **1 medium onion, chopped**
- **1 medium green pepper, chopped**
- **2 celery ribs, chopped**
- **4 oz. boneless skinless chicken breast, cut into 1-in. pieces**
- **2 fully cooked andouille sausage links, sliced**
- **4 garlic cloves, minced**
- **3 Tbsp. olive oil**
- **4 tsp. reduced-sodium Creole seasoning, divided**
- **1 pkg. (10 oz.) frozen riced cauliflower**
- **½ lb. uncooked shrimp (26-30 per lb.), peeled and deveined**
- **2 cups cherry tomatoes, halved**

1. Preheat oven to 425°. Place first 6 ingredients in a 15x10x1-in. baking pan. Drizzle with olive oil and sprinkle with 2 tsp. Creole seasoning; toss to coat. Bake 8 minutes.
2. Meanwhile, cook cauliflower according to package directions. Toss shrimp with remaining 2 tsp. Creole seasoning. Add shrimp, tomatoes and cauliflower to pan; stir to combine. Bake until shrimp turn pink, 5-7 minutes longer.
1½ CUPS: *366 cal., 23g fat (6g sat. fat), 158mg chol., 1301mg sod., 14g carb. (6g sugars, 4g fiber), 29g pro.*

SHEET-PAN JAMBALAYA WITH CAULIFLOWER RICE

MAIN DISHES

CATFISH PARMESAN

Mississippi is the nation's largest producer of farm-raised catfish. My family loves this dish, and asks for it often. One of the reasons I like it is that it's so simple to prepare.
—Mrs. W.D. Baker, Starkville, MS

PREP: 15 min. • **BAKE:** 20 min. • **MAKES:** 6 servings

- **¾ cup dry bread crumbs**
- **3 Tbsp. grated Parmesan cheese**
- **2 Tbsp. chopped fresh parsley**
- **½ tsp. salt**
- **¼ tsp. paprika**
- **⅛ tsp. each pepper, dried oregano and basil**
- **6 fresh or frozen catfish fillets (3 to 5 oz. each)**
- **½ cup butter, melted**
- **Optional: Tartar sauce and lemon wedges**

1. In a shallow bowl, combine the bread crumbs, Parmesan cheese, parsley and seasonings. Dip catfish in melted butter, then in crumb mixture. Arrange in a greased 13x9-in. baking dish.
2. Bake, uncovered, at 375° until fish just begins to flake easily with a fork, 20-25 minutes. If desired, serve with tartar sauce and lemon wedges.

1 FILLET: *219 cal., 18g fat (10g sat. fat), 50mg chol., 522mg sod., 10g carb. (0 sugars, 0 fiber), 5g pro.*

CATFISH PARMESAN

SKEWERED LAMB WITH BLACKBERRY-BALSAMIC GLAZE

SKEWERED LAMB WITH BLACKBERRY-BALSAMIC GLAZE

This dish proves it takes only a few quality ingredients to make a classy main dish.
—Elynor Townsend, Summerfield, FL

PREP: 10 min. + marinating • **GRILL:** 10 min. • **MAKES:** 6 servings

- **½ cup seedless blackberry spreadable fruit**
- **⅓ cup balsamic vinegar**
- **1 Tbsp. minced fresh rosemary or 1 tsp. dried rosemary, crushed**
- **1 Tbsp. Dijon mustard**
- **1½ lbs. lean boneless lamb, cut into 1-in. cubes**
- **¼ tsp. salt**

1. In a small bowl, combine the spreadable fruit, vinegar, rosemary and mustard. Pour ⅔ cup marinade into a shallow dish; add lamb. Turn to coat; cover and refrigerate for at least 1 hour. Cover and refrigerate remaining marinade for basting.
2. Drain lamb, discarding marinade in dish. Thread lamb onto 6 metal or soaked wooden skewers. Place kabobs on greased grill rack. Grill, covered, over medium heat or broil 4 in. from the heat until lamb reaches desired doneness (for medium-rare, a thermometer should read 135°; medium, 140°; medium-well, 145°), 10-12 minutes, turning once and basting frequently with reserved marinade. Sprinkle with salt before serving.

1 kabob: *255 cal., 9g fat (4g sat. fat), 103mg chol., 264mg sod., 9g carb. (7g sugars, 0 fiber), 32g pro.* **Diabetic exchanges:** *5 lean meat, ½ starch.*

TEST KITCHEN TIP

Do you avoid lamb because you've heard it has a strong flavor? Then try grain-fed lamb, which has a milder flavor than grass-fed lamb. Domestic lamb is usually grain-fed.

CHIPOTLE PUMPKIN CHICKEN PIZZA

(SHOWN ON PAGE 62)

Think pizza and pumpkin can't go together? Think again. The sweetness of the pumpkin paired with the spice of the chipotle peppers makes for a delicious, balanced sauce. I love the way this recipe incorporates healthy ingredients in a fun, family-friendly way.
—Julie Peterson, Crofton, MD

PREP: 20 min. • **BAKE:** 15 min./batch
MAKES: 2 pizzas (4 pieces each)

- **2 pkg. (7½ oz. each) frozen cauliflower pizza crust or 2 prebaked 12-in. thin whole wheat pizza crusts**
- **1 Tbsp. olive oil**
- **¾ cup canned pumpkin**
- **2 chipotle peppers in adobo sauce, minced**
- **¼ tsp. salt**
- **⅛ tsp. pepper**
- **1½ cups cubed cooked chicken**
- **½ cup mild chunky salsa**
- **1½ cups shredded part-skim mozzarella cheese**
- **¼ cup thinly sliced red onion**
- **Minced fresh cilantro, optional**

1. Preheat oven to 425°. Place crusts on ungreased baking sheets; brush with oil. Combine pumpkin, minced chipotle peppers, salt and pepper; spread over crusts. Combine chicken and salsa; spoon over pumpkin layer. Top with cheese and red onion.
2. Bake until edges are lightly browned and cheese is melted, 12-15 minutes. Let stand for 5 minutes before cutting. If desired, sprinkle with cilantro.

1 PIECE: *225 cal., 9g fat (3g sat. fat), 37mg chol., 504mg sod., 21g carb. (4g sugars, 3g fiber), 15g pro.* **Diabetic exchanges:** *2 lean meat, 1 starch, 1 vegetable, ½ fat.*

SPAGHETTI WITH BACON

As children, we always requested this dish for our birthday dinners. Our mother got the recipe from her grandmother. Now I pass on our tasty tradition.
—Ruth Keogh, North St. Paul, MN

PREP: 20 min. • **BAKE:** 40 min.
MAKES: 4 servings

- **8 oz. uncooked spaghetti**
- **½ lb. bacon strips, chopped**
- **1 medium onion, chopped**
- **1 can (14½ oz.) diced tomatoes, undrained**
- **1 can (8 oz.) tomato sauce**
- **Minced fresh parsley, optional**

1. Preheat oven to 350°. Cook spaghetti according to package directions for al dente.
2. In a large skillet, cook bacon and onion over medium heat until bacon is crisp, stirring occasionally; drain. Stir in tomatoes and tomato sauce; bring to a boil.
3. Drain spaghetti; transfer to a greased 11x7-in. baking dish. Spread sauce over top. Bake, covered, until bubbly, 40-45 minutes. If desired, sprinkle with parsley.

1 SERVING: *159 cal., 6g fat (2g sat. fat), 11mg chol., 498mg sod., 18g carb. (4g sugars, 2g fiber), 7g pro.*

SPAGHETTI WITH BACON

AIR-FRYER NASHVILLE
HOT CHICKEN
MAIN DISHES

AIR-FRYER NASHVILLE HOT CHICKEN

I live in Tennessee and absolutely love the famous Nashville hot chicken. In an attempt to make it easier to prepare, I thought I'd try cooking it in my air fryer. I'm so glad I did; this is almost better than the original.
—April H. Lane, Greeneville, TN

PREP: 30 min. • **COOK:** 10 min./batch
MAKES: 6 servings

- 2 **Tbsp. dill pickle juice, divided**
- 2 **Tbsp. hot pepper sauce, divided**
- 1 **tsp. salt, divided**
- 2 **lbs. chicken tenderloins**
- 1 **cup all-purpose flour**
- ½ **tsp. pepper**
- 1 **large egg**
- ½ **cup buttermilk**
- **Cooking spray**
- ½ **cup olive oil**
- 2 **Tbsp. cayenne pepper**
- 2 **Tbsp. dark brown sugar**
- 1 **tsp. paprika**
- 1 **tsp. chili powder**
- ½ **tsp. garlic powder**
- **Dill pickle slices**

1. In a bowl or shallow dish, combine 1 Tbsp. pickle juice, 1 Tbsp. hot sauce and ½ tsp. salt. Add chicken and turn to coat. Refrigerate, covered, at least 1 hour. Drain, discarding any marinade.
2. Preheat air fryer to 375°. In a shallow bowl, mix flour, remaining ½ tsp. salt and the pepper. In another shallow bowl, whisk egg, buttermilk, and the remaining 1 Tbsp. pickle juice and 1 Tbsp. hot sauce. Dip chicken in flour to coat both sides; shake off excess. Dip in egg mixture, then again in flour mixture.
3. In batches, arrange chicken in a single layer on well-greased tray in air-fryer basket; spritz with cooking spray. Cook until golden brown, 5-6 minutes. Turn; spritz with cooking spray. Cook until golden brown, 5-6 minutes longer.
4. Whisk together oil, cayenne pepper, brown sugar and seasonings; pour over hot chicken and toss to coat. Serve with pickles.
5 OZ. COOKED CHICKEN: *413 cal., 21g fat (3g sat. fat), 96mg chol., 170mg sod., 20g carb. (5g sugars, 1g fiber), 39g pro.*

MINT LAMB STEW

MINT LAMB STEW

The lamb here isn't just tender—it melts in your mouth! This recipe is an adaptation of a stew my mother used to make while I was growing up in England. Now I round it out with local root vegetables.
—Maureen Evans, Rancho Cucamonga, CA

PREP: 40 min. • **COOK:** 6 hours
MAKES: 6 servings (2¼ qt.)

- ½ **cup all-purpose flour**
- ½ **tsp. salt**
- ¼ **tsp. pepper**
- 1½ **lbs. lamb stew meat, cubed**
- 2 **shallots, sliced**
- 2 **Tbsp. olive oil**
- ½ **cup red wine**
- 2 **cans (14½ oz. each) beef broth**
- 2 **medium potatoes, cubed**
- 1 **large sweet potato, peeled and cubed**
- 2 **large carrots, cut into 1-in. pieces**
- 2 **medium parsnips, peeled and cubed**
- 1 **garlic clove, minced**
- 1 **Tbsp. mint jelly**
- 4 **bacon strips, cooked and crumbled**
- **Minced fresh mint, optional**

1. In a large shallow dish, combine the flour, salt and pepper. Add the meat, a few pieces at a time, and turn to coat. In a large skillet, brown meat and shallots in oil in batches.
2. Transfer to a 5- or 6-qt. slow cooker. Add the red wine to the skillet, stirring to loosen any browned bits from pan. Bring to a boil. Reduce the heat; simmer, uncovered, for 1-2 minutes. Add to slow cooker.
3. Stir in the broth, potatoes, sweet potato, carrots, parsnips and garlic. Cover and cook on low for 6-8 hours or until meat is tender. Stir in jelly; sprinkle with bacon. If desired, sprinkle with fresh mint before serving.
1½ CUPS: *442 cal., 13g fat (4g sat. fat), 79mg chol., 1016mg sod., 46g carb. (11g sugars, 5g fiber), 31g pro.*

MAIN DISHES

HEARTY CHICKEN ENCHILADAS

My husband, Nathan, and I really like Mexican food, and this is our favorite dish. You can modify it to suit your taste by adding corn, rice or refried beans.
—Jenny Miller, Raleigh, NC

PREP: 30 min. + simmering • **BAKE:** 25 min.
MAKES: 2 casseroles (2 servings each)

- 1 **lb. boneless skinless chicken breasts**
- 2 **cans (15 oz. each) enchilada sauce**
- 1 **can (4 oz.) chopped green chiles**
- 1 **can (15 oz.) black beans, rinsed and drained**
- 8 **flour tortillas (6 in.)**
- 1 **cup shredded Mexican cheese blend**

Optional toppings: Sour cream, shredded lettuce, pico de gallo and sliced avocado

1. In a 3-qt. slow cooker, combine the chicken, enchilada sauce and chiles. Cover and cook on low for 6-8 hours or until meat is tender.

2. Remove chicken and shred with 2 forks. Reserve 1⅔ cups cooking juices. Pour the remaining cooking juices into a large bowl; add the beans and shredded chicken. Coat 2 freezer-safe 8-in. square baking dishes with cooking spray; add ½ cup reserved juices to each.

3. Place about ⅓ cup chicken mixture down the center of each tortilla. Roll up and place seam side down in prepared dishes. Pour remaining reserved juices over top; sprinkle with cheese.

4. Cover 1 dish and freeze for up to 3 months. Cover and bake second dish at 350° for 20 minutes. Uncover; bake until cheese is lightly browned, about 5 minutes longer. Serve with toppings as desired.

To use frozen enchiladas: Thaw in the refrigerator overnight. Remove from the refrigerator 30 minutes before baking. Bake as directed.

2 ENCHILADAS: *577 cal., 20g fat (4g sat. fat), 83mg chol., 1541mg sod., 57g carb. (8g sugars, 8g fiber), 46g pro.*

DID YOU KNOW?

Enchilada sauce is a blend of tomatoes, oil and spices thickened with a little flour or cornstarch. Green enchilada sauce, which is made from tomatillos instead of tomatoes, is also available.

HEARTY CHICKEN ENCHILADAS

MOM'S OVEN-BARBECUED RIBS

My mom made these tender ribs for special Sunday suppers when we were growing up. A few common ingredients are all you need to make the zesty sauce that coats them. Everyone's eyes light up when I bring these ribs to the table.
—Yvonne White, Williamson, NY

PREP: 10 min. • **BAKE:** 2¾ hours
MAKES: 6 servings

- **3 to 4 lbs. country-style pork ribs**
- **1½ cups water**
- **1 cup ketchup**
- **⅓ cup Worcestershire sauce**
- **1 tsp. salt**
- **1 tsp. chili powder**
- **½ tsp. onion powder**
- **⅛ tsp. hot pepper sauce**

Preheat oven to 350°. Place ribs in a greased roasting pan. Bake, uncovered, for 45 minutes. Meanwhile, in a saucepan, combine the remaining ingredients. Bring to a boil; cook 1 minute. Drain ribs. Spoon sauce over ribs. Cover and bake 1½ hours. Uncover ribs; bake 30 minutes longer, basting once.

1 SERVING: *289 cal., 14g fat (5g sat. fat), 86mg chol., 1084mg sod., 14g carb. (4g sugars, 1g fiber), 27g pro.*

MALAI KOFTA

Malai kofta consists of delicious potato and cheese balls in a velvety tomato-based curry sauce. The air fryer lightens up the dumplings, which are usually deep-fried, while the pressure cooker makes the curry sauce effortless.
—Soniya Saluja, Chantilly, VA

PREP: 30 min. • **COOK:** 25 min.
MAKES: 20 kofta (4 cups gravy)

KOFTA

- **2 large potatoes, peeled and cubed**
- **8 oz. paneer, crumbled, or 1 cup 4% cottage cheese**
- **½ tsp. ground cardamom**
- **½ tsp. salt**
- **2 Tbsp. raisins**
- **2 Tbsp. salted cashews**

GRAVY

- **3 large tomatoes, chopped**
- **½ cup plain yogurt**
- **½ cup water**
- **¼ cup chopped cashews**
- **1 Tbsp. ginger garlic paste**
- **2 tsp. red chili powder, divided**
- **1 Tbsp. ghee or canola oil**
- **2 tsp. garam masala**
- **2 Tbsp. sugar**
- **2 Tbsp. dried fenugreek leaves**
- **2 to 4 Tbsp. heavy whipping cream, optional**

MALAI KOFTA

1. Place potatoes in a large saucepan and cover with water. Bring to a boil. Reduce heat and cook for 10 minutes or until tender; drain. Mash potatoes; cool to room temperature.

2. Preheat air fryer to 375°. In a large bowl, stir together potatoes, paneer, cardamom and salt until combined. Spoon 2 Tbsp. of potato mixture in lightly greased hands and flatten to ⅛ in. thick. Press a raisin and cashew in the center; bring sides up to enclose. Gently roll into a ball. Repeat with remaining potato mixture. Spritz fryer basket with cooking spray. Working in batches if needed, place balls in a single layer in basket lined with parchment. Cook until golden brown, 10-15 minutes.

3. Meanwhile, for the gravy, in a 6-qt. electric pressure cooker, combine tomatoes, yogurt, water, cashews, ginger garlic paste and 1 tsp. red chili powder. Lock lid; close pressure-release valve. Adjust to pressure-cook on high for 6 minutes. Quick-release pressure. Using an immersion blender, puree mixture until smooth. Strain mixture, pressing to extract as much liquid as possible; discard solids. Wipe insert clean.

4. Select saute setting and adjust for medium heat; add ghee. When ghee is hot, add garam masala and remaining 1 tsp. red chili powder; cook, stirring constantly, until very fragrant, 1-2 minutes. Stir in the strained tomato mixture and sugar. Simmer, uncovered, until mixture is slightly thickened, 5-8 minutes. Add fenugreek and, if desired, cream; cook 1 minute. Pour mixture over kofta.

4 KOFTA WITH ABOUT ¾ CUP GRAVY: *442 cal., 26g fat (13g sat. fat), 63mg chol., 386mg sod., 40g carb. (15g sugars, 4g fiber), 16g pro.*

VEGAN BUTTER CAULIFLOWER

VEGAN BUTTER CAULIFLOWER

I created this Indian butter cauliflower recipe for all the picky eaters in my family who love ethnic food. It's also vegan-friendly.
—Mihaela Metaxa-Albu, London, NY

PREP: 25 min. • **COOK:** 20 min.
MAKES: 4 servings

- **1 large head cauliflower, cut into florets**
- **2 Tbsp. coconut oil, melted**
- **1 Tbsp. minced fresh gingerroot**
- **2 garlic cloves, minced**
- **1 tsp. garam masala**
- **¼ tsp. salt**
- **¼ tsp. pepper**

SAUCE
- **1 Tbsp. olive oil**
- **½ cup chopped onion**
- **1 Tbsp. minced fresh gingerroot**
- **2 garlic cloves, minced**
- **2 tsp. garam masala**
- **2 tsp. curry powder**
- **1 tsp. cayenne pepper, optional**
- **1 can (15 oz.) crushed tomatoes**
- **1 can (13.66 oz.) coconut milk**
- **¼ tsp. salt**
- **¼ tsp. pepper**
- **¼ cup chopped fresh cilantro**
- **Optional: Hot cooked rice, naan flatbreads and lime wedges**

1. Preheat broiler. In a bowl, combine first 7 ingredients; toss to coat. Transfer to a rimmed baking sheet. Broil 3-4 in. from heat until the cauliflower is brown and crisp-tender, 12-15 minutes, turning once.
2. Meanwhile, in a large skillet, heat oil over medium-high heat. Add chopped onion; cook and stir until tender, 4-5 minutes. Add next 4 ingredients and, if desired, cayenne pepper; cook 1 minute longer. Stir in the tomatoes, coconut milk, salt and pepper. Bring to a boil; reduce heat. Simmer, uncovered, until thickened, 10-12 minutes, stirring occasionally. Stir in cauliflower; sprinkle with cilantro. If desired, serve with rice, naan and lime wedges.
1½ CUPS: *349 cal., 27g fat (22g sat. fat), 0 chol., 584mg sod., 24g carb. (11g sugars, 7g fiber), 8g pro.*

QUICK & EASY CHICKEN POKE BOWL

This poke bowl is a great alternative when sushi-grade fish isn't in the budget. I love it because it's quick, easy and inexpensive. While it's not a traditional poke recipe, the chicken still rocks in this bowl.
—Emily Cresta, Oxford, OH

PREP: 25 min. + chilling • **COOK:** 5 min.
MAKES: 4 servings

- **1 cup uncooked sushi (short grain) rice**

PICKLED ONIONS
- **½ cup cider vinegar**
- **1 Tbsp. sugar**
- **1 small red onion, thinly sliced**

SPICY MAYONNAISE
- **⅓ cup mayonnaise**
- **4 tsp. Sriracha chili sauce**

POKE BOWL
- **2 cups shredded rotisserie chicken**
- **2 Tbsp. reduced-sodium soy sauce**
- **2 tsp. toasted sesame oil**
- **1 tsp. honey**
- **1 medium ripe avocado, peeled and sliced**
- **½ small cucumber, thinly sliced**
- **1 cup alfalfa or bean sprouts**
- **Optional: Sliced green onions and sesame seeds**

1. Cook the rice according to package directions. Meanwhile, in a resealable jar, whisk vinegar and sugar until dissolved; add red onion. Seal and refrigerate 30 minutes or up to 2 weeks. In a small bowl, stir together mayonnaise and chili sauce; refrigerate, covered, until serving.
2. In a large skillet or wok, toss chicken, soy sauce, sesame oil and honey. Cook and stir over medium-low heat until chicken is heated through, 5-7 minutes. To serve, divide rice among 4 serving bowls. Top with chicken mixture, avocado, cucumber, sprouts, pickled onions, spicy mayonnaise and, if desired, sliced green onions and sesame seeds.
1 BOWL: *539 cal., 26g fat (5g sat. fat), 64mg chol., 606mg sod., 49g carb. (4g sugars, 4g fiber), 25g pro.*

QUICK & EASY
CHICKEN POKE BOWL

HOME-STYLE ROAST BEEF

HOME-STYLE ROAST BEEF

A very tender roast, this gains richness from the gravy, and the bacon gives it a different taste. For variety, you can cube the roast and serve it over rice with gravy...or cube and mix it with noodles, gravy and vegetables if you'd like to make it into a casserole.
—Sandra Furman-Krajewski, Amsterdam, NY

PREP: 10 min. • **BAKE:** 2½ hours + standing
MAKES: 10 servings

- **1 beef rump roast or bottom round roast (3 to 4 lbs.)**
- **1 can (14½ oz.) chicken broth**
- **1 can (10¼ oz.) beef gravy**
- **1 can (10¾ oz.) condensed cream of celery soup, undiluted**
- **¼ cup water**
- **¼ cup Worcestershire sauce**
- **¼ cup soy sauce**
- **3 Tbsp. dried parsley flakes**
- **3 Tbsp. dill weed**
- **2 Tbsp. dried thyme**
- **4½ tsp. garlic powder**
- **1 tsp. celery salt**
- **Pepper to taste**
- **1 large onion, sliced ¼ in. thick**
- **8 bacon strips**
- **¼ cup butter, cubed**

1. Place roast in a large roasting pan with fat side up. In a small bowl, combine the broth, gravy, soup, water, Worcestershire sauce and soy sauce; pour over roast. Sprinkle with seasonings. Arrange onion slices over roast. Place bacon strips diagonally over onion. Dot with butter.
2. Bake, uncovered, at 325° until the meat reaches desired doneness (for medium-rare, a thermometer should read 135°; medium, 140°; medium-well, 145°), 2½-3 hours. Let stand for 15 minutes before slicing.

4 OZ. COOKED BEEF: *368 cal., 22g fat (8g sat. fat), 112mg chol., 1277mg sod., 9g carb. (2g sugars, 2g fiber), 32g pro.*

TASTY TUNA CASSEROLE

This is not your usual tuna casserole. The macaroni and tuna are coated in a rich and creamy sauce with a kiss of tomato.
—Elsie Epp, Newton, KS

PREP: 20 min. • **BAKE:** 20 min.
MAKES: 4 servings

- **2 cups uncooked elbow macaroni**
- **1 can (12 oz.) albacore white tuna in water**
- **1 can (8 oz.) tomato sauce**
- **4 oz. reduced-fat cream cheese, cubed**
- **1 small onion, finely chopped**
- **¼ tsp. salt**
- **½ tsp. dried oregano**

1. Cook macaroni according to package directions. Meanwhile, in a large bowl, combine the remaining ingredients. Drain macaroni; stir into tuna mixture.
2. Transfer mixture to a 2-qt. baking dish coated with cooking spray. Cover and bake at 350° until heated through, 20-25 minutes.

1½ CUPS: *334 cal., 9g fat (5g sat. fat), 56mg chol., 851mg sod., 33g carb. (4g sugars, 2g fiber), 29g pro.*

TUNA MAC & CHEESE: Prepare 1 package (7¼ oz.) macaroni and cheese according to package directions; stir in 1 can (10¾ oz.) condensed cream of celery soup, the tuna and ½ cup milk. Sprinkle with 1 cup shredded cheddar cheese. Bake as directed.

TUNA VEGGIE MACARONI: Substitute 10 oz. cubed Velveeta, 4 cups frozen peas and carrots (thawed), 1 cup milk and ½ tsp. dill weed for the tomato sauce, cream cheese, onion, salt and oregano. Proceed as directed.

STEAKHOUSE PIZZA

One of my first jobs was in a steakhouse restaurant. This recipe gives me a chance to celebrate two favorite foods: steak and pizza. I love the addition of eggs baked onto the pizza for a steak and eggs dish.
—Lisa Benoit, Cookeville, TN

PREP: 35 min. • **BAKE:** 10 min. + standing
MAKES: 8 servings

- 1 **loaf (1 lb.) frozen pizza dough, thawed**
- 1 **pkg. (8 oz.) frozen spinach and artichoke cheese dip, thawed**
- ¾ **cup grape tomatoes, halved**
- 1 **lb. boneless beef top loin steak, thinly sliced**
- 1½ **tsp. Montreal steak seasoning**
- ⅓ **cup torn fresh basil**
- 3 **Tbsp. pine nuts**
- 2 **bacon strips, cooked and crumbled**
- ⅓ **cup prepared ranch salad dressing**
- 1 **Tbsp. prepared horseradish**

1. Preheat oven to 400°. Press dough to fit a greased 14-in. pizza pan. Pinch edges to form a rim. Bake until edges are lightly browned, 10-12 minutes. Cool 10 minutes.
2. Spread with dip; top with tomatoes. Toss steak with steak seasoning; place over tomatoes. Bake on a lower oven rack until steak reaches desired doneness and crust is golden brown, 10-12 minutes. Let stand 10 minutes. Sprinkle with basil, pine nuts and crumbled bacon. Combine dressing and horseradish; serve with pizza.
1 PIECE: *290 cal., 12g fat (2g sat. fat), 28mg chol., 434mg sod., 27g carb. (2g sugars, 1g fiber), 18g pro.*

HOW-TO

Save Bacon Grease

Bacon grease is so tasty, it's worth saving for other uses. Once cooled, strain grease through cheesecloth or a coffee filter. Cover and refrigerate grease up to 6 months.

Use the bacon fat for popping corn, cooking potatoes or frying eggs.

MADRAS CURRIED EGGS WITH RICE

Whoever said that gourmet foods take ages to prepare did not know about this traditional Indian dish, which my mother-in-law shared with me. Its meatless simplicity and all the accompaniments make it unique, delicious and unforgettable.
—Judy Batson, Tampa, FL

PREP: 20 min. + standing • **COOK:** 15 min.
MAKES: 4 servings

- 8 **large eggs**
- ¼ **cup butter**
- 1 **small onion, chopped**
- 2 **tsp. curry powder**
- 2 **tsp. tomato paste**
- 1 **garlic clove, minced**
- 1 **cup water**
- 1 **can (14½ oz.) petite diced tomatoes, optional**
- 1 **tsp. lemon juice**
- 2 **pkg. (8.8 oz. each) ready-to-serve long grain rice**

Optional: Chopped salted peanuts, raisins, granted orange zest, chutney and shredded coconut

1. Place eggs in a single layer in a large saucepan; add enough cold water to cover by 1 in. Cover and quickly bring to a boil. Remove from heat. Let stand 15 minutes for large eggs (18 minutes for extra-large eggs and 12 minutes for medium eggs). Rinse eggs in cold water until cool enough to handle; peel and cut in half lengthwise.
2. Meanwhile, melt butter in a large skillet over medium-high heat. Add onion; cook and stir until tender, 4-5 minutes. Add curry powder, tomato paste and garlic; cook 30 seconds. Stir in water and, if desired, tomatoes. Bring to a boil; reduce heat and simmer until sauce slightly thickens, 8-10 minutes. Stir in lemon juice. Gently stir in eggs; cook until heated through. Serve eggs and sauce with rice and desired toppings.
1 SERVING: *464 cal., 24g fat (10g sat. fat), 403mg chol., 236mg sod., 43g carb. (1g sugars, 2g fiber), 17g pro.*

MADRAS CURRIED EGGS WITH RICE

AIR-FRYER SPICY GINGER BEEF SKEWERS

AIR-FRYER SPICY GINGER BEEF SKEWERS

My family loves the flavors of these zippy kabobs. I usually grill them outside, but if it's cold or rainy, I love cooking them in my air fryer.
—Jasey McBurnett, Rock Springs, WY

PREP: 20 min. + marinating • **COOK:** 5 min.
MAKES: 6 servings

- 1 **beef flank steak (1½ lbs.)**
- 1 **cup rice vinegar**
- 1 **cup soy sauce**
- ¼ **cup packed brown sugar**
- 2 **Tbsp. minced fresh gingerroot**
- 6 **garlic cloves, minced**
- 3 **tsp. sesame oil**
- 2 **tsp. Sriracha chili sauce or 1 tsp. hot pepper sauce**
- ½ **tsp. cornstarch**
- **Optional: Sesame seeds and thinly sliced green onions**

1. Cut beef into ¼-in.-thick strips. In a large bowl, whisk the next 7 ingredients until blended. Pour 1 cup of the marinade into a shallow dish. Add beef; turn to coat. Cover and refrigerate 2-8 hours. Cover and refrigerate remaining marinade.
2. Preheat air fryer to 400°. Drain beef, discarding marinade in dish. Thread beef onto 12 metal or soaked wooden skewers that fit into air fryer. Working in batches if necessary, arrange skewers in a single layer on greased tray in air-fryer basket. Cook until meat reaches desired doneness (for medium-rare, a thermometer should read 135°; medium, 140°; medium-well, 145°), 4-5 minutes, turning skewers occasionally and basting frequently, using ½ cup of the reserved marinade.
3. Meanwhile, to make glaze, bring the remaining marinade (about ¾ cup) to a boil; whisk in ½ tsp. cornstarch. Cook, whisking constantly, until thickened, 1-2 minutes. Brush skewers with glaze just before serving. If desired, top with sesame seeds and sliced green onions.
2 KABOBS: *264 cal., 10g fat (4g sat. fat), 54mg chol., 1480mg sod., 18g carb. (15g sugars, 0 fiber), 24g pro.*

COCONUT CHICKEN NUGGETS WITH CREAMY CARIBBEAN SALSA

COCONUT CHICKEN NUGGETS WITH CREAMY CARIBBEAN SALSA

This coconut chicken recipe is such a fun change of pace. The salsa's tropical flavor makes the dish fresh and bright.
—Jane Estrin, Jacksonville, FL

PREP: 45 min. + marinating • **BAKE:** 15 min.
MAKES: 8 servings

- 1 **can (8 oz.) crushed pineapple, drained**
- 1 **medium jicama, peeled and chopped**
- 1 **medium sweet red pepper, chopped**
- 1 **medium mango, peeled and chopped**
- 1 **jalapeno pepper, seeded and quartered**
- 2 **Tbsp. minced fresh cilantro**
- 2 **Tbsp. fresh lime juice**
- 1 **Tbsp. minced fresh gingerroot**
- 1 **tsp. grated lime zest**
- ¼ **tsp. salt**
- ¾ **cup reduced-fat sour cream**

CHICKEN NUGGETS

- 2 **lbs. boneless skinless chicken breasts, cut into 1-in. cubes**
- 2 **cups buttermilk**
- 1½ **cups all-purpose flour**
- 1 **tsp. salt**
- ½ **tsp. pepper**
- 4 **large egg whites**
- ¼ **cup water**
- 3 **cups panko bread crumbs**
- 1 **cup unsweetened shredded coconut**
- 2 **Tbsp. sesame seeds**
- 2 **tsp. paprika**
- **Cooking spray**

1. Place the first 10 ingredients in a food processor; pulse until finely chopped but not pureed, 5-6 times. Transfer to a bowl; fold in sour cream. Cover and refrigerate until serving. In a shallow dish, combine chicken and buttermilk. Cover and refrigerate 30 minutes.
2. Preheat oven to 400°. In a shallow dish, combine flour, salt and pepper. In another shallow dish, whisk together egg whites and water. In a third shallow dish, stir together panko, coconut, sesame seeds and paprika. Drain chicken. Dip chicken, a few pieces at a time, in flour mixture to coat; shake off excess. Dip in egg mixture, then in panko mixture, patting to help coating adhere.
3. Place chicken on lightly greased baking sheets; spritz with cooking spray. Bake until chicken is no longer pink, 15-20 minutes, turning halfway through cooking and spritzing with additional cooking spray. Serve with salsa.
NOTE: Wear disposable gloves when cutting hot peppers; the oils can burn skin. Avoid touching your face.
1 SERVING: *402 cal., 13g fat (7g sat. fat), 65mg chol., 315mg sod., 41g carb. (15g sugars, 6g fiber), 31g pro.*

THE BEST GRILLED SIRLOIN TIP ROAST

If you're looking for a flavorful cut of meat that's still pretty lean, give this sirloin tip roast recipe a try. I like to cook it slowly over indirect heat, mopping it frequently with red wine sauce.
—James Schend, Pleasant Prairie, WI

PREP: 40 min. + chilling
GRILL: 1½ hours + standing
MAKES: 6 servings

- 1 **beef sirloin tip roast or beef tri-tip roast (2 to 3 lbs.)**
- 1 **Tbsp. kosher salt**
- 2 **tsp. dried thyme**
- 2 **tsp. garlic powder**
- 1 **tsp. coarsely ground pepper**
- 2 **Tbsp. olive oil, divided**
- 1 **small onion, chopped**
- 1 **bottle (750 ml) dry red wine**
- 6 **fresh thyme sprigs**
- 1 **garlic cloves, crushed**
- ½ **tsp. whole peppercorns**
- 3 **whole cloves**

HORSERADISH-THYME BUTTER (OPTIONAL)
- 6 **Tbsp. softened butter**
- 2 **Tbsp. prepared horseradish**
- 3 **Tbsp. fresh thyme leaves**

1. Sprinkle roast with salt, thyme, garlic powder and ground pepper. Cover and refrigerate at least 8 hours or up to 24 hours. Meanwhile, in a saucepan, saute onion in 1 Tbsp. olive oil until tender, about 5 minutes. Add wine, thyme sprigs, garlic, peppercorns and cloves. Simmer until reduced to ¾ cup. Cool; strain, discarding solids, and refrigerate.
2. Remove roast from the refrigerator 1 hour before grilling. Prepare grill for indirect heat, using a drip pan. Add wood chips according to the manufacturer's directions.
3. Pat roast dry with paper towels. Brush with remaining 1 Tbsp. oil; place over drip pan. Grill, covered, over medium-low indirect heat, brushing with mop sauce every 20 minutes, until meat reaches desired doneness (for medium-rare, a thermometer should read 135°; medium, 140°; medium-well, 145°), 1½-2 hours. Let stand 15 minutes before slicing.
4. If desired, in a small bowl, stir together butter, horseradish and thyme. Serve on top of roast.
4 OZ. COOKED BEEF: *262 cal., 13g fat (4g sat. fat), 91mg chol., 1027mg sod., 3g carb. (1g sugars, 1g fiber), 32g pro.*

THE BEST GRILLED SIRLOIN TIP ROAST

GREEK TILAPIA

While on a trip through the Greek islands, my husband and I had a dish that we loved. I tried to duplicate it by combining several different recipes and came up with this.
—Sally Burrell, Idaho Falls, ID

PREP: 30 min. • **BAKE:** 10 min.
MAKES: 4 servings

- 4 **tilapia fillets (4 oz. each)**
- 4 **tsp. butter**
- 1 **large egg**
- ¾ **cup crumbled tomato and basil feta cheese**
- ¼ **cup fat-free milk**
- ¼ **tsp. cayenne pepper**
- 1 **large tomato, seeded and chopped**
- ¼ **cup chopped ripe olives**
- ¼ **cup pine nuts, toasted**
- 1 **Tbsp. minced fresh parsley**
- 1 **Tbsp. lemon juice**
- ⅛ **tsp. pepper**

1. In a large cast-iron or other ovenproof skillet, brown fish in butter.
2. In a small bowl, combine the egg, cheese, milk and cayenne; spoon over fish. Sprinkle with tomato, olives and pine nuts. Bake, uncovered, at 425° until fish just begins to flake easily with a fork, 10-15 minutes.
3. In a small bowl, combine the parsley, lemon juice and pepper; drizzle over fish.
1 FILLET: *279 cal., 16g fat (6g sat. fat), 123mg chol., 362mg sod., 5g carb. (2g sugars, 2g fiber), 29g pro.*

SIMPLE SALSA CHICKEN

SIMPLE SALSA CHICKEN

My husband and I prefer our food a little spicier than our children, so one evening I baked plain chicken for the kids and created this dish for us. My husband liked it so well that it is now a regular menu item at our house.
—Jan Cooper, Troy, AL

PREP: 10 min. • **BAKE:** 25 min. • **MAKES:** 2 servings

2 boneless skinless chicken breast halves (5 oz. each)
⅛ tsp. salt
⅓ cup salsa
2 Tbsp. taco sauce
⅓ cup shredded Mexican cheese blend
Optional: Lime wedges and sliced avocado

1. Place chicken in a shallow 2-qt. baking dish coated with cooking spray. Sprinkle with salt. Combine salsa and taco sauce; drizzle over chicken. Sprinkle with cheese.
2. Cover and bake at 350° until a thermometer reads 165°, 25-30 minutes. If desired, serve chicken with lime wedges and sliced avocado.
1 SERVING: *226 cal., 7g fat (3g sat. fat), 92mg chol., 628mg sod., 3g carb. (2g sugars, 0 fiber), 34g pro.* **Diabetic exchanges:** *5 lean meat, 1 fat.*

MUSHROOM PORK RAGOUT

Savory slow-cooked pork is luscious served in a delightful tomato gravy over noodles. It's a nice change from a regular pork roast. I serve it with broccoli or green beans on the side.
—Connie McDowell, Greenwood, DE

PREP: 20 min. • **COOK:** 3 hours • **MAKES:** 2 servings

1 pork tenderloin (¾ lb.)
⅛ tsp. salt
⅛ tsp. pepper
1 Tbsp. cornstarch
¾ cup canned crushed tomatoes, divided
1 Tbsp. chopped sun-dried tomatoes (not packed in oil)
1¼ tsp. dried savory
1½ cups sliced fresh mushrooms
⅓ cup sliced onion
1½ cups hot cooked egg noodles

1. Rub pork with salt and pepper; cut in half. In a 1½-qt. slow cooker, combine the cornstarch, ½ cup crushed tomatoes, sun-dried tomatoes and savory. Top with mushrooms, onion and pork. Pour remaining tomatoes over pork. Cover and cook on low 3-4 hours, until meat is tender.
2. Remove meat and cut into slices. Stir cooking juices until smooth; serve with pork and noodles.
1 SERVING: *360 cal., 7g fat (2g sat. fat), 122mg chol., 309mg sod., 32g carb. (3g sugars, 3g fiber), 40g pro.* **Diabetic exchanges:** *5 lean meat, 2 vegetable, 1 starch.*

MUSHROOM PORK RAGOUT

RAVIOLI CASSEROLE

HERBED ROAST TURKEY BREAST

I made this turkey breast for my first formal dinner party as a newlywed. It was such a success that it's become a standby on all my entertaining menus.
—Lisa Mahon Fluegeman, Cincinnati, OH

PREP: 10 min. • **BAKE:** 2 hours + standing
MAKES: 12 servings

- **1 bone-in turkey breast (5 to 6 lbs.)**
- **5 tsp. lemon juice**
- **1 Tbsp. olive oil**
- **1 to 2 tsp. pepper**
- **1 tsp. dried rosemary, crushed**
- **1 tsp. dried thyme**
- **1 tsp. garlic salt**
- **1 medium onion, cut into wedges**
- **1 celery rib, cut into 2-in. pieces**
- **½ cup white wine or chicken broth**

1. Preheat oven to 325°. With fingers, carefully loosen the skin from both sides of turkey breast. Combine lemon juice and oil; brush under the skin. Combine pepper, rosemary, thyme and garlic salt; rub over the turkey.
2. Place onion and celery in a 3-qt. baking dish. Top with turkey breast, skin side up. Pour wine into the dish.
3. Bake, uncovered, until a thermometer reads 170°, 2-2½ hours. (Cover loosely with foil if turkey browns too quickly.) Cover turkey and let stand 15 minutes before carving.
5 OZ COOKED TURKEY: *285 cal., 11g fat (3g sat. fat), 102mg chol., 241mg sod., 2g carb. (1g sugars, 0 fiber), 40g pro.* **Diabetic exchanges:** *5 medium-fat meat.*

RAVIOLI CASSEROLE

The whole family will love this yummy dish that tastes like lasagna without all the fuss. Timesaving ingredients like frozen ravioli and prepared spaghetti sauce make it a cinch to prepare. It's so easy, children can help you assemble it.
—Mary Ann Rothert, Austin, TX

PREP: 10 min. • **BAKE:** 30 min.
MAKES: 8 servings

- **1 pkg. (20 oz.) refrigerated cheese ravioli**
- **3½ cups pasta sauce**
- **2 cups small-curd 4% cottage cheese**
- **4 cups shredded mozzarella cheese**
- **¼ cup grated Parmesan cheese**
- **Minced fresh parsley, optional**

1. Preheat the oven to 350°. Prepare ravioli according to package directions; drain. Spread 1 cup of the spaghetti sauce in an ungreased 13x9-in. baking dish. Layer with half of the ravioli, 1¼ cups sauce, 1 cup cottage cheese and 2 cups mozzarella cheese. Repeat layers. Sprinkle with Parmesan cheese.
2. Bake, uncovered, until casserole is bubbly, 30-40 minutes. Let stand for 5-10 minutes before serving. If desired, sprinkle with parsley.
1 CUP: *518 cal., 25g fat (12g sat. fat), 88mg chol., 1411mg sod., 44g carb. (13g sugars, 5g fiber), 30g pro.*

HERBED ROAST
TURKEY BREAST

MAIN DISHES

(5i)

DAD'S LEMONY GRILLED CHICKEN

Lemon juice, onions and garlic add tangy, savory flavor to chicken when firing up the grill.
—Mike Schulz, Tawas City, MI

PREP: 20 min. + marinating • **GRILL:** 30 min.
MAKES: 8 servings

- **1 cup olive oil**
- **⅔ cup lemon juice**
- **6 garlic cloves, minced**
- **1 tsp. salt**
- **½ tsp. pepper**
- **2 medium onions, chopped**
- **8 chicken drumsticks (2 lbs.)**
- **8 bone-in chicken thighs (2 lbs.)**

1. In a small bowl, whisk first 5 ingredients until blended; stir in onions. Pour 1½ cups marinade into a large shallow dish. Add chicken and turn to coat. Cover; refrigerate overnight. Cover and refrigerate remaining marinade.
2. Prepare grill for indirect heat. Drain chicken, discarding marinade in dish. Place chicken on grill rack, skin side up. Grill, covered, over indirect medium heat 15 minutes. Turn; grill until a thermometer reads 170°-175°, 15-20 minutes longer, basting occasionally with reserved marinade.

1 DRUMSTICK AND 1 THIGH: *528 cal., 39g fat (8g sat. fat), 129mg chol., 318mg sod., 6g carb. (3g sugars, 1g fiber), 38g pro.*

DAD'S LEMONY GRILLED CHICKEN

HAMBURGER NOODLE CASSEROLE

People have a hard time believing this homey and hearty casserole uses lighter ingredients because the taste is so rich and creamy. It's a great weeknight family entree!
—Martha Henson, Winnsboro, TX

PREP: 30 min. • **BAKE:** 35 min.
MAKES: 10 servings

- **5 cups uncooked egg noodles**
- **1½ lbs. lean ground beef (90% lean)**
- **2 garlic cloves, minced**
- **3 cans (8 oz. each) tomato sauce**
- **½ tsp. sugar**
- **½ tsp. salt**
- **⅛ tsp. pepper**
- **1 pkg. (8 oz.) reduced-fat cream cheese**
- **1 cup reduced-fat ricotta cheese**
- **¼ cup reduced-fat sour cream**
- **3 green onions, thinly sliced, divided**
- **⅔ cup shredded reduced-fat cheddar cheese**

1. Preheat oven to 350°. Cook noodles according to package directions.
2. Meanwhile, in a large nonstick skillet over medium heat, cook beef until no longer pink. Add garlic; cook 1 minute longer. Drain. Stir in tomato sauce, sugar, salt and pepper; heat through. Drain noodles; stir into beef mixture.
3. In a small bowl, beat cream cheese, ricotta cheese and sour cream until blended. Stir in half of the onions.
4. Spoon half the noodle mixture into a 13x9-in. baking dish coated with cooking spray. Top with the cheese mixture and remaining noodle mixture.
5. Cover and bake 30 minutes. Uncover and sprinkle with cheddar cheese. Bake until heated through and cheese is melted, 5-10 minutes longer. Sprinkle with the remaining onions.

1 CUP: *319 cal., 14g fat (8g sat. fat), 92mg chol., 635mg sod., 23g carb. (5g sugars, 1g fiber), 24g pro.*

MEXICAN LASAGNA

I collect cookbooks and recipes (this one is from my son's mother-in-law). My husband teases me that I won't live long enough to try half of the recipes in my files!
—Rose Ann Buhle, Minooka, IL

PREP: 20 min. • **BAKE:** 65 min. + standing
MAKES: 12 servings

- **2 lbs. ground beef**
- **1 can (16 oz.) refried beans**
- **1 can (4 oz.) chopped green chiles**
- **1 envelope taco seasoning**
- **2 Tbsp. hot salsa**
- **12 oz. uncooked lasagna noodles**
- **4 cups shredded Colby-Monterey Jack cheese, divided**
- **1 jar (16 oz.) mild salsa**
- **2 cups water**
- **2 cups sour cream**
- **1 can (2¼ oz.) sliced ripe olives, drained**
- **3 green onions, chopped**
- **1 medium tomato, chopped, optional**

1. Preheat oven to 350°. In a large skillet, cook beef over medium heat until no longer pink; drain. Stir in refried beans, chiles, taco seasoning and hot salsa.
2. In a greased 13x9-in. baking dish, layer a third of the noodles and meat mixture. Top with 1 cup of cheese. Repeat layers twice.
3. Combine the mild salsa and water; pour over top. Cover and bake 1 hour or until heated through.
4. Top with sour cream, olives, onions, tomatoes if desired, and remaining cheese. Bake, uncovered, 5 minutes. Let stand 10-15 minutes before cutting.
1 SERVING: *521 cal., 28g fat (16g sat. fat), 110mg chol., 909mg sod., 36g carb. (4g sugars, 3g fiber), 29g pro.*

READER REVIEW

"My kids loved this! I loved the fact that I did not have to precook the noodles. I followed the directions closely and my kids really loved the beef, bean and cheese combination. As a Community Cook for Taste of Home, I enjoy preparing classic dishes with a twist. Trust this five-star recipe!"
—MAMAKNOWSBEST, TASTEOFHOME.COM

SLOW-COOKER BEEF BRISKET

SLOW-COOKER BEEF BRISKET

This brisket is so easy to prepare and has been a family favorite for years. I added the fresh mushrooms to give it more flavor.
—Mary Ann Lee, Clifton Park, NY

PREP: 20 min. • **COOK:** 6 hours
MAKES: 8 servings

- **1 fresh beef brisket (3 to 4 lbs.)**
- **½ lb. sliced fresh mushrooms**
- **2 bay leaves**
- **1 can (15 oz.) crushed tomatoes**
- **1 cup chopped onion**
- **½ cup packed brown sugar**
- **½ cup balsamic vinegar**
- **½ cup ketchup**
- **¼ cup cornstarch**
- **¼ cup cold water**

1. Cut brisket in half; place in a 5-qt. slow cooker. Add mushrooms and bay leaves. Combine the tomatoes, onion, brown sugar, vinegar and ketchup; pour over beef. Cover and cook on low for 6-7 hours or until meat is tender.
2. Remove beef and keep warm. Discard bay leaves. In a large saucepan, combine cornstarch and cold water until smooth. Gradually stir in cooking liquid. Bring to a boil; cook and stir until thickened, about 2 minutes. Slice meat across the grain; serve with gravy.
1 SERVING: *341 cal., 8g fat (3g sat. fat), 72mg chol., 339mg sod., 31g carb. (21g sugars, 2g fiber), 37g pro.*

BEER & BACON
MACARONI & CHEESE

BEER & BACON MACARONI & CHEESE

We put a creative spin on classic mac and cheese by adding our favorite beer and bacon. Six tests later, we are happy.
—Cindy Worth, Lapwai, ID

PREP: 25 min. • **BAKE:** 15 min.
MAKES: 6 servings

- **2 cups uncooked elbow macaroni**
- **6 bacon strips, chopped**
- **3 garlic cloves, minced**
- **¼ cup all-purpose flour**
- **1¾ cups 2% milk**
- **⅔ cup brown ale or chicken broth**
- **1 cup shredded Parmesan cheese**
- **1 cup shredded extra-sharp cheddar cheese**
- **2 green onions, chopped**
- **½ tsp. salt**
- **¼ tsp. pepper**
- **Additional green onions**

1. Preheat oven to 375°. Cook macaroni according to package directions for al dente; drain.
2. Meanwhile, in a 10-in. cast-iron or other ovenproof skillet, cook bacon over medium heat until crisp. Remove to paper towels. In the same pan, add garlic; cook and stir for 30 seconds. Stir in flour until blended; gradually whisk in milk and beer. Bring mixture to a boil, stirring constantly; cook until thickened, 2-3 minutes. Stir in cheeses until blended. Add macaroni, green onions, salt, pepper and half the bacon; stir to combine. Bake, uncovered, until bubbly, 15-20 minutes. Sprinkle with remaining bacon and additional green onions.
1¼ CUPS: *398 cal., 23g fat (11g sat. fat), 52mg chol., 767mg sod., 28g carb. (5g sugars, 1g fiber), 19g pro.*

NEW ENGLAND LAMB BAKE

This hearty dish is perfect for warming up on a chilly winter evening. When you smell it baking, you'll be glad you stayed home.
—Frank Grady, Fort Kent, ME

PREP: 25 min. • **BAKE:** 1½ hours
MAKES: 8 servings

- **1 Tbsp. canola oil**
- **2 lbs. boneless leg of lamb, cut into 1-in. cubes**
- **1 large onion, chopped**
- **¼ cup all-purpose flour**
- **3 cups chicken broth**
- **2 large carrots, sliced**
- **2 large leeks (white portion only), cut into ½-in. slices**
- **2 Tbsp. minced fresh parsley, divided**
- **½ tsp. dried rosemary, crushed**
- **½ tsp. salt**
- **¼ tsp. pepper**
- **¼ tsp. dried thyme**
- **3 large potatoes, peeled and sliced**
- **3 Tbsp. butter, melted and divided**

1. Preheat oven to 375°. In a Dutch oven, heat oil over medium heat. Add lamb and onion; cook and stir until meat is no longer pink. Stir in flour until blended. Gradually add chicken broth. Bring to a boil; cook until thickened, 1-2 minutes, stirring to loosen browned bits from pan. Add the carrots, leeks, 1 Tbsp. parsley, rosemary, salt, pepper and thyme.
2. Spoon into a greased 13x9-in. or 3-qt. baking dish. Cover with potato slices; brush with 2 Tbsp. melted butter. Bake for 1 hour; brush the potatoes with remaining 1 Tbsp. butter. Return to oven; bake until meat is tender and potatoes are golden, 30 minutes to 1 hour longer. Cool briefly; sprinkle with remaining 1 Tbsp. parsley.
FREEZE OPTION: Before adding parsley, cover and freeze the baked, cooled casserole. To use, partially thaw in refrigerator overnight. Remove from the refrigerator 30 minutes before baking. Preheat oven to 350°. Reheat, covered, until a thermometer reads 165°, about 1 hour. Sprinkle with parsley.
1 PIECE: *356 cal., 13g fat (5g sat. fat), 82mg chol., 631mg sod., 34g carb. (4g sugars, 4g fiber), 25g pro.* **Diabetic exchanges:** *3 starch, 3 lean meat, 1½ fat.*

NEW ENGLAND LAMB BAKE

HOMEMADE MARINARA SAUCE, PAGE 98

ALFREDO SAUCE PAGE 97

CLASSIC PESTO PAGE 99

Meal Planner

A great cook always has a few meal-planning tricks up a sleeve. Here are dozens of timesaving ideas.

OUR ALL-TIME FAVORITES

Savory Roasted Chicken p. 92

Spinach Chicken Frittata p. 93

Seafood Alfredo p. 97

Meatball Subs p. 98

Basic Cookie Dough p. 104

The Roast with the Most

Goodbye, grocery-store chicken! Roast your own at home with just a few minutes' prep, then turn it into two delish dishes later.

SAVORY ROASTED CHICKEN

5i

SAVORY ROASTED CHICKEN

When you want an impressive centerpiece for Sunday dinner or a special-occasion meal, you can't go wrong with this golden chicken. The moist, tender meat is enhanced with hints of orange, savory and thyme.
—Taste of Home *Test Kitchen*

PREP: 10 min. • **BAKE:** 1½ hours + standing
MAKES: 10 servings

- **1 roasting chicken (6 to 7 lbs.)**
- **1 tsp. onion salt**
- **½ tsp. dried thyme**
- **½ tsp. dried savory**
- **¼ tsp. grated orange zest**
- **¼ tsp. pepper**
- **1 tsp. vegetable oil**

1. Place chicken on a rack in a shallow roasting pan. Carefully loosen the skin above the breast meat. Combine the onion salt, thyme, savory, orange zest and pepper; rub half of the herb mixture under the loosened skin. Rub chicken skin with oil; sprinkle with remaining herb mixture.
2. Bake at 375° until a thermometer inserted in thickest part of thigh reads 170°-175°, 1½-2 hours. Let stand for 10-15 minutes. Remove skin before carving. Skim fat and thicken pan juices for gravy if desired.

4 OZ. COOKED CHICKEN: *197 cal., 8g fat (2g sat. fat), 86mg chol., 267mg sod., 0 carb. (0 sugars, 0 fiber), 29g pro.* **Diabetic exchanges:** *4 lean meat.*

SPINACH CHICKEN FRITTATA

POPPY SEED CHICKEN

This simple yet delicious dish is terrific for dinner, but the leftovers are a bonus for lunch. It reheats really well in a microwave, so you may want to double the recipe.
—Janet Zoss, Jackson, MI

PREP: 15 min. • **BAKE:** 30 min. • **MAKES:** 6 servings

- **1 cup sour cream**
- **1 can (10¾ oz.) condensed cream of chicken soup, undiluted**
- **1 Tbsp. poppy seeds**
- **1 tsp. dill weed**
- **4 cups cubed cooked chicken**
- **3 cups cooked rice**
- **1½ cups butter-flavored cracker crumbs**
- **½ cup butter, melted**

1. In a large bowl, combine the sour cream, soup, poppy seeds and dill. Stir in chicken and rice.
2. Spread into a greased 11x7-in. baking dish. Combine crumbs and butter; sprinkle over casserole. Bake, uncovered, at 350° until bubbly, about 30 minutes.
1⅓ CUPS: *668 cal., 40g fat (18g sat. fat), 137mg chol., 771mg sod., 44g carb. (4g sugars, 2g fiber), 33g pro.*

SPINACH CHICKEN FRITTATA

When we were growing up, spinach was one of the few vegetables my brothers and I enjoyed. So our mom found all kinds of ways to include it in meals. This dish is one of my favorites. Be creative; feel free to vary the vegetables, cheeses and meat to suit your tastes and budget.
—Paula Tuduri, Bozeman, MT

TAKES: 30 min. • **MAKES:** 4 servings

- **½ cup julienned sweet red pepper**
- **½ cup chopped onion**
- **2 Tbsp. olive oil**
- **3 large eggs**
- **½ cup 2% milk**
- **1 cup shredded cooked chicken**
- **1 pkg. (10 oz.) frozen chopped spinach, thawed and squeezed dry**
- **½ cup shredded part-skim mozzarella cheese**
- **1 Tbsp. grated Parmesan cheese**
- **½ tsp. salt**
- **¼ tsp. pepper**

In a large skillet, saute the red pepper and onion in oil until tender. In a large bowl, beat eggs and milk. Stir in the chicken if desired, ½ cup spinach, mozzarella and Parmesan cheeses, salt and pepper (save remaining spinach for another use). Add to the skillet. Cover and cook over medium heat until a knife inserted in the center comes out clean, 7-10 minutes. Cut into wedges.
1 PIECE: *270 cal., 17g fat (5g sat. fat), 185mg chol., 560mg sod., 8g carb. (4g sugars, 3g fiber), 22g pro.*

POPPY SEED CHICKEN

Get Grillin'

Quick and easy summer meals abound when you start with scrumptious grilled flank steak. Savor the leftovers in quick tacos or a sun-kissed salad.

EASY MARINATED GRILLED FLANK STEAK

EASY MARINATED GRILLED FLANK STEAK

Friends shared this three-ingredient marinade years ago, and it's been a favorite since. Serve the steak with salad and grilled potatoes for a quick meal.
—Beverly Dietz, Surprise, AZ

PREP: 5 min. + marinating • **GRILL:** 15 min.
MAKES: 8 servings

- 1 **cup barbecue sauce**
- ½ **cup burgundy wine or beef broth**
- ¼ **cup lemon juice**
- 1 **beef flank steak (2 lbs.)**

1. In a small bowl, whisk barbecue sauce, wine and lemon juice until blended. Pour 1 cup marinade into a shallow dish. Add beef and turn to coat. Cover; refrigerate 4 hours or overnight. Cover and refrigerate remaining marinade.

2. Drain beef, discarding marinade in dish. Grill steak, covered, over medium heat until meat reaches desired doneness (for medium-rare, a thermometer should read 135°; medium, 140°; medium-well, 145°), 6-8 minutes on each side. Let stand for 5 minutes before thinly slicing across the grain. Serve with reserved marinade.

3 OZ. COOKED STEAK WITH 1½ TBSP. RESERVED MARINADE: *195 cal., 9g fat (4g sat. fat), 54mg chol., 271mg sod., 4g carb. (3g sugars, 0 fiber), 22g pro.* **Diabetic exchanges:** *3 lean meat, 1 fat.*

STEAK TORTILLAS

When I grill steak, I always cook extra so I have leftovers to make these delicious filled tortillas. The steak strips are seasoned with salsa, chili powder and cumin, then tucked inside soft flour tortillas with tasty toppings. —*Kris Wells, Hereford, AZ*

TAKES: 15 min. • **MAKES:** 6 servings

- **2 cups thinly sliced cooked beef steak (about ¾ lb.)**
- **1 small onion, chopped**
- **¼ cup salsa**
- **½ tsp. ground cumin**
- **½ tsp. chili powder**
- **¼ tsp. garlic powder**
- **1½ tsp. all-purpose flour**
- **½ cup cold water**
- **6 flour tortillas (8 in.), warmed**
- **Optional: Shredded cheese, chopped lettuce and tomatoes, and additional salsa**

1. In a large nonstick skillet, saute steak and onion for 1 minute. Stir in the salsa, cumin, chili powder and garlic powder.
2. In a small bowl, combine flour and water until smooth; gradually add to the skillet. Bring to a boil; cook and stir until thickened, 1-2 minutes. Place beef mixture on tortillas; top as desired with cheese, lettuce, tomatoes and additional salsa. Fold in sides.
1 FILLED TORTILLA: *253 cal., 6g fat (1g sat. fat), 43mg chol., 313mg sod., 28g carb. (1g sugars, 0 fiber), 22g pro.* **Diabetic exchanges:** *3 lean meat, 2 starch.*

MANDARIN STEAK SALAD

Your family will think you spent hours on this luscious summery salad. What a great way to use up your leftover flank steak. —Taste of Home *Test Kitchen*

TAKES: 25 min. • **MAKES:** 4 servings (1 cup)

- **⅓ cup olive oil**
- **¼ cup cider vinegar**
- **¼ cup orange juice**
- **2 Tbsp. minced fresh parsley**
- **2 Tbsp. honey**
- **1 garlic clove, minced**
- **1 tsp. chili sauce**
- **½ tsp. salt**
- **4 cups torn romaine**
- **1 lb. cooked beef steak, sliced**
- **1 cup sliced fresh strawberries**
- **1 small red onion, sliced**
- **1 can (11 oz.) mandarin oranges, drained**
- **2 cups pecan halves, toasted**
- **1 (5.3 oz.) fresh goat cheese, crumbled**

In a small bowl, whisk the first 8 ingredients; set aside. Divide romaine among 4 plates; top with steak, strawberries, onion, oranges, pecans and cheese. Serve with vinaigrette.
1 SERVING: *926 cal., 69g fat (12g sat. fat), 118mg chol., 549mg sod., 39g carb. (28g sugars, 8g fiber), 45g pro.*

MANDARIN STEAK SALAD

The Secret's in the Sauce

Start with three homemade sauces, then turn 'em into nine delish dishes for your family. Boom. Dinner's done!

Turn creamy Alfredo sauce into these creations!

This classic sauce is so easy to make. It's creamy and comforting, and it coats fettuccine noodles in fine fashion. You can also use it to top grilled meats and veggies.
—Jo Gray, Park City, MT

TAKES: 25 min. • **MAKES:** 2½ cups

- **6 Tbsp. butter**
- **2 cups heavy whipping cream**
- **½ cup Parmesan cheese**
- **½ cup grated Romano cheese**
- **2 large egg yolks, lightly beaten**
- **¼ tsp. salt**
- **Dash each pepper and ground nutmeg**

In a medium saucepan, melt the butter over medium-low heat. Stir in cream, Parmesan and Romano cheeses, egg yolks, salt, pepper and nutmeg. Cook and stir over medium-low heat until a thermometer reads 160° (do not boil).

¼ CUP: *356 cal., 36g fat (23g sat. fat), 145mg chol., 408mg sod., 3g carb. (2g sugars, 0 fiber), 8g pro.*

Chicken Alfredo Sandwiches

Sprinkle ½ tsp. **Italian seasoning** and ¼ tsp. each **salt** and **pepper** over 4 boneless skinless **chicken breasts.** Cook in 1 Tbsp. **canola oil** over medium heat until a thermometer reads 170°, 8-10 minutes. Top with 2 **roasted red pepper strips.** On a piece of toasted **garlic bread,** layer ¼ cup fresh **spinach,** 1 Tbsp. warmed **Alfredo sauce,** the chicken and another 1 Tbsp. Alfredo sauce. Cover with another piece of garlic bread if desired.

Fettuccine Alfredo

Cook 4 oz. **fettuccine** according to package directions. Drain; combine with ½ cup **Alfredo sauce** and 2 Tbsp. grated **Parmesan.** If desired, sprinkle with minced fresh **parsley.**

Seafood Alfredo

In a skillet, saute 1 tsp. minced **garlic** in 2 Tbsp. **olive oil** until tender. Stir in 8 oz. **imitation crab,** 5 oz. cooked **salad shrimp,** 1 Tbsp. **lemon juice** and ½ tsp. **pepper.** Cook for 1 minute. Add 2 cups **Alfredo sauce** and ½ cup thawed frozen **peas.** Cook until heated through. Pour over 12 oz. hot cooked **bowtie pasta.** Sprinkle with ¼ cup grated **Parmesan cheese.**

Turn marinara into 3 easy entrees

Homemade Marinara Sauce

This quick and easy homemade marinara sauce is my kids' favorite. It works wonderfully with spaghetti as well as in meatball subs.
—Cara Bjornlie, Detroit Lakes, MN

TAKES: 30 min. • **MAKES:** 7 cups

- **1 Tbsp. olive oil**
- **1 small onion, chopped**
- **2 garlic cloves, minced**
- **2 cans (28 oz. each) Italian crushed tomatoes**
- **1 Tbsp. Italian seasoning**
- **1 to 2 Tbsp. sugar**
- **½ tsp. salt**
- **½ tsp. pepper**

In a large saucepan, heat oil over medium heat. Add the onion; cook and stir until softened, 3-4 minutes. Add garlic; cook 1 minute longer. Add tomatoes, Italian seasoning, sugar, salt and pepper; bring to a boil. Reduce heat; simmer, covered, 10 minutes.

¾ CUP: *91 cal., 2g fat (0 sat. fat), 0 chol., 489mg sod., 12g carb. (8g sugars, 3g fiber), 3g pro.* **Diabetic exchanges:** *2 vegetable, ½ fat.*

Meatball Subs

Combine 2 large **eggs,** 1 cup dry **bread crumbs,** 2 Tbsp. grated **Parmesan,** 2 Tbsp. diced **onion,** ½ tsp. each **salt, pepper** and **garlic powder,** and ¼ tsp. **Italian seasoning.** Crumble 2 lbs. **ground beef** over mixture; mix. Shape into 1-in. balls. Place in a 3-qt. microwave-safe dish. Cover; microwave on high 4 minutes. Turn meatballs; cook until no longer pink, 3-4 minutes. Drain. Add 3 cups **marinara.** Cook 2-4 minutes or until heated through. Serve on **rolls,** with sliced **onions** and **peppers** if desired.

Italian Chicken Stew

Cook 1 lb. cubed boneless skinless **chicken breasts,** 4 medium peeled, cut **potatoes,** 1 chopped **red pepper** and 2 minced **garlic cloves** in 2 Tbsp. **olive oil** until chicken is no longer pink and vegetables are tender. Stir in 3 cups **marinara,** 1¾ cups frozen **green beans,** 1 tsp. dried **basil,** ¼ tsp. **salt** and ¼ tsp. crushed **red pepper flakes;** cook and stir until heated through.

Spicy Bratwurst Supper

Cook 6 **bacon strips** and ½ cup chopped **onion** over medium heat until bacon is crisp; drain. In the same skillet, saute 5 cooked sliced **bratwursts,** ½ lb. **sliced mushrooms** and 1 Tbsp. diced **jalapeno** until mushrooms are tender. Stir in 2 cups **marinara** and the bacon mixture; heat through. Serve over hot cooked **rice** with ¼ cup shredded **Gouda.**

Turn pesto into 3 easy entrees

This versatile pesto boasts a peppy basil flavor.
—Iola Egle, Bella Vista, AR

TAKES: 10 min. • **MAKES:** 1 cup

- 4 **cups loosely packed basil leaves**
- ½ **cup grated Parmesan cheese**
- 2 **garlic cloves, halved**
- ¼ **tsp. salt**
- ½ **cup pine nuts, toasted**
- ½ **cup olive oil**

Place basil, cheese, garlic and salt in a food processor; cover and pulse until chopped. Add pine nuts. Cover; process until blended. While processing, gradually add oil in a steady stream.

2 TBSP. *196 cal., 19g fat (3g sat. fat), 4mg chol., 152mg sod., 3g carb. (0 sugars, 1g fiber), 5g pro.*

Easy Pesto Pizza

Place 1 loaf **frozen bread dough,** thawed, on a floured surface; let rest 10 minutes. Knead in ¼ cup shredded **Parmesan** and ½ tsp. each dried **basil** and **oregano.** Roll into a 12-in. circle; place on a greased pizza pan. Prick with a fork. Bake at 425° 10 minutes. Spread ¼ cup **pesto** over crust. Sprinkle with 1 cup sliced fresh **mushrooms,** 1 cup shredded **mozzarella** and ¼ cup shredded **Parmesan.** Bake until golden, 8-10 minutes.

BLT Bruschetta

In a bowl, combine 5 **maple bacon strips,** cooked and crumbled, ½ cup chopped **tomato,** ½ cup chopped **lettuce,** 2 Tbsp. **pesto,** 2 Tbsp. minced fresh **basil,** ¼ tsp. **salt** and ¼ tsp. **pepper;** set aside. Cut a **French baguette** into 36 slices; place slices on ungreased baking sheets. Brush with **olive oil.** Bake at 400° until golden brown, 9-11 minutes. Spread with 6 Tbsp. **pesto;** top each slice with 2 tsp. bacon mixture.

Pesto Hamburgers

Shape 1½ lbs. **ground beef** into four ¾-in.-thick patties. Season with **salt** and **pepper.** Cook patties over medium heat until meat is no longer pink, about 5 minutes on each side. Top each with a slice of **mozzarella,** 2 Tbsp. **pesto** and 2 **roasted pepper strips.** Cook, covered, until cheese is melted. Serve on buns.

MEAL PLANNER

Wholly Guacamole

Guac lovers, rejoice! A basic guac gets a dozen variations, plus you'll find bright mealtime ideas for all that avocado goodness.

PEACHY JALAPENO GUACAMOLE

PEACHY JALAPENO GUACAMOLE

Fresh jalapenos and summer-ripe peaches give this creamy guacamole so much flavor. It has a little kick, but I love that it's not so spicy it burns off my taste buds!
—Colleen Delawder, Herndon, VA

TAKES: 15 min. • **MAKES:** 1½ cups

- **2 medium ripe avocados, peeled and cubed**
- **2 Tbsp. lime juice**
- **½ tsp. kosher salt**
- **½ tsp. ground cumin**
- **¼ tsp. pepper**
- **1 medium peach, peeled and finely chopped**
- **1 jalapeno pepper, seeded and minced**
- **2 Tbsp. finely chopped red onion**
- **Tortilla chips**

Mash avocados with lime juice, salt, cumin and pepper. Gently stir in peach, jalapeno and red onion. Serve with tortilla chips.

NOTE: Wear disposable gloves when cutting hot peppers; the oils can burn skin. Avoid touching your face.

¼ CUP: *90 cal., 7g fat (1g sat. fat), 0 chol., 164mg sod., 7g carb. (2g sugars, 4g fiber), 1g pro.* **Diabetic exchanges:** *1 fat, ½ starch.*

FETA CHEESE & POMEGRANATE GUAC: Mash avocados with lime juice and salt. Omit remaining ingredients. Top guacamole with ½ cup pomegranate seeds and ½ cup crumbled feta cheese.

DID YOU KNOW?

Avocado is high in monounsaturated fat, a so-called "good fat" that can lower your blood cholesterol along with the risk of stroke and heart disease. Each fruit also contains about 9 grams of healthy fiber.

SPICY HASH BROWN WAFFLES WITH FRIED EGGS

Refrigerated hash brown potatoes help you make quick work of these crunchy waffles. Put out lots of toppings so everyone can design his or her own.
—Nancy Judd, Alpine, UT

TAKES: 30 min. • **MAKES:** 4 servings

- **5 large eggs, divided use**
- **½ tsp. salt**
- **½ tsp. ground cumin**
- **½ tsp. pepper**
- **¼ tsp. chili powder**
- **1¾ cups refrigerated shredded hash brown potatoes**
- **1 small onion, finely chopped**
- **¼ cup canned chopped green chiles**
- **2 Tbsp. salsa**
- **2 Tbsp. canola oil**
- **½ cup shredded cheddar-Monterey Jack cheese**
- **Optional: Salsa, guacamole, sour cream and minced fresh cilantro**

1. In a large bowl, whisk 1 egg, salt, cumin, pepper and chili powder. Stir in potatoes, onion, green chiles and salsa. Bake in a preheated waffle iron coated with cooking spray until golden brown and potatoes are tender, 8-12 minutes.
2. In a large skillet, heat oil over medium-high heat. Break remaining eggs, 1 at a time, into pan. Reduce heat to low. Cook to desired doneness, turning after whites are set if desired. Remove from heat. Sprinkle with cheese; cover and let stand 3 minutes or until melted.
3. Serve eggs with waffles and toppings of your choice.

1 WAFFLE WITH 1 FRIED EGG: *273 cal., 17g fat (5g sat. fat), 245mg chol., 570mg sod., 17g carb. (2g sugars, 2g fiber), 12g pro.*

SALSA BLACK BEAN BURGERS

SALSA BLACK BEAN BURGERS

Meatless meals are so tasty when these hearty bean burgers are on the menu. Guacamole and sour cream make them seem decadent.
—Jill Reichardt, St. Louis, MO

TAKES: 20 min. • **MAKES:** 4 servings

- **1 can (15 oz.) black beans, rinsed and drained**
- **⅔ cup dry bread crumbs**
- **1 small tomato, seeded and finely chopped**
- **1 jalapeno pepper, seeded and finely chopped**
- **1 large egg**
- **1 tsp. minced fresh cilantro**
- **1 garlic clove, minced**
- **1 Tbsp. olive oil**
- **4 whole wheat hamburger buns, split**
- **Optional: Reduced-fat sour cream and guacamole**

1. Place beans in a food processor; cover and process until blended. Transfer to a large bowl. Add the bread crumbs, tomato, jalapeno, egg, cilantro and garlic. Mix until combined. Shape into 4 patties.
2. In a large nonstick skillet, cook patties in oil over medium heat until lightly browned, 4-6 minutes on each side. Serve on buns. If desired, top with sour cream and guacamole.

NOTE: Wear disposable gloves when cutting hot peppers; the oils can burn skin. Avoid touching your face.

1 BURGER: *323 cal., 8g fat (1g sat. fat), 53mg chol., 557mg sod., 51g carb. (6g sugars, 9g fiber), 13g pro.*

ROCK THAT GUAC

Grab some tortilla chips and get ready to dunk into these sweet and savory spins on the classic, creamy avocado snack.

RADISH + MANDARIN ORANGE

Radishes are often overlooked as a salad garnish, but their crisp bite is a welcome addition here. For balance, pair radish's peppery crunch with the soft, sweet tang of mandarin oranges.

GUACAMOLE

In a bowl, mash 3 ripe avocados until almost smooth. Stir in 2-3 Tbsp. fresh lime juice and ½-1 tsp. kosher salt. Let stand 10 minutes to allow flavors to blend. Then get to topping!

GRILLED CHICKEN + CHERRY TOMATO

Chicken breasts hot off the grill and cherry tomatoes plucked from your garden turn a simple snack into a gourmet meal.

BASIL + TOASTED PINE NUTS

For a pesto-inspired take, top guac off with toasted pine nuts and fresh basil ribbons. You can also substitute lemon juice for the traditional lime.

CAJUN SHRIMP + RED PEPPER

Here's a way to not only spice up your guac but also make it dinnerworthy: Top it with a Louisiana classic and a handful of crunchy chopped red pepper.

MANGO + HABANERO

For the ultimate sweet-spicy combo, pair mango with fresh habanero chile peppers. You can control the guac's heat by adjusting how much of the peppers' seeds and ribs you stir into the dip.

BLACK BEAN + CORN

Bright colors and contrasting textures make this combination especially delightful. For extra flavor, start by grilling fresh ears of corn on the cob.

BLUE CHEESE + TOASTED ALMONDS

The crumbly tang of blue cheese paired with the sweet, toasty crunch of almonds is a mind-blowing duo when it's stirred into cool, creamy avocado.

JICAMA + PINEAPPLE

If you're a fan of chunky guac, this combo is for you. Crunchy diced jicama and juicy chopped pineapple make for seriously satisfying bites. To add some smoky flavor, toss the pineapple on the grill for a few minutes before chopping.

BACON + COTIJA CHEESE

Take your game-day snack to a new level. Bacon adds crisp, rich texture while Cotija cheese makes things extra creamy. If you're feeling bold, go with applewood smoked bacon for more complex flavor.

APPLE + WHITE ONION

A little bit sweet, a little bit sharp, this matchup is unexpectedly delicious on your guac. Depending on the type of apple you use, this can taste fruity, sugary or tart.

MEAL PLANNER

Smart Cookie

A Utah baker shares her treats-tray secret weapon: one basic cookie dough turned into five sensational sweets. Here's how!

BASIC COOKIE DOUGH

BASIC COOKIE DOUGH

Skip the store-bought stuff and learn how to make cookies from scratch—it's easy! Thanks to this basic cookie dough recipe, you can turn everyday ingredients into five sensational sweets. Bake some right away, then pop the extra dough into the freezer to bake later.
—Gloria McBride, Payson, UT

TAKES: 15 min. • **MAKES:** 8 cups dough

- **2½ cups butter, softened**
- **2 cups sugar**
- **2 large eggs, room temperature**
- **¼ cup 2% milk**
- **2 tsp. vanilla extract**
- **7½ to 8 cups (30 to 32 oz.) all-purpose flour**
- **4 tsp. baking powder**
- **1 tsp. salt**

1. In a large bowl, cream butter and sugar until light and fluffy, 5-7 minutes. Beat in eggs, milk and vanilla. In another bowl, whisk 7½ cups flour, baking powder and salt; gradually beat into creamed mixture, adding more flour if necessary. Divide dough into four 2-cup portions. Refrigerate, covered, until needed.
2. Basic Cookie Dough may be used to prepare the following recipes: Chocolate Mallow Cookies, Jelly Sandwich Cookies, Crumb-Topped Date Bars, Cherry Surprise Cookies and Classic Sugar Cookies.
4 TSP. DOUGH: *98 cal., 5g fat (3g sat. fat), 17mg chol., 91mg sod., 12g carb. (4g sugars, 0 fiber), 1g pro.*

TEST KITCHEN TIPS

- Be sure to not overmix the cookie dough ingredients; this will help to prevent the dough from spreading excessively if you prefer to bake some or all of the cookies later.
- Throw in some handfuls of your favorite chocolate chips for chocolate chip cookie dough.

CHOCOLATE MALLOW COOKIES

CHOCOLATE MALLOW COOKIES

Cocoa, marshmallows and ready-made frosting transform the basic dough into these delightful treats. I like to top each with a pecan half.
—Gloria McBride, Payson, UT

PREP: 20 min. • **BAKE:** 10 min./batch • **MAKES:** 40 cookies

2 cups Basic Cookie Dough
½ cup sugar
½ cup baking cocoa
1 large egg, room temperature
¼ cup 2% milk
½ cup chopped pecans
20 large marshmallows, halved
1 can (16 oz.) chocolate frosting

1. In a bowl, combine the cookie dough, sugar, cocoa, egg and milk; mix well. Stir in pecans. Drop by tablespoonfuls 2 in. apart onto ungreased baking sheets. Bake at 375° for 8 minutes. Press a marshmallow half onto the top of each cookie. Bake 2 minutes longer or until marshmallow is puffed. Remove to wire racks to cool.
2. Cut a hole in the corner of a pastry bag or plastic bag; insert a medium star tip. Fill bag with frosting. Pipe a star onto each cookie.
1 COOKIE: *140 cal., 6g fat (3g sat. fat), 15mg chol., 72mg sod., 21g carb. (14g sugars, 1g fiber), 1g pro.*

5i

JELLY SANDWICH COOKIES

Sandwiching jelly between two layers of the basic dough creates designs that look like stained glass. Your favorite raisin filling is excellent in these cookies, too.
—Gloria McBride, Payson, UT

PREP: 20 min. • **BAKE:** 10 min./batch • **MAKES:** about 2 dozen

2 cups Basic Cookie Dough
Assorted jellies or jams

1. On a lightly floured surface, roll out dough to ⅛-in. thickness. Cut with a 2½-in. round cookie cutter. Using a 1½-in. cookie cutter of your choice, cut out the center of half of the cookies.
2. Place whole cookies 2 in. apart on greased baking sheets. Spread each with 1 tsp. jelly or jam; top each with a cutout cookie. Pinch edges with a fork to seal. Bake at 375° for 10-12 minutes or until edges are golden brown. Remove to wire racks to cool.
1 COOKIE: *98 cal., 5g fat (3g sat. fat), 17mg chol., 77mg sod., 12g carb. (4g sugars, 0 fiber), 1g pro.*

JELLY SANDWICH COOKIES

CRUMB-TOPPED DATE BARS

5i
CRUMB-TOPPED DATE BARS

Basic dough doubles as a shortbread-like crust and crumbly topping for these sweet date bars.
—Gloria McBride, Payson, UT

PREP: 20 min. • **BAKE:** 25 min. • **MAKES:** 2 dozen

- **1 pkg. (8 oz.) chopped dates**
- **½ cup sugar**
- **½ cup water**
- **1 Tbsp. lemon juice**
- **2 cups Basic Cookie Dough**

1. In a saucepan, bring the dates, sugar, water and lemon juice to a boil. Reduce heat; simmer, uncovered, for 5 minutes, stirring occasionally. Remove from the heat; cool.
2. Press half of the cookie dough into a greased 9-in. square baking pan. Spread with date mixture. Crumble remaining dough over filling. Bake at 375° for 25-30 minutes or until top is golden brown. Cool on a wire rack. Cut into bars.
1 BAR: *141 cal., 5g fat (3g sat. fat), 17mg chol., 77mg sod., 23g carb. (15g sugars, 1g fiber), 2g pro.*

5i
CHERRY SURPRISE COOKIES

There's a rich chocolate surprise tucked into each of these cute bites. Candied cherries add a colorful finishing touch.
—Gloria McBride, Payson, UT

PREP: 15 min. • **BAKE:** 15 min./batch • **MAKES:** 3 dozen

- **2 cups Basic Cookie Dough**
- **36 chocolate stars or chocolate kisses**
- **36 candied cherry halves**

Drop cookie dough by teaspoonfuls 2 in. apart onto greased baking sheets. Top each with a chocolate star and wrap dough around it. Top each with a candied cherry half. Bake at 375° for 10-12 minutes or until bottoms are lightly browned. Remove to wire racks to cool.
1 COOKIE: *96 cal., 5g fat (3g sat. fat), 12mg chol., 57mg sod., 13g carb. (7g sugars, 0 fiber), 1g pro.*

CHERRY SURPRISE COOKIES

5i

CLASSIC SUGAR COOKIES

Use cookie cutters to cut seasonal shapes from a few cups of this dough. Prepared frosting and colored sugar make it a snap to decorate the cookies according to the season or holiday.
—Gloria McBride, Payson, UT

PREP: 10 min. • **BAKE:** 10 min./batch + cooling
MAKES: about 3 dozen

- **2 cups Basic Cookie Dough**
- **Colored sugar and frosting of your choice**

On a lightly floured surface, roll out dough to ¼-in. thickness. Using 2½-in. cookie cutters, cut out desired shapes. Place 2 in. apart on ungreased baking sheets. Leave plain or sprinkle with colored sugar. Bake at 375° for 8-10 minutes or until the edges are golden brown. Remove to wire racks to cool. Frost plain cookies; sprinkle with colored sugar if desired.

1 COOKIE: *65 cal., 3g fat (2g sat. fat), 11mg chol., 51mg sod., 8g carb. (3g sugars, 0 fiber), 1g pro.*

TEST KITCHEN TIP

Most cookie doughs may be refrigerated or frozen, then baked later. When stored in airtight containers, unbaked cookie doughs can be refrigerated for a week or frozen for up to 3 months.

Freeze cookie dough by dropping tablespoonfuls onto baking sheets. Cover and freeze until firm. When the dough is frozen, transfer the dough balls into airtight containers.

To use frozen dough, place dough balls 2 in. apart on greased or ungreased baking sheets. Bake as the recipe directs, until the cookies are lightly browned.

CLASSIC SUGAR COOKIES

GARDEN CHICKEN CACCIATORE
PAGE 121

Cook It Fast or Slow

Choose your weapon: pressure cooker or slow cooker. Either way, you win when dinner's ready for the table on your schedule.

OUR ALL-TIME FAVORITES

Southwestern Pork & Squash Soup p. 110

Lora's Red Beans & Rice p. 112

Potato Soup p. 120

SOUTHWESTERN PORK & SQUASH SOUP

SOUTHWESTERN PORK & SQUASH SOUP

I adapted a pork and squash stew recipe, using tomatoes and southwestern-style seasonings. My husband and sons loved it, and the leftovers were even better the next day! Try it with fresh corn muffins.
—Molly Andersen, Portland, OR

PREP: 20 min. • **MAKES:** 6 servings (2¼ qt.)

- **1 lb. pork tenderloin, cut into 1-in. cubes**
- **1 medium onion, chopped**
- **1 Tbsp. canola oil**
- **3 cups reduced-sodium chicken broth**
- **1 medium butternut squash, peeled and cubed**
- **2 medium carrots, sliced**
- **1 can (14½ oz.) diced tomatoes with mild green chiles, undrained**
- **1 Tbsp. chili powder**
- **1 tsp. ground cumin**
- **1 tsp. dried oregano**
- **½ tsp. pepper**
- **¼ tsp. salt**

Fast Cook: **3 MIN.**
Select saute setting on a 6-qt. electric pressure cooker and adjust for medium heat; add oil. When oil is hot, cook and stir the pork and onion in oil until browned. Press cancel. Stir in remaining ingredients. Lock lid; close pressure-release valve. Adjust to pressure-cook on high for 3 minutes. Quick-release pressure. (A thermometer inserted into pork should read at least 145°.)

Slow Cook: **4 HOURS**
In a large skillet, brown pork and onion in oil; drain. Transfer to a 4- or 5-qt. slow cooker. Stir in the remaining ingredients. Cover and cook on low for 4-5 hours or until meat is tender.

FREEZE OPTION: In a freezer container, layer pork, butternut squash, onions, carrots and seasonings. Seal. Freeze for up to 6 months. Thaw overnight in refrigerator before use. Add broth and tomatoes; cook as directed in appliance of choice.

1½ CUPS: *228 cal., 5g fat (1g sat. fat), 42mg chol., 637mg sod., 27g carb. (9g sugars, 8g fiber), 19g pro.* **Diabetic exchanges:** *2 starch, 1 lean meat, 1 fat.*

CHICKEN TIKKA MASALA

This Indian-style entree has flavors that keep me coming back for more—a simple dish spiced with garam masala, gingerroot and cumin that's simply amazing.
—Jaclyn Bell, Logan, UT

PREP: 25 min. • **MAKES:** 8 servings

- 2 **Tbsp. olive oil**
- ½ **large onion, finely chopped**
- 4½ **tsp. minced fresh gingerroot**
- 4 **garlic cloves, minced**
- 1 **Tbsp. garam masala**
- 2½ **tsp. salt**
- 1½ **tsp. ground cumin**
- 1 **tsp. paprika**
- ¾ **tsp. pepper**
- ½ **tsp. cayenne pepper**
- ¼ **tsp. ground cinnamon**
- 2½ **lbs. boneless skinless chicken breasts, cut into 1½-in. cubes**
- 1 **can (29 oz.) tomato puree**
- 1 **jalapeno pepper, halved and seeded**
- 1 **bay leaf**
- ⅓ **cup water (Fast version only)**
- 1½ **cups plain yogurt**
- 1 **Tbsp. cornstarch**
- 1 **cup heavy whipping cream (Slow version only)**
- **Hot cooked basmati rice**
- **Chopped fresh cilantro, optional**

CHICKEN TIKKA MASALA

Fast Cook: **20 MIN.**

1. Select saute setting on a 6-qt. electric pressure cooker and adjust for medium heat; add oil. When oil is hot, cook onion until tender. Add ginger and garlic; cook 1 minute. Stir in seasonings and cook 30 seconds. Press cancel. Add chicken, tomato puree, jalapeno, bay leaf and ⅓ cup water.

2. Lock lid; close pressure-release valve. Adjust to pressure-cook on high and cook for 10 minutes. Quick-release pressure. Discard bay leaf and jalapeno.

3. Select saute setting and adjust for medium heat; bring mixture to a boil. In a small bowl, mix yogurt with cornstarch until smooth; gradually stir into sauce. Cook and stir until sauce is thickened, about 3 minutes. Serve with rice. If desired, sprinkle with cilantro.

Slow Cook: **4¼ HOURS**

1. In a 5-qt. slow cooker, combine the oil, onion, ginger, garlic and seasonings with the yogurt. Add chicken, tomato puree, jalapeno and bay leaf.

2. Cook, covered, on low 4 hours or until chicken is tender. Remove jalapeno and bay leaf.

3. In a small bowl, mix cornstarch and cream until smooth; gradually stir into sauce. Cook, covered, on high 15-20 minutes or until sauce is thickened. Serve with rice. If desired, sprinkle with cilantro.

NOTE: Wear disposable gloves when cutting hot peppers; the oils can burn skin. Avoid touching your face.

1 CUP: *279 cal., 8g fat (2g sat. fat), 84mg chol., 856mg sod., 13g carb. (5g sugars, 2g fiber), 32g pro.* **Diabetic exchanges:** *4 lean meat, 1 starch, 1 fat.*

1 CUP: *381 cal., 19g fat (2g sat. fat), 84mg chol., 856mg sod., 13g carb. (5g sugars, 2g fiber), 33g pro.*

LORA'S RED BEANS & RICE

LORA'S RED BEANS & RICE

My dear mother-in-law passed this simple recipe to me. With meats, beans and savory veggies that simmer all day, it's tasty, easy and economical, too!
—Carol Simms, Madison, MS

PREP: 15 min. + soaking • **MAKES:** 10 servings

- 1 lb. dried kidney beans (about 2½ cups)
- 2 cups cubed fully cooked ham (about 1 lb.)
- 1 pkg. (12 oz.) fully cooked andouille chicken sausage links or flavor of choice, sliced
- 1 medium green pepper, chopped
- 1 medium onion, chopped
- 2 celery ribs, chopped
- 1 Tbsp. hot pepper sauce
- 2 garlic cloves, minced
- 1½ tsp. salt
- Hot cooked rice

TEST KITCHEN TIP

Celery, onion and green pepper are a classic Creole combination called holy trinity or Cajun mirepoix. Standard mirepoix uses carrots instead of green pepper.

Fast Cook: **30 MIN.**

1. Rinse and sort beans. Soak overnight according to package directions. Drain, discarding water; rinse with cool water.
2. In a 6-qt. electric pressure cooker, combine beans, ham, sausage, vegetables, pepper sauce, garlic, salt and enough water to cover (about 4 cups). Lock lid; close pressure-release valve. Adjust to pressure-cook on high for 30 minutes. Quick-release pressure. Serve with rice.

Slow Cook: **8 HOURS**

1. Rinse and sort beans. Soak overnight according to package directions. Drain, discarding water; rinse with cool water.
2. Place beans in a greased 6-qt. slow cooker. Stir in ham, sausage, vegetables, pepper sauce, garlic and salt. Add enough water to cover by 1 in.
3. Cook, covered, on low, 8-9 hours or until beans are tender. Serve with rice.

1 CUP BEAN MIXTURE: *249 cal., 5g fat (1g sat. fat), 43mg chol., 788mg sod., 31g carb. (2g sugars, 7g fiber), 23g pro.* **Diabetic exchanges:** *2 starch, 1 lean meat.*

BEEF SHORT RIBS VINDALOO

My sister shared this dish with me, and I've made a few modifications to fit my tastes. The kitchen smells wonderful when I make it!
—Lorraine Carlstrom, Nelson, BC

PREP: 30 min. + marinating
MAKES: 4 servings

- 1 **Tbsp. cumin seeds**
- 2 **tsp. coriander seeds**
- 1 **Tbsp. butter**
- 1 **medium onion, finely chopped**
- 8 **garlic cloves, minced**
- 1 **Tbsp. minced fresh gingerroot**
- 2 **tsp. mustard seed**
- ½ **tsp. ground cloves**
- ¼ **tsp. kosher salt**
- ¼ **tsp. ground cinnamon**
- ¼ **tsp. cayenne pepper**
- ½ **cup red wine vinegar**
- 4 **bay leaves**
- 2 **lbs. bone-in beef short ribs**
- 1 **cup fresh sugar snap peas, halved**
- **Optional: Hot cooked rice, plain yogurt and minced fresh cilantro**

BEEF SHORT RIBS VINDALOO

Fast Cook: **40 MIN. + RELEASING**

1. Select saute setting on a 6-qt. electric pressure cooker and adjust for medium heat. Add cumin and coriander seeds; toast until aromatic, stirring frequently. Cool. Remove from cooker; coarsely crush seeds in a spice grinder or with a mortar and pestle.
2. Melt butter over medium heat. Add onion, garlic and ginger; cook and stir for 1 minute. Add mustard seed, ground cloves, salt, cinnamon, cayenne pepper and crushed seeds; cook and stir 1 minute longer. Remove and cool completely.
3. In a large shallow dish, combine the vinegar, bay leaves and onion mixture. Add ribs; turn to coat. Refrigerate, covered, overnight.
4. Transfer rib mixture to pressure cooker; add broth. Lock lid; close the pressure-release valve. Adjust to pressure-cook on high for 40 minutes. Let pressure release naturally for 10 minutes; quick-release any remaining pressure. Select saute setting; adjust for medium heat. Stir in peas; cook 8-10 minutes longer or until peas are crisp-tender. Skim fat; discard bay leaves. Serve rib mixture with rice, yogurt and cilantro if desired.

Slow Cook: **8¼ HOURS**

1. In a dry small skillet over medium heat, toast cumin and coriander seeds until aromatic, stirring frequently. Cool. Coarsely crush seeds in a spice grinder or with a mortar and pestle.
2. In a large saucepan, heat butter over medium heat. Add the onion, garlic and ginger; cook and stir for 1 minute. Add the mustard seed, cloves, salt, cinnamon, cayenne pepper and crushed seeds; cook and stir 1 minute longer. Cool completely.
3. In a large shallow dish, combine the vinegar, bay leaves and onion mixture. Add ribs; turn to coat. Refrigerate, covered, overnight.
4. Transfer rib mixture to a 4-qt. slow cooker. Cover and cook on low for 8-10 hours or until meat is tender. Stir in peas; cook 8-10 minutes longer or until peas are crisp-tender. Skim fat; discard bay leaves. Serve rib mixture with rice, yogurt and cilantro if desired.

FREEZE OPTION: Prepare recipe as directed, placing onion mixture, vinegar, bay leaves and beef in a freezer container. Freeze for up to 6 months. Thaw overnight in refrigerator before use.

1 SERVING: *256 cal., 15g fat (6g sat. fat), 64mg chol., 295mg sod., 12g carb. (3g sugars, 3g fiber), 21g pro.*

LEMON RED POTATOES

LEMON RED POTATOES

Butter, lemon juice, parsley and chives enhance this simple side dish. I usually prepare these potatoes when I'm having company. I like that this leaves room on the stove for preparing other dishes.
—Tara Branham, Austin, TX

PREP: 5 min. • **MAKES:** 6 servings

- **1½ lbs. medium red potatoes**
- **¼ cup water**
- **¼ cup butter, melted**
- **3 Tbsp. minced fresh parsley**
- **1 Tbsp. lemon juice**
- **1 Tbsp. minced chives**
- **Salt and pepper to taste**

HOW-TO

Get the Most Juice

Next time you squeeze a fresh lemon or lime, first warm the fruit in the microwave for 7-10 seconds. Then roll it back and forth under your palm on the counter, giving it firm pressure. You'll get more juice and it'll be easier to squeeze, too.

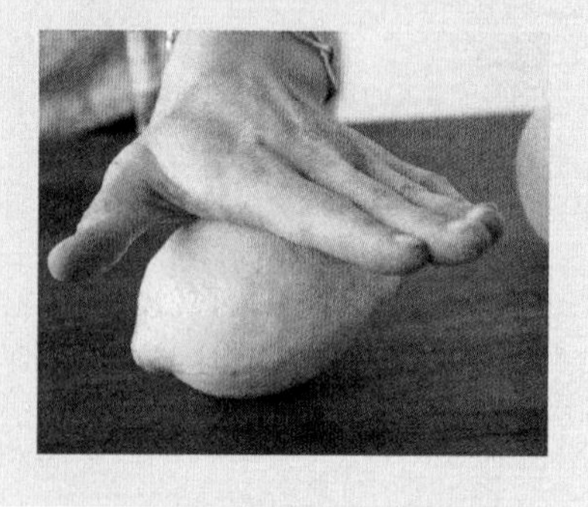

Fast Cook: **25 MIN.**

1. Cut a strip of peel around the middle of each potato. Place potatoes and ¼ cup water in a 6-qt. electric pressure cooker. Lock lid; close pressure-release valve. Adjust to pressure-cook on high for 12 minutes. Quick-release pressure. Drain any cooking liquid; transfer potatoes to large bowl.

2. In a small bowl, combine butter, parsley, lemon juice and chives. Pour over potatoes; toss to coat. Sprinkle with salt and pepper.

Slow Cook: **2½ HOURS**

1. Cut a strip of peel from around the middle of each potato. Place potatoes and water in a 3-qt. slow cooker. Cover and cook on high 2½-3 hours or until tender (do not overcook); drain.

2. In a small bowl, combine the butter, parsley, lemon juice and chives. Pour over the potatoes and toss to coat. Season with salt and pepper.

1 SERVING: *150 cal., 8g fat (5g sat. fat), 20mg chol., 85mg sod., 18g carb. (1g sugars, 2g fiber), 2g pro.*

LENTIL PUMPKIN SOUP

Plenty of herbs and spices brighten up my hearty pumpkin soup. It's just the thing we need on nippy fall days and nights.
—Laura Magee, Houlton, WI

PREP: 15 min. • **MAKES:** 6 servings

- 1 lb. red potatoes (about 4 medium), cut into 1-in. pieces
- 1 can (15 oz.) pumpkin
- 1 cup dried lentils, rinsed
- 1 medium onion, chopped
- 3 garlic cloves, minced
- ½ tsp. ground ginger
- ½ tsp. pepper
- ⅛ tsp. salt
- 2 cans (14½ oz. each) vegetable broth
- 1½ cups water

LENTIL PUMPKIN SOUP

Fast Cook: **12 MIN. + RELEASING**
In a 6-qt. electric pressure cooker, combine all the ingredients. Lock the lid; close pressure-release valve. Adjust to pressure-cook on high for 12 minutes. Allow pressure to release naturally for 10 minutes, then quick-release any remaining pressure.

Slow Cook: **7 HOURS**
In a 3- or 4-qt. slow cooker, combine all ingredients. Cook, covered, on low for 7-9 hours or until potatoes and lentils are tender.

1½ CUPS: *210 cal., 1g fat (0 sat. fat), 0 chol., 463mg sod., 42g carb. (5g sugars, 7g fiber), 11g pro.* **Diabetic exchanges:** *3 starch, 1 lean meat.*

SAUCY INDIAN-STYLE CHICKEN & VEGETABLES

SAUCY INDIAN-STYLE CHICKEN & VEGETABLES

This dish always seems to develop a devoted following. Prepared sauce makes it easy to bring the rich flavors of Indian cuisine to your family. Feel free to use more or less of the tikka masala sauce according to your personal taste.
—Erica Polly, Sun Prairie, WI

PREP: 15 min. • **MAKES:** 8 servings

- 2 **medium sweet potatoes, peeled and cut into 1½-in. pieces**
- 2 **Tbsp. water**
- 2 **medium sweet red peppers, cut into 1-in. pieces**
- 3 **cups fresh cauliflowerets**
- 2 **lbs. boneless skinless chicken thighs, cubed**
- 2 **jars (15 oz. each) tikka masala curry sauce**
- ¾ **tsp. salt**
- **Minced fresh cilantro, optional**
- **Naan flatbreads, warmed**

Fast Cook: **5 MIN.**
In a 6-qt. electric pressure cooker, combine chicken and vegetables; add sauce, water and salt. Lock lid; close pressure-release valve. Adjust to pressure-cook on high for 3 minutes. Quick-release pressure. A thermometer inserted in chicken should read at least 170°. If desired, top with minced fresh cilantro; serve with warmed naan.

Slow Cook: **4 HOURS**
1. Microwave sweet potatoes and water, covered, on high just until potatoes begin to soften, 3-4 minutes.
2. In a 5- or 6-qt. slow cooker, combine vegetables and chicken; add sauce and salt. Cook, covered, on low 4-5 hours or until meat is tender. If desired, top with cilantro; serve with warmed naan.

FREEZE OPTION: Omitting cilantro and naan, freeze cooled chicken and vegetable mixture in freezer containers. To use, partially thaw in refrigerator overnight. Microwave, covered, on high in a microwave-safe dish until heated through, stirring gently and adding a little water if necessary. If desired, sprinkle with cilantro. Serve with warmed naan.

1¼ CUPS: *334 cal., 15g fat (4g sat. fat), 80mg chol., 686mg sod., 25g carb. (12g sugars, 5g fiber), 25g pro.* **Diabetic exchanges:** *3 lean meat, 2 fat, 1½ starch.*

WINTER FRUIT COMPOTE

You can make this colorful and easy fruit relish up to a week in advance. It's an outstanding accompaniment to turkey, chicken or pork throughout the holiday season.
—Esther Chesney, Carthage, MO

PREP: 10 min. • **MAKES:** 2½ cups

- **1 pkg. (12 oz.) fresh or frozen cranberries, thawed**
- **⅔ cup packed brown sugar**
- **¼ cup thawed orange juice concentrate**
- **2 Tbsp. raspberry vinegar**
- **½ cup chopped dried apricots**
- **½ cup golden raisins**
- **½ cup chopped walnuts, toasted**

TEST KITCHEN TIP

Dark brown sugar contains more molasses than light or golden brown sugar. The types are generally interchangeable in recipes. But if you prefer a bolder flavor, choose dark brown sugar.

WINTER FRUIT COMPOTE

Fast Cook: **20 MIN. + RELEASING**

1. In a 6-qt. electric pressure cooker, combine the cranberries, brown sugar, orange juice concentrate and vinegar. Lock lid; close pressure-release valve. Adjust to pressure-cook on high for 3 minutes. Let pressure release naturally for 5 minutes; quick-release any remaining pressure.

2. Stir in apricots, raisins and walnuts. Refrigerate leftovers.

Slow Cook: **1¼ HOURS**

1. In a 1½-qt. slow cooker, combine cranberries, brown sugar, orange juice concentrate and vinegar. Cook, covered, on low for 1¼-1¾ hours, until cranberries pop and mixture is thickened.

2. Turn off heat; stir in the apricots, raisins and walnuts. Refrigerate leftovers.

2 TBSP.: *161 cal., 4g fat (0 sat. fat), 0 chol., 32mg sod., 32g carb. (28g sugars, 3g fiber), 2g pro.*

TURKEY CHILI

TURKEY CHILI

I've taken my mother's milder recipe for chili and made it thicker and more robust. It's a favorite, especially in fall and winter.
—Celesta Zanger, Bloomfield Hills, MI

PREP: 20 min. • **MAKES:** 12 servings (3 qt.)

- 1 lb. lean ground turkey
- ¾ cup chopped celery
- ¾ cup chopped onion
- ¾ cup chopped green pepper
- 2 Tbsp. chili powder
- 1 tsp. ground cumin
- ¼ tsp. pepper
- ⅛ to ¼ tsp. cayenne pepper
- 2 cans (14½ oz. each) no-salt-added diced tomatoes, undrained
- 1 jar (24 oz.) meatless pasta sauce
- 1 can (16 oz.) hot chili beans, undrained
- 1½ cups water
- ½ cup frozen corn
- 1 can (16 oz.) kidney beans, rinsed and drained
- 1 can (15 oz.) pinto beans, rinsed and drained
- Optional toppings: Sour cream, cubed avocado, diced jalapeno peppers

Fast Cook: **5 MIN. + RELEASING**

1. Select saute or browning setting on a 6-qt. electric pressure cooker; adjust for medium heat. Cook turkey until no longer pink, 6-8 minutes, breaking it into crumbles; remove and drain turkey. Add water to pressure cooker. Cook 1 minute, stirring to loosen browned bits from pan. Return turkey to pressure cooker. Stir in celery, onion, green pepper, tomatoes, pasta sauce, beans, corn and seasonings.
2. Lock lid; close pressure-release valve. Adjust to pressure-cook on high for 5 minutes. Allow pressure to release naturally for 10 minutes, then quick-release any remaining pressure. If desired, serve with sour cream, avocado and jalapeno.

Slow Cook: **6½ HOURS**

1. In a large skillet, cook and crumble turkey with celery, onion and green pepper over medium-high heat until the turkey is no longer pink, 6-8 minutes. Transfer to a 5-qt. slow cooker. Stir in seasonings, tomatoes, pasta sauce, chili beans, water and corn.
2. Cook, covered, on high 1 hour. Reduce setting to low; cook, covered, 5-6 hours or until flavors are blended.
3. Stir in kidney and pinto beans; cook, covered, on low 30 minutes longer. If desired, serve with sour cream, avocado and jalapeno.

FREEZE OPTION: Freeze cooled chili in freezer containers. To use, partially thaw in refrigerator overnight. Heat through in a saucepan, stirring occasionally; add a little water if necessary.

1 CUP: *200 cal., 4g fat (1g sat. fat), 26mg chol., 535mg sod., 29g carb. (8g sugars, 8g fiber), 15g pro.* **Diabetic exchanges:** *2 lean meat, 2 vegetable, 1 starch.*

APPLE BALSAMIC CHICKEN

I just love the sweet and tart flavor balsamic vinegar gives to this dish. It's such an easy meal to prepare, and the chicken thighs are tender and flavorful.
—Juli Snaer, Enid, OK

PREP: 15 min. • **MAKES:** 4 servings

- 4 bone-in chicken thighs (about 1½ lbs.), skin removed
- ½ cup chicken broth
- ¼ cup apple cider or juice
- ¼ cup balsamic vinegar
- 2 Tbsp. lemon juice
- ½ tsp. salt
- ½ tsp. garlic powder
- ½ tsp. dried thyme
- ½ tsp. paprika
- ½ tsp. pepper
- 2 Tbsp. butter
- 2 Tbsp. all-purpose flour

READER REVIEW

"This was amazing. I used chicken breasts instead of thighs. I served it with noodles cooked in broth. I'm going to try again and add some mushrooms."
—SHANNONDOBOS, TASTEOFHOME.COM

APPLE BALSAMIC CHICKEN

Fast Cook: **15 MIN. + RELEASING**

1. In a small bowl, combine the chicken broth, cider, vinegar, lemon juice and seasonings. Place chicken in a 6-qt. electric pressure cooker; pour broth mixture over meat. Lock lid; close pressure-release valve. Adjust to pressure-cook on high for 10 minutes. Allow pressure to naturally release for 10 minutes, then quick-release any remaining pressure.

2. Remove chicken; keep warm. Skim fat from cooking liquid. In a small saucepan, melt butter; whisk in flour until smooth. Gradually add the cooking liquid. Cook and stir until the sauce is thickened, 2-3 minutes. Serve with chicken.

Slow Cook: **4 HOURS**

1. Place chicken in a 1½-qt. slow cooker. In a small bowl, combine the broth, cider, vinegar, lemon juice and seasonings; pour over meat. Cover and cook on low for 4-5 hours, until chicken is tender.

2. Remove chicken; keep warm. Skim fat from cooking liquid. In a small saucepan, melt butter; stir in flour until smooth. Gradually add cooking liquid. Bring to a boil; cook and stir for 2-3 minutes or until thickened. Serve with chicken.

1 SERVING: *277 cal., 15g fat (6g sat. fat), 103mg chol., 536mg sod., 9g carb. (4g sugars, 0 fiber), 25g pro.*

POTATO SOUP

POTATO SOUP

I decided to add some character to a basic potato chowder with roasted red peppers. The extra flavor gives a deliciously unique twist to an otherwise ordinary soup.
—Mary Shivers, Ada, OK

PREP: 20 min. • **MAKES:** 12 servings (3 qt.)

- **3 lbs. potatoes, peeled and cut into ½-in. cubes (8 cups)**
- **1 large onion, chopped**
- **1 jar (7 oz.) roasted sweet red peppers, drained and chopped**
- **1 small celery rib, chopped**
- **6 cups chicken broth**
- **½ tsp. garlic powder**
- **½ tsp. seasoned salt**
- **½ tsp. pepper**
- **⅛ tsp. rubbed sage**
- **⅓ cup all-purpose flour**
- **2 cups heavy whipping cream, divided**
- **1 cup grated Parmesan cheese, divided**
- **8 bacon strips, cooked and crumbled**
- **2 Tbsp. minced fresh cilantro**

Fast Cook: **25 MIN.**

1. Place first 9 ingredients in a 6-qt. electric pressure cooker. Lock lid; close pressure-release valve. Adjust pressure to pressure-cook on high for 15 minutes. Quick-release pressure.

2. Select saute setting and adjust for low heat. Mix flour and ½ cup cream until smooth; stir into soup. Stir in ¾ cup Parmesan cheese, bacon, cilantro and remaining cream. Cook and stir until slightly thickened, 6-8 minutes. Serve with remaining cheese.

Slow Cook: **5½ HOURS**

1. Place first 9 ingredients in a 5- or 6-qt. slow cooker. Cook, covered, on low 5-6 hours or until potatoes are tender.

2. Mix flour and ½ cup cream until smooth; stir into soup. Stir in ¾ cup cheese and the bacon, cilantro and remaining cream. Cook, covered, on low until slightly thickened, about 30 minutes. Serve with remaining cheese.

1 CUP: *289 cal., 19g fat (11g sat. fat), 59mg chol., 848mg sod., 23g carb. (4g sugars, 1g fiber), 7g pro.*

GARDEN CHICKEN CACCIATORE

Treat company to this perfect Italian dish. My guests always rave about how good it is. I like to serve it with pasta and a green salad for a balanced meal. Mangia!
—Martha Schirmacher, Sterling Heights, MI

PREP: 15 min. • **MAKES:** 12 servings

- 12 boneless skinless chicken thighs (about 3 lbs.)
- 2 medium green peppers, chopped
- 1 can (14½ oz.) diced tomatoes with basil, oregano and garlic, undrained
- 1 can (6 oz.) tomato paste
- 1 medium onion, chopped
- ½ cup reduced-sodium chicken broth
- ¼ cup dry red wine or additional reduced-sodium chicken broth
- 3 garlic cloves, minced
- ¾ tsp. salt
- ⅛ tsp. pepper
- 2 Tbsp. cornstarch
- 2 Tbsp. cold water
- Minced fresh parsley, optional

GARDEN CHICKEN CACCIATORE

Fast Cook: **10 MIN.**

1. Place chicken in an 6- or 8-qt. electric pressure cooker. Combine green peppers, tomatoes, tomato paste, onion, broth, wine, garlic, salt and pepper; pour over chicken. Lock lid; close pressure-release valve. Adjust to pressure-cook on high for 10 minutes. Quick-release pressure. A thermometer inserted in chicken should read at least 170°. Remove chicken to a serving patter; keep warm.
2. In a small bowl, mix cornstarch and water until smooth; stir into the broth mixture. Select saute setting and adjust for low heat. Simmer, stirring constantly, until thickened, 1-2 minutes.

Slow Cook: **8½ HOURS**

1. Place chicken in a 4- or 5-qt. slow cooker. In a medium bowl, combine green peppers, tomatoes, tomato paste, onion, broth, wine, garlic, salt and pepper; pour over chicken. Cook, covered, on low 8-10 hours or until chicken is tender.
2. In a small bowl, mix the cornstarch and water until smooth; gradually stir into slow cooker. Cook, covered, on high 30 minutes or until sauce is thickened. If desired, sprinkle with minced parsley before serving.

FREEZE OPTION: In a freezer container, layer chopped green peppers, onions, garlic, salt, pepper and chicken. Seal. Freeze for up to 6 months. Thaw overnight in refrigerator before use.

3 OZ. COOKED CHICKEN WITH ABOUT ½ CUP SAUCE: *206 cal., 8g fat (2g sat. fat), 76mg chol., 353mg sod., 8g carb. (3g sugars, 2g fiber), 23g pro.*
Diabetic exchanges: *3 lean meat, 1 vegetable.*

CHICKPEA & POTATO CURRY

CHICKPEA & POTATO CURRY

Here's my recipe for chana masala, the classic Indian dish. Browning the onion, ginger and garlic first really makes the sauce amazing.
—Anjana Devasahayam, San Antonio, TX

PREP: 25 min. • **MAKES:** 6 servings

- 1 Tbsp. canola oil
- 1 medium onion, chopped
- 2 garlic cloves, minced
- 2 tsp. minced fresh gingerroot
- 2 tsp. ground coriander
- 1 tsp. garam masala
- 1 tsp. chili powder
- ½ tsp. salt
- ½ tsp. ground cumin
- ¼ tsp. ground turmeric
- 1 can (15 oz.) crushed tomatoes
- 2 cans (15 oz. each) chickpeas or garbanzo beans, rinsed and drained
- 1 large baking potato, peeled and cut into ¾-in. cubes
- 2½ cups vegetable stock
- 1 Tbsp. lime juice
- Chopped fresh cilantro
- Hot cooked rice
- Optional: Sliced red onion and lime wedges

Fast Cook: **5 MIN. + RELEASING**

1. Select saute setting on a 6-qt. electric pressure cooker. Adjust for medium heat; add oil. When oil is hot, cook and stir onion until crisp-tender, 2-4 minutes. Add garlic, ginger and dry seasonings; cook and stir 1 minute. Add stock to pressure cooker. Cook for 30 seconds, stirring to loosen browned bits from pan. Press cancel. Stir in tomatoes, chickpeas and potato.

2. Lock lid; close pressure-release valve. Adjust to pressure-cook on high for 3 minutes. Let pressure release naturally for 10 minutes; quick-release any remaining pressure.

3. Stir in lime juice; sprinkle with cilantro. Serve with rice and, if desired, red onion and lime wedges.

Slow Cook: **6 HOURS**

1. In a large skillet, heat oil over medium-high heat; saute onion until tender, 2-4 minutes. Add garlic, ginger and dry seasonings; cook and stir 1 minute. Stir in tomatoes; transfer to a 3- or 4-qt. slow cooker.

2. Stir in chickpeas, potato and stock. Cook, covered, on low for 6-8 hours, until potato is tender and flavors are blended.

3. Stir in lime juice; sprinkle with cilantro. Serve with rice and, if desired, red onion and lime wedges.

1¼ CUPS: *240 cal., 6g fat (0 sat. fat), 0 chol., 767mg sod., 42g carb. (8g sugars, 9g fiber), 8g pro.*

BEEFY CABBAGE BEAN STEW

While on one of our small group quilting retreats, one of my friends made this wonderful recipe for dinner. We all loved it and have since passed it around for others to enjoy—now I'm passing it on to you.
—Melissa Glancy, La Grange, KY

PREP: 20 min. • **MAKES:** 6 servings

- ½ **lb. lean ground beef (90% lean)**
- 3 **cups shredded cabbage or angel hair coleslaw mix**
- 1 **can (16 oz.) red beans, rinsed and drained**
- 1 **can (14½ oz.) diced tomatoes, undrained**
- 1 **can (8 oz.) tomato sauce**
- ¾ **cup salsa or picante sauce**
- 1 **medium green pepper, chopped**
- 1 **small onion, chopped**
- 3 **garlic cloves, minced**
- 1 **tsp. ground cumin**
- ½ **tsp. pepper**
- **Optional: Shredded cheddar cheese and sliced jalapeno peppers**

BEEFY CABBAGE BEAN STEW

Fast Cook: **5 MIN.**

1. Select saute or browning setting on a 6-qt. electric pressure cooker; adjust for medium heat. Cook beef until no longer pink, 6-8 minutes, breaking into crumbles; drain. Press cancel. Return beef to pressure cooker.

2. Stir in remaining ingredients. Lock lid; close pressure-release valve. Adjust to pressure-cook on high for 3 minutes. Quick-release pressure.

Slow Cook: **6 HOURS**

1. In a large skillet, cook beef over medium heat until no longer pink, 4-6 minutes, breaking into crumbles; drain.

2. Transfer meat to a 4-qt. slow cooker. Stir in remaining ingredients. Cook, covered, on low 6-8 hours or until cabbage is tender. If desired, top with shredded cheddar cheese and sliced jalapeno peppers.

FREEZE OPTION: Freeze cooled stew in freezer containers. To use, partially thaw in refrigerator overnight. Heat through in a saucepan, stirring occasionally; add a little water if necessary.

1 CUP: *177 cal., 4g fat (1g sat. fat), 24mg chol., 591mg sod., 23g carb. (5g sugars, 7g fiber), 13g pro.* **Diabetic exchanges:** *1 starch, 1 lean meat, 1 vegetable.*

STIR-FRIED ZUCCHINI
PAGE 137

Side Dishes & Condiments

Celebrate seasonal flavor with garden-fresh green veggie sides, homey fall casseroles, stewed vegetables, and a slew of spreads, jams and butters.

CHECK OUT THESE SPECIALTIES

Homemade Taco Seasoning Mix p. 128

Mashed Cauliflower with Parmesan p. 128

Cinnamon Blueberry Jam p. 129

Stir-Fried Zucchini p. 137

Pumpkin Butter p. 141

BEST EVER CASHEW CHEESE SAUCE

SUCCOTASH

You can't get more southern than succotash. This recipe comes from my mother, who was a fantastic cook. This dish made her famous at least with everyone who ever tasted it.
—Rosa Boone, Mobile, AL

PREP: 1¾ hours + cooling • **COOK:** 1 hour
MAKES: 16 servings

- 1 smoked ham hock (about 1½ lbs.)
- 4 cups water
- 1 can (28 oz.) diced tomatoes, undrained
- 1½ cups frozen lima beans, thawed
- 1 pkg. (10 oz.) crowder peas, thawed, or 1 can (15½ oz.) black-eyed peas, drained
- 1 pkg. (10 oz.) frozen corn, thawed
- 1 medium green pepper, chopped
- 1 medium onion, chopped
- ⅓ cup ketchup
- 1½ tsp. salt
- 1½ tsp. dried basil
- 1 tsp. rubbed sage
- 1 tsp. paprika
- ½ tsp. pepper
- 1 bay leaf
- 1 cup sliced fresh or frozen okra
- Snipped fresh dill and chives, optional

1. In a Dutch oven or large saucepan, simmer ham hock in water until tender, 1½ hours. Cool; remove meat from the bone and return to pan. (Discard bone and broth or save for another use.) Add the tomatoes, beans, peas, corn, green pepper, onion, ketchup and seasonings. Simmer, uncovered, for 45 minutes.

2. Add okra; simmer, uncovered, until tender, 15 minutes. Discard bay leaf before serving. Garnish with dill and chives if desired.

¾ CUP: *79 cal., 0 fat (0 sat. fat), 2mg chol., 442mg sod., 16g carb. (5g sugars, 3g fiber), 4g pro.* **Diabetic exchanges:** *1 starch.*

BEST EVER CASHEW CHEESE SAUCE

This is a versatile cashew cream sauce that's totally plant-based. I use it as a pasta sauce, as a pizza topping, over roasted veggies, on tacos and for grilled cheese. Because it doesn't reheat well, I don't suggest making a double batch.
—Max Gregor, Santa Fe, NM

PREP: 15 min. + soaking • **COOK:** 10 min.
MAKES: 4 cups

- 2 cups organic raw cashews
- 1 Tbsp. olive oil
- ½ medium onion, chopped
- 2 garlic cloves, minced
- ¼ tsp. salt
- ¼ tsp. pepper
- 2 cups vegetable broth, divided
- 1 Tbsp. nutritional yeast
- Paprika, optional

1. Rinse cashews in cold water; drain. Place in a large bowl; add enough water to cover by 3 in. Cover and let stand overnight.

2. In a large skillet, heat oil over medium heat. Add onion; cook and stir until tender, 4-6 minutes. Add garlic, salt and pepper; cook 1 minute longer. Add 1½ cups broth; bring to a boil. Reduce heat to a simmer.

3. Drain and rinse cashews, discarding liquid. Add cashews to skillet; heat through. Transfer mixture to a blender. Add nutritional yeast; cover and process until pureed, adding enough remaining broth to achieve desired consistency. If desired, sprinkle with paprika.

⅔ CUP: *245 cal., 18g fat (3g sat. fat), 0 chol., 329mg sod., 13g carb. (3g sugars, 2g fiber), 7g pro.*

QUICK PICKLED RADISHES

QUICK PICKLED RADISHES

These pickled radishes are the perfect addition to tacos, barbecue or just about any sandwich you can dream of. Each sliced radish is just a little bit sweet and slightly crunchy and has a lot of zing. You're probably going to want to have a batch in your fridge at all times!
—Colleen Delawder, Herndon, VA

PREP: 25 min. + chilling • **MAKES:** 3 cups

- **1 lb. radishes**
- **½ cup water**
- **½ cup cider vinegar**
- **¼ cup sugar**
- **¼ cup packed light brown sugar**
- **1 Tbsp. mustard seed**
- **1 tsp. kosher salt**
- **1 tsp. whole peppercorns**
- **1 to 2 bay leaves**

With a mandoline or vegetable peeler, cut radishes into very thin slices. Place radishes in a 1-qt. jar. In a large saucepan, bring remaining ingredients to a boil. Carefully ladle hot liquid over radishes. Cover and refrigerate overnight.
¼ CUP: *11 cal., 0 fat (0 sat. fat), 0 chol., 296mg sod., 2g carb. (1g sugars, 1g fiber), 0 pro.*

JALAPENO GREEN BEANS

This simple green bean dish gets a bit of a kick from jalapeno pepper. If you don't like things too spicy, reduce the amount of jalapeno by half—or eliminate it completely.
—Deirdre Cox, Kansas City, MO

TAKES: 25 min. • **MAKES:** 4 servings

- **2 Tbsp. olive oil**
- **1 jalapeno pepper, thinly sliced**
- **1 shallot, thinly sliced**
- **1 lb. fresh green beans, cut into 2-in. pieces**
- **½ tsp. salt**
- **2 Tbsp. lemon juice**

In a large cast-iron or other heavy skillet, heat oil over medium-high heat. Add jalapeno and shallot; cook and stir until tender, 2-3 minutes. Add beans and salt; cook and stir until beans are tender, reducing heat if necessary, 8-10 minutes. Drizzle with lemon juice. Serve immediately.
NOTE: Wear disposable gloves when cutting hot peppers; the oils can burn skin. Avoid touching your face.
½ CUP: *106 cal., 7g fat (1g sat. fat), 0 chol., 303mg sod., 11g carb. (4g sugars, 4g fiber), 2g pro.* **Diabetic exchanges:** *1½ fat, 1 vegetable.*

JALAPENO GREEN BEANS

HOMEMADE TACO SEASONING MIX

HOMEMADE TACO SEASONING MIX

This seasoning mix is right on. It tastes like purchased mixes but is cheaper and has only about half the sodium. Your heart and wallet will surely thank you!
—Taste of Home *Test Kitchen*

TAKES: 20 min. • **MAKES:** 16 servings (1 cup mix)

- **¼ cup all-purpose flour**
- **¼ cup chili powder**
- **3 Tbsp. dried minced onion**
- **1 Tbsp. garlic powder**
- **2½ tsp. salt**
- **2 tsp. dried oregano**
- **2 tsp. ground cumin**
- **1½ tsp. cayenne pepper**
- **1 tsp. ground coriander**

ADDITIONAL INGREDIENTS

- **1 lb. lean ground beef (90% lean)**
- **¾ cup water**
- **4 whole wheat tortillas (8 in.), warmed**

1. Combine the first 9 ingredients. Store in an airtight container in a cool, dry place for up to 1 year. Makes 4 batches (about 1 cup total).

2. To prepare tacos: In a large skillet, cook beef over medium heat until no longer pink; drain. Add ¼ cup taco seasoning mix and water. Bring to a boil; cook and stir for 2 minutes. Fill each tortilla with ½ cup beef mixture.

1 PREPARED TACO: *338 cal., 13g fat (4g sat. fat), 71mg chol., 619mg sod., 26g carb. (2g sugars, 3g fiber), 27g pro.*

MASHED CAULIFLOWER WITH PARMESAN

I couldn't shake my mashed potato habit—until I tried cauliflower mashed to a similar consistency. I started making my own, and my family loves it.
—Meredith Howard, Franklin, KY

TAKES: 30 min. • **MAKES:** 6 servings

- **1 large head cauliflower (about 2½ lbs.), broken into florets**
- **1 cup shredded Parmesan cheese, divided**
- **⅓ cup heavy whipping cream or half-and-half cream**
- **1 Tbsp. butter**
- **½ tsp. pepper**
- **Minced fresh parsley, optional**

1. Place 1 in. of water and the cauliflower in a large saucepan; bring to a boil over high heat. Cook, covered, until cauliflower is softened, 10-12 minutes. Drain.

2. Mash cauliflower to desired consistency. Stir in ½ cup cheese, cream, butter and pepper. Sprinkle with remaining ½ cup cheese and, if desired, parsley.

⅔ CUP: *154 cal., 11g fat (7g sat. fat), 33mg chol., 290mg sod., 8g carb. (3g sugars, 3g fiber), 8g pro.*

MASHED CAULIFLOWER WITH PARMESAN

CINNAMON BLUEBERRY JAM

Watching my grandmother can hundreds of jars of tomatoes, peaches and pears inspired me to try making jams and jellies myself. I remember going down into her cellar as a girl—all those jars on the shelves gave me such a warm, homey feeling! My family enjoys this jam on warm corn or blueberry muffins. The cinnamon's a bit of a surprise.
—Barbara Burns, Phillipsburg, NJ

PREP: 15 min. • **PROCESS:** 10 min.
MAKES: 4 half-pints

- 1 **lb. fresh or frozen blueberries (about 1 qt.)**
- 3½ **cups sugar**
- 1 **Tbsp. bottled lemon juice**
- ¼ **tsp. ground cinnamon**
- ⅛ **tsp. ground cloves**
- 1 **pouch (3 oz.) liquid fruit pectin**

1. Crush blueberries; measure 2½ cups and place in a large saucepan. Add the sugar, lemon juice, cinnamon and cloves; bring to a rolling boil over high heat, stirring constantly. Quickly stir in the pectin. Return to a full rolling boil; boil for 1 minute, stirring constantly.
2. Remove from the heat; skim off foam. Carefully ladle hot mixture into hot half-pint jars, leaving ¼-in. headspace. Remove air bubbles; wipe rims and adjust lids. Process for 10 minutes in a boiling-water canner.
NOTE: The processing time listed is for altitudes of 1,000 feet or less. Add 1 minute to the processing time for each 1,000 feet of additional altitude.
2 TBSP.: *93 cal., 0 fat (0 sat. fat), 0 chol., 1mg sod., 24g carb. (23g sugars, 0 fiber), 0 pro.*

READER REVIEW

"I used a food mill to crush the berries since I didn't want all the skins and I didn't add the ground cloves. I have made three batches so far. Excellent!"
—MILLERTAND, TASTEOFHOME.COM

CHERRY TOMATO PASTA WITH AVOCADO SAUCE

CHERRY TOMATO PASTA WITH AVOCADO SAUCE

Heart-healthy avocado makes this pasta dish feel indulgent without being overly rich. The flavorful sauce is so luscious, you'll think there is cream hiding in there. It's guilt-free and dairy-free, but with a texture and consistency that's similar to traditional cream-based sauces.
—Julie Peterson, Crofton, MD

TAKES: 30 min. • **MAKES:** 10 servings

- 1 **pkg. (14½ oz.) protein-enriched rotini (about 3½ cups uncooked)**
- 2 **medium ripe avocados, peeled and pitted**
- 1 **cup fresh spinach**
- ¼ **cup loosely packed basil leaves**
- 2 **garlic cloves, halved**
- 2 **Tbsp. lime juice**
- ½ **tsp. kosher salt**
- ¼ **tsp. coarsely ground pepper**
- ⅓ **cup olive oil**
- 1 **cup assorted cherry tomatoes, halved**
- ½ **cup pine nuts**
- **Optional: Shredded Parmesan cheese, shredded mozzarella cheese and grated lime zest**

1. Cook rotini according to package directions for al dente. Meanwhile, place avocados, spinach, basil, garlic, lime juice, salt and pepper in a food processor; pulse until chopped. Continue processing while gradually adding oil in a steady stream.
2. Drain rotini; transfer to a large bowl. Add avocado mixture and tomatoes; toss to coat. Top with pine nuts and toppings of your choice.
¾ CUP: *314 cal., 18g fat (2g sat. fat), 0 chol., 125mg sod., 32g carb. (2g sugars, 5g fiber), 9g pro.*

CITRUS CANTALOUPE BUTTER

CITRUS CANTALOUPE BUTTER

This sweet cantaloupe butter gets its warm spice flavor from the cinnamon sticks. Orange sections and fresh lime juice and zest lend a lovely citrus twist.
—Mary M. Leverette, Columbia, SC

PREP: 20 min. + simmering
PROCESS: 10 min. • **MAKES:** 5 half-pints

- **2 medium cantaloupes, peeled, seeded and cubed**
- **2 cups orange sections, pith and seeds removed**
- **5 cups sugar**
- **½ cup bottled lime juice**
- **2 cinnamon sticks (3 in.)**
- **1 Tbsp. grated lime zest**

1. Process cantaloupe and orange sections in batches in a blender until pureed. Transfer to a Dutch oven.
2. Add sugar, lime juice, cinnamon and zest. Bring to a boil. Reduce heat; simmer, uncovered, until mixture is reduced to 5 cups and reaches a thick, spreadable consistency, about 2 hours, stirring frequently. Discard cinnamon sticks.
3. Carefully ladle hot mixture into 5 hot half-pint jars, leaving ¼-in. headspace. Remove air bubbles and adjust headspace, if necessary, by adding hot mixture. Wipe rims. Center lids on jars; screw on bands until fingertip tight.
4. Submerge jars in a canner with simmering water, ensuring that they are completely covered. Bring to a boil; process for 10 minutes. Remove jars and cool.
NOTE: The processing time listed is for altitudes of 1,000 feet or less. Add 1 minute to the processing time for each 1,000 feet of additional altitude.
2 TBSP.: *112 cal., 0 fat (0 sat. fat), 0 chol., 5mg sod., 29g carb. (28g sugars, 0 fiber), 0 pro.*

GRILLED ELOTE FLATBREAD

Here's a fun twist on a classic Mexican dish! Keep your kitchen cooled down during the summer months by grilling this fresh flatbread outdoors.
—Amanda Phillips, Portland, OR

PREP: 20 min. • **GRILL:** 15 min.
MAKES: 12 servings

- **2 medium ears sweet corn, husked**
- **3 Tbsp. olive oil, divided**
- **1 lb. fresh or frozen pizza dough, thawed**
- **½ cup mayonnaise**
- **⅓ cup crumbled Cotija cheese, divided**
- **⅓ cup chopped fresh cilantro, divided**
- **1 Tbsp. lime juice**
- **½ tsp. chili powder**
- **⅛ tsp. pepper**

1. Brush corn with 1 Tbsp. oil. Grill corn, covered, over medium heat until lightly browned and tender, 10-12 minutes, turning occasionally. Cool slightly. Cut corn from cobs; transfer to a large bowl.
2. On a lightly floured surface, roll or press dough to a 15x10-in. oval (about ¼ in. thick); place on a greased sheet of foil. Brush top with 1 Tbsp. oil.
3. Carefully invert crust onto grill rack, removing foil. Brush top with remaining 1 Tbsp. oil. Grill, covered, over medium heat until bottom is golden brown, 2-3 minutes on each side. Remove from grill; cool slightly.
4. Add mayonnaise, 3 Tbsp. cheese, 3 Tbsp. cilantro, lime juice, chili powder and pepper to corn; stir to combine. Spread over warm crust. Sprinkle with remaining cheese and cilantro.
1 PIECE: *211 cal., 13g fat (2g sat. fat), 4mg chol., 195mg sod., 20g carb. (2g sugars, 1g fiber), 5g pro.*

GRILLED ELOTE FLATBREAD

ASH'S SWEET & SPICY ENCHILADA SAUCE

This enchilada sauce recipe is both sweet and spicy—just as the name implies. Spoon it over enchiladas, burritos and spicy casseroles.
—Lauren Ash, Van Nuys, CA

TAKES: 30 min. • **MAKES:** 1¼ cups

2 Tbsp. olive oil
2 Tbsp. all-purpose flour
3 Tbsp. chili powder
2 Tbsp. packed brown sugar
1½ tsp. ground cumin
1½ tsp. paprika
1 tsp. salt
1 tsp. garlic powder
1 tsp. onion powder
½ tsp. pepper
1¾ cups vegetable broth

In a saucepan, heat oil over medium heat. Whisk in flour until blended. Add chili powder, brown sugar and remaining seasonings; cook, stirring constantly, until fragrant, 2-3 minutes. Gradually whisk in broth. Bring to a boil; cook and stir until thickened, about 20 minutes.

2 TBSP.: *53 cal., 3g fat (0 sat. fat), 0 chol., 424mg sod., 6g carb. (3g sugars, 1g fiber), 1g pro.*

ASH'S SWEET & SPICY ENCHILADA SAUCE

MINT CHUTNEY

MINT CHUTNEY

This versatile mint chutney recipe pairs well with samosas, sandwiches and salads! Its herby, bright flavor dresses up any dish.
—Soniya Saluja, Chantilly, VA

TAKES: 10 min. • **MAKES:** ⅔ cup

1 bunch fresh cilantro leaves, stems removed (about 2 cups)
1 bunch fresh mint leaves, stems removed (about 1 cup)
3 to 4 whole green chile peppers
3 garlic cloves, halved
Juice of 1 lemon or lime
1 Tbsp. sugar
1 tsp. cumin seeds
½ tsp. salt
1 to 2 Tbsp. water

In a blender, combine the first 8 ingredients; cover and process until smooth, adding water to reach desired consistency.

2 TBSP.: *31 cal., 0 fat (0 sat. fat), 0 chol., 248mg sod., 7g carb. (3g sugars, 2g fiber), 1g pro.* **Diabetic exchanges:** *½ starch.*

FRIJOLES Y CHORIZO

Chorizo (pork sausage) and frijoles (beans) make a tasty and authentic side dish. The flavorful meat combined with the zippy mixture of beans, peppers and seasonings is unforgettable.
—Taste of Home *Test Kitchen*

PREP: 40 min. + soaking • **COOK:** 2 hours
MAKES: 16 servings (2 qt.)

- 1 **lb. dried pinto beans**
- 2 **poblano peppers**
- 2 **serrano peppers**
- 6 **cups water**
- 1 **bay leaf**
- ½ **lb. uncooked chorizo, casing removed**
- 2 **Tbsp. lard**
- 1 **cup chopped onion**
- 2 **tsp. salt**
- ¼ **cup chopped fresh cilantro**

1. Place beans in a Dutch oven; add water to cover by 2 in. Bring to a boil; boil for 2 minutes. Remove from the heat; cover and let stand for 1 hour.
2. Place peppers on a baking sheet; broil 4 in. from the heat until skins blister, about 4 minutes. With tongs, rotate peppers a quarter turn. Broil and rotate until all sides are blistered and blackened. Immediately place peppers in a bowl; cover and let stand for 15 minutes. Peel off and discard charred skin. Remove stems and seeds. Chop peppers and set aside.
3. Drain and rinse pinto beans, discarding liquid. Return beans to the Dutch oven. Add 6 cups water and bay leaf; bring to a boil. Reduce heat; simmer, uncovered, for 1½- 2 hours or until beans are tender.
4. Meanwhile, crumble chorizo into a skillet; cook over medium heat for 6-8 minutes or until fully cooked. Drain and set aside. In the same skillet, melt lard. Add onion and reserved peppers; cook and stir until tender, about 5 minutes.
5. Add the chorizo, pepper mixture and salt to beans. Simmer, uncovered, for 30 minutes. Discard bay leaf. Just before serving, stir in cilantro.
NOTE: Wear disposable gloves when cutting hot peppers; the oils can burn skin. Avoid touching your face.
½ CUP: *173 cal., 6g fat (2g sat. fat), 14mg chol., 472mg sod., 20g carb. (2g sugars, 5g fiber), 9g pro.*

ZUCCHINI PICKLES

Preserve garden-fresh zucchini by pickling your harvest.
—Susan Court, Pewaukee, WI

PREP: 25 min. + standing • **PROCESS:** 15 min.
MAKES: about 4 half-pints

- 2 **lbs. firm fresh zucchini, cut into ¼-in. slices**
- 2 **small onions, sliced**
- ¼ **cup canning salt**
- 3 **cups white vinegar**
- 2 **cups sugar**
- 2 **tsp. mustard seed**
- 1 **tsp. celery seed**
- 1 **tsp. turmeric**

1. Combine zucchini and onions in a large bowl; sprinkle with canning salt and cover with cold water. Let stand 2 hours; rinse and drain.
2. In a large saucepan, bring remaining ingredients to a boil. Pour over zucchini and onions; cover and let stand 2 hours.
3. Transfer to a large saucepan. Bring to a boil; reduce heat and simmer 5 minutes. Carefully ladle hot mixture into 4 hot half-pint jars, leaving ½-in. headspace. Remove air bubbles and adjust headspace, if necessary, by adding hot mixture. Wipe rims. Center lids on jars; screw on bands until fingertip tight.
4. Place jars in canner with simmering water, ensuring that they are completely covered with water. Bring to a boil; process for 15 minutes. Remove jars and cool.
NOTE: The processing time listed is for altitudes of 1,000 feet or less. For altitudes up to 3,000 feet, add 5 minutes; 6,000 feet, add 10 minutes; 8,000 feet, add 15 minutes; 10,000 feet, add 20 minutes.
¼ CUP: *111 cal., 0 fat (0 sat. fat), 0 chol., 1772mg sod., 28g carb. (26g sugars, 1g fiber), 1g pro.*

ZUCCHINI PICKLES

GRANNY'S APPLE SCALLOPED POTATOES

I created this dish because I love scalloped potatoes and apples. It is delicious with breaded baked pork chops, which you could cook at the same time in another cast-iron pan. We are retired and it's just the two of us, but you could easily double the recipe.
—Shirley Rickis, The Villages, FL

PREP: 25 min. • **BAKE:** 55 min. + standing
MAKES: 4 servings

- **1 medium Granny Smith apple, peeled and thinly sliced**
- **1 tsp. sugar**
- **1 tsp. lemon juice**
- **2 Tbsp. butter**
- **½ cup sliced sweet onion**
- **4 medium red potatoes, thinly sliced (about 1 lb.)**
- **¾ cup plus 2 Tbsp. shredded Parmesan cheese, divided**
- **½ cup heavy whipping cream**
- **½ tsp. minced fresh thyme or ¼ tsp. dried thyme**
- **¼ tsp. salt**
- **¼ tsp. pepper**
- **4 bacon strips, cooked and crumbled**
- **Chopped fresh parsley, optional**

1. Preheat oven to 350°. In a small bowl, combine apple slices, sugar and lemon juice; toss to coat. Set aside. In an 8- or 9-in. cast-iron or other ovenproof skillet, heat butter over medium heat. Add onion; cook and stir until crisp-tender, about 3 minutes. Remove from the heat.
2. Alternately arrange potato and apple slices in a single layer in same skillet. Combine ¾ cup Parmesan cheese, cream, thyme, salt and pepper; pour over top.
3. Bake, uncovered, 50 minutes. Top with bacon and remaining 2 Tbsp. Parmesan cheese. Bake until potatoes are tender and top is lightly browned, 5-10 minutes longer. Let stand 10 minutes before serving. If desired, sprinkle with parsley.
1 SERVING: *376 cal., 25g fat (15g sat. fat), 70mg chol., 651mg sod., 27g carb. (7g sugars, 3g fiber), 13g pro.*

GRANNY'S APPLE SCALLOPED POTATOES

VIOLET JELLY

For a beautiful jelly to give as gifts, this one can't be beat. It is not only delicious but also guaranteed to impress all!
—Bernard Bellin, Franklin, WI

PREP: 40 min. + standing • **PROCESS:** 5 min.
MAKES: about 5 half-pints

- **8 cups fresh violet blossoms**
- **3½ cups boiling water**
- **1 pkg. (1¾ oz.) powdered fruit pectin**
- **½ cup lemon juice**
- **4 cups sugar**

1. Rinse and drain blossoms; place in a large heat-resistant glass bowl. Pour boiling water over the blossoms and let stand for 2 hours, stirring occasionally.
2. Strain and reserve violet liquid, pressing with a spatula to extract all possible color. Discard blossoms.
3. Measure violet liquid; add enough water to measure 3½ cups (liquid will be blue-green). Stir in pectin, lemon juice and sugar (the liquid will turn a violet color).
4. Pour into a large stainless steel saucepan; bring to a rolling boil, stirring constantly. Boil 1 minute.
5. Remove from the heat; skim off foam. Carefully ladle hot liquid into hot sterilized half-pint jars, leaving ¼-in. headspace. Remove air bubbles; wipe rims and adjust lids. Process for 5 minutes in a boiling-water canner.
NOTE: Only pick flowers from chemical-free woods or lawns. The processing time listed is for altitudes of 1,000 feet or less. Add 1 minute to the processing time for each 1,000 feet of additional altitude.
2 TBSP.: *86 cal., 0 fat (0 sat. fat), 0 chol., 1mg sod., 22g carb. (21g sugars, 0 fiber), 0 pro.*

SPICY BEET RELISH

SPICY BEET RELISH

We love the taste of this relish with any type meat or bean dish. You can adjust the pepper and horseradish to taste.
—Norma Leatherwood, Sevierville, TN

PREP: 1 hour • **PROCESS:** 15 min. • **MAKES:** 3 pints

- **4 lbs. fresh beets**
- **1 cup sugar**
- **1 cup cider vinegar**
- **2 Tbsp. grated peeled horseradish**
- **2 tsp. canning salt**
- **½ tsp. cayenne pepper**
- **¼ tsp. pepper**
- **Optional: Sliced baguette and grated lemon zest**

1. Scrub beets and trim tops to 1 in. Place in a Dutch oven; add water to cover. Bring to a boil. Reduce heat; simmer, covered, 45-60 minutes or until tender. Remove from water; cool. Peel and shred beets.
2. In a Dutch oven, combine sugar and vinegar; cook and stir over medium heat until sugar is dissolved. Stir in shredded beets, horseradish, salt, cayenne and pepper; bring to a boil.
3. Ladle hot mixture into hot 1-pint jars, leaving ½-in. headspace. Remove air bubbles and adjust headspace, if necessary, by adding hot relish. Wipe rims. Center lids on jars; screw on bands until fingertip tight.
4. Place jars in canner, ensuring that they are completely covered with water. Bring to a boil; process for 15 minutes. Remove jars and cool. If desired, serve on baguette slices and sprinkle with lemon zest.
NOTE: The processing time listed is for altitudes of 1,000 feet or less. For altitudes up to 3,000 feet, add 5 minutes; 6,000 feet, add 10 minutes; 8,000 feet, add 15 minutes; 10,000 feet, add 20 minutes.
¼ CUP: *70 cal., 0 fat (0 sat. fat), 0 chol., 256mg sod., 17g carb. (15g sugars, 2g fiber), 1g pro.*

GREEN BEAN BUNDLES

I found this recipe in a rural newspaper years ago and have made it often. The bean bundles are excellent with chicken or beef. Sometimes I'll arrange them around a mound of wild rice to make an appetizing side dish.
—Virginia Stadler, Nokesville, VA

TAKES: 25 min. • **MAKES:** 8 servings

- **1 lb. fresh green beans, trimmed**
- **8 bacon strips, partially cooked**
- **1 Tbsp. finely chopped onion**
- **3 Tbsp. butter**
- **1 Tbsp. white wine vinegar**
- **1 Tbsp. sugar**
- **¼ tsp. salt**

1. Cook the beans until crisp-tender. Wrap about 10 beans in each bacon strip; secure with a toothpick. Place on a foil-covered baking sheet. Bake at 400° until bacon is done, 10-15 minutes.
2. In a skillet, saute onion in butter until tender. Add vinegar, sugar and salt; heat through. Remove bundles to a serving bowl or platter; pour sauce over and serve immediately.
1 BUNDLE: *186 cal., 17g fat (7g sat. fat), 27mg chol., 286mg sod., 5g carb. (3g sugars, 2g fiber), 3g pro.*

GREEN BEAN BUNDLES

SUMMER ZUCCHINI PASTA

SUMMER ZUCCHINI PASTA

I'm always experimenting when my garden is cranking out zucchini and summer squash. This simple and healthy pasta dish is one of my latest wins. It's meatless, but you can add shredded chicken or grilled salmon for a heartier dish.
—Beth Berlin, Oak Creek, WI

TAKES: 25 min. • **MAKES:** 10 servings

- **1 pkg. (16 oz.) pappardelle or tagliatelle pasta**
- **¼ cup olive oil**
- **2 small zucchini, cut into thin ribbons**
- **2 small yellow summer squash, cut into thin ribbons**
- **4 garlic cloves, thinly sliced**
- **2 cans (14½ oz. each) diced tomatoes with roasted garlic, undrained**
- **⅓ cup loosely packed basil leaves, torn**
- **1 Tbsp. coarsely chopped fresh rosemary**
- **½ tsp. salt**
- **¼ tsp. crushed red pepper flakes**

Cook pasta according to package directions. Meanwhile, in a Dutch oven, heat oil over medium-high heat. Add zucchini and yellow squash; cook and stir until crisp-tender, 3-4 minutes. Add garlic; cook 1 minute longer. Add tomatoes, basil, rosemary, salt and pepper flakes; heat through. Drain pasta; serve with zucchini mixture. If desired, top with additional basil.
1 CUP: *254 cal., 7g fat (1g sat. fat), 0 chol., 505mg sod., 42g carb. (8g sugars, 3g fiber), 7g pro.*

ROMESCO SAUCE

Whether you pair it with fish, roasted veggies or some other creation, this flavor-packed sauce will take your dish to a new level.
—Lauren McAnelly, Des Moines, IA

TAKES: 10 min. • **MAKES:** 10 servings

- **½ cup slivered almonds, toasted**
- **½ cup soft whole wheat or white bread crumbs**
- **½ cup fire-roasted crushed tomatoes**
- **1 jar (8 oz.) roasted sweet red peppers, drained**
- **2 Tbsp. minced fresh parsley**
- **2 garlic cloves**
- **1 tsp. sweet paprika**
- **½ tsp. salt**
- **¼ tsp. freshly ground pepper**
- **¼ cup sherry**
- **½ cup olive oil**

Pulse almonds, bread crumbs, tomatoes, roasted peppers, parsley, garlic, paprika, salt and pepper in a food processor until finely chopped. Add sherry; process until blended. Continue processing while gradually adding oil in a steady stream.
¼ CUP: *164 cal., 14g fat (2g sat. fat), 0 chol., 268mg sod., 5g carb. (2g sugars, 1g fiber), 2g pro.*

ROMESCO SAUCE

STIR-FRIED ZUCCHINI

(SHOWN ON PAGE 124)

I plant many vegetables to use in cooking. Zucchini is among our favorites and is often in abundance. That's why this dish is so popular at our house.
—Deborah Elliot, Ridge Spring, SC

TAKES: 10 min. • **MAKES:** 8 servings

- 2 lbs. sliced zucchini
- 2 garlic cloves, minced
- ¼ cup olive oil
- 1 tsp. salt
- ½ tsp. Italian seasoning
- ¼ tsp. pepper

In a large skillet, saute the zucchini and garlic in oil until zucchini is crisp-tender, about 5 minutes. Sprinkle with seasonings. Serve immediately.

½ CUP: *77 cal., 7g fat (1g sat. fat), 0 chol., 299mg sod., 4g carb. (2g sugars, 1g fiber), 1g pro.*

READER REVIEW

"Delicious summertime recipe! Perfect side to go along with burgers or grilled pork chops. I used garlic salt, but the fresh garlic called for in the recipe is probably even more flavorful!"

—REMENEC, TASTEOFHOME.COM

BACON MAC & CHEESE CORNBREAD SKILLET

BACON MAC & CHEESE CORNBREAD SKILLET

My cast-iron skillet is a workhorse. I just love it for cooking and baking. And this cast-iron mac and cheese recipe can be served as a main dish or as a smaller portion side.
—Lisa Keys, Kennett Square, PA

PREP: 35 min. • **BAKE:** 30 min. + standing
MAKES: 8 servings

- 1¾ cups uncooked elbow macaroni
- 8 bacon strips, chopped
- 1 cup shredded smoked Gouda or cheddar cheese
- 1 cup shredded pepper jack cheese
- 4 oz. cream cheese, cubed
- 6 large eggs, divided use
- 3 cups 2% milk, divided
- 4 green onions, chopped
- 1 tsp. kosher salt, divided
- ½ tsp. pepper, divided
- 1 pkg. (8½ oz.) cornbread/muffin mix
- ½ tsp. smoked paprika
- Additional green onions

1. Preheat oven to 400°. Cook macaroni according to the package directions. Meanwhile, in a 12-in. ovenproof skillet, cook bacon over medium heat until crisp, stirring occasionally. Remove with a slotted spoon; drain on paper towels. Discard drippings, reserving 1 Tbsp. in pan.

2. Drain macaroni; add to drippings. Stir in shredded cheeses and cream cheese; cook and stir over medium heat until cheese is melted, 2-3 minutes. Whisk 2 eggs, 1 cup milk, green onions, ½ tsp. kosher salt and ¼ tsp. pepper; pour into skillet. Cook and stir until slightly thickened, 3-4 minutes. Remove from heat.

3. Reserve ¼ cup bacon for topping; sprinkle remaining bacon over macaroni. Place cornbread mix, paprika and remaining 4 eggs, 2 cups milk, ½ tsp. kosher salt and ¼ tsp. pepper in a blender; cover and process until smooth. Pour over bacon.

4. Bake until puffed and golden brown, 30-35 minutes. Let stand 10 minutes before serving. Sprinkle with reserved ¼ cup bacon and additional green onions.

1 CUP: *497 cal., 27g fat (13g sat. fat), 203mg chol., 978mg sod., 40g carb. (12g sugars, 3g fiber), 23g pro.*

GOBI ALOO

GOBI ALOO

Aloo gobi is a very popular Indian dish. In northern India, where I'm from, we call it gobi aloo. The vegetarian dish gets its flavors from turmeric, ginger, garlic and lime.
—Soniya Saluja, Chantilly, VA

PREP: 25 min. • **COOK:** 5 min.
MAKES: 4 servings

- **1 Tbsp. olive oil**
- **1 tsp. cumin seeds**
- **1 medium red onion, thinly sliced**
- **2 large plum tomatoes, chopped**
- **2 tsp. minced fresh gingerroot**
- **1 tsp. red chili powder**
- **1 tsp. garam masala**
- **1 tsp. ground cumin**
- **¾ tsp. salt**
- **¼ tsp. ground turmeric**
- **1 medium head cauliflower, cut into 2- or 3-in. pieces**
- **2 small potatoes, peeled and cut into thin wedges**
- **2 Tbsp. water**
- **Chopped fresh cilantro, optional**

1. Select saute setting on a 6-qt. electric pressure cooker. Adjust for medium heat; add oil. When oil is hot, cook and stir cumin seeds until fragrant and they start to pop. Add onion; cook until crisp-tender, about 2 minutes. Add tomatoes and ginger; cook 1 minute. Add chili powder, garam masala, cumin, salt and turmeric; cook until fragrant, about 1 minute. Stir in cauliflower, potatoes and water. Press cancel.
2. Lock lid; close pressure-release valve. Adjust to pressure-cook on high for 3 minutes. Let pressure release naturally for 5 minutes; quick-release any remaining pressure. Sprinkle with cilantro if desired.
1¼ CUPS: *164 cal., 4g fat (1g sat. fat), 0 chol., 514mg sod., 29g carb. (6g sugars, 6g fiber), 5g pro.* **Diabetic exchanges:** *2 starch, 1 fat.*

DID YOU KNOW?

Gobi aloo is a popular dish in northern India. (Gobi means cauliflower and aloo means potato.) Like dal, it has become a staple of Indian cuisine that's enjoyed worldwide. You can adjust the levels of turmeric, ginger, garlic and lime to suit your tastes.

FRIED MASHED POTATO BALLS

FRIED MASHED POTATO BALLS

The key to making this recipe is to use mashed potatoes that start firm from chilling. Serve the potato balls with sour cream or ranch salad dressing on the side.
—Taste of Home Test Kitchen

PREP: 25 min. + standing • **COOK:** 5 min./batch
MAKES: 6 servings

- **2 cups cold mashed potatoes**
- **1 large egg, lightly beaten**
- **¾ cup shredded cheddar cheese**
- **½ cup chopped green onions**
- **4 bacon strips, cooked and crumbled**
- **½ cup dry bread crumbs**
- **Oil for frying**

1. Place mashed potatoes in a large bowl; let stand at room temperature for 30 minutes. Stir in the egg, cheese, onions and bacon. Shape into 1-in. balls; roll in bread crumbs. Let stand for 15 minutes.
2. In an electric skillet, heat 1 in. of oil to 375°. Fry potato balls, a few at a time, until golden brown, 2½-3 minutes. Remove with a slotted spoon to paper towels to drain. Serve warm.
5 POTATO BALLS: *290 cal., 19g fat (5g sat. fat), 55mg chol., 496mg sod., 21g carb. (1g sugars, 1g fiber), 9g pro.*

QUICK ROASTED RED PEPPER SPREAD

PINEAPPLE SWEET POTATO CASSEROLE WITH MARSHMALLOWS

Pineapple, sugar and marshmallows lend extra sweetness to sweet potatoes. I've been making the casserole for years, for both special occasions and casual dinners.
—Ruth Leach, Shreveport, LA

PREP: 45 min. • **BAKE:** 40 min.
MAKES: 8 servings

- **6 medium sweet potatoes**
- **½ cup butter, cubed**
- **¾ cup sugar**
- **1 can (20 oz.) crushed pineapple, drained**
- **2 large eggs, beaten**
- **1 tsp. vanilla extract**
- **½ tsp. ground nutmeg**
- **½ tsp. salt**
- **15 large marshmallows**

1. Place sweet potatoes in a large kettle and cover with water; bring to a boil. Boil gently until potatoes can easily be pierced with the tip of a sharp knife, 30-45 minutes. Drain; cool slightly.
2. Preheat oven to 350°. Peel potatoes and place in a large bowl with butter and sugar; mash. Add pineapple, eggs, vanilla, nutmeg and salt; stir to combine.
3. Spoon into a greased 2-qt. baking dish. Top with marshmallows. Bake, uncovered, until a knife inserted in the center comes out clean, 40-45 minutes.

1 CUP: *367 cal., 13g fat (8g sat. fat), 84mg chol., 295mg sod., 62g carb. (43g sugars, 3g fiber), 4g pro.*

QUICK ROASTED RED PEPPER SPREAD

This spread is easy to make and can be used in many ways! It's amazing on top of grilled meats, mixed into a hearty stew for extra flavor, stirred into cream for a rich pasta sauce, or combined with mayonnaise as a sandwich condiment. I always keep this spread on hand: By freezing it in small portions, I can remove exactly the amount needed for each use.
—Josh Rink, Milwaukee, WI

TAKES: 10 min. • **MAKES:** 8 servings (1 cup)

- **1 jar (12 oz.) roasted sweet red peppers, drained**
- **1 Tbsp. fresh rosemary leaves**
- **2 garlic cloves, minced**
- **2 tsp. grated lemon zest**
- **½ tsp. kosher salt**

Place ingredients in the bowl of a food processor fitted with the blade attachment; process until smooth, scraping down side of bowl as needed. Red pepper spread can be refrigerated up to 2 weeks or frozen up to 3 months.

2 TBSP.: *16 cal., 0 fat (0 sat. fat), 0 chol., 276mg sod., 2g carb. (1g sugars, 0 fiber), 0 pro.*

TEST KITCHEN TIPS

Pepper Spread Uses

- Mix 1 Tbsp. with 1 cup of mayonnaise for a unique spread on sandwiches or as a topping for crab cakes.
- Whisk ¼ cup with 2 Tbsp. olive oil and brush onto chicken or steak just before removing from the grill.
- Stir 1-2 Tbsp. into soups or stews for added richness and flavor.

FIESTA CORN

Corn with tomatoes and jalapenos is one of the first dishes I cooked for my husband. Don't like heat? Use green bell peppers instead of jalapenos.
—Cassandra Ramirez, Bardstown, KY

TAKES: 25 min. • **MAKES:** 8 servings

- **¼ cup butter, cubed**
- **1 small onion, chopped**
- **2 to 3 jalapeno peppers, seeded and chopped**
- **6 plum tomatoes, seeded and chopped**
- **5 cups fresh or frozen corn**
- **1½ tsp. salt**
- **Lime wedges, optional**

1. In a 6-qt. stockpot, heat butter over medium heat. Add onion and jalapenos; cook and stir until onion is crisp-tender, 3-4 minutes. Stir in tomatoes; cook 3 minutes longer.
2. Add corn; cook, uncovered, until tender, stirring occasionally, 8-10 minutes. Stir in salt. If desired, serve with lime wedges.
NOTE: Wear disposable gloves when cutting hot peppers; the oils can burn skin. Avoid touching your face.
¾ CUP: *142 cal., 7g fat (4g sat. fat), 15mg chol., 505mg sod., 20g carb. (7g sugars, 3g fiber), 4g pro.*

FIESTA CORN

PUMPKIN BUTTER

PUMPKIN BUTTER

Biting into this spiced butter on a hot biscuit is absolutely heavenly. With a dash of whipped cream, you might think you were eating pumpkin pie!
—June Barrus, Springville, UT

PREP: 5 min. • **COOK:** 20 min. + cooling • **MAKES:** 6 cups

- **3 cans (15 oz. each) pumpkin**
- **2 cups sugar**
- **1½ cups water**
- **3 Tbsp. lemon juice**
- **1 Tbsp. grated lemon zest**
- **3 tsp. ground cinnamon**
- **¾ tsp. salt**
- **¾ tsp. ground nutmeg**
- **¾ tsp. ground ginger**

1. In a large saucepan, combine all ingredients. Bring to a boil, stirring frequently. Reduce heat; cover and simmer for 20 minutes to allow flavors to blend.
2. Cool. Spoon into jars. Cover and store in the refrigerator for up to 3 weeks.
2 TBSP.: *42 cal., 0 fat (0 sat. fat), 0 chol., 38mg sod., 11g carb. (9g sugars, 1g fiber), 0 pro.*

CREAMY CAULIFLOWER RICE

What began as a quick fix dish has become a staple in our house. It's a great way to add veggies to a meal, and it's a nice change from traditional cauliflower.
—Caresse Caton, Mobile, AL

TAKES: 30 min. • **MAKES:** 10 servings

- **3 cups uncooked long grain rice**
- **3 cups frozen cauliflower, thawed**
- **6 cups reduced-sodium chicken broth**
- **6 oz. cream cheese, cubed**
- **¾ tsp. salt**
- **¼ tsp. pepper**

In a large saucepan, combine rice, cauliflower and broth; bring to a boil. Reduce heat; simmer, covered, 15-20 minutes or until liquid is absorbed and rice is tender. Remove from heat. Add cream cheese, salt and pepper; stir until melted.

¾ CUP: *301 cal., 6g fat (4g sat. fat), 17mg chol., 584mg sod., 52g carb. (2g sugars, 2g fiber), 8g pro.*

CREAMY CAULIFLOWER RICE

GLAZED CARROTS WITH GREEN GRAPES

GLAZED CARROTS WITH GREEN GRAPES

After receiving a slow cooker many years ago and not knowing what to do with the thing, I finally branched out and read up on what it was all about. This is one of the recipes I make that is enjoyed by all at any time of the year. It is so colorful and a delightful side for any meal.
—Lorraine Caland, Shuniah, ON

PREP: 20 min. • **COOK:** 3½ hours • **MAKES:** 7 servings

- **8 medium carrots, sliced (14 oz.)**
- **⅓ cup orange marmalade**
- **2 Tbsp. water**
- **¼ tsp. salt**
- **1 cup halved green grapes**
- **1 Tbsp. butter**
- **Chopped fresh parsley, optional**

In a 3-qt. slow cooker, combine carrots, marmalade, water and salt. Cook, covered, on low heat until carrots are almost tender, 2¾ hours. Add the grapes and butter. Cover and cook on low until tender, 45 minutes longer. If desired, sprinkle with parsley.

½ CUP: *98 cal., 2g fat (1g sat. fat), 4mg chol., 157mg sod., 21g carb. (16g sugars, 2g fiber), 1g pro.*

5i
STRAWBERRY BUTTER

There are several farms in our community where families can pick their own strawberries. We usually pick a big bucketful and can't resist sampling some in the car on the way home. But we make sure to save enough for this delicious spread.
—Kim Hammond, Watsonville, CA

PREP: 10 min. + chilling • **MAKES:** 2 cups

- **1 pkg. (8 oz.) cream cheese, softened**
- **½ cup butter, softened**
- **1 cup confectioners' sugar**
- **1 tsp. vanilla extract**
- **1 cup fresh strawberries, pureed**

In a bowl, beat cream cheese and butter until smooth. Gradually add sugar and vanilla; mix well. Stir in strawberries. Cover tightly and refrigerate for several hours or overnight. May be stored in the refrigerator for up to 1 week. Serve with English muffins, toast, waffles or pancakes.
2 TBSP.: *132 cal., 11g fat (7g sat. fat), 31mg chol., 100mg sod., 8g carb. (8g sugars, 0 fiber), 1g pro.*

STRAWBERRY BUTTER

ALABAMA WHITE BBQ SAUCE

5i
ALABAMA WHITE BBQ SAUCE

When my boys spent their summers with their grandmother in Alabama, she would treat them to a restaurant that served chicken with white barbecue sauce. Making this reminds me of those times. Apply the sauce only at the very end of the grilling.
—Sabrina Everett, Thomasville, GA

PREP: 5 min. + chilling • **MAKES:** 3 cups

- **2 cups mayonnaise**
- **1 cup cider vinegar**
- **2 Tbsp. pepper**
- **2 Tbsp. lemon juice**
- **1 tsp. salt**
- **½ tsp. cayenne pepper**

In a small bowl, whisk all ingredients. Refrigerate for at least 8 hours. Brush sauce over meats during the last few minutes of grilling. Serve remaining sauce on the side for dipping.
2 TBSP.: *124 cal., 13g fat (2g sat. fat), 1mg chol., 192mg sod., 1g carb. (0 sugars, 0 fiber), 0 pro.*

TEST KITCHEN TIP

Alabama white sauce is traditionally slathered on barbecued chicken. Try it with chicken wings or pulled pork sandwiches, too. You can also use it as a coleslaw dressing or a dip for vegetables.

CHOCOLATE YEAST BREAD
PAGE 148

Breads, Rolls & Muffins

Put the butter out to soften, because hot homemade bread is just pages away! Discover sweet and savory delights for all occasions here.

OUR ALL-TIME FAVORITES

Wonderful English Muffins p. 146

Green Onion Rolls p. 147

Garlic Rosemary Pull-Apart Bread p. 149

Cristen's Giant Cinnamon Rolls p. 153

CARROT ZUCCHINI BREAD

This flavorful low-sugar bread satisfies my husband's sweet tooth surprisingly well—and I like it too.
—Edna Bright, Paris, IL

PREP: 10 min. • **BAKE:** 45 min. + cooling
MAKES: 2 loaves (12 pieces each)

- **1 cup unsweetened applesauce**
- **¾ cup shredded carrots**
- **¾ cup shredded peeled zucchini**
- **½ cup sugar**
- **2 lage eggs, room temperature**
- **1½ tsp. pumpkin pie spice**
- **1 tsp. ground cinnamon**
- **½ tsp. ground nutmeg**
- **3 cups all-purpose flour**
- **1 Tbsp. baking powder**
- **½ tsp. baking soda**
- **½ tsp. salt**
- **¾ cup orange juice**

1. Preheat oven to 350°. In a bowl, combine the first 8 ingredients. Combine flour, baking powder, baking soda and salt; add alternately with orange juice to carrot mixture. Pour into 2 greased and floured 8x4-in. loaf pans.

2. Bake until a toothpick inserted in the center comes out clean, about 45 minutes. Cool for 10 minutes; remove from pans to a wire rack to cool completely.

1 PIECE: *90 cal., 1g fat (0 sat. fat), 16mg chol., 145mg sod., 19g carb. (6g sugars, 1g fiber), 2g pro.* **Diabetic exchanges:** *1 starch.*

CARROT ZUCCHINI BREAD

WONDERFUL ENGLISH MUFFINS

When I was growing up on a farm, my mom always seemed to be making homemade bread...and nothing tasted so good! Now I like to make these simple, delicious muffins for my own family.
—Linda Rasmussen, Twin Falls, ID

PREP: 30 min. + rising • **COOK:** 25 min.
MAKES: 12 muffins

- **1 cup whole milk**
- **¼ cup butter, cubed**
- **2 Tbsp. sugar**
- **1 tsp. salt**
- **2 pkg. (¼ oz. each) active dry yeast**
- **1 cup warm water (110° to 115°)**
- **2 cups all-purpose flour**
- **3 to 3½ cups whole wheat flour**
- **1 Tbsp. sesame seeds**
- **1 Tbsp. poppy seeds**
- **Cornmeal**

1. Scald milk in a saucepan; add butter, sugar and salt. Stir until butter melts; cool to lukewarm. In a small bowl, dissolve yeast in warm water; add to milk mixture. Stir in all-purpose flour and 1 cup whole wheat flour until smooth. Add sesame seeds, poppy seeds and enough remaining whole wheat flour to make a soft dough.

2. Turn onto a floured surface; knead until smooth and elastic, 8-10 minutes. Place in a greased bowl, turning once to grease top. Cover and let rise until doubled, about 1 hour.

3. Punch dough down. Roll to ⅓-in. thickness on a cornmeal-covered surface. Cut into circles with a 3½-in. or 4-in. cutter; cover with a towel and let rise until nearly doubled, about 30 minutes.

4. Place muffins, cornmeal side down, in a greased skillet; cook over medium-low heat until bottoms are browned, 12-14 minutes. Turn and cook until other side is browned, 12-14 minutes. Cool on wire racks; split and toast to serve.

1 MUFFIN: *240 cal., 6g fat (3g sat. fat), 13mg chol., 248mg sod., 41g carb. (4g sugars, 4g fiber), 7g pro.*

DOUBLE CHOCOLATE SCONES

DOUBLE CHOCOLATE SCONES

Chocolate lovers will adore these moist, decadent scones that earned me a blue ribbon in a baking competition. They're perfect for a tea or brunch, and the mix of cocoa and chocolate chips makes them sweet enough for dessert.
—Stephanie Sorbie, Peoria, AZ

PREP: 15 min. • **BAKE:** 20 min. • **MAKES:** 8 scones

- 1¾ **cups all-purpose flour**
- ½ **cup baking cocoa**
- ⅓ **cup sugar**
- 1½ **tsp. baking powder**
- ½ **tsp. salt**
- 4 **oz. cream cheese, cubed**
- ¼ **cup cold butter, cubed**
- 2 **large eggs, room temperature, divided use**
- ¾ **cup heavy whipping cream**
- 2 **tsp. vanilla extract**
- ⅔ **cup semisweet chocolate chips**

1. Preheat oven to 375°. In a large bowl, whisk the first 5 ingredients. Cut in cream cheese and butter until mixture resembles coarse crumbs. In another bowl, whisk 1 egg, cream and vanilla; stir into crumb mixture just until moistened. Stir in chocolate chips.
2. Turn onto a floured surface; knead gently 10 times. Pat dough into a 6-in. circle. Cut into 8 wedges. Place wedges on a greased baking sheet. In a small bowl, whisk remaining egg; brush over scones. Bake 18-20 minutes or until a toothpick inserted in center comes out clean. Serve warm.
1 SCONE: *412 cal., 25g fat (15g sat. fat), 114mg chol., 334mg sod., 42g carb. (17g sugars, 3g fiber), 8g pro.*

5i

GREEN ONION ROLLS

Better double the batch—these savory, elegant rolls are sure to disappear fast.
—Jane Kroeger, Key Largo, FL

PREP: 30 min. + rising • **BAKE:** 20 min. • **MAKES:** 1 dozen

- 1 **Tbsp. butter**
- 1½ **cups chopped green onions**
- ½ **tsp. pepper**
- ¾ **tsp. garlic salt, optional**
- 1 **loaf (1 lb.) frozen bread dough, thawed**
- ½ **cup shredded part-skim mozzarella cheese**
- ⅓ **cup grated Parmesan cheese**

1. Preheat oven to 375°. In a large skillet, heat the butter over medium-high heat; saute green onions until tender. Stir in pepper and, if desired, garlic salt. Remove from heat.
2. On a lightly floured surface, roll dough into a 12x8-in. rectangle. Spread with onion mixture. Sprinkle with cheeses.
3. Roll up jelly-roll style, starting with a long side; pinch seam to seal. Cut into 12 slices; place in greased muffin cups. Cover; let rise in a warm place until doubled, about 30 minutes. Preheat the oven to 375°.
4. Bake rolls until golden brown, 18-20 minutes. Remove from pan to a wire rack. Serve warm.
1 ROLL: *142 cal., 4g fat (1g sat. fat), 7mg chol., 415mg sod., 20g carb. (2g sugars, 2g fiber), 6g pro.*

GREEN ONION ROLLS

GLUTEN-FREE SPICED SWEET POTATO MUFFINS

GLUTEN-FREE SPICED SWEET POTATO MUFFINS

I have a family member with special dietary needs, so I came up with this muffin recipe that we could all enjoy. Gluten-free muffins can sometimes have an unpleasant texture, but these are just as good as any traditional recipe, maybe even better! If you don't have sweet potato on hand, canned pumpkin can be used instead.
—Kallee Krong-McCreery, Escondido, CA

PREP: 20 min. • **BAKE:** 25 min.
MAKES: 1 dozen

- **2¼ cups gluten-free all-purpose baking flour**
- **¼ cup sugar**
- **1 tsp. baking powder**
- **1 tsp. ground cinnamon**
- **½ tsp. baking soda**
- **½ tsp. salt**
- **¼ tsp. ground allspice**
- **¼ tsp. ground ginger**
- **3 large eggs, room temperature**
- **1 cup mashed sweet potatoes**
- **⅔ cup honey**
- **2 Tbsp. coconut oil, melted**
- **1 Tbsp. olive oil**
- **1 tsp. vanilla extract**

TOPPING

- **3 Tbsp. sugar**
- **¼ tsp. ground cinnamon**

1. Preheat oven to 350°. In a large bowl, whisk the first 8 ingredients. In another bowl, whisk eggs, sweet potatoes, honey, coconut oil, olive oil and vanilla until blended. Add to flour mixture; stir just until moistened.

2. Fill 12 greased or paper-lined muffin cups three-fourths full. Combine topping ingredients; sprinkle over batter. Bake until a toothpick inserted in center comes out clean, 25-30 minutes. Cool 5 minutes before removing from pan to a wire rack. Serve warm.

1 MUFFIN: *231 cal., 5g fat (3g sat. fat), 47mg chol., 217mg sod., 44g carb. (25g sugars, 3g fiber), 4g pro.*

CHOCOLATE YEAST BREAD

(SHOWN ON PAGE 144)

Your family will love this tender loaf of chocolate bread. Slices are excellent when toasted and spread with butter, cream cheese or peanut butter.
—Laura Cryts, Derry, NH

PREP: 30 min. + rising • **BAKE:** 25 min.
MAKES: 2 loaves (12 pieces each)

- **4½ cups all-purpose flour**
- **⅓ cup baking cocoa**
- **2 Tbsp. sugar**
- **1 pkg. (¼ oz.) active dry yeast**
- **1 tsp. salt**
- **¼ tsp. baking soda**
- **1 cup water**
- **½ cup 2% milk**
- **½ cup semisweet chocolate chips**
- **2 Tbsp. butter**
- **1 large egg, room temperature**
  Optional: Baking cocoa and/or confectioners' sugar

1. In a bowl, combine 1¼ cups flour, cocoa, sugar, yeast, salt and baking soda. In a saucepan, heat the water, milk, chocolate chips and butter; stir until chocolate is melted. Cool to 120°-130°. Add to dry ingredients; beat on medium speed for 2 minutes. Add ½ cup flour and egg; beat on high for 2 minutes. Stir in enough remaining flour to form a stiff dough.

2. Turn onto a floured surface; knead until smooth and elastic, 6-8 minutes. Place in a greased bowl, turning once to grease top. Cover and let rise in a warm place until doubled, about 1 hour.

3. Punch dough down. Turn onto a lightly floured surface; divide in half. Shape into loaves. Place in 2 greased 8x4-in. loaf pans. Cover and let rise until doubled, about 1 hour.

4. Bake at 375° until loaves are browned, 25-30 minutes. Remove from pans to cool on wire racks. Dust with baking cocoa and/or confectioners' sugar if desired.

1 PIECE: *124 cal., 3g fat (1g sat. fat), 11mg chol., 125mg sod., 22g carb. (3g sugars, 1g fiber), 3g pro.*

CARAWAY PUFFS

Our daughter took these light-as-a-feather rolls to a 4-H event and came home with a Grand Champion ribbon! We think they're especially delectable served straight from the oven.
—Glennis Endrud, Buxton, ND

PREP: 15 min. + rising • **BAKE:** 15 min.
MAKES: 1 dozen

- **1 pkg. (¼ oz.) active dry yeast**
- **¼ cup warm water (110° to 115°)**
- **1 cup warm 4% cottage cheese (110° to 115°)**
- **2 Tbsp. sugar**
- **1 Tbsp. butter, softened**
- **2 tsp. caraway seeds**
- **1 tsp. salt**
- **¼ tsp. baking soda**
- **2⅓ cups all-purpose flour**
- **1 large egg, room temperature**

1. In a large bowl, dissolve yeast in warm water. Add the cottage cheese, sugar, butter, caraway seeds, salt, baking soda and 1⅓ cups flour. Beat on medium speed for 3 minutes. Add egg and ½ cup flour; beat 2 minutes longer. Stir in enough remaining flour to form a firm dough (batter will be stiff). Do not knead. Cover and let rise in a warm place until doubled, about 45 minutes. Stir dough down.
2. Spoon into greased muffin cups. Cover and let rise in a warm place until doubled, about 35 minutes.
3. Bake at 400° for 12-14 minutes or until golden brown. Cool in pan for 1 minute. Serve immediately.
1 PUFF: *128 cal., 2g fat (1g sat. fat), 21mg chol., 315mg sod., 22g carb. (3g sugars, 1g fiber), 6g pro.*

TEST KITCHEN TIP

Batter Up!

Easy batter bread lets you enjoy homemade yeast bread without the work of kneading. It dirties fewer dishes and leaves your counter clean, since the dough stays in its mixing bowl for the first rise. Batter bread dough is looser and stickier than traditional kneaded doughs.

GARLIC ROSEMARY PULL-APART BREAD

This recipe is a different type of pull-apart bread. Eat it by itself, dipped in marinara, or as part of a meal. For a variation on the flavor, add sun-dried tomatoes, pesto, or an onion soup mix packet instead of the rosemary-garlic combo.
—Christina Trikoris, Clarksville, TN

PREP: 25 min. + rising
BAKE: 55 min. + cooling • **MAKES:** 16 servings

- **3 tsp. active dry yeast**
- **1 tsp. salt**
- **5¼ to 6 cups all-purpose flour**
- **1 cup water**
- **1 cup butter, cubed**
- **½ cup 2% milk**
- **2 large eggs, room temperature**

FLAVORING
- **½ cup butter, melted**
- **6 garlic cloves, minced**
- **2 Tbsp. minced fresh rosemary or 2 tsp. dried rosemary, crushed**
- **1 tsp. salt**
- **1 cup grated Parmesan cheese**

1. In a large bowl, mix yeast, salt and 2 cups flour. In a small saucepan, heat water, cubed butter and milk to 120°-130°. Add to dry ingredients; beat on medium speed for 2 minutes. Add eggs; beat on high for 2 minutes. Stir in enough remaining flour to form a soft dough (dough will be sticky).
2. Turn dough onto a floured surface; knead until smooth and elastic, 6-8 minutes. Place in a greased bowl, turning once to grease the top. Cover and let rise in a warm place until doubled, about 1 hour.
3. Punch dough down. Turn onto a lightly floured surface; shape into 1½-in. balls. Combine melted butter, garlic, rosemary and salt. Dip 10 dough balls into butter mixture. Place in a greased 10-in. fluted tube pan; sprinkle with a scant ¼ cup Parmesan cheese. Repeat with remaining balls and Parmesan cheese. Drizzle with any remaining butter mixture. Cover and let rise until doubled, about 45 minutes. Preheat oven to 350°.
4. Bake until golden brown, 55-70 minutes or until a thermometer inserted in bread reads 200°. Cool for 10 minutes before inverting onto a serving plate. Serve warm.
1 SERVING: *341 cal., 20g fat (12g sat. fat), 74mg chol., 536mg sod., 33g carb. (1g sugars, 1g fiber), 7g pro.*

GARLIC ROSEMARY PULL-APART BREAD

HEALTHY AVOCADO PINEAPPLE MUFFINS

HEALTHY AVOCADO PINEAPPLE MUFFINS

These healthy muffins are a real treat for breakfast, a luncheon or a coffee break. The avocado adds an extra-special touch to the yummy muffins. They are delicious served warm from the oven, and they also freeze well. The muffins would be a nice touch for breakfast on St. Patrick's Day.
—Joan Hallford, North Richland Hills, TX

PREP: 20 min. • **BAKE:** 20 min.
MAKES: 1 dozen

- **⅔ cup cubed ripe avocado**
- **3 large eggs, room temperature**
- **¼ cup honey**
- **2 Tbsp. canola oil**
- **1 can (8 oz.) unsweetened crushed pineapple, undrained**
- **2 cups all-purpose flour**
- **½ tsp. salt**
- **½ tsp. baking powder**
- **½ tsp. baking soda**
- **½ tsp. ground cinnamon**
- **¾ cup toasted chopped pecans, divided**

1. Preheat oven to 375°. In a large bowl, beat avocado until only small lumps remain. Add eggs, honey and oil; beat until blended. Stir in pineapple. In another bowl, whisk flour, salt, baking powder, baking soda and cinnamon. Add to avocado mixture; stir just until moistened. Fold in ½ cup pecans.
2. Fill 12 greased or foil-lined muffin cups; sprinkle tops with remaining ¼ cup pecans. Bake until a toothpick inserted in center comes out clean, 20-25 minutes. Cool for 5 minutes before removing from pan to a wire rack. Serve warm.

1 MUFFIN: *208 cal., 10g fat (1g sat. fat), 47mg chol., 190mg sod., 26g carb. (9g sugars, 2g fiber), 5g pro.* **Diabetic exchanges:** *2 fat, 1½ starch.*

SNICKERDOODLE PUMPKIN BREAD

This luscious bread is well worth the occasional splurge. When we first discovered how fantastic it was, I made four loaves on three separate occasions in just over a week!
—Jaleen Burkholder, Waterloo, NY

PREP: 35 min. • **BAKE:** 45 min. + cooling
MAKES: 12 pieces

- **½ cup butter, softened**
- **½ cup sugar**
- **2 large eggs, room temperature**
- **½ cup canned pumpkin**
- **1½ cups all-purpose flour**
- **1 tsp. baking powder**
- **½ tsp. salt**
- **¼ tsp. baking soda**
- **⅓ cup buttermilk**
- **½ tsp. ground cinnamon**
- **1 tsp. molasses**

COATING

- **5 Tbsp. butter, melted**
- **1 Tbsp. maple syrup**
- **¼ cup sugar**
- **¼ cup packed brown sugar**
- **½ tsp. ground cinnamon**

1. Preheat oven to 350°. In a large bowl, cream butter and sugar until light and fluffy, 5-7 minutes. Add eggs, 1 at a time, beating well after each addition. Beat in pumpkin. In another bowl, whisk flour, baking powder, salt and baking soda; add to creamed mixture alternately with buttermilk, beating well after each addition. Batter will be thick.
2. Remove ½ cup batter to a small bowl; stir in cinnamon and molasses until blended. Pour half of the remaining plain batter into a greased 8x4-in. loaf pan; dot with half of the cinnamon batter. Repeat layers. Cut through batter with a knife to swirl.
3. Bake until a toothpick inserted in center comes out clean, 45-50 minutes. Cool in pan 20 minutes before removing to a wire rack. For coating, in a small bowl combine melted butter and maple syrup. In another shallow bowl, combine sugar, brown sugar and cinnamon. Brush loaf with butter mixture, allowing butter to soak into bread; gently roll loaf in sugar mixture, pressing lightly to coat.

1 PIECE: *254 cal., 14g fat (8g sat. fat), 64mg chol., 291mg sod., 31g carb. (18g sugars, 1g fiber), 3g pro.*

SNICKERDOODLE PUMPKIN BREAD

SWEET POTATO SPICE BREAD

It's a good thing this recipe makes two mini loaves because they'll go fast! For a small household, eat one loaf now and freeze the other for later.
—Ronnie Littles, Virginia Beach, VA

PREP: 15 min. • **BAKE:** 25 min. + cooling
MAKES: 2 mini loaves (6 pieces each)

- **1 cup all-purpose flour**
- **1½ tsp. baking powder**
- **¼ tsp. each ground cinnamon, nutmeg and allspice**
- **⅛ tsp. salt**
- **1 large egg, room temperature**
- **⅓ cup mashed sweet potato**
- **⅓ cup honey**
- **3 Tbsp. canola oil**
- **2 Tbsp. molasses**
- **⅓ cup chopped walnuts**

1. In a small bowl, combine the flour, baking powder, spices and salt. In another small bowl, whisk the egg, sweet potato, honey, oil and molasses. Stir into dry ingredients just until moistened. Fold in walnuts.
2. Transfer to 2 greased 5¾x3x2-in. loaf pans. Bake at 325° for 25-30 minutes or until a toothpick inserted in the center comes out clean. Cool for 10 minutes before removing from pans to wire racks.
1 PIECE: *142 cal., 6g fat (1g sat. fat), 18mg chol., 85mg sod., 20g carb. (10g sugars, 1g fiber), 3g pro.*

SWEET POTATO SPICE BREAD

GARDEN HERB DROP BISCUITS

This biscuit recipe is a great complement to homemade soup, stew and chili. It's also wonderful for making a sandwich with leftover ham! I enjoy coming up with new recipes for my husband and me using garden-fresh herbs and veggies.
—Dreama Crump, Hephzibah, GA

PREP: 20 min. • **BAKE:** 15 min.
MAKES: 1 dozen

- **2¼ cups biscuit/baking mix**
- **1 cup shredded cheddar cheese**
- **2 green onions, finely chopped**
- **1 Tbsp. minced fresh parsley or 1 tsp. dried parsley flakes**
- **1 Tbsp. minced fresh basil or 1 tsp. dried basil**
- **2 tsp. minced fresh oregano or ½ tsp. dried oregano**
- **½ tsp. sugar**
- **¼ tsp. garlic powder**
- **⅔ cup plus 1 Tbsp. 2% milk, divided**
- **⅓ cup sour cream**
- **2 tsp. spicy brown mustard**
- **1 large egg**

1. Preheat oven to 425°. In a large bowl, mix the first 8 ingredients. In a small bowl, whisk ⅔ cup milk, sour cream and mustard until blended. Add to baking mix mixture; stir just until moistened.
2. Drop by ¼ cupfuls 2 in. apart onto a greased baking sheet. In a small bowl, whisk egg with remaining milk; brush over tops. Bake 12-14 minutes or until golden brown. Serve warm.
1 BISCUIT: *153 cal., 7g fat (3g sat. fat), 28mg chol., 319mg sod., 17g carb. (2g sugars, 1g fiber), 5g pro.*

"I made this recipe for a topping on a turkey potpie. It added great flavor to the pie. I omitted the cheese and green onions. It's a winner. It was easy to prepare, especially since it started with a baking mix. This Community Cook deems it a keeper!"
—JON.RUTH.ALUMBAUGH, TASTEOFHOME.COM

RAISIN RYE MUFFINS

These wholesome muffins sweetened with honey are egg-, wheat- and milk-free, so they are wonderful for people with food allergies. —Edna Hoffman, Hebron, IN

TAKES: 30 min. • **MAKES:** 6 muffins

- **1 cup rye flour**
- **2 tsp. baking powder**
- **½ tsp. ground cinnamon**
- **¼ tsp. salt**
- **½ cup water**
- **2 Tbsp. honey**
- **2 Tbsp. canola oil**
- **½ cup raisins**

1. In a large bowl, combine the flour, baking powder, cinnamon and salt. Combine water, honey and oil; stir into dry ingredients just until moistened. Fold in raisins.

2. Fill 6 muffin cups coated with cooking spray two-thirds full. Bake at 400° for 15-20 minutes or until a toothpick comes out clean. Cool for 5 minutes before removing from the pan to a wire rack. Serve warm.

1 MUFFIN: *160 cal., 5g fat (0 sat. fat), 0 chol., 234mg sod., 29g carb. (14g sugars, 3g fiber), 2g pro.*

CRISTEN'S GIANT CINNAMON ROLLS

CRISTEN'S GIANT CINNAMON ROLLS

As a young newlywed, I took it upon myself to make cinnamon rolls because I thought that was the hallmark of a good baker. The first rolls were dense like hockey pucks and somewhat flavorless. Our dear black Lab Annie wouldn't even eat one. I practiced for a couple of months and entered a contest at the Iowa State Fair—and I won! —Cristen Clark, Runnells, IA

PREP: 45 min. + rising
BAKE: 25 min. + cooling • **MAKES:** 1 dozen

- **2 pkg. (¼ oz. each) quick-rise yeast**
- **½ cup warm water (110° to 115°)**
- **2 tsp. honey**
- **1½ cups warm 2% milk (110° to 115°)**
- **½ cup sugar**
- **½ cup butter, softened**
- **½ cup mashed potatoes**
- **3 large eggs, room temperature, lightly beaten**
- **2 tsp. salt**
- **7½ to 8 cups all-purpose flour**

FILLING

- **1 cup packed brown sugar**
- **2 Tbsp. ground cinnamon**
- **1½ tsp. all-purpose flour**
- **Dash salt**
- **½ cup butter, softened**

VANILLA ICING

- **3 cups confectioners' sugar**
- **¼ cup 2% milk**
- **1 tsp. vanilla bean paste or vanilla extract**
- **Dash salt**

1. In a small bowl, dissolve yeast in warm water and honey. In a large bowl, combine milk, sugar, butter, potatoes, eggs, salt, yeast mixture and 4 cups flour; beat on medium speed until smooth. Stir in enough remaining flour to form a soft dough (dough will be sticky). Turn dough onto a floured surface; knead until smooth and elastic, 6-8 minutes. Place in a greased large bowl, turning once to grease the top. Cover and let rise in a warm place until doubled, about 1 hour.

2. For filling, combine brown sugar, cinnamon, flour and salt. Punch down dough. Turn onto a lightly floured surface; roll into a 24x12-in. rectangle. Spread butter to within ½ in. of edges; sprinkle with brown sugar mixture. Roll up jelly-roll style, starting with a long side; pinch seam to seal. Cut into 12 slices. Place in 2 greased 13x9-in. baking pans (6 slices per pan), cut side down. Cover with kitchen towels; let rise in a warm place until doubled, about 30 minutes.

3. Preheat oven to 350°. Bake until lightly browned, 25-30 minutes, covering loosely with foil during the last 10 minutes of baking. Cool in pan 30 minutes. In a small bowl, mix icing ingredients; drizzle over the rolls.

1 ROLL: *695 cal., 18g fat (11g sat. fat), 90mg chol., 588mg sod., 122g carb. (59g sugars, 3g fiber), 11g pro.*

CHOCOLATE CHIP MUFFINS

Both of my daughters love these muffins! I usually double this recipe so I have extras to keep in the freezer for a quick breakfast or snack.
—Lori Thompson, New London, TX

PREP: 15 min. • **BAKE:** 20 min. • **MAKES:** 1 dozen

- **2 cups all-purpose flour**
- **½ cup sugar**
- **1 Tbsp. baking powder**
- **½ tsp. salt**
- **1 large egg, room temperature**
- **¾ cup 2% milk**
- **⅓ cup vegetable oil**
- **¾ cup miniature semisweet chocolate chips**

1. Preheat oven to 400°. In a large bowl, combine the first 4 ingredients. In a small bowl, beat egg, milk and oil. Stir into dry ingredients just until moistened. Fold in chocolate chips.
2. Fill 12 greased or paper-lined muffin cups three-fourths full. Bake until a toothpick comes out clean, 18-20 minutes. Cool for 5 minutes before removing to a wire rack.
1 MUFFIN: *229 cal., 10g fat (3g sat. fat), 20mg chol., 213mg sod., 32g carb. (15g sugars, 1g fiber), 4g pro.*

CHOCOLATE CHIP MUFFINS

APPLE CIDER BISCUITS

APPLE CIDER BISCUITS

My family enjoys these tender, flaky biscuits warm from the oven. We have a lot of apple trees, so we're always looking for apple recipes. This is a tasty way to use some of our cider.
—Harriet Stichter, Milford, IN

TAKES: 30 min. • **MAKES:** about 1 dozen

- **2 cups all-purpose flour**
- **1 Tbsp. baking powder**
- **2 tsp. sugar**
- **½ tsp. salt**
- **⅓ cup cold butter**
- **¾ cup apple cider**
- **⅛ tsp. ground cinnamon**
- **Honey, optional**

1. In a bowl, combine the flour, baking powder, sugar and salt. Cut in butter until mixture resembles coarse crumbs. Stir in cider just until moistened. Turn onto a lightly floured surface and knead 8-10 times.
2. Roll out to ½-in. thickness; cut with a 2½-in. biscuit cutter. Place on ungreased baking sheets. Sprinkle with cinnamon; pierce tops of biscuits with a fork.
3. Bake at 425° until golden brown, 12-14 minutes. If desired, serve with honey.
1 BISCUIT: *131 cal., 5g fat (3g sat. fat), 14mg chol., 252mg sod., 18g carb. (3g sugars, 1g fiber), 2g pro.*

HEAVENLY CHEESE DANISH

This tempting cheese Danish is baked to flaky perfection and made to shine with a simple egg wash gloss. It tastes just as decadent as any breakfast pastry you'd find in a bakery or coffee shop.
—Josephine Triton, Lakewood, OH

PREP: 50 min. + chilling • **BAKE:** 15 min.
MAKES: 16 rolls

- 2 **pkg. (¼ oz. each) active dry yeast**
- ½ **cup warm water (110° to 115°)**
- 4 **cups all-purpose flour**
- ⅓ **cup sugar**
- 2 **tsp. salt**
- 1 **cup cold butter, cubed**
- 1 **cup 2% milk**
- 4 **large egg yolks, room temperature**

ASSEMBLY

- 3 **tsp. ground cinnamon**
- 12 **oz. cream cheese, softened**
- ⅓ **cup sugar**
- 1 **large egg, separated, room temperature**
- 1 **Tbsp. water**
- 2 **Tbsp. maple syrup**

1. Dissolve yeast in warm water. In another bowl, mix flour, sugar and salt; cut in butter until crumbly. Add milk, egg yolks and yeast mixture; stir to form a soft dough (dough will be sticky). Cover and refrigerate for 8-24 hours.
2. To assemble, punch down dough; divide into 4 portions. On a lightly floured surface, pat each portion into a 9x4-in. rectangle; sprinkle each with ¾ tsp. cinnamon. Cut each rectangle lengthwise into four 9x1-in. strips. Twist each strip, then loosely wrap strip around itself to form a coil; tuck the end under and pinch to seal. Place 3 in. apart on greased baking sheets.
3. Beat cream cheese, sugar and egg yolk until smooth. Press an indentation in center of each roll; fill with 1 rounded Tbsp. cream cheese mixture. Cover; let rise in a warm place until doubled, about 45 minutes. Preheat oven to 350°.
4. Whisk egg white with water; brush over rolls. Bake until rolls are golden brown, 15-20 minutes. Remove to wire racks brush with syrup. Serve warm. Refrigerate leftovers.

1 ROLL: *359 cal., 21g fat (12g sat. fat), 111mg chol., 468mg sod., 37g carb. (12g sugars, 1g fiber), 7g pro.*

CHERRY-GO-ROUND

This fancy coffee cake is surprisingly easy. It makes a great gift.
—Kathy McCreary, Wichita, KS

PREP: 30 min. + chilling • **BAKE:** 20 min.
MAKES: 2 coffee cakes (12 servings each)

- 1 **pkg. (¼ oz.) active dry yeast**
- ¼ **cup warm water (110° to 115°)**
- 1 **cup warm whole milk (110° to 115°)**
- ½ **cup sugar**
- ½ **cup butter, softened**
- 1 **large egg, room temperature**
- 1 **tsp. salt**
- 4½ **to 5 cups all-purpose flour**

FILLING

- 2 **cans (16 oz. each) pitted tart cherries, well drained and roughly chopped**
- ½ **cup all-purpose flour**
- ½ **cup packed brown sugar**
- ½ **cup chopped pecans**

ICING

- 1 **cup confectioners' sugar**
- ¼ **tsp. vanilla extract**
- 1 **to 2 Tbsp. whole milk**

1. In a large bowl, dissolve yeast in warm water. Add the milk, sugar, butter, egg, salt and 2 cups flour. Beat until smooth. Stir in enough remaining flour to form a soft dough.
2. Turn onto a lightly floured surface; knead until smooth and elastic, 6-8 minutes. Place in a greased bowl, turning once to grease top. Cover and refrigerate overnight.
3. Line 2 baking sheets with parchment; set aside. Punch dough down. Turn onto a lightly floured surface; divide in half. Roll each portion into a 14x7-in. rectangle. Spread cherries over dough to within ½ in. of edges. Combine the flour, brown sugar and pecans; sprinkle over cherries.
4. Roll up jelly-roll style, starting with a long side; pinch seams and tuck ends under. Place each seam side down on a prepared baking sheet; pinch ends together to form a ring. With kitchen scissors, cut from outside edge two-thirds of the way toward center of ring at 1-in. intervals. Separate strips slightly and twist to allow filling to show. Cover and let rise until doubled, about 1 hour.
5. Bake at 350° until golden brown, 20-25 minutes. Remove from pans to wire racks.
6. In a small bowl, for icing, combine the confectioners' sugar, vanilla and enough milk to reach desired consistency; drizzle over warm coffee cakes.

1 PIECE: *223 cal., 6g fat (3g sat. fat), 21mg chol., 149mg sod., 38g carb. (18g sugars, 1g fiber), 4g pro.*

CHERRY-GO-ROUND

PEACHES & CREAM WHISKEY LOAF

I love when fresh peaches are in season! This recipe is sweet from the peaches, but it also has a slight tang from the whiskey. It will star as a perfect after-dinner sweet but is just as good with morning coffee. It also makes a welcome gift for neighbors and friends.
—Anne Ormond, Dover, NH

PREP: 20 min. • **BAKE:** 1 hour + cooling
MAKES: 1 loaf (12 pieces)

- **1½ cups all-purpose flour**
- **1 cup packed brown sugar**
- **1¼ tsp. baking soda**
- **2 large eggs, room temperature**
- **⅓ cup sour cream**
- **¼ cup canola oil**
- **2 Tbsp. peach whiskey or whiskey**
- **1 cup chopped peeled fresh peaches**
- **½ cup chopped pecans**

GLAZE

- **1 cup confectioners' sugar**
- **1 to 2 Tbsp. 2% milk**
- **1 Tbsp. peach whiskey or whiskey**

1. Preheat oven to 350°. In a large bowl, whisk flour, brown sugar and baking soda. In another bowl, whisk eggs, sour cream, oil and whiskey until blended. Add to flour mixture; stir just until moistened. Fold in peaches and pecans.

2. Transfer to a greased 8x4-in. loaf pan. Bake until a toothpick inserted in center comes out clean, 60-65 minutes. Cool in pan 10 minutes before removing to a wire rack to cool completely. Combine glaze ingredients; drizzle over cooled bread. Let stand until set.

FREEZE OPTION: Securely wrap the cooled loaf in foil, then freeze. To use, thaw at room temperature.

1 PIECE: *273 cal., 10g fat (2g sat. fat), 33mg chol., 151mg sod., 42g carb. (29g sugars, 1g fiber), 3g pro.*

PEACHES & CREAM WHISKEY LOAF

BOSTON BROWN BREAD

This bread is one of my favorites, and I'm sure it will become one of yours, as well. The loaf's dense, chewy texture and slight sweetness from the molasses make it irresistible.
—NannyKay Novalue, tasteofhome.com

PREP: 15 min. • **BAKE:** 45 min. + cooling
MAKES: 1 loaf (16 pieces)

- **1 cup all-purpose flour**
- **1 cup whole wheat flour**
- **½ cup steel-cut oats**
- **½ cup cornmeal**
- **½ cup rye flour**
- **1 tsp. salt**
- **1 tsp. baking soda**
- **1 tsp. baking powder**
- **1 large egg, room temperature**
- **2 cups buttermilk**
- **¼ cup molasses**

1. Preheat oven to 325°. In a large bowl, combine first 8 ingredients. In another bowl, whisk egg, buttermilk and molasses. Stir into dry ingredients just until moistened. Transfer to a greased 9x5-in. loaf pan.

2. Bake 45-50 minutes or until a toothpick inserted in the center comes out clean. Cool 10 minutes before removing from pan to a wire rack.

NOTE: Steel-cut oats are also known as Scotch oats or Irish oatmeal.

1 PIECE: *131 cal., 1g fat (0 sat. fat), 14mg chol., 290mg sod., 26g carb. (5g sugars, 2g fiber), 5g pro.*

PEPPER JACK MUFFINS

This is a delicious muffin recipe to serve with any soup or chili recipe. Regular cheddar cheese can be used instead of the pepper jack for a milder muffin.
—Deborah Forrest, Ocean Springs, MS

TAKES: 25 min. • **MAKES:** 5 muffins

- 1 **cup all-purpose flour**
- 1 **Tbsp. sugar**
- 1 **tsp. baking powder**
- ¼ **tsp. salt**
- 1 **large egg, room temperature**
- ½ **cup milk**
- 2 **Tbsp. butter, melted**
- ⅓ **cup shredded pepper jack cheese**

1. In a small bowl, combine the flour, sugar, baking powder and salt. In another bowl, combine the egg, milk and butter. Stir into dry ingredients just until moistened. Fold in cheese.
2. Fill greased muffin cups three-fourths full. Bake at 400° for 15-20 minutes or until a toothpick comes out clean. Cool for 5 minutes before removing from pan to a wire rack. Serve warm.
1 SERVING: *199 cal., 9g fat (5g sat. fat), 65mg chol., 300mg sod., 23g carb. (4g sugars, 1g fiber), 7g pro.*

CONCHAS (SEASHELLS)

CONCHAS (SEASHELLS)

A fun-to-make pan dulce or sweet bread is a breakfast or snack pastry found all over Mexico. A fluffy brioche-like dough gets a crispy streusel topping that is scored to resemble a shell. The breads come in a variety of colors and other shapes, but I prefer them topped with plain and chocolate streusel.
—Johnna Johnson, Scottsdale, AZ

PREP: 45 min. + rising
BAKE: 15 min. + cooling • **MAKES:** 1 dozen

- ⅓ **cup sugar**
- 1 **pkg. (¼ oz.) active dry yeast**
- 1 **tsp. salt**
- 1 **tsp. ground cinnamon**
- 5 **to 5½ cups all-purpose flour**
- 1 **cup 2% milk**
- ½ **cup unsalted butter, cubed**
- 2 **large eggs, room temperature**

STREUSEL
- ½ **cup unsalted butter, softened**
- 1 **cup all-purpose flour**
- ⅔ **cup sugar**
- 1 **tsp. vanilla extract**
- 1 **oz. semisweet chocolate, ground**
- 1 **large egg**
- 2 **Tbsp. 2% milk**

1. In a large bowl, mix sugar, yeast, salt, cinnamon and 2 cups flour. In a small saucepan, heat milk and butter to 120°-130°. Add to dry ingredients; beat on medium speed 2 minutes. Add eggs; beat on high 2 minutes. Stir in enough remaining flour to form a stiff dough (dough will be sticky). Turn dough onto a floured surface; knead dough until smooth and elastic, 6-8 minutes. Place in a greased bowl, turning once to grease the top. Cover and let rise in a warm place until doubled, about 1 hour. Meanwhile, to make streusel, in a large bowl, beat butter, flour, sugar and vanilla until combined. Divide in half. Mix chocolate into 1 half; set aside. Punch down dough.
2. Divide dough into 12 portions; form each into a 3-in. oval. Place ovals 2 in. apart on parchment-lined baking sheets. In a small bowl, whisk egg with milk; brush over dough. Divide plain streusel into 6 portions; roll each into a 3-in. circle. Place over half the rolls. Repeat with chocolate streusel and remaining rolls. Using a sharp knife, cut through streusel on top of rolls to resemble a clamshell. Cover with kitchen towels; let rise in a warm place until almost doubled, about 30 minutes. Preheat oven to 375°. Brush rolls with remaining egg wash. Bake until the tops are lightly browned, 15-20 minutes. Remove to a wire rack to cool completely.
1 ROLL: *475 cal., 19g fat (11g sat. fat), 89mg chol., 229mg sod., 67g carb. (19g sugars, 2g fiber), 9g pro.*

TEST KITCHEN TIP

The sweet streusel topping creates a crispy crust on the baked conchas. You can add a little food coloring to color the plain streusel for different occasions.

CHILES RELLENOS
CROQUE-MADAME, PAGE 160

Breakfast & Brunch

Discover the perfect dish for holiday company, lazy Saturday mornings and even the busiest weekday with the 26 recipes here.

DISHES WE LOVE

Chiles Rellenos Croque-Madame p. 160

The Best French Toast p. 162

Finnish Cheese Pie p. 164

Easy Cheesy Cauliflower Breakfast Casserole p. 169

MEAN GREEN SMOOTHIE BOWLS

This delicious bright green blend contains powerful antioxidants. Pour smoothies into serving bowls and top with cucumber slices and fresh parsley sprigs for a pretty presentation.
—Laura Wilhelm, West Hollywood, CA

TAKES: 20 min. • **MAKES:** 6 servings

- **2 medium green apples, chopped**
- **2 celery ribs (with leaves), chopped**
- **2 cups fresh baby spinach**
- **8 sprigs fresh parsley, stems removed, chopped**
- **1 medium cucumber, peeled and chopped**
- **1 Tbsp. minced fresh gingerroot**
- **1 cup unfiltered or filtered apple juice**
- **¼ cup fresh lemon juice**
- **2 Tbsp. raw honey**
- **Optional toppings: Sliced or chopped cucumber, sliced or chopped apples, minced fresh parsley and additional celery leaves**

Place all ingredients except toppings in a blender; cover and process until blended. Pour into chilled bowls; top as desired. Serve immediately.

1 SMOOTHIE BOWL: *79 cal., 0 fat (0 sat. fat), 0 chol., 22mg sod., 20g carb. (16g sugars, 2g fiber), 1g pro.* **Diabetic exchanges:** *1 starch, 1 vegetable.*

MEAN GREEN SMOOTHIE BOWLS

CHILES RELLENOS CROQUE-MADAME

(SHOWN ON PAGE 158)

A traditional croque-madame is a heartier version of a croque-monsieur because it's served with an egg on top of the sandwich. Instead of bechamel and Gruyere, this playful version includes pepper jack, chiles and chipotle mayo.
—Lauren Wyler, Dripping Springs, TX

TAKES: 30 min. • **MAKES:** 4 servings

- **1 can (7 oz.) whole green chiles, drained**
- **8 slices country-style white bread**
- **3 Tbsp. chipotle mayonnaise**
- **4 slices pepper jack cheese**
- **½ lb. sliced deli ham**
- **5 Tbsp. butter, softened, divided**
- **1 cup shredded sharp cheddar cheese**
- **4 large eggs**
- **⅛ tsp. salt**
- **⅛ tsp. pepper**
- **Fresh minced chives, optional**

1. Slice chiles into long strips; pat dry with paper towels and set aside. Spread 4 bread slices with chipotle mayonnaise. Layer with pepper jack cheese, ham and chiles; top with remaining 4 bread slices. Spread outside of sandwiches with 4 Tbsp. butter.
2. On a griddle, toast sandwiches over medium heat until bottom is golden brown, 2-3 minutes. Flip and sprinkle with cheddar cheese. Cover and cook until bottom is golden brown and cheese just starts to melt, 2-3 minutes longer.
3. Meanwhile, for eggs, heat remaining 1 Tbsp. butter in a large nonstick skillet over medium-high heat. Break eggs, 1 at a time, into pan. Reduce heat to low. Cook until whites are set and yolks begin to thicken, turning once if desired. Sprinkle with salt and pepper. Top sandwiches with eggs. Sprinkle with chives if desired.

1 SERVING: *709 cal., 48g fat (23g sat. fat), 308mg chol., 1529mg sod., 34g carb. (6g sugars, 2g fiber), 35g pro.*

PUMPKIN & CHICKEN SAUSAGE HASH

PUMPKIN & CHICKEN SAUSAGE HASH

This can be served as a side or as the main dish for breakfast, lunch or dinner. I like to serve it topped with poached or fried eggs for breakfast.
—Valerie Donn, Gaylord, MI

PREP: 15 min. • **COOK:** 25 min. • **MAKES:** 4 servings

- 2 **Tbsp. olive oil**
- 2 **cups cubed fresh pumpkin or butternut squash**
- ¼ **tsp. salt**
- ¼ **tsp. pepper**
- ½ **cup chopped onion**
- 1 **pkg. (12 oz.) fully cooked apple chicken sausage links or flavor of your choice, cut into ½-in. slices**
- 1 **cup sliced fresh mushrooms**
- ½ **cup chopped sweet red pepper**
- ½ **cup chopped green pepper**
- 1 **tsp. garlic powder**
- ¼ **cup minced fresh parsley**

In a large skillet, heat oil over medium heat. Add pumpkin; sprinkle with salt and pepper. Cook and stir until crisp-tender, 8-10 minutes. Add onion; cook 3 minutes longer. Add sausage, mushrooms, red and green peppers, and garlic powder. Cook and stir until pumpkin is tender, 10-12 minutes. Top with parsley before serving.

1 SERVING: *260 cal., 14g fat (3g sat. fat), 60mg chol., 634mg sod., 19g carb. (13g sugars, 2g fiber), 16g pro.* **Diabetic exchanges:** *2 lean meat, 1½ fat, 1 starch.*

BACON BREAKFAST COOKIES

I tried this recipe when I was a 4-H leader. Before morning chores, the young members would grab a glass of milk or juice and a handful of these crisp cookies, which are chock-full of bacon, cornflakes and raisins.
—Louise Gangwish, Shelton, NE

PREP: 10 min. • **BAKE:** 15 min./batch • **MAKES:** 2 dozen

- ½ **cup butter, softened**
- ¾ **cup sugar**
- 1 **large egg, room temperature**
- 1 **cup all-purpose flour**
- ¼ **tsp. baking soda**
- 10 **bacon strips, cooked and crumbled**
- 2 **cups cornflakes**
- ½ **cup raisins**

1. In a large bowl, cream butter and sugar until light and fluffy, 5-7 minutes. Beat in egg. Combine flour and baking soda; gradually add to creamed mixture. Stir in bacon, cornflakes and raisins.

2. Drop by rounded tablespoonfuls 2 in. apart onto ungreased baking sheets. Bake at 350° for 15-18 minutes or until lightly browned. Cool for 2 minutes before removing to wire racks. Store in the refrigerator.

2 BREAKFAST COOKIES: *225 cal., 11g fat (6g sat. fat), 43mg chol., 228mg sod., 29g carb. (17g sugars, 1g fiber), 4g pro.*

BACON BREAKFAST COOKIES

THE BEST FRENCH TOAST

THE BEST FRENCH TOAST

There's no question that this is the best French toast recipe ever. The caramelized exterior meets a soft custardlike center that practically melts in your mouth. Not only that, but it's quick and easy, too!
—Audrey Rompon, Milwaukee, WI

TAKES: 15 min. • **MAKES:** 4 servings

- **1½ cups half-and-half cream**
- **3 large egg yolks**
- **3 Tbsp. brown sugar**
- **2 tsp. vanilla extract**
- **¾ tsp. ground cinnamon**
- **½ tsp. salt**
- **¼ tsp. ground nutmeg**
- **8 slices day-old brioche bread (1 in. thick)**
  Optional toppings: Butter, maple syrup, fresh berries, whipped cream and confectioners' sugar

1. In a shallow dish, whisk together the first 7 ingredients. Preheat a greased griddle over medium heat.
2. Dip bread into egg mixture, letting it soak 5 seconds on each side. Cook on griddle until golden brown on both sides. Serve with toppings as desired.

2 PIECES: *546 cal., 24g fat (15g sat. fat), 263mg chol., 786mg sod., 64g carb. (25g sugars, 2g fiber), 13g pro.*

TEST KITCHEN TIP

Using day-old bread from a bakery helps the French toast hold its shape. If you're using commercially produced brioche, be sure to allow the bread to become slightly stale for best results.

OATMEAL BREAKFAST BARS

These soft and chewy treats have a hint of orange marmalade, so they're a fun change of pace from typical granola bars. They're easy to put together and so delicious, you'll find yourself making them all the time.
—Barbara Nowakowski, North Tonawanda, NY

TAKES: 25 min. • **MAKES:** 2½ dozen

- **4 cups quick-cooking oats**
- **1 cup packed brown sugar**
- **1 tsp. salt**
- **1½ cups chopped walnuts**
- **1 cup sweetened shredded coconut**
- **¾ cup butter, melted**
- **¾ cup orange marmalade**

In a large bowl, combine the oats, brown sugar and salt. Stir in remaining ingredients. Press into a greased 15x10x1-in. baking pan. Bake at 425° for 15-17 minutes or until golden brown. Cool on a wire rack. Cut into 30 bars.

1 BAR: *182 cal., 10g fat (4g sat. fat), 12mg chol., 141mg sod., 22g carb. (13g sugars, 1g fiber), 3g pro.*

OATMEAL BREAKFAST BARS

PUMPKIN FRENCH TOAST WITH BACON MAPLE SYRUP

My two great-grandsons helped me create this recipe. Each of the boys took turns prepping and offering suggestions. It's a wonderful holiday brunch dish, and it can even be made a day ahead and baked when you're ready to serve.
—Barbara Estabrook, Appleton, WI

PREP: 35 min. + chilling • **BAKE:** 40 min.
MAKES: 8 servings

- 4 **bacon strips**
- 1¼ **cups 2% milk**
- 3 **large eggs**
- ½ **cup plus 3 Tbsp. packed light brown sugar, divided**
- ½ **cup canned pumpkin**
- 2 **Tbsp. maple syrup**
- 2½ **tsp. pumpkin pie spice, divided**
- 12 **oz. challah or brioche bread, cut into ½-in. cubes**
- ¼ **cup quick-cooking oats**
- ¼ **cup chopped pecans, toasted**
- 3 **Tbsp. all-purpose flour**
- 3 **Tbsp. cold butter**

SAUCE
- 3 **Tbsp. butter**
- 3 **Tbsp. light brown sugar**
- 3 **Tbsp. maple syrup**
- 3 **Tbsp. 2% milk**
- 3 **Tbsp. canned pumpkin**

1. In a large skillet, cook bacon over medium heat until crisp. Remove to paper towels to drain; crumble bacon. Discard drippings, reserving 1 Tbsp. for sauce. In a large bowl, whisk milk, eggs, ½ cup brown sugar, pumpkin, maple syrup and 2 tsp. pie spice until blended. Place half the bread cubes in a greased 2-qt. baking dish. Top with half the crumbled bacon and half the egg mixture. Repeat layers. Refrigerate, covered, overnight.
2. Preheat oven to 350°. Remove casserole from refrigerator while the oven heats. Combine oats, pecans, flour, and the remaining 3 Tbsp. brown sugar and ½ tsp. pie spice. Cut in cold butter until mixture resembles coarse crumbs. Sprinkle over casserole. Bake, uncovered, until a knife inserted near the center comes out clean, 40-45 minutes. Let stand 5-10 minutes before serving. Meanwhile, for sauce, in a small saucepan, melt butter and reserved bacon grease over medium heat. Stir in brown sugar and maple syrup. Add milk and pumpkin; heat through. Serve with French toast.
1 SERVING: *486 cal., 23g fat (12g sat. fat), 137mg chol., 386mg sod., 62g carb. (39g sugars, 2g fiber), 10g pro.*

PEAR QUINOA BREAKFAST BAKE

PEAR QUINOA BREAKFAST BAKE

In an effort to eat more healthfully, I've been trying to incorporate extra whole grains into our diet. My husband and I enjoy quinoa, so I created this breakfast bake for our Sunday brunch. The quinoa is a nice change of pace from oatmeal.
—Sue Gronholz, Beaver Dam, WI

PREP: 15 min. • **BAKE:** 55 min. + standing
MAKES: 2 servings

- 1 **cup water**
- ¼ **cup quinoa, rinsed**
- ¼ **cup mashed peeled ripe pear**
- 1 **Tbsp. honey**
- ¼ **tsp. ground cinnamon**
- ¼ **tsp. vanilla extract**
- **Dash ground ginger**
- **Dash ground nutmeg**

TOPPING
- ¼ **cup sliced almonds**
- 1 **Tbsp. brown sugar**
- 1 **Tbsp. butter, softened**
- **Plain Greek yogurt, optional**

1. Preheat oven to 350°. In a small bowl, combine the first 8 ingredients; transfer to a greased 3-cup baking dish. Cover and bake for 50 minutes. In another small bowl, combine almonds, brown sugar, and butter; sprinkle over quinoa mixture.
2. Bake, uncovered, until lightly browned, 5-10 minutes longer. Let stand 10 minutes before serving. If desired, serve with Greek yogurt.
1 SERVING: *267 cal., 13g fat (4g sat. fat), 15mg chol., 49mg sod., 35g carb. (18g sugars, 4g fiber), 6g pro.* **Diabetic exchanges:** *2½ fat, 2 starch.*

FINNISH CHEESE PIE

Being of Finnish heritage, I am always thrilled when I find a family recipe. This salmon and dill pie came tumbling out of one of my grandmother's books. It's a winner.
—Judy Batson, Tampa, FL

PREP: 20 min. • **BAKE:** 30 min. + standing
MAKES: 6 servings

- **1 Tbsp. butter**
- **⅓ cup finely chopped green onions**
- **¾ cup flaked smoked salmon fillets**
- **¼ cup snipped fresh dill**
- **Dough for single-crust pie**
- **3 large eggs**
- **1 cup half-and-half cream**
- **¼ cup all-purpose flour**
- **½ tsp. salt**
- **½ tsp. ground nutmeg**
- **½ tsp. pepper**
- **1 cup shredded Swiss cheese**

1. Preheat oven to 400°. In a small skillet, melt butter over medium heat. Add green onions; cook and stir until crisp-tender, about 3 minutes. Remove from heat. Gently stir in salmon and dill; set aside.

2. On a lightly floured surface, roll dough to a ⅛-in.-thick circle; transfer to a 9-in. pie plate. Trim crust to ½ in. beyond rim of plate; flute edge. Spoon salmon mixture into crust. In a small bowl, whisk eggs, cream, flour and seasonings until blended; pour over top. Sprinkle with cheese.

3. Bake on a lower oven rack until a knife inserted near the center comes out clean, 35-40 minutes. Cover edge loosely with foil during the last 10 minutes if needed to prevent overbrowning. Remove foil. Let stand 10 minutes before cutting.

1 PIECE: *448 cal., 30g fat (18g sat. fat), 179mg chol., 642mg sod., 26g carb. (2g sugars, 1g fiber), 16g pro.*

DOUGH FOR SINGLE-CRUST PIE (9 IN.): Combine 1¼ cups all-purpose flour and ¼ tsp. salt; cut in ½ cup cold butter until crumbly. Gradually add 3-5 Tbsp. ice water, tossing with a fork until dough holds together when pressed. Wrap and refrigerate 1 hour.

FINNISH CHEESE PIE

CARAMELIZED MUSHROOM & ONION FRITTATA

When I was young, my grandmother used to make buttery sauteed mushrooms for me. Now I enjoy them in a hearty breakfast frittata.
—Melissa D'Antonio, Poughkeepsie, NY

PREP: 15 min. • **COOK:** 45 min.
MAKES: 4 servings

- **1 lb. sliced fresh mushrooms**
- **1 medium red onion, chopped**
- **3 Tbsp. butter**
- **3 Tbsp. olive oil**
- **1 shallot, chopped**
- **1 garlic clove, minced**
- **½ cup shredded cheddar cheese**
- **¼ cup shredded Parmesan cheese**
- **8 large eggs**
- **3 Tbsp. heavy whipping cream**
- **¼ tsp. salt**
- **¼ tsp. pepper**

1. In a 10-in. ovenproof skillet, saute mushrooms and onion in butter and oil until softened. Reduce heat to medium-low; cook for 30 minutes or until deep golden brown, stirring occasionally. Add shallot and garlic; cook 1 minute longer.

2. Reduce heat; sprinkle with cheeses. In a large bowl, whisk the eggs, cream, salt and pepper; pour over top. Cover and cook for 4-6 minutes or until eggs are nearly set.

3. Uncover skillet. Broil 3-4 in. from the heat for 2-3 minutes or until eggs are completely set. Let stand for 5 minutes. Cut into 4 wedges.

1 WEDGE: *465 cal., 38g fat (16g sat. fat), 479mg chol., 529mg sod., 11g carb. (4g sugars, 2g fiber), 22g pro.*

READER REVIEW

"This was my first time making frittata, and this recipe was so easy. You can make everything at your convenience and clean as you go. The mushroom and onion flavors went wonderfully with the egg. I don't think I will ever make another omelet again!"

—BMHUNTER, TASTEOFHOME.COM

HIGH-OCTANE PANCAKES

HIGH-OCTANE PANCAKES

Fluffy and health-packed, these hotcakes are what we rely on to jump-start frosty winter mornings in Colorado. They keep us satisfied all morning long and are scrumptious!
—Kelly Hanlon, Strasburg, CO

TAKES: 20 min. • **MAKES:** 4 pancakes

- ⅓ **cup plus 1 Tbsp. all-purpose flour**
- ¼ **cup quick-cooking oats**
- 3 **Tbsp. toasted wheat germ**
- 2 **tsp. sugar**
- 1¼ **tsp. baking powder**
- ⅛ **tsp. salt**
- ⅔ **cup fat-free milk**
- ¼ **cup fat-free plain yogurt**
- 1 **Tbsp. canola oil**

1. In a small bowl, mix the first 6 ingredients. In another bowl, whisk milk, yogurt and oil until blended. Add to flour mixture; stir just until moistened.
2. Lightly coat a nonstick griddle with cooking spray; heat over medium heat. Pour batter by ⅓ cupfuls onto griddle. Cook until bubbles form on top of pancake; cook until the second side is golden brown.
FREEZE OPTION: Freeze cooled pancakes between layers of waxed paper in a freezer container. To use, place a stack of 2 pancakes on a microwave-safe plate, and microwave on high until heated through, about 1 minute.
2 PANCAKES: *281 cal., 9g fat (1g sat. fat), 2mg chol., 450mg sod., 41g carb. (10g sugars, 3g fiber), 11g pro.* **Diabetic exchanges:** *3 starch, 1½ fat.*

FREEZER BREAKFAST SANDWICHES

On busy mornings, these freezer breakfast sandwiches save the day. A hearty combo of eggs, Canadian bacon and cheese will keep you fueled until lunchtime.
—Christine Rukavena, Milwaukee, WI

PREP: 25 min. • **COOK:** 15 min. • **MAKES:** 12 sandwiches

- 12 **large eggs**
- ⅔ **cup 2% milk**
- ½ **tsp. salt**
- ¼ **tsp. pepper**

SANDWICHES

- 12 **English muffins, split**
- 4 **Tbsp. butter, softened**
- 12 **slices Colby-Monterey Jack cheese**
- 12 **slices Canadian bacon**

1. Preheat oven to 325°. In a large bowl, whisk eggs, milk, salt and pepper until blended. Pour into a 13x9-in. baking pan coated with cooking spray. Bake until set, 15-18 minutes. Cool on a wire rack.
2. Meanwhile, toast English muffins (or bake them at 325° until lightly browned, 12-15 minutes). Spread 1 tsp. butter on each muffin bottom.
3. Cut eggs into 12 portions. Layer muffin bottoms with an egg portion, a cheese slice (tearing cheese to fit) and Canadian bacon. Replace muffin tops. Wrap sandwiches in waxed paper and then in foil; freeze in a freezer container.
To use frozen sandwiches: Remove foil. Microwave a waxed paper-wrapped sandwich at 50% power until thawed, 1-2 minutes. Turn sandwich over; microwave at 100% power until hot and a thermometer reads at least 160°, 30-60 seconds. Let stand 2 minutes before serving.
1 SANDWICH: *334 cal., 17g fat (9g sat. fat), 219mg chol., 759mg sod., 26g carb. (3g sugars, 2g fiber), 19g pro.*

FREEZER BREAKFAST SANDWICHES

BREAKFAST BLT WAFFLES

PEACHY DANISH PANCAKE BALLS (AEBLESKIVER)

Years ago, a friend returned from visiting her family in Denmark and brought back her family recipe for aebleskiver. After hearing her rave about the tasty round treats sold in bakeries and in street markets there, I ordered an aebleskiver pan and have been making these tender filled pancake balls ever since.
—Kristine Chayes, Smithtown, NY

PREP: 20 min. • **COOK:** 5 min./batch
MAKES: about 3 dozen

- 3 **large eggs, separated, room temperature**
- 2 **cups buttermilk**
- 2 **cups all-purpose flour**
- 1 **tsp. baking soda**
- 1 **tsp. salt**
- ½ **tsp. ground cinnamon**
- 2 **medium peaches, peeled and chopped**
- **Confectioners' sugar**

In a large bowl, whisk egg yolks and buttermilk until blended. In another bowl, whisk flour, baking soda, salt and cinnamon. Stir into egg mixture just until moistened. In a small bowl, beat egg whites on high speed until stiff but not dry. With a rubber spatula, gently stir a fourth of the egg whites into batter. Fold in remaining egg whites. Place a greased aebleskiver pan over medium heat. In batches, pour 1 Tbsp. batter into each cup. Top with a peach piece and another 1 Tbsp. batter. Cook until bubbles on top begin to pop and bottoms are golden brown. Turn; cook until second side is golden brown. Serve warm with confectioners' sugar.

FREEZE OPTION: Freeze cooled pancakes between layers of waxed paper in a freezer container. To use, place pancakes on an ungreased baking sheet, cover with foil and reheat in a preheated 375° oven until heated through, 5-10 minutes. Or, place on a microwave-safe plate and microwave on high until heated through, 45-90 seconds.

4 PIECES: *160 cal., 2g fat (1g sat. fat), 64mg chol., 530mg sod., 27g carb. (5g sugars, 1g fiber), 7g pro.* **Diabetic exchanges:** *2 starch.*

BREAKFAST BLT WAFFLES

I'm not a big fan of sweets for breakfast, but I love a crisp waffle. My son and I tried these BLT waffles, and they were a huge success! We used gluten-free, dairy-free waffles with fantastic results.
—Courtney Stultz, Weir, KS

PREP: 10 min. • **COOK:** 25 min.
MAKES: 4 servings

- 8 **bacon strips**
- 4 **cups chopped fresh kale**
- 4 **large eggs**
- 4 **frozen waffles**
- 1 **large tomato, sliced**
- ½ **cup shredded cheddar cheese**
- **Optional: Chipotle mayonnaise and minced fresh parsley**

1. In a large nonstick skillet, cook bacon over medium heat until crisp. Remove to paper towels to drain. Discard drippings, reserving 2 Tbsp. Cook and stir kale in 1 Tbsp. drippings in same pan over medium heat until tender, 6-8 minutes. Remove and keep warm. Add remaining 1 Tbsp. drippings to pan. Break eggs, 1 at a time, into pan; reduce heat to low. Cook until whites are set and yolks begin to thicken, turning once if desired.

2. Meanwhile, prepare waffles according to package directions. Top each waffle with kale, tomato slices, 1 egg, cheese and bacon strips. If desired, serve with chipotle mayonnaise and parsley.

1 SERVING: *382 cal., 26g fat (9g sat. fat), 228mg chol., 695mg sod., 19g carb. (3g sugars, 2g fiber), 18g pro.*

PEACHY DANISH PANCAKE BALLS (AEBLESKIVER)

MUFFIN-TIN SCRAMBLED EGGS

I made these one year at Christmas as a way to save time, and they were a big hit. I have to make a large batch because my husband and boys can polish them off in a short amount of time. These also freeze very well—if there are any left!
—Jill Darin, Geneseo, IL

PREP: 15 min. • **BAKE:** 20 min. • **MAKES:** 2 dozen

- **24 large eggs**
- **1 tsp. salt**
- **½ tsp. pepper**
- **¼ tsp. garlic powder**
- **1 jar (4 oz.) sliced mushrooms, finely chopped**
- **1 can (4 oz.) chopped green chiles**
- **3 oz. sliced deli ham, finely chopped**
- **½ medium onion, finely chopped**
- **½ cup shredded cheddar cheese**
- **Pico de gallo, optional**

1. Preheat oven to 350°. In a large bowl, whisk eggs, salt, pepper and garlic powder until blended. Stir in mushrooms, chiles, ham, onion and cheese. Spoon about ¼ cup mixture into each of 24 greased muffin cups.
2. Bake 18-20 minutes or until eggs are set, rotating pans halfway. Let stand 10 minutes before removing from pans. If desired, serve with pico de gallo.
FREEZE OPTION: Freeze cooled, baked eggs in airtight containers. To use, microwave each serving on high for 1¼-1½ minutes or until heated through.
1 EGG CUP: *88 cal., 6g fat (2g sat. fat), 190mg chol., 257mg sod., 1g carb. (0 sugars, 0 fiber), 8g pro.* **Diabetic exchanges:** *1 medium-fat meat.*

MUFFIN-TIN SCRAMBLED EGGS

CRISPY FRENCH TOAST

CRISPY FRENCH TOAST

Cornflakes add irresistible crunch to this easy baked French toast recipe. My light version uses egg substitute and skim milk but still gets plenty of flavor from vanilla, spice and a kiss of orange.
—Flo Burtnett, Gage, OK

PREP: 20 min. • **BAKE:** 15 min. • **MAKES:** 6 servings

- **½ cup egg substitute**
- **½ cup fat-free milk**
- **¼ cup orange juice**
- **1 tsp. vanilla extract**
- **Dash ground nutmeg**
- **12 slices day-old French bread (¾ in. thick)**
- **1½ cups crushed cornflakes**

1. In a shallow dish, combine the egg substitute, milk, orange juice, vanilla and nutmeg. Add bread; soak for 5 minutes, turning once. Coat both sides of each slice with cornflake crumbs.
2. Place in a 15x10x1-in. baking pan coated with cooking spray. Bake at 425° for 10 minutes; turn. Bake 5-8 minutes longer or until golden brown.
FREEZE OPTION: Remove baked French toast from pan to wire racks to cool. Freeze between layers of waxed paper in an airtight freezer container. To use, place frozen French toast on a greased baking sheet. Bake in a preheated 425° oven for 5-7 minutes or until heated through. Or, microwave each French toast on high for 30-60 seconds or until heated through.
2 SLICES: *200 cal., 1g fat (0 sat. fat), 0 chol., 421mg sod., 40g carb. (4g sugars, 1g fiber), 7g pro.* **Diabetic exchanges:** *3 starch.*

EASY CHEESY CAULIFLOWER BREAKFAST CASSEROLE

I love finding new ways to add veggies to my meals. This twist on a breakfast favorite swaps in riced cauliflower for the usual hash browns to make it not only keto-friendly but also a real crowd-pleasing addition to the brunch rotation.
—Robyn Warren, Lead Hill, AR

PREP: 30 min. • **BAKE:** 40 min. + standing
MAKES: 12 servings

- 1 **lb. bacon strips, chopped**
- 1 **cup chopped sweet onion**
- ½ **large sweet red pepper, chopped**
- ½ **large green pepper, chopped**
- 9 **large eggs, lightly beaten**
- 1½ **cups whole-milk ricotta cheese**
- 4 **cups frozen riced cauliflower, thawed**
- 2 **cups shredded cheddar cheese**
- 1 **cup shredded Swiss cheese**
- ½ **tsp. pepper**
- ¼ **tsp. salt**

1. Preheat oven to 350°. In a large skillet, cook bacon over medium heat until crisp, stirring occasionally. Remove with a slotted spoon; drain on paper towels. Discard drippings, reserving 1 Tbsp. in pan.
2. Add onion and chopped peppers to drippings; cook and stir over medium-high heat until tender, 6-8 minutes. In a large bowl, whisk eggs and ricotta. Stir in riced cauliflower, shredded cheeses, bacon, onion mixture, pepper and salt. Pour into a greased 13x9-in. baking dish. Bake, uncovered, until a knife inserted near the center comes out clean, 40-45 minutes. Let stand 10 minutes before serving.
FREEZE OPTION: Cool baked casserole completely; cover tightly and freeze. To use, partially thaw in refrigerator overnight. Remove from refrigerator 30 minutes before baking. Preheat oven to 350°. Bake casserole as directed, increasing time as necessary to heat through and for a thermometer inserted in center to read 165°.
1 PIECE: *307 cal., 22g fat (11g sat. fat), 194mg chol., 534mg sod., 7g carb. (4g sugars, 2g fiber), 21g pro.*

SALMON CROQUETTE BREAKFAST SANDWICH

I'm obsessed with smoked salmon on bagels with all the accouterments! I could seriously eat it every day for breakfast! But smoked salmon can get pricey, so I found a cheaper alternative without losing the flavor.
—Jessi Hampton, Richmond Hill, GA

PREP: 25 min. • **COOK:** 10 min.
MAKES: 2 servings

- 1 **large egg, lightly beaten**
- ¼ **cup dry bread crumbs**
- 1 **tsp. garlic powder**
- 1 **tsp. smoked paprika**
- 1 **pouch (6 oz.) boneless skinless pink salmon**
- 1 **Tbsp. olive oil**
- 2 **everything bagels, split and toasted**
- 4 **Tbsp. cream cheese, softened**
- 1 **Tbsp. capers, drained**
- 1 **medium tomato, sliced**
- ½ **medium red onion, thinly sliced into rings**
- **Snipped fresh dill, optional**

1. In a small bowl, combine egg, bread crumbs, garlic powder and smoked paprika. Add salmon and mix lightly but thoroughly. Shape into 2 patties.
2. In a large skillet, cook patties in oil over medium heat until browned, 5-6 minutes on each side. Spread cut sides of bagels with cream cheese; sprinkle with capers. Serve patties on bagels with tomato, red onion and, if desired, dill.
1 SANDWICH: *656 cal., 25g fat (10g sat. fat), 152mg chol., 1205mg sod., 75g carb. (14g sugars, 4g fiber), 34g pro.*

SALMON CROQUETTE BREAKFAST SANDWICH

MAPLE BACON WALNUT COFFEE CAKE

THE BEST QUICHE LORRAINE

Nestled in a buttery, rustic crust, this quiche is filled with sweet onions, bacon bits and cheese. It's the perfect addition to brunch.
—Shannon Norris, Cudahy, WI

PREP: 1 hour • **BAKE:** 1¼ hours + cooling
MAKES: 8 servings

- **Dough for single-crust deep-dish pie**
- 1 **pkg. (12 oz.) thick-sliced bacon strips, coarsely chopped**
- 3 **large sweet onions, chopped**
- 1 **Tbsp. minced fresh thyme**
- ½ **tsp. coarsely ground pepper**
- ⅛ **tsp. ground nutmeg**
- 1½ **cups shredded Gruyere cheese**
- ½ **cup grated Parmesan cheese**
- 8 **large eggs, room temperature**
- 2 **cups whole milk**
- 1 **cup heavy whipping cream**

1. On a lightly floured surface, roll dough to a 14-in. circle. Transfer to a 9-in. springform pan; press firmly against bottom and sides. Refrigerate while preparing filling.
2. In a large skillet, cook bacon over medium heat until crisp, stirring occasionally. Remove with a slotted spoon; drain on paper towels. Discard drippings, reserving 1 Tbsp. in pan. Add onions to drippings; cook and stir over medium heat until caramelized, 20-25 minutes. Stir in thyme, pepper and nutmeg; remove from the heat. Cool slightly. Stir in cheeses and reserved bacon; spoon into crust. Preheat oven to 350°. In a large bowl, whisk eggs, milk, and cream until blended; pour over top. Place springform pan on a rimmed baking sheet.
3. Bake on a lower oven rack until a knife inserted near the center comes out clean, 75-85 minutes. Cool on a wire rack for 15 minutes. Loosen sides from pan with a knife. Remove rim from pan.
DOUGH FOR SINGLE-CRUST DEEP-DISH PIE: Combine 1½ cups all-purpose flour and ¼ tsp. salt; cut in ⅔ cup cold butter until crumbly. Gradually add 3-6 Tbsp. ice water, tossing with a fork until dough holds together when pressed. Shape into a disk; wrap and refrigerate 1 hour.
1 PIECE: *671 cal., 49g fat (27g sat. fat), 308mg chol., 841mg sod., 33g carb. (10g sugars, 2g fiber), 25g pro.*

MAPLE BACON WALNUT COFFEE CAKE

The sleepyheads will roll out of bed when they smell this sweet and savory coffee cake baking. Nuts and bacon in the crumbly topping blend with maple, nutmeg and cinnamon.
—Angela Spengler, Niceville, FL

PREP: 25 min. • **BAKE:** 35 min. + cooling
MAKES: 24 servings

- 2½ **cups all-purpose flour**
- 1 **cup packed brown sugar**
- ½ **tsp. salt**
- ⅓ **cup cold butter**
- 2 **tsp. baking powder**
- ½ **tsp. baking soda**
- ½ **tsp. ground cinnamon**
- ¼ **tsp. ground nutmeg**
- 2 **large eggs, room temperature**
- 1½ **cups buttermilk**
- ½ **cup maple syrup**
- ⅓ **cup unsweetened applesauce**
- 5 **bacon strips, cooked and crumbled**
- ½ **cup chopped walnuts**

1. In a large bowl, combine the flour, brown sugar and salt. Cut in butter until crumbly. Set aside ½ cup for topping. Combine the baking powder, baking soda, cinnamon and nutmeg; stir into remaining flour mixture.
2. In a small bowl, whisk the eggs, buttermilk, syrup and applesauce until well blended. Gradually stir into flour mixture until combined.
3. Spread into a 13x9-in. baking pan coated with cooking spray. Sprinkle with reserved topping, then bacon and walnuts. Bake at 350° until a toothpick inserted in the center comes out clean, 35-40 minutes. Cool on a wire rack.
1 PIECE: *160 cal., 5g fat (2g sat. fat), 27mg chol., 183mg sod., 25g carb. (14g sugars, 1g fiber), 3g pro.* **Diabetic exchanges:** *1½ starch, 1 fat.*

STRAWBERRY OVERNIGHT OATS

With gluten-free oats, this is an easy gluten-free and dairy-free breakfast that is ready and waiting for you in the morning. Use more or less sugar depending on the sweetness of your strawberries.
—Jolene Martinelli, Fremont, NH

PREP: 1¼ hours + chilling • **MAKES:** 1 serving

- **1 cup sliced fresh strawberries**
- **½ tsp. sugar**
- **¾ cup old-fashioned oats**
- **3 Tbsp. powdered peanut butter**
- **1½ tsp. chia seeds**
- **1 cup unsweetened almond milk**

In a small bowl, combine strawberries and sugar. Let stand 1 hour; mash if desired. In a pint jar, layer ¼ cup oats, 1 Tbsp. powdered peanut butter, ½ tsp. chia seeds and ⅓ cup strawberry mixture. Repeat layers twice. Pour the almond milk over top; seal and refrigerate overnight.

1 SERVING: *352 cal., 10g fat (1g sat. fat), 0 chol., 183mg sod., 60g carb. (12g sugars, 12g fiber), 10g pro.*

STRAWBERRY OVERNIGHT OATS

SAUSAGE & PANCAKE BAKE

SAUSAGE & PANCAKE BAKE

Trial and error made this recipe one that my family asks for time and time again. It's so easy and very good.
—Ethel Sanders, Oklahoma City, OK

PREP: 15 min. • **BAKE:** 30 min. • **MAKES:** 8 servings

- **1 lb. bulk pork sausage**
- **2 cups biscuit/baking mix**
- **1⅓ cups 2% milk**
- **2 large eggs**
- **¼ cup canola oil**
- **2 medium apples, peeled and thinly sliced**
- **2 Tbsp. cinnamon sugar**
- **Maple syrup**

Preheat oven to 350°. In a large skillet over medium heat, cook and crumble sausage until no longer pink, 5-7 minutes; drain. Mix biscuit mix, milk, eggs and oil until blended; stir in sausage. Transfer biscuit mixture to a greased 13x9-in. baking dish. Top with apples; sprinkle with cinnamon sugar. Bake until set, 30-45 minutes. Serve with syrup.

TO MAKE AHEAD: Refrigerate, covered, several hours or overnight. To use, preheat oven to 350°. Remove casserole from refrigerator; uncover and let stand while the oven heats. Bake as directed, increasing time as necessary until a knife inserted in the center comes out clean.

1 PIECE: *379 cal., 24g fat (6g sat. fat), 80mg chol., 692mg sod., 30g carb. (9g sugars, 1g fiber), 11g pro.*

TEX-MEX GRAIN BOWL

WARM GRAPEFRUIT WITH GINGER-SUGAR

Sweetly broiled grapefruit is a specialty at my bed-and-breakfast. In addition to serving it at breakfast or brunch, you can try it as a light snack or dessert.
—Stephanie Levy, Lansing, NY

TAKES: 15 min. • **MAKES:** 2 servings

- **1 large red grapefruit**
- **2 to 3 tsp. chopped crystallized ginger**
- **2 tsp. sugar**

1. Preheat broiler. Cut grapefruit crosswise in half. With a small knife, cut around the membrane in the center of each half and discard. Cut around each section to loosen fruit. Place on a baking sheet, cut side up.

2. Mix ginger and sugar; sprinkle over fruit. Broil 4 in. from heat until sugar is melted, about 4 minutes.

½ GRAPEFRUIT: *85 cal., 0 fat (0 sat. fat), 0 chol., 3mg sod., 22g carb. (17g sugars, 2g fiber), 1g pro.* **Diabetic exchanges:** *1 fruit, ½ starch.*

WARM GRAPEFRUIT WITH GINGER-SUGAR

TEX-MEX GRAIN BOWL

This recipe is special because it is not only healthy but also delicious. Oatmeal is one of those dishes often eaten sweetened. People rarely think about using it in a savory dish—and they really should!
—Athena Russell, Greenville, SC

TAKES: 20 min. • **MAKES:** 4 servings

- **4 cups water**
- **2 Tbsp. reduced-sodium taco seasoning**
- **2 cups old-fashioned oats or multigrain hot cereal**
- **1 cup black beans, rinsed, drained and warmed**
- **1 cup salsa**
- **½ cup finely shredded cheddar cheese**
- **1 medium ripe avocado, peeled and cubed**
- **Optional: Pitted ripe olives, sour cream and chopped cilantro**

In a large saucepan, bring water and taco seasoning to a boil. Stir in oats; cook 5 minutes over medium heat, stirring occasionally. Remove from heat. Divide oatmeal among 4 bowls. Top with beans, salsa, cheese, avocado and toppings as desired. Serve immediately.

1 SERVING: *345 cal., 13g fat (4g sat. fat), 14mg chol., 702mg sod., 46g carb. (5g sugars, 9g fiber), 12g pro.*

VEGAN LEMON POPPY SEED DOUGHNUTS

These doughnuts are anything but boring! They are super fluffy, soft and moist—a delicious sweet treat that comes loaded with lemony flavor enhanced by a slight nuttiness from the poppy seeds. Their popping vibrant yellow color makes them especially awesome for springtime brunches.
—Shanika Graham-White, Brooklyn, NY

PREP: 25 min. • **BAKE:** 10 min. + cooling
MAKES: 1 dozen

- **2 cups organic all-purpose flour**
- **½ cup organic sugar**
- **2 tsp. baking powder**
- **½ tsp. baking soda**
- **2 Tbsp. poppy seeds**
- **1 Tbsp. grated lemon zest**
- **¼ tsp. sea salt**
- **1⅓ cups unsweetened almond milk**
- **3 Tbsp. coconut oil, melted**
- **2 Tbsp. lemon juice**
- **1 tsp. vanilla extract**

LEMON GLAZE
- **1 cup organic confectioners' sugar plus more as needed**
- **1 to 2 Tbsp. unsweetened almond milk**
- **1 tsp. lemon juice**
- **1 tsp. grated lemon zest**
- **½ tsp. vanilla extract**
- **2 tsp. vegan-approved yellow gel food coloring**

1. Preheat oven to 400°. Lightly grease doughnut baking pans with coconut oil; set aside.
2. In a medium bowl, whisk together flour, sugar, baking powder, baking soda, poppy seeds, zest and salt. In a separate bowl, stir together almond milk, coconut oil, lemon juice and vanilla; add to dry mixture, mixing until combined. Transfer batter to a pastry bag; pipe batter into prepared pans.
3. Bake until light golden brown and a toothpick comes out clean, 10-12 minutes. Cool in pans 5 minutes before removing to wire racks to cool completely.
4. For glaze, whisk confectioners' sugar, almond milk, lemon juice, zest and vanilla until smooth; whisk in food coloring. Dip tops of doughnuts into glaze; let stand until set.

1 DOUGHNUT: *192 cal., 5g fat (3g sat. fat), 0 chol., 195mg sod., 35g carb. (18g sugars, 1g fiber), 3g pro.*

CHOCOLATE-HAZELNUT ESPRESSO CINNAMON ROLLS

CHOCOLATE-HAZELNUT ESPRESSO CINNAMON ROLLS

These jumbo cinnamon rolls will stand alone at your next brunch. Bursting with chocolate, hazelnut, espresso and cinnamon, they'll please any palate and bring to mind your favorite coffee shop bakery.
—Pam Ivbuls, Elkhorn, NE

PREP: 45 min. + chilling • **BAKE:** 25 min.
MAKES: 8 servings

- **2 pkg. (¼ oz. each) active dry yeast**
- **½ cup warm water (110° to 115°)**
- **½ cup half-and-half cream (110° to 115°)**
- **½ cup 2% milk (110° to 115°)**
- **2 Tbsp. sugar**
- **2 Tbsp. butter, softened**
- **2 Tbsp. Nutella**
- **1 Tbsp. hazelnut flavoring syrup**
- **1 tsp. salt**
- **1 tsp. instant espresso powder**
- **3¾ to 4¼ cups bread flour**

FILLING
- **1 cup Nutella**
- **¼ cup butter, melted**
- **1 Tbsp. all-purpose flour**
- **1 Tbsp. ground cinnamon**
- **1 tsp. hazelnut flavoring syrup**
- **½ tsp. instant espresso powder**

GLAZE
- **½ cup confectioners' sugar**
- **2 tsp. butter, softened**
- **2 tsp. buttermilk**
- **2 tsp. hazelnut flavoring syrup**
- **Chopped hazelnuts, optional**

1. In a large bowl, dissolve yeast in warm water. Add cream, milk, sugar, butter, Nutella, hazelnut syrup, salt, espresso powder and 2 cups flour; beat on medium speed until smooth. Stir in enough remaining flour to form a soft dough (dough will be sticky).
2. Turn dough onto a floured surface; knead until smooth and elastic, 6-8 minutes. Place in a greased bowl, turning once to grease the top. Cover and let rise in a warm place until doubled, about 45 minutes.
3. Punch dough down. Turn onto a lightly floured surface. Roll into a 20x16-in. rectangle. Combine filling ingredients until smooth. Spread over dough to within ½ in. of edges. Roll up jelly-roll style, starting with a short side; pinch seam to seal. Cut into 8 slices. Place in a greased or parchment-lined 13x9-in. baking pan. Cover and refrigerate overnight.
4. Remove from refrigerator; cover and let rise in a warm place until almost doubled, about 45 minutes.
5. Preheat oven to 350°. Bake until golden brown, 25-30 minutes. Meanwhile, combine confectioners' sugar, butter, buttermilk and hazelnut syrup until smooth. Drizzle over warm rolls. Sprinkle with hazelnuts if desired. Serve warm.

1 ROLL: *616 cal., 25g fat (9g sat. fat), 35mg chol., 407mg sod., 89g carb. (37g sugars, 4g fiber), 12g pro.*

CRANBERRY NUTELLA SANDWICH COOKIES
PAGE 183

Cookies, Bars & Candies

Who doesn't have a soft spot for crumbly cookies, gooey bars and snackable candies? Turn here for the treats we love to share.

BEST OF THE BEST

Candy Bar Fudge p. 176

Butter Brickle Biscotti p. 176

Gumdrop Cookies p. 182

Cranberry Pecan Cookies p. 185

Caramel Heavenlies p. 186

CANDY BAR FUDGE

BUTTER BRICKLE BISCOTTI

These twice-baked toffee cookies are a must with coffee at Christmastime. They also make great gifts from the kitchen.
—Darlene Brenden, Salem, OR

PREP: 20 min. + chilling
BAKE: 50 min. + cooling
MAKES: about 2½ dozen

- **½ cup butter, softened**
- **½ cup sugar**
- **¼ cup packed brown sugar**
- **3 large eggs, room temperature**
- **2 tsp. vanilla extract**
- **3 cups all-purpose flour**
- **2 tsp. baking powder**
- **¼ tsp. salt**
- **1 pkg. (8 oz.) milk chocolate English toffee bits**

1. Preheat oven to 350°. In a large bowl, cream butter and sugars until light and fluffy, 5-7 minutes. Add eggs, 1 at a time, beating well after each addition. Beat in vanilla. Combine the flour, baking powder and salt; gradually add to creamed mixture and mix well. Stir in toffee bits.
2. Divide dough in half. On a parchment-lined baking sheet, shape each portion of dough into a 10x2½-in. rectangle. Cover and refrigerate for 30 minutes.
3. Bake until golden brown, 30-35 minutes. Cool for 10 minutes. Transfer to a cutting board; cut diagonally with a serrated knife into ½-in. slices.
4. Place slices cut side down on ungreased baking sheets. Bake until golden brown, 20-24 minutes, turning once. Remove to wire racks to cool. Store biscotti in an airtight container.

1 COOKIE: *141 cal., 6g fat (3g sat. fat), 29mg chol., 109mg sod., 19g carb. (10g sugars, 0 fiber), 2g pro.*

READER REVIEW

"These are always a winner. Everyone loves them. They are my go-to baking gift."
—CWINDLAB, TASTEOFHOME.COM

CANDY BAR FUDGE

My manager at work, who knows I like to try new treat recipes, shared this one with me. I've made this chewy and chocolaty fudge many times since. Packed with nuts and caramel, it's like a candy bar. Everyone who's tried it loves it.
—Lois Freeman, Oxford, MI

PREP: 20 min. + chilling • **MAKES:** 2¾ lbs.

- **½ cup butter**
- **⅓ cup baking cocoa**
- **¼ cup packed brown sugar**
- **¼ cup whole milk**
- **3½ cups confectioners' sugar**
- **1 tsp. vanilla extract**
- **30 caramels, unwrapped**
- **1 Tbsp. water**
- **2 cups salted peanuts**
- **½ cup semisweet chocolate chips**
- **½ cup milk chocolate chips**

1. In a microwave-safe bowl, combine the butter, cocoa, brown sugar and milk. Microwave on high until mixture boils, about 2 minutes. Stir in confectioners' sugar and vanilla. Pour into a greased 8-in. square dish.
2. In another microwave-safe bowl, heat caramels and water on high until melted, about 75 seconds. Stir in peanuts; spread over chocolate layer. Microwave semisweet chocolate chips on high until melted, about 30 seconds; spread over caramel layer. Chill until firm. Cut into 1-in. squares.

1 PIECE: *101 cal., 5g fat (2g sat. fat), 5mg chol., 48mg sod., 14g carb. (12g sugars, 1g fiber), 2g pro.*

5i

ROLLED BUTTER ALMOND COOKIES

These delicate cookies look like they could come from a bakery. You can leave them plain or drizzle melted chocolate over the ends.
—Jane Haskell, Huron, SD

PREP: 10 min. • **BAKE:** 5 min./batch + cooling • **MAKES:** 4 dozen

- **6 Tbsp. butter, cubed**
- **2 Tbsp. heavy whipping cream**
- **½ cup sugar**
- **½ cup ground almonds, walnuts or pecans**
- **2 Tbsp. all-purpose flour**

1. Preheat oven to 350°. In a small saucepan, melt butter with cream. Combine sugar, almonds and flour; stir into butter mixture until smooth. Cook and stir over low heat for 1 minute; remove from heat.
2. Working in batches of 4, drop batter by teaspoonfuls 4 in. apart onto a parchment-lined baking sheet. Bake until light golden brown, 5-6 minutes. Cool on pan 1 minute before quickly rolling into a cylinder, using handle of wooden spoon. Remove to wire racks to cool completely.
1 COOKIE: *30 cal., 2g fat (1g sat. fat), 5mg chol., 12mg sod., 3g carb. (2g sugars, 0 fiber), 0 pro.*

ROLLED BUTTER ALMOND COOKIES

CHOCOLATE ZUCCHINI COOKIES

CHOCOLATE ZUCCHINI COOKIES

This recipe started out as a plain zucchini cookie. But over the years, I added nuts and chocolate chips. These soft cookies never make it to the cookie jar!
—Tina Lunt, Bass Harbor, ME

PREP: 15 min. • **BAKE:** 10 min./batch • **MAKES:** 8 dozen

- **2 cups finely shredded zucchini**
- **1 cup butter, softened**
- **2 cups sugar**
- **2 large eggs, room temperature**
- **4 cups all-purpose flour**
- **2 tsp. baking soda**
- **2 tsp. ground cinnamon**
- **1 tsp. salt**
- **1 tsp. ground nutmeg**
- **1 tsp. ground cloves**
- **1 cup chopped nuts**
- **½ cup semisweet chocolate chips**

1. Place shredded zucchini on a clean towel; roll up and squeeze to remove excess liquid. Set aside. In a large bowl, cream butter and sugar until light and fluffy, 5-7 minutes. Add the eggs, 1 at a time, beating well after each addition. Combine the flour, baking soda, cinnamon, salt, nutmeg and cloves; gradually add to the creamed mixture and mix well. Stir in the zucchini, nuts and chocolate chips.
2. Drop by tablespoonfuls 3 in. apart onto ungreased baking sheets. Bake at 375° until lightly browned, 10-12 minutes. Remove to wire racks to cool.
1 COOKIE: *67 cal., 3g fat (1g sat. fat), 9mg chol., 68mg sod., 9g carb. (5g sugars, 0 fiber), 1g pro.*

SPICY OATMEAL COOKIE MIX

SPICY OATMEAL COOKIE MIX

Brown sugar and spice and everything nice—cinnamon, coconut, oats and chips—are all layered together in pretty jars of yummy, ready-to-bake cookie mix. This quick and easy gift idea is appreciated any time of year. Remember to include preparation instructions and a list of the additional ingredients needed with your gift tag.
—Taste of Home *Test Kitchen*

PREP: 15 min. • **BAKE:** 10 min./batch • **MAKES:** about 3½ dozen

- **1 cup all-purpose flour**
- **1 tsp. ground cinnamon**
- **¾ tsp. baking soda**
- **¼ tsp. salt**
- **⅛ tsp. ground nutmeg**
- **½ cup packed brown sugar**
- **½ cup sugar**
- **1 cup old-fashioned oats**
- **½ cup milk chocolate chips**
- **½ cup butterscotch chips**
- **½ cup sweetened shredded coconut**

ADDITIONAL INGREDIENTS

- **½ cup butter, softened**
- **1 large egg, room temperature**
- **¾ tsp. vanilla extract**

In a small bowl, combine the first 5 ingredients. In a 1-qt. glass jar, layer flour mixture, brown sugar, sugar, oats, chips and coconut, packing well between each layer. Cover and store in a cool, dry place up to 6 months. **Makes:** 1 batch (4 cups).

TO PREPARE COOKIES: Preheat oven to 350°. In a large bowl, beat butter, egg and vanilla. Add cookie mix and mix well. Drop by rounded teaspoonfuls 2 in. apart onto ungreased baking sheets. Bake until golden brown, 9-11 minutes. Cool 2 minutes before removing to wire racks.

1 COOKIE: *90 cal., 4g fat (3g sat. fat), 11mg chol., 63mg sod., 12g carb. (8g sugars, 0 fiber), 1g pro.*

CLASSIC LEMON BARS

These bars are simple enough for no-fuss dinners yet elegant enough for special celebrations. Regardless of when you serve them, I'm sure they'll be a hit at your home.
—Melissa Mosness, Loveland, CO

PREP: 15 min. • **BAKE:** 25 min. + cooling • **MAKES:** 9 servings

- **½ cup butter, softened**
- **¼ cup sugar**
- **1 cup all-purpose flour**

FILLING

- **¾ cup sugar**
- **2 large eggs, room temperature**
- **3 Tbsp. lemon juice**
- **2 Tbsp. all-purpose flour**
- **1 tsp. grated lemon zest**
- **¼ tsp. baking powder**
- **Confectioners' sugar**

1. In a small bowl, cream butter and sugar until light and fluffy, 5-7 minutes; gradually beat in flour until blended.

2. Press into an ungreased 8-in. square baking dish. Bake at 350° for 15-20 minutes or until edges are lightly browned.

3. For filling, in a small bowl, beat the sugar, eggs, lemon juice, flour, lemon zest and baking powder until frothy. Pour over crust.

4. Bake 10-15 minutes longer or until set and lightly browned. Cool on a wire rack. Sprinkle with confectioners' sugar. Cut into squares.

1 PIECE: *250 cal., 11g fat (7g sat. fat), 74mg chol., 99mg sod., 35g carb. (23g sugars, 0 fiber), 3g pro.*

CLASSIC LEMON BARS

MOCHA-WALNUT MACARONS

BIRTHDAY CAKE FUDGE

This decadent treat is the perfect thing to make your birthday special. Or prepare it ahead and package it as a surprise gift for a friend.
—Rashanda Cobbins, Milwaukee, WI

PREP: 10 min. + chilling • **MAKES:** 64 servings

- **1 can (14 oz.) sweetened condensed milk**
- **1½ cups white baking chips**
- **3 Tbsp. butter**
- **⅛ tsp. salt**
- **1½ cups unprepared funfetti cake mix**
- **3 Tbsp. sprinkles**

1. Line an 8-in. square pan with foil or parchment; grease foil lightly. In a large heavy saucepan, cook and stir milk, baking chips, butter and salt over low heat until smooth. Remove from heat; stir in cake mix until dissolved. Spread into prepared pan; top with sprinkles. Refrigerate, covered, until firm, about 2 hours.
2. Using foil, lift fudge out of pan. Remove foil; cut fudge into 1-in. squares. Store in an airtight container in the refrigerator.

1 PIECE: *59 cal., 2g fat (2g sat. fat), 4mg chol., 47mg sod., 9g carb. (7g sugars, 0 fiber), 1g pro.*

BIRTHDAY CAKE FUDGE

MOCHA-WALNUT MACARONS

This cookie perfectly captures the chocolate, nutty flavor of my favorite gourmet coffee. Store in an airtight container.
—Christine Venzon, Peoria, IL

PREP: 30 min. + standing • **BAKE:** 20 min./batch + cooling
MAKES: 3½ dozen

- **2 large egg whites**
- **1 cup confectioners' sugar**
- **½ cup chopped walnuts, toasted**
- **2 Tbsp. baking cocoa**
- **1 Tbsp. instant coffee granules**
- **Dash salt**
- **⅓ cup superfine sugar**

1. Place egg whites in a large bowl; let stand at room temperature 30 minutes.
2. Preheat oven to 275°. Place confectioners' sugar, walnuts, cocoa and coffee in a food processor; process until finely ground and set aside.
3. Add salt to egg whites; beat on medium speed until soft peaks form. Gradually add superfine sugar, 1 Tbsp. at a time, beating on high after each addition until sugar is dissolved. Continue beating until stiff glossy peaks form. Carefully fold in the walnut mixture until blended.
4. Pipe or drop by rounded teaspoonfuls 1 in. apart onto parchment-lined baking sheets. Air-dry for 30 minutes before baking. Bake 18-20 minutes. Remove macarons from baking sheet to a wire rack; cool completely. Remove from parchment; store in an airtight container.

1 COOKIE: *22 cal., 1g fat (0 sat. fat), 0 chol., 3mg sod., 3g carb. (3g sugars, 0 fiber), 0 pro.*

SNAP, CRACKLE, SWAP!

Give the crispy-chewy cereal treat a little extra pop with fun and flavorful stir-ins.

START HERE

In a large saucepan over low heat or in a microwave, melt a 10-oz. pkg. of miniature marshmallows in 3 Tbsp. canola oil; stir until smooth. Remove from the heat; stir in 5 cups Rice Krispies cereal plus any mix-ins. Press mixture into a lightly greased 13x9-in. baking pan using waxed paper or a lightly greased spatula. Cool to room temperature. Cut into bars.

5

2

4

3

1

1. ROCKY ROAD
Stir in 5 whole graham crackers, crumbled; 1 cup chopped salted almonds; and 1 cup chocolate chunks when adding the cereal. Melt an 11½-oz. pkg. chocolate chunks; spread over cooled bars. Top with a 10-oz. pkg. mini marshmallows. Using a kitchen torch, toast the marshmallows until golden brown. Sprinkle bars with ¼ cup almonds and ¾ cup chocolate chunks.

2. SPARKLY PRINCESS
Stir 2 tsp. strawberry extract into the melted marshmallows. Stir in ⅔ cup rainbow sprinkles when adding cereal. Melt an 11½-oz. pkg. white baking chips; spread over cooled bars. Sprinkle with ⅓ cup rainbow sprinkles. Use cookie cutters to cut out shapes if desired.

3. MAPLE BACON
Stir 2 tsp. maple flavoring into melted marshmallows. Add 9 cooked, crumbled bacon strips when adding the cereal.

4. SALTED CARAMEL PRETZEL
Add ⅔ cup each chopped caramels and pretzels when adding the cereal. Melt an 11½-oz. pkg. milk chocolate chips; spread over the cooled bars. Top with ⅓ cup each coarsely chopped caramels and pretzels. Sprinkle bars with sea salt.

5. WATERMELON
Stir 1 tsp. watermelon extract into the melted marshmallows. Stir ¼ tsp. green food coloring paste into half the marshmallow mixture. Add 3 cups cereal. Press mixture around inside edge of 2 lightly greased 9-in. round cake pans. Stir ¼ tsp. pink food coloring paste and ⅛ tsp. red food coloring paste into the remaining marshmallow mixture; add 3 cups cereal. Press into center of the cake pans. Press mini chocolate chips into pink portion for seeds.

6. CHOCOLATE RASPBERRY
Stir 1 tsp. raspberry extract into the melted marshmallows. Add 1 cup mini chocolate chips and 1 cup freeze-dried raspberries when adding the cereal.

7. FUNKY MONKEY
Stir 1½ tsp. banana extract into the melted marshmallows. Add a 10-oz. pkg. peanut butter chips, 1 cup dried banana chips and ½ cup chopped dry-roasted peanuts when adding cereal. Press ½ cup chopped dry-roasted peanuts on top of the warm bars.

8. MORNING BUZZ
Stir 2 tsp. coffee extract into the melted marshmallows. Add ½ cup coarsely chopped chocolate-covered espresso beans when adding cereal. Melt an 11-oz. pkg. dark chocolate chips; spread on top of the cooled bars. Sprinkle with ½ cup coarsely chopped chocolate-covered espresso beans.

9. CARAMEL APPLE
Add 1 cup chopped dried apples when adding cereal. Shape ½ cup mixture into an apple shape. Insert pop stick into center; repeat with remaining mixture. Let cool. Melt an 11-oz. pkg. caramels according to the package directions. Spread caramel onto apples; set on waxed paper to cool.

10. OREO
Add 1 cup coarsely chopped Oreo cookies when adding the cereal. Melt a 10-oz. pkg. white baking chips and spread over cooled bars. Sprinkle with 1 cup coarsely chopped Oreo cookies.

GLUTEN-FREE BROWNIE BARS

I can't eat dairy or gluten, but I crave the delicious brownies that I used to eat before these restrictions. This recipe sure is a satisfying substitute! The brownies will still seem soft when you pull them from the oven. They are done when the edges look very lightly browned.
—Linda Speranza, Buckeye, AZ

PREP: 20 min. • **BAKE:** 30 min. + cooling • **MAKES:** 16 servings

1 cup almond butter
½ cup agave nectar
1 large egg, room temperature
½ tsp. salt
½ tsp. baking powder
1 pkg. (10 oz.) dairy-free semisweet chocolate chips
1 cup chopped walnuts, lightly toasted

1. Preheat oven to 325°. Line an 8-in. square baking pan with parchment, letting ends extend up sides; set aside. In a large bowl, beat the first 5 ingredients until blended. Stir in chocolate chips and walnuts. Spread into prepared pan.
2. Bake until edges begin to brown and a toothpick inserted in center comes out with moist crumbs (do not overbake), 30-35 minutes. Cool completely in pan on a wire rack, at least 2 hours. Lifting with parchment, remove brownies from pan. Cut into bars. Store in an airtight container.
NOTE: This recipe was tested with Enjoy Life semisweet chocolate chips.
1 BAR: *266 cal., 19g fat (5g sat. fat), 12mg chol., 131mg sod., 23g carb. (17g sugars, 3g fiber), 6g pro.*

GLUTEN-FREE BROWNIE BARS

GUMDROP COOKIES

GUMDROP COOKIES

These fun cookies are chock-full of chewy gumdrops. I use red and green ones at Christmas, black and orange for Halloween, and pastel shades for Easter. I've made this recipe for years and I find that kids really get a kick out of the cookies with a candy surprise inside!
—Carolyn Stromberg, Wever, IA

PREP: 20 min. • **BAKE:** 15 min./batch + cooling • **MAKES:** about 3 dozen

¾ cup shortening
1 cup sugar, divided
½ tsp. almond extract
1¾ cups all-purpose flour
½ tsp. baking soda
¼ tsp. salt
1 cup chopped fruit-flavored or spiced gumdrops
2 large egg whites, room temperature

1. Preheat oven to 350°. Cream shortening and ¾ cup sugar until light and fluffy, 5-7 minutes. Beat in almond extract. In another bowl, whisk flour, baking soda and salt; gradually add to creamed mixture and mix well. Stir in gumdrops.
2. In a separate bowl, beat egg whites until soft peaks form. Gradually add remaining sugar, beating until stiff peaks form. Fold into dough.
3. Drop by level tablespoonfuls 2 in. apart onto ungreased baking sheets. Bake until golden brown, 12-15 minutes. Cool 1 minute before removing from pans to wire racks to cool completely.
1 COOKIE: *102 cal., 4g fat (1g sat. fat), 0 chol., 39mg sod., 15g carb. (9g sugars, 0 fiber), 1g pro.*

CRANBERRY NUTELLA SANDWICH COOKIES

(SHOWN ON PAGE 174)

I created these cookies for my family after I realized that we had been without Nutella for far too long! Tart dried cranberries are a natural pairing to the hazelnut flavor. We can't get enough of these sweet cookies!
—Nancy Mock, Colchester, VT

PREP: 25 min. + chilling
BAKE: 20 min./batch + cooling
MAKES: 16 sandwich cookies

- 1 **cup unsalted butter, softened**
- 1 **cup confectioners' sugar**
- 3 **tsp. vanilla extract**
- 2¼ **cups all-purpose flour**
- ¼ **tsp. salt**
- ½ **cup dried cranberries, finely chopped**
- ¼ **cup 2% milk**
- ¾ **cup Nutella**

1. In a large bowl, cream butter and confectioners' sugar on high speed until light and fluffy, 5-7 minutes. Beat in vanilla. In another bowl, whisk the flour and salt; gradually beat into creamed mixture. Stir in cranberries. Divide dough in half. Shape each half into a disk. Wrap and refrigerate 30 minutes or until firm enough to roll.
2. Preheat oven to 325°. On a lightly floured surface, roll each portion of dough to ¼-in. thickness. Cut with a floured 2-in. diamond-shaped cookie cutter. Place 2 in. apart on parchment paper-lined baking sheets. Brush with milk.
3. Bake until the edges begin to brown, 18-20 minutes. Remove from pans to wire racks to cool completely. Spread Nutella over bottoms of half of the cookies; top with the remaining cookies. Store in an airtight container.
1 SANDWICH COOKIE: *284 cal., 16g fat (8g sat. fat), 31mg chol., 47mg sod., 34g carb. (19g sugars, 1g fiber), 3g pro.*

FRENCH TOAST SPIRALS

These little spiral cookies taste just like French toast. They're not too sweet, and they're pretty enough for a Christmas cookie plate.
—Ellen Riley, Murfreesboro, TN

PREP: 30 min. + chilling
BAKE: 15 min./batch + cooling
MAKES: 4 dozen

- 1 **cup butter, softened**
- ¾ **cup confectioners' sugar**
- ¼ **cup sugar**
- 1 **large egg, room temperature**
- 2 **Tbsp. maple syrup**
- 1 **tsp. vanilla extract**
- 2½ **cups all-purpose flour**
- ½ **tsp. salt**
- ½ **tsp. ground cinnamon**

FILLING

- ⅓ **cup butter, softened**
- 3 **Tbsp. all-purpose flour**
- 3 **Tbsp. brown sugar**
- 2 **Tbsp. maple syrup**
- 1 **tsp. instant coffee granules**
- **Confectioners' sugar, optional**

1. Cream butter and sugars until light and fluffy, 5-7 minutes. Beat in egg, maple syrup and vanilla. In another bowl, whisk flour, salt and cinnamon; gradually beat into creamed mixture. On a baking sheet, roll dough between 2 sheets of waxed paper into a 12-in. square. Refrigerate 30 minutes.
2. For filling, beat first 5 ingredients until blended. Remove top sheet of waxed paper; spread filling over dough to within ¼ in. of edges. Using waxed paper, roll up tightly, jelly-roll style, removing paper as you roll. Wrap and refrigerate until firm, about 2 hours.
3. Preheat oven to 375°. Unwrap and cut dough crosswise into ¼-in. slices. Place 2 in. apart on parchment-lined baking sheets. Bake until edges are light brown, 12-14 minutes. Cool on pans 5 minutes. Remove to wire racks to finish cooling. If desired, dust with confectioners' sugar.
1 COOKIE: *92 cal., 5g fat (3g sat. fat), 17mg chol., 67mg sod., 10g carb. (5g sugars, 0 fiber), 1g pro.*

FRENCH TOAST SPIRALS

FRUIT & ALMOND BITES

APRICOT BARS

These tender bars have a great flavor. Everyone in my family loves them, and I get lots of requests for the recipe.
—Kim Gilliland, Simi Valley, CA

PREP: 15 min. • **BAKE:** 50 min.
MAKES: 16 bars

- **⅔ cup dried apricots**
- **½ cup water**
- **½ cup butter, softened**
- **¼ cup confectioners' sugar**
- **1⅓ cups all-purpose flour, divided**
- **2 large eggs, room temperature**
- **1 cup packed brown sugar**
- **½ tsp. vanilla extract**
- **½ tsp. baking powder**
- **¼ tsp. salt**
- **½ cup chopped walnuts**
- **Additional confectioners' sugar**

1. In a small saucepan, cook apricots in water over medium heat for 10 minutes or until softened. Drain, cool and chop; set aside. In a large bowl, cream butter and confectioners' sugar until light and fluffy, 5-7 minutes. Gradually add 1 cup flour until well blended.

2. Press into a greased 8-in. square baking dish. Bake at 350° until lightly browned, about 20 minutes.

3. Meanwhile, in a small bowl, beat eggs and brown sugar until blended. Beat in vanilla. In a small bowl, combine the baking powder, salt and remaining flour; gradually add to egg mixture. Stir in apricots and nuts. Pour over crust.

4. Bake at 350° until set, about 30 minutes. Cool on wire rack. Dust with confectioners' sugar; cut into bars.

1 BAR: *197 cal., 9g fat (4g sat. fat), 42mg chol., 121mg sod., 28g carb. (18g sugars, 1g fiber), 3g pro.*

FRUIT & ALMOND BITES

With big handfuls of dried apricots, cherries, almonds and pistachios, these are some seriously tasty and satisfying no-bake treats. You can take them anywhere.
—Donna Pochoday-Stelmach, Morristown, NJ

PREP: 40 min. + chilling
MAKES: about 4 dozen

- **3¾ cups sliced almonds, divided**
- **¼ tsp. almond extract**
- **¼ cup honey**
- **2 cups finely chopped dried apricots**
- **1 cup finely chopped dried cherries or cranberries**
- **1 cup finely chopped pistachios, toasted**

1. Place 1¼ cups almonds in a food processor; pulse until finely chopped. Remove almonds to a shallow bowl; reserve for coating.

2. Add remaining 2½ cups almonds to food processor; pulse until finely chopped. Add extract. While processing, gradually add honey. Remove to a large bowl; stir in apricots and cherries. Divide mixture into 6 portions; shape each into a ½-in.-thick roll. Wrap and refrigerate until firm, about 1 hour .

3. Unwrap and cut rolls into 1½-in. pieces. Roll half of the pieces in reserved almonds, pressing gently to adhere. Roll remaining half in chopped pistachios. If desired, wrap individually in waxed paper, twisting ends to close. Store in airtight containers, layered between waxed paper if unwrapped.

NOTE: To toast nuts, bake in a shallow pan in a 350°; oven for 5-10 minutes or cook in a skillet over low heat until lightly browned, stirring occasionally.,

1 PIECE: *86 cal., 5g fat (0 sat. fat), 0 chol., 15mg sod., 10g carb. (7g sugars, 2g fiber), 2g pro.* **Diabetic exchanges:** *1 fat, ½ starch.*

PACOCA (BRAZILIAN PEANUT CANDY)

This tasty sweet treat is such an easy recipe with only a few ingredients! It's a popular candy in Brazil and after you try it, I'm sure you'll love it, too.
—Francine Lizotte, Surrey, BC

PREP: 15 min. + chilling • **MAKES:** 81 pieces (about 2 lbs.)

- **9 whole graham crackers**
- **1¾ cups dry-roasted peanuts**
- **2 Tbsp. sugar**
- **1 can (14 oz.) sweetened condensed milk**
- **½ tsp. vanilla extract**
- **Dash Himalayan sea salt**

1. Line a 9-in. square baking pan with parchment, letting ends extend up sides. Place graham crackers and peanuts in a food processor; pulse until just ground. Add sugar; process 10 seconds. Add sweetened condensed milk, vanilla and salt; pulse until dough comes together.
2. Press dough into prepared pan. Refrigerate, covered, at least 4 hours or overnight. Lifting with parchment, remove from pan. Cut into squares. Store in an airtight container.
1 PIECE: *42 cal., 2g fat (1g sat. fat), 2mg chol., 44mg sod., 5g carb. (4g sugars, 0 fiber), 1g pro.*

TEST KITCHEN TIP

For a twist, drizzle melted chocolate on top after pressing the mixture down in the baking dish.

PACOCA (BRAZILIAN PEANUT CANDY)

CRANBERRY PECAN COOKIES

5i

CRANBERRY PECAN COOKIES

Each delightful little cookie is loaded with cranberries, nuts and a sweet hint of vanilla. But these little gems start with ready-made cookie dough! Let that be your little secret.
—Louise Hawkins, Lubbock, TX

PREP: 10 min. • **BAKE:** 10 min./batch • **MAKES:** 3½ dozen

- **1 tube (16½ oz.) refrigerated sugar cookie dough, softened**
- **1 cup chopped pecans**
- **⅔ cup white baking chips**
- **⅔ cup dried cranberries**
- **1 tsp. vanilla extract**

1. Preheat oven to 350°. In a large bowl, combine cookie dough, pecans, chips, cranberries and vanilla. Drop by tablespoonfuls 2 in. apart onto ungreased baking sheets.
2. Bake until lightly browned, 10-12 minutes. Cool 2 minutes before removing from pans to wire racks. Store in an airtight container.
1 COOKIE: *87 cal., 5g fat (1g sat. fat), 4mg chol., 50mg sod., 10g carb. (5g sugars, 0 fiber), 1g pro.*

SALTED PEANUT SQUARES

SALTED PEANUT SQUARES

Want to make something a little out of the ordinary? This recipe makes nearly 10 dozen chewy, nutty, sweet-and-salty bars.
—Barb Timm, Lakeville, MN

PREP: 20 min. + standing • **MAKES:** 9¾ dozen

- **3½ cups dry-roasted peanuts, divided**
- **1 pkg. (10 oz.) peanut butter chips**
- **2 Tbsp. butter**
- **1 can (14 oz.) sweetened condensed milk**
- **1 jar (7 oz.) marshmallow creme**
- **36 miniature Snickers candy bars, chopped**

1. Sprinkle half of the peanuts into a greased 13x9-in. baking pan. In a large microwave-safe bowl, heat chips and butter at 50% power for 1 minute; stir. Microwave in 20-second intervals until melted; stir until smooth. Stir in sweetened condensed milk; cook, uncovered, on high for 1 minute.
2. Stir in marshmallow creme and chopped candy bars. Spread into prepared pan. Sprinkle with remaining peanuts. Cover with plastic wrap; press down lightly.
3. Refrigerate until set. Cut into 1-in. squares. Store squares in an airtight container.
1 PIECE: *64 cal., 3g fat (1g sat. fat), 2mg chol., 47mg sod., 7g carb. (5g sugars, 0 fiber), 2g pro.*

CARAMEL HEAVENLIES

Before I cut these bars into triangles, I usually trim the edges so all the cookies look the same. My husband and daughter love this part because they get to eat the scraps.
—Dawn Burns, Lake St. Louis, MO

PREP: 20 min. • **BAKE:** 15 min. + cooling • **MAKES:** about 3 dozen

- **12 whole graham crackers**
- **2 cups miniature marshmallows**
- **¾ cup butter, cubed**
- **¾ cup packed brown sugar**
- **1 tsp. ground cinnamon**
- **1 tsp. vanilla extract**
- **1 cup sliced almonds**
- **1 cup sweetened shredded coconut**

1. Preheat oven to 350°. Line a 15x10x1-in. baking pan with foil, letting foil extend over sides by 1 in.; lightly coat foil with cooking spray. Arrange graham crackers in prepared pan; sprinkle with marshmallows.
2. In a small saucepan, combine the butter, brown sugar and cinnamon; cook and stir over medium heat until butter is melted and sugar is dissolved. Remove from heat; stir in vanilla.
3. Spoon butter mixture over marshmallows. Sprinkle with almonds and coconut. Bake until browned,14-16 minutes. Cool completely in pan on a wire rack.
4. Using foil, lift out of pan. Cut into triangles; discard foil.
1 PIECE: *110 cal., 7g fat (3g sat. fat), 10mg chol., 68mg sod., 13g carb. (8g sugars, 1g fiber), 1g pro.*

CARAMEL HEAVENLIES

POPCORN COOKIES

It's so much fun to surprise people with the crushed popcorn in these yummy cookies. They're definitely a distinctive cookie on any holiday cookie tray.
—Leigh Anne Preston, Palmyra, IN

PREP: 15 min. • **BAKE:** 15 min./batch + cooling
MAKES: about 2½ dozen

- **½ cup butter, softened**
- **1 cup sugar**
- **1 large egg, room temperature**
- **1 tsp. vanilla extract**
- **1¼ cups all-purpose flour**
- **½ tsp. baking soda**
- **Dash salt**
- **2 cups popped popcorn, lightly crushed**
- **1 cup semisweet chocolate chips**
- **½ cup chopped pecans**

1. Preheat oven to 350°. Cream butter and sugar until light and fluffy, 5-7 minutes; beat in egg and vanilla. In a separate bowl, whisk flour, baking soda and salt; gradually beat into creamed mixture. Stir in popcorn, chocolate chips and pecans.
2. Drop by tablespoonfuls 2 in. apart onto greased baking sheets. Bake cookies until golden brown, 13-14 minutes. Remove to wire racks to cool.
1 COOKIE: *119 cal., 7g fat (3g sat. fat), 15mg chol., 66mg sod., 15g carb. (10g sugars, 1g fiber), 1g pro.*

HOW-TO

Keep Cookies Fresh

To keep baked goods soft and moist when storing, add a slice of white bread to the container. It will help preserve moisture in cookies, cakes, muffins and more.

TWO-TONE CARAMEL BROWNIES

TWO-TONE CARAMEL BROWNIES

This dessert is a mashup of two of my favorite bar recipes. A woman I worked with just after high school gave me the recipe for chocolate caramel brownies, and I have an easy recipe for bars that are made with yellow cake mix. I wondered what they would taste like baked together, so I tried it—and I've been making them ever since!
—Staci Perry Mergenthal, Verdi, MN

PREP: 40 min. • **BAKE:** 20 min. + cooling
MAKES: 40 servings

- **1 pkg. chocolate cake mix (regular size)**
- **¾ cup butter, melted**
- **1 can (5 oz.) evaporated milk, divided**
- **1 pkg. (11 oz.) Kraft caramel bits**
- **1 cup semisweet chocolate chips**
- **1 pkg. yellow cake mix (regular size)**
- **1 large egg, room temperature**
- **½ cup plus 1 Tbsp. butter, softened, divided**
- **1 can (14 oz.) sweetened condensed milk**
- **1 pkg. (11½ oz.) milk chocolate chips**

1. Preheat oven to 350°. Line a 13x9-in. baking pan with parchment; grease paper. In a large bowl, beat chocolate cake mix, melted butter and ⅓ cup evaporated milk until blended; batter will be thick. Reserve ¼ cup batter for topping. Spread remaining batter into prepared pan. Bake 6 minutes.
2. Meanwhile, in a microwave, melt caramel bits and remaining ⅓ cup evaporated milk; stir until smooth. Sprinkle hot chocolate crust with semisweet chips; pour caramel mixture over top. Set aside.
3. In another large bowl, beat yellow cake mix, egg and ½ cup softened butter until combined; batter will be thick. Reserve half for topping. Crumble remaining mixture over caramel layer. Bake 6 minutes.
4. In a microwave, melt the sweetened condensed milk, milk chocolate chips and the remaining 1 Tbsp. softened butter; stir until smooth. Pour over yellow cake layer. Sprinkle with the reserved yellow and chocolate cake batters. Bake until the top is golden brown, 20-25 minutes. Cool completely on a wire rack. Store in an airtight container.
1 BROWNIE: *272 cal., 13g fat (8g sat. fat), 27mg chol., 260mg sod., 38g carb. (28g sugars, 1g fiber), 3g pro.*

HAZELNUT MACARONS

You don't have to be an expert in French cooking to whip up these sandwich cookies. The crisp, chewy macarons require attention to detail, but they're not hard to make—and they're simply a delight, both for personal snacking and giving as gifts!
—Taste of Home *Test Kitchen*

PREP: 50 min. • **BAKE:** 10 min./batch + cooling • **MAKES:** about 5 dozen

- 6 **large egg whites**
- 1½ **cups hazelnuts, toasted**
- 2½ **cups confectioners' sugar**
- **Dash salt**
- ½ **cup superfine sugar**

COFFEE BUTTERCREAM

- 1 **cup sugar**
- 6 **Tbsp. water**
- 6 **large egg yolks**
- 4 **tsp. instant espresso powder**
- 1 **tsp. vanilla extract**
- 1½ **cups butter, softened**
- 6 **Tbsp. confectioners' sugar**

1. Place egg whites in a small bowl; let stand at room temperature for 30 minutes.
2. Preheat oven to 350°. Place hazelnuts and confectioners' sugar in a food processor; pulse until nuts are finely ground.
3. Add salt to egg whites; beat on medium speed until soft peaks form. Gradually add superfine sugar, 1 Tbsp. at a time, beating on high until stiff peaks form. Fold in hazelnut mixture.
4. With a pastry bag, pipe 1-in.-diameter cookies 2 in. apart onto parchment-lined baking sheets. Bake until cookies are lightly browned and firm to the touch, 9-12 minutes. Transfer cookies on the parchment to wire racks; cool completely.
5. For the buttercream, in a heavy saucepan, combine sugar and water. Bring to a boil; cook over medium-high heat until sugar is dissolved. Remove from heat. In a small bowl, whisk a small amount of hot syrup into egg yolks; return all to pan, whisking constantly. Cook until thickened, 2-3 minutes, stirring constantly; remove from heat. Stir in espresso powder and vanilla extract; cool completely.
6. In a stand mixer with the whisk attachment, beat butter until creamy. Gradually beat in cooled syrup. Beat in confectioners' sugar until fluffy. Refrigerate until mixture firms to a spreading consistency, about 10 minutes.
7. Spread about 1½ tsp. buttercream onto the bottoms of half the cookies; top with remaining cookies. Store in airtight containers in the refrigerator.

1 SANDWICH COOKIE: *117 cal., 8g fat (3g sat. fat), 31mg chol., 67mg sod., 12g carb. (11g sugars, 0 fiber), 1g pro.*

TO TOAST WHOLE HAZELNUTS: Bake in a shallow pan in a 350° oven until fragrant and lightly browned, 7-10 minutes, stirring occasionally. To remove skins, wrap hazelnuts in a tea towel; rub with towel to loosen skins.

CHOCOLATE CARAMELS

5i

CHOCOLATE CARAMELS

When I was growing up, my mom would make these delicious candies every Christmas. They were my favorite then and still are today.
—Sue Gronholz, Beaver Dam, WI

PREP: 5 min. • **COOK:** 55 min. + cooling • **MAKES:** 32 pieces (1¼ lb.)

- 1 **tsp. butter, softened**
- 1 **cup sugar**
- ¾ **cup light corn syrup**
- 2 **oz. unsweetened chocolate, chopped**
- 1½ **cups heavy whipping cream, divided**

1. Line a 9x5-in. loaf pan with foil and grease the foil with butter; set aside.
2. In a large heavy saucepan, bring the sugar, corn syrup and chocolate to a boil over medium heat; stir until smooth. Add ½ cup cream; cook, stirring constantly, until a candy thermometer reads 234° (soft-ball stage). Add another ½ cup cream; return mixture to 234° (soft-ball stage). Add the remaining cream; cook to 245° (firm-ball stage).
3. Immediately pour into prepared pan (do not scrape saucepan). Let stand until firm, about 5 hours or overnight. Using foil, lift candy out of pan. Discard foil; cut candy into 1-in. squares using a buttered knife. Wrap individually in waxed paper; twist ends.

NOTE: We recommend that you test your candy thermometer before each use by bringing water to a boil; the thermometer should read 212°. Adjust your recipe temperature up or down based on your test.

1 CARAMEL: *94 cal., 5g fat (3g sat. fat), 16mg chol., 10mg sod., 13g carb. (8g sugars, 0 fiber), 0 pro.*

COCONUT EGG NESTS

Looking for an Easter activity that kids will enjoy assembling and eating? Try these sweet birds' nest cookies. They're a snap to make and call for just a few ingredients.
—Tonya Hamrick, Wallace, WV

TAKES: 20 min. • **MAKES:** 1 dozen

- **6 oz. white candy coating, coarsely chopped**
- **6 drops green food coloring**
- **1 drop yellow food coloring**
- **1 cup sweetened shredded coconut**
- **36 jelly beans**

In a microwave-safe bowl, melt candy coating; stir in food coloring until blended. Stir in coconut. Drop by tablespoonfuls onto waxed paper into 12 mounds. Make an indentation in the center of each with the end of a wooden spoon handle. Fill each with three jelly beans. Let stand until set.

1 SERVING: *127 cal., 7g fat (6g sat. fat), 0 chol., 22mg sod., 17g carb. (15g sugars, 0 fiber), 0 pro.*

COCONUT EGG NESTS

ORANGE GUMDROPS

ORANGE GUMDROPS

I get nothing but rave reviews when I make these gumdrops and usually have to prepare three batches. The refreshing orange flavor is a nice change from the usual chocolate holiday candies.
—Becky Burch, Marceline, MO

PREP: 10 min. • **COOK:** 10 min. + standing • **MAKES:** about 6 dozen

- **1 tsp. plus 1 Tbsp. butter, softened, divided**
- **1 cup sugar**
- **1 cup light corn syrup**
- **¾ cup water**
- **1 pkg. (1¾ oz.) powdered fruit pectin**
- **½ tsp. baking soda**
- **1½ tsp. orange extract**
- **1 tsp. grated orange zest**
- **4 drops yellow food coloring**
- **1 drop red food coloring**
- **Additional sugar, optional**

1. Line the bottom and sides of a 9x5-in. loaf pan with foil. Grease the foil with 1 tsp. butter; set aside.

2. Grease the bottom and sides of a large heavy saucepan with the remaining butter; add sugar and corn syrup. Cook and stir over medium heat until mixture comes to a boil, about 9 minutes. Cook over medium-high heat until a candy thermometer reads 280° (soft-crack stage), stirring occasionally.

3. Meanwhile, in another large saucepan, combine the water, pectin and baking soda (mixture will foam slightly). Cook and stir over high heat until mixture boils, about 2 minutes. Remove from the heat; set aside.

4. When corn syrup mixture reaches 280° (soft-crack stage), remove from the heat. Return pectin mixture to medium-high heat; cook until mixture begins to simmer. Carefully and slowly ladle corn syrup mixture in a very thin stream into pectin mixture, stirring constantly. Cook and stir 1 minute longer.

5. Remove from the heat; stir in the extract, zest and food coloring. Transfer to prepared pan. Let stand until firm, about 2 hours. Cut into squares. If desired, roll in additional sugar.

1 SERVING: *30 cal., 0 fat (0 sat. fat), 1mg chol., 16mg sod., 7g carb. (6g sugars, 0 fiber), 0 pro.*

THE BEST SWEET POTATO PIE
PAGE 195

Cakes & Pies

The crowning glory of any meal—whether it's a casual barbecue or holiday celebration—is a beautiful pie, cake or tart.

OUR ALL-TIME FAVORITES

Southern Lane Cake p. 196

Brownie Kiss Cupcakes p. 201

Peanut Butter Silk Pie p. 203

Huckleberry Cheese Pie p. 204

Maple-Glazed Apple Pie p. 207

GANACHE-TOPPED PUMPKIN TART

EGGNOG TRES LECHES CAKE

When the holidays roll around, my family eagerly anticipates tasting this dessert. By poking holes in the cake, you ensure the creamy eggnog sauce is absorbed into every last crumb.

—Jan Valdez, Chicago, IL

PREP: 40 min. + standing
BAKE: 25 min. + chilling • **MAKES:** 15 servings

- **1 pkg. white cake mix (regular size)**
- **1⅓ cups water**
- **2 Tbsp. canola oil**
- **3 large egg whites, room temperature**
- **2 cups eggnog**
- **1 can (14 oz.) sweetened condensed milk**
- **½ cup 2% milk**
- **1½ cups heavy whipping cream**
- **¼ cup sugar**
- **⅛ tsp. ground cinnamon**
- **⅛ tsp. ground nutmeg**

1. Preheat oven to 350°. In a large bowl, combine cake mix, water, oil and egg whites; beat on low speed 30 seconds. Beat on medium 2 minutes. Pour into a greased and floured 13x9-in. baking pan.

2. Bake until a toothpick inserted in center comes out clean, 25-30 minutes. Cool on a wire rack. Using a skewer, poke holes in cake 1 in. apart.

3. In a large bowl, combine the eggnog, sweetened condensed milk and 2% milk. Pour ¾ cup mixture over cake; let stand until liquid is absorbed, 20-30 minutes. Repeat 4 times. Cover and refrigerate for 8 hours or overnight.

4. In a large bowl, beat the cream until it begins to thicken. Add sugar; beat until soft peaks form. Spread over cake. Sprinkle with cinnamon and nutmeg. Refrigerate the leftovers.

1 PIECE: *394 cal., 19g fat (10g sat. fat), 62mg chol., 309mg sod., 51g carb. (36g sugars, 0 fiber), 6g pro.*

GANACHE-TOPPED PUMPKIN TART

I love the flavor combination of spiced pumpkin and chocolate, which inspired me to create this tart. Sometimes I like to sprinkle chopped crystallized ginger over the chocolate ganache for extra flavor and texture.

—Bernice Janowski, Stevens Point, WI

PREP: 20 min. + chilling
BAKE: 55 min. + cooling • **MAKES:** 8 servings

- **1 cup all-purpose flour**
- **¾ cup sugar**
- **½ cup baking cocoa**
- **1 tsp. pumpkin pie spice**
- **½ tsp. salt**
- **½ cup butter, melted**

FILLING

- **1 can (15 oz.) pumpkin**
- **3 large eggs**
- **¾ cup packed dark brown sugar**
- **2 tsp. grated orange zest**
- **2 tsp. pumpkin pie spice**
- **¼ tsp. salt**
- **½ cup heavy whipping cream**

GANACHE

- **¾ cup semisweet chocolate chips**
- **½ cup heavy whipping cream**
- **Crystallized ginger, chopped, optional**

1. Preheat oven to 425°. In a large bowl, combine flour, sugar, baking cocoa, pie spice and salt. Stir in butter until crumbly. Press onto bottom and up sides of a 9-in. tart pan with removable bottom; place on a baking sheet. Bake 10 minutes; cool on a wire rack.

2. Meanwhile, in another large bowl, whisk pumpkin, eggs, brown sugar, orange zest, pie spice and salt. Slowly whisk in cream. Pour into crust. Bake 15 minutes. Reduce oven temperature to 350°. Bake until filling is set, 40-45 minutes. Cool on a wire rack.

3. For ganache, place chocolate chips in a small bowl. In a small saucepan, bring cream just to a boil. Pour over chocolate; let stand 10 minutes. Stir with a whisk until smooth. Spread over tart; chill until set. If desired, garnish with crystallized ginger.

1 PIECE: *551 cal., 30g fat (18g sat. fat), 134mg chol., 358mg sod., 70g carb. (50g sugars, 4g fiber), 7g pro.*

SWEDISH FLOP

This was one of my Gramma Esther's favorites. Found mainly in the Chicago area, this combination of fluffy yeasted cake and buttercream is, like Esther herself, a showstopper.
—Shauna Sever, Oak Park, IL

PREP: 45 min. + rising
BAKE: 30 min. + cooling • **MAKES:** 12 servings

- **1 pkg. (¼ oz.) quick-rise yeast**
- **⅔ cup warm whole milk (110° to 115°)**
- **4 Tbsp. unsalted butter, melted**
- **¼ cup sugar**
- **2 large eggs, room temperature**
- **2 tsp. grated lemon zest**
- **1 tsp. vanilla extract**
- **2 cups all-purpose flour**
- **½ tsp. fine sea salt**

STREUSEL

- **¾ cup all-purpose flour**
- **⅓ cup packed light brown sugar**
- **⅛ tsp. fine sea salt**
- **5 Tbsp. unsalted butter, room temperature**

ERMINE FROSTING

- **¼ cup all-purpose flour**
- **1 cup whole milk**
- **1 cup sugar**
- **¼ tsp. fine sea salt**
- **1 cup unsalted butter, room temperature**
- **1 tsp. vanilla extract**
- **¼ tsp. almond extract**
- **½ cup rhubarb or raspberry jam**
- **¼ cup confectioners' sugar**

1. In the bowl of a stand mixer, combine yeast and milk; let stand 5 minutes. Whisk in butter, sugar, eggs, zest and vanilla. With the paddle attachment, beat in flour and salt until shiny, 3-4 minutes (batter will be very loose and sticky). Place in a greased bowl; lightly sprinkle surface with additional flour. Cover and let rise in a warm place until doubled, about 1 hour.

2. Lightly grease a 13x9-in. baking pan; line pan with parchment, letting ends extend up sides. Transfer dough to prepared pan; cover and let rise until doubled, about 45 minutes.

3. Preheat oven to 350°. Meanwhile, for streusel, in a bowl, combine flour, brown sugar and salt. Add butter and rub together until coarse crumbs form; refrigerate while dough rises.

4. Sprinkle streusel evenly over the dough. Bake on the center rack until edges start to brown, about 30 minutes. Cool in pan on a wire rack.

5. For frosting, whisk flour, milk, sugar, and salt in a large saucepan. Cook, whisking constantly, over medium heat until mixture thickens, about 1 minute. Remove and let cool completely. Whisk butter and extracts on high speed until fluffy, about 2 minutes. Add cooled flour mixture; beat until fluffy and mousselike, about 5 minutes.

6. Remove cake from pan. Using a serrated knife, cut ¼ in. off outside edges; slice cake horizontally into 2 layers. Spread frosting evenly over bottom layer; top with jam. Replace the top of cake; dust cake with confectioners' sugar.

1 PIECE: *510 cal., 26g fat (16g sat. fat), 98mg chol., 173mg sod., 64g carb. (39g sugars, 1g fiber), 6g pro.*

READER REVIEW

"Definitely a sweet treat! It takes some time to make but well worth it."
—STEPHENNORTHCUTT, TASTEOFHOME.COM

SWEDISH FLOP

SUMMER SQUASH POUND CAKE

SUMMER SQUASH POUND CAKE

This golden brown, tender pound cake is the perfect treat to make when you have an abundance of summer squash in your garden. It's not overly sweet, so it appeals to everyone.
—Lisa Brockwell, Necedah, WI

PREP: 20 min. • **BAKE:** 50 min. + cooling • **MAKES:** 12 servings

- **½ cup butter, softened**
- **1¼ cups sugar**
- **2 large eggs, room temperature**
- **1 tsp. lemon juice**
- **¼ tsp. almond extract**
- **2½ cups all-purpose flour**
- **1½ tsp. baking powder**
- **¼ tsp. baking soda**
- **¼ tsp. salt**
- **½ cup sour cream or plain Greek yogurt**
- **2 cups shredded yellow summer squash**

GLAZE

- **¾ cup confectioners' sugar**
- **2 to 3 tsp. water**
- **1½ tsp. lemon juice**

1. Preheat oven to 350°. Grease and flour a 10-in. fluted tube pan. In a large bowl, beat butter and sugar until crumbly. Add eggs, 1 at a time, beating well after each addition. Beat in lemon juice and extract. In another bowl, whisk flour, baking powder, baking soda and salt; add to creamed mixture alternately with sour cream, beating after each addition just until combined. Stir in squash.
2. Transfer to prepared pan. Bake until a toothpick inserted in center comes out clean, 50-55 minutes. Cool in pan 10 minutes before removing to a wire rack to cool completely. Combine glaze ingredients; pour over cake.
1 PIECE: *310 cal., 11g fat (6g sat. fat), 54mg chol., 213mg sod., 50g carb. (29g sugars, 1g fiber), 4g pro.*

5i

FIVE-MINUTE BLUEBERRY PIE

If you like the taste of fresh blueberries, you'll love this pie. Since it's a breeze to whip up, I make it often, especially in summer.
—Milda Anderson, Osceola, WI

PREP: 15 min. + chilling • **MAKES:** 8 servings

- **½ cup sugar**
- **2 Tbsp. cornstarch**
- **¾ cup water**
- **4 cups fresh or frozen blueberries, thawed**
- **1 graham cracker crust (9 in.)**
- **Whipped cream, optional**

In a large saucepan, combine sugar and cornstarch. Stir in the water until smooth. Bring to a boil over medium heat; cook and stir for 2 minutes. Add blueberries. Cook for 3 minutes, stirring occasionally. Pour into crust. Chill. Garnish with whipped cream if desired.
1 PIECE: *202 cal., 6g fat (1g sat. fat), 0 chol., 122mg sod., 39g carb. (29g sugars, 2g fiber), 1g pro.*

FIVE-MINUTE BLUEBERRY PIE

THE BEST SWEET POTATO PIE

(SHOWN ON PAGE 190)

I love this dessert's rich sweet potato flavor and irresistibly buttery crust. Sour cream makes the filling super smooth, and the brown sugar and spices make it extra cozy. There's no doubt that this is the best sweet potato pie!
—Rashanda Cobbins, Milwaukee, WI

PREP: 1½ hours + chilling
BAKE: 35 min. + cooling • **MAKES:** 8 servings

CRUST:

- 1 **large egg yolk**
- ¼ **to ½ cup ice water, divided**
- 2½ **cups all-purpose flour**
- 3 **Tbsp. sugar**
- ½ **tsp. salt**
- ½ **cup cold shortening, cubed**
- ½ **cup cold butter, cubed**

FILLING:

- 2½ **lbs. sweet potatoes**
- ⅔ **cup packed brown sugar**
- ½ **cup sour cream**
- 3 **large eggs, lightly beaten**
- ⅓ **cup butter, melted**
- 1 **Tbsp. bourbon**
- 2 **tsp. vanilla extract**
- 1½ **tsp. ground cinnamon**
- ½ **tsp. ground nutmeg**
- ½ **tsp. salt**
- **Optional toppings: Whipped cream and sugared cranberries**

1. In a small bowl, mix egg yolk with ¼ cup ice water; set aside. Place the flour, sugar and salt in a food processor; pulse until blended. Add shortening and butter; pulse until shortening and butter are the size of peas. While pulsing, add egg yolk mixture. Add just enough of remaining ice water to form moist crumbs. Divide dough in half. Shape each into a disk; wrap and refrigerate 1 hour or overnight.

2. Preheat oven to 400°. Scrub the sweet potatoes; place in a 13x9-in. baking pan with 1½ cups water. Bake until tender, 45-50 minutes. Meanwhile, on a lightly floured surface, roll 1 disk of dough to a ⅛-in.-thick circle; transfer to a 9-in. deep-dish pie plate. Trim crust to ½ in. beyond rim of plate; flute edge. Roll remaining disk to ⅛-in. thickness; cut into desired shapes with floured 1-in. cookie cutters. Place on a parchment-lined baking sheet. Refrigerate crust and cutouts for at least 30 minutes.

RED VELVET CAKE IN A JAR

3. Peel potatoes when they are cool enough to handle; place in a food processor. Pulse to coarsely mash. Add brown sugar and the next 8 ingredients; blend until smooth. Pour filling into chilled crust. Bake on lowest oven rack 15 minutes. Reduce oven setting to 350°; bake until center is just set, 20-25 minutes. Bake crust cutouts on an upper oven rack until golden brown, 10-12 minutes. Cool on a wire rack; decorate pie with cutouts and toppings as desired.

1 PIECE: *726 cal., 37g fat (18g sat. fat), 147mg chol., 500mg sod., 88g carb. (38g sugars, 6g fiber), 10g pro.*

TO MAKE SUGARED CRANBERRIES: Place ⅓ cup sugar in a small bowl. In a microwave, warm 1 Tbsp. light corn syrup, about 10 seconds; toss with 1 cup fresh cranberries. Add to sugar and toss; let stand on waxed paper until set, about 1 hour.

RED VELVET CAKE IN A JAR

I love to make these for friends, family and teachers. Red velvet is my favorite during the holidays, but you can use any cake and frosting flavors you like. Then dress up the jars with homemade labels and ribbons for gifting. Don't forget to tie a spoon to the jar; everyone likes to dig right in!
—Lillie Collier, Mobile, AL

PREP: 30 min. • **BAKE:** 35 min. + cooling
MAKES: 16 servings

- 1 **pkg. red velvet cake mix (regular size)**
- 1 **pkg. (3.9 oz.) instant chocolate pudding mix**
- 3 **cups miniature semisweet chocolate chips**

ICING

- 2 **pkg. (8 oz. each) cream cheese, softened**
- 1 **tsp. vanilla extract**
- 2 **cups confectioners' sugar**
- 1 **Tbsp. 2% milk**
- 16 **half-pint jars**

1. Grease a 13x9-in. baking pan.

2. Prepare cake mix batter according to package directions, adding pudding mix before mixing batter, and folding 1 cup chocolate chips into prepared batter. Transfer to prepared pan. Bake and cool as package directs. Cut into ¼-in. cubes.

3. In a large bowl, beat cream cheese and vanilla until blended. Gradually beat in confectioners' sugar and milk until smooth.

4. In each of 16 half-pint jars, layer ½ cup cake cubes, 1 Tbsp. icing and 1 Tbsp. remaining chocolate chips. Repeat layers. Refrigerate leftovers.

1 SERVING: *530 cal., 28g fat (13g sat. fat), 64mg chol., 358mg sod., 70g carb. (52g sugars, 2g fiber), 6g pro.*

SOUTHERN LANE CAKE

SOUTHERN LANE CAKE

I just love this impressive cake, and so do my dinner guests. With the fruit filling and topping, it's reminiscent of a fruitcake but so much more delicious!
—Mabel Parvi, Ridgefield, WA

PREP: 40 min. • **BAKE:** 20 min. + cooling
MAKES: 12 servings

- **6 large egg whites**
- **¾ cup butter, softened**
- **1½ cups sugar**
- **1 tsp. vanilla extract**
- **2¼ cups all-purpose flour**
- **2½ tsp. baking powder**
- **½ tsp. salt**
- **¾ cup 2% milk**

FILLING

- **6 large egg yolks**
- **1 cup sugar**
- **½ cup butter, cubed**
- **¼ cup bourbon**
- **1 Tbsp. grated orange zest**
- **¼ tsp. salt**
- **¾ cup raisins**
- **¾ cup sweetened shredded coconut**
- **¾ cup chopped pecans**
- **¾ cup coarsely chopped red candied cherries**
- **1 cup heavy whipping cream, whipped and sweetened**

1. Line bottoms of 3 greased 9-in. round baking pans with parchment. Grease paper; set aside. Place egg whites in a large bowl; let stand at room temperature 30 minutes.
2. In another large bowl, cream butter and sugar until light and fluffy, 5-7 minutes. Beat in vanilla. In another bowl, whisk flour, baking powder and salt; add to creamed mixture alternately with milk, beating well after each addition. Beat egg whites until stiff peaks form; fold into batter. Transfer to prepared pans.
3. Bake at 325° until a toothpick inserted in the center comes out clean, 20-25 minutes. Cool for 10 minutes before removing from pans to wire racks; remove paper. Cool completely.
4. For filling, combine egg yolks and sugar in a large saucepan. Add butter; cook and stir over medium-low heat until sugar is dissolved and mixture thickens (do not boil). Remove from heat. Stir in bourbon, orange zest and salt. Fold in the raisins, coconut, pecans and cherries. Cool.
5. Place 1 cake layer on a serving plate; spread with a third of the filling. Repeat layers twice. Frost sides of cake with whipped cream. Refrigerate until serving.

1 PIECE: *677 cal., 36g fat (20g sat. fat), 167mg chol., 469mg sod., 81g carb. (58g sugars, 2g fiber), 8g pro.*

CHERRY PLUM SLAB PIE WITH WALNUT STREUSEL

I love to make desserts with fruit all summer! This one is great because you can quickly make pie for a crowd, plus the crumbly, nutty streusel is perfect with fruit. If you make your own pastry, you can easily roll it out to size. It's also easy with store-bought pie crust! I recommend stacking your two pie crusts on top of each other and then rolling them to the correct size.
—Elisabeth Larsen, Pleasant Grove, UT

PREP: 25 min. • **BAKE:** 50 min. + cooling
MAKES: 20 servings

- **1 lb. fresh sweet cherries, pitted**
- **4 medium red plums, thinly sliced**
- **½ cup sugar**
- **¼ cup cornstarch**
- **2 Tbsp. lemon juice**
- **Dough for double-crust pie**

TOPPING

- **½ cup old-fashioned oats**
- **½ cup chopped walnuts**
- **⅓ cup all-purpose flour**
- **¼ cup sugar**
- **¼ cup packed brown sugar**
- **1 tsp. ground cinnamon**
- **¼ tsp. salt**
- **½ cup cold unsalted butter**

1. Preheat oven to 375°. In a large bowl, combine cherries, plums, sugar, cornstarch and lemon juice; toss to coat.
2. On a lightly floured surface, roll dough into a 16x12-in. rectangle; transfer to an ungreased 13x9-in. baking dish. Trim even with rim of dish. Add filling. For topping, in a small bowl, mix oats, walnuts, flour, sugar, brown sugar, cinnamon and salt; cut in the butter until crumbly. Sprinkle over filling.
3. Bake until filling is bubbly and crust is golden brown, 50-55 minutes. Cool on a wire rack.

1 PIECE: *279 cal., 16g fat (9g sat. fat), 36mg chol., 155mg sod., 32g carb. (15g sugars, 2g fiber), 3g pro.*

DOUGH FOR DOUBLE-CRUST PIE: Combine 2½ cups all-purpose flour and ½ tsp. salt; cut in 1 cup cold butter until crumbly. Gradually add ⅓-⅔ cup ice water, tossing with a fork until dough holds together when pressed. Divide dough in half. Shape each into a disk; wrap and refrigerate 1 hour.

CHERRY PLUM SLAB PIE
WITH WALNUT STREUSEL

CAKES & PIES

VANILLA BEAN CUPCAKES

My 3-year-old son loves these! Tiny flecks of vanilla bean elevate the moist, tender cupcakes to special-occasion status.
—Alysha Braun, St. Catharines, ON

PREP: 30 min. • **BAKE:** 20 min. + cooling
MAKES: 1½ dozen

- **¾ cup unsalted butter, softened**
- **1¼ cups sugar**
- **2 large eggs, room temperature**
- **2 vanilla beans**
- **2 cups cake flour**
- **2 tsp. baking powder**
- **½ tsp. salt**
- **⅔ cup 2% milk**

FROSTING

- **1 pkg. (8 oz.) cream cheese, softened**
- **6 Tbsp. unsalted butter, softened**
- **1½ tsp. vanilla extract**
- **3 cups confectioners' sugar**
- **Assorted sprinkles and coarse sugar**

1. Preheat oven to 375°. Line 18 muffin cups with paper liners.
2. In a large bowl, cream butter and sugar until light and fluffy, 5-7 minutes. Add eggs, 1 at a time, beating well after each addition. Split vanilla beans lengthwise; using the tip of a sharp knife, scrape seeds from the center into creamed mixture. In another bowl, whisk flour, baking powder and salt; add to creamed mixture alternately with milk, beating well after each addition.
3. Fill prepared cups half full. Bake until a toothpick inserted in center comes out clean, 18-20 minutes. Cool in pans for 10 minutes before removing to wire racks to cool completely.
4. In a large bowl, beat cream cheese, butter and vanilla until blended. Gradually beat in confectioners' sugar until smooth. Frost cupcakes. Decorate with sprinkles and coarse sugar as desired. Refrigerate leftovers.
FREEZE OPTION: Freeze cooled cupcakes in resealable freezer containers. To use, thaw at room temperature. Frost as directed.

1 CUPCAKE: *266 cal., 13g fat (8g sat. fat), 56mg chol., 143mg sod., 36g carb. (24g sugars, 0 fiber), 3g pro.*

VANILLA BEAN CUPCAKES

PINEAPPLE POKE CAKE

This is a delicious dessert that's especially good on a hot day, but we like it year-round. With several store-bought ingredients, it's a snap to prepare any time.
—Sandra Etelamaki, Ishpeming, MI

PREP: 20 min. • **BAKE:** 25 min. + cooling
MAKES: 20 servings

- **1 pkg. yellow cake mix (regular size)**
- **1 pkg. (1 oz.) sugar-free instant vanilla pudding mix**
- **½ cup water**
- **2 large eggs, room temperature, lightly beaten**
- **½ cup egg substitute**
- **½ cup fat-free milk**
- **¼ cup unsweetened applesauce**
- **1 can (8 oz.) unsweetened crushed pineapple, undrained**
- **¼ cup packed brown sugar**

FROSTING

- **1½ cups cold fat-free milk**
- **1 pkg. (1 oz.) sugar-free instant vanilla pudding mix**
- **1 carton (8 oz.) frozen reduced-fat whipped topping, thawed**

1. In a bowl, combine the first 7 ingredients. Beat on medium speed for 2 minutes. Pour batter into a 13x9-in. baking pan coated with cooking spray.
2. Bake at 350° for 25-30 minutes or until a toothpick inserted in the center comes out clean.
3. Meanwhile, in a small saucepan, combine pineapple and brown sugar. Cook and stir until mixture comes to a boil. Boil until most of the liquid is evaporated, 4-5 minutes; cool slightly. Remove cake from the oven; place on a wire rack. Poke holes in warm cake with a fork. Spoon pineapple mixture evenly over cake; cool completely.
4. For frosting, in a small bowl, whisk milk and pudding mix for 2 minutes. Let stand until soft-set, about 2 minutes. Spread over cake. Spread whipped topping over pudding. Store in the refrigerator.
1 PIECE: *180 cal., 4g fat (2g sat. fat), 22mg chol., 313mg sod., 31g carb. (18g sugars, 1g fiber), 3g pro.*

(5i)

CLASSIC BUTTER PIE PASTRY

This all-butter pastry makes a flavorful, flaky pie crust that's easy to handle and bakes up golden brown and beautiful. It's just like Mom's—only better!
—Taste of Home *Test Kitchen*

PREP: 10 min. + chilling
MAKES: pastry for one 9-in. pie

INGREDIENTS FOR SINGLE-CRUST PIE
- **1¼ cups all-purpose flour**
- **¼ tsp. salt**
- **½ cup cold butter, cubed**
- **3 to 4 Tbsp. ice water**

INGREDIENTS FOR DOUBLE-CRUST PIE
- **2½ cups all-purpose flour**
- **½ tsp. salt**
- **1 cup cold butter, cubed**
- **⅓ to ⅔ cup ice water**

1. Combine flour and salt; cut in butter until crumbly. Gradually add ice water, tossing with a fork until the dough holds together when pressed.
2. Shape dough into a disk for a single-crust pie; for a double-crust pie, divide dough in half, with 1 piece slightly larger than the other. Shape into 2 disks. Wrap and refrigerate 1 hour or overnight.
On a lightly floured surface, roll 1 disk of dough to a ⅛-in.-thick circle; transfer to a 9-in. pie plate.
FOR A SINGLE-CRUST PIE: Trim crust to ½ in. beyond rim of plate; flute edge. Fill or bake according to recipe directions.
FOR A DOUBLE-CRUST PIE: Add the filling to crust. Roll remaining dough to a ⅛-in.-thick circle. Place over filling. Trim, seal and flute edge. Cut slits in top. Bake according to recipe directions.
1 PIECE (⅛ RECIPE) SINGLE-CRUST PASTRY: *173 cal., 12g fat (7g sat. fat), 31mg chol., 165mg sod., 15g carb. (0 sugars, 1g fiber), 2g pro.*

MAPLE PECAN PIE

MAPLE PECAN PIE

Our Vermont maple syrup can't be beat, and this is one of my favorite pies. It's also quick and easy to make.
—*Mildred Wescom, Belvidere, VT*

PREP: 10 min. • **BAKE:** 40 min. + cooling
MAKES: 8 servings

- **Dough for single-crust pie (9 in.)**
- **3 large eggs, room temperature**
- **½ cup sugar**
- **1 cup maple syrup**
- **3 Tbsp. butter, melted**
- **½ tsp. vanilla extract**
- **¼ tsp. salt**
- **2 cups pecan halves**
- **Whipped cream, optional**

1. Preheat oven to 375°. On a lightly floured surface, roll dough to a ⅛-in.-thick circle; transfer to a 9-in. pie plate. Trim crust to ½ in. beyond rim of plate; flute edge. Refrigerate while preparing filling.
2. In a bowl, whisk eggs and sugar until smooth. Add maple syrup, butter, vanilla, salt and pecans. Pour into crust.
3. Bake until a knife inserted in the center comes out clean, 30-40 minutes. Cool on a wire rack for 1 hour. If desired, top pie with whipped cream to serve. Store in the refrigerator.
1 PIECE: *561 cal., 35g fat (12g sat. fat), 111mg chol., 294mg sod., 58g carb. (38g sugars, 3g fiber), 7g pro.*

GRANDMA'S APPLE CAKE

GRANDMA'S APPLE CAKE

My husband's grandma's apple cake recipe is perfect for all your fall gatherings. With lightly spiced apples and a sweet glaze, each slice is comforting.
—Zainab Storms, Damascus, MD

PREP: 30 min. • **BAKE:** 55 min. + cooling
MAKES: 20 servings

- 3 **cups all-purpose flour**
- 1 **tsp. baking soda**
- 1 **tsp. kosher salt**
- 1 **tsp. ground cinnamon**
- ¼ **tsp. ground nutmeg**
- ¼ **tsp. ground ginger**
- 1½ **cups vegetable or canola oil**
- 2 **cups sugar**
- 3 **large eggs, room temperature**
- 2 **tsp. vanilla extract**
- 1 **tsp. fresh lemon juice**
- 3 **medium apples, peeled and thinly sliced**
- 1 **cup chopped walnuts, toasted**

GLAZE
- 1 **cup confectioners' sugar**
- 2 **tsp. fresh lemon juice**

1. Preheat oven to 300°. Line bottom of a 10-in. springform pan or a 13x9-in. baking pan with parchment; grease parchment. In a bowl, whisk together flour and the next 5 ingredients. In a large bowl, beat oil, sugar and eggs until pale and slightly thick, about 2 minutes. Beat in vanilla extract and lemon juice. Add dry ingredients; stir just until moistened. Fold in apples and walnuts (batter will be thick).

2. Transfer to prepared pan. Bake until a toothpick inserted in center comes out clean, 55- 60 minutes. Cool cake in pan on a wire rack.

3. For glaze, mix confectioners' sugar and lemon juice; drizzle over cake.

1 PIECE: *378 cal., 22g fat (2g sat. fat), 28mg chol., 170mg sod., 44g carb. (28g sugars, 1g fiber), 4g pro.*

CRAN-APPLE PRALINE GINGERBREAD

Start with a spice-rich batter baked atop apples and cranberries in a creamy caramel sauce, then invert when done for a topsy-turvy dessert that's a real beauty. The old-time holiday taste will delight family and friends!
—Jeanne Holt, St. Paul, MN

PREP: 25 min. • **BAKE:** 30 min. + cooling
MAKES: 8 servings

- ⅔ **cup fat-free caramel ice cream topping**
- 2 **medium tart apples, peeled and thinly sliced**
- ⅔ **cup fresh or frozen cranberries**
- ¼ **cup butter, softened**
- ¼ **cup sugar**
- 1 **large egg, room temperature**
- 6 **Tbsp. molasses**
- ¼ **cup unsweetened applesauce**
- 1½ **cups all-purpose flour**
- ¾ **tsp. baking soda**
- ½ **tsp. ground ginger**
- ½ **tsp. apple pie spice**
- ¼ **tsp. salt**
- ¼ **cup hot water**

YOGURT CREAM
- ¾ **cup reduced-fat whipped topping**
- ½ **cup fat-free vanilla yogurt**

1. Coat a 9-in. round baking pan with cooking spray. Pour caramel topping into pan and tilt to coat bottom evenly. Arrange the apples and cranberries in a single layer over caramel.

2. In a large bowl, beat butter and sugar until crumbly, about 2 minutes. Add egg; mix well. Beat in molasses and applesauce (mixture may appear curdled). Combine the flour, baking soda, ginger, apple pie spice and salt; add to butter mixture just until moistened. Stir in hot water.

3. Pour over fruit; smooth top. Bake at 350° for 30-35 minutes or until a toothpick inserted in the center comes out clean. Cool for 10 minutes before inverting onto a serving plate. Combine whipped topping and yogurt; serve with gingerbread.

1 PIECE WITH 2 TBSP. YOGURT CREAM: *289 cal., 7g fat (5g sat. fat), 42mg chol., 284mg sod., 53g carb. (28g sugars, 2g fiber), 4g pro.*

LADY BALTIMORE CAKE

I first made this cake for my father's birthday, and now it is the only cake that he requests. It has complex flavors and is very unique.
—Cleo Gonske, Redding, CA

PREP: 30 min. + standing
BAKE: 20 min. + cooling • **MAKES:** 16 servings

- **1⅔ cups raisins, chopped**
- **8 dried figs, finely chopped**
- **½ cup brandy**

CAKE

- **2½ cups all-purpose flour**
- **2 cups sugar**
- **2 tsp. grated orange zest**
- **1 tsp. baking powder**
- **½ tsp. baking soda**
- **⅛ tsp. salt**
- **1⅓ cups buttermilk**
- **½ cup butter, softened**
- **1 tsp. vanilla extract**
- **4 large egg whites, room temperature**

FROSTING

- **2 cups butter, softened**
- **6 cups confectioners' sugar, sifted**
- **2 tsp. vanilla extract**
- **¼ to ⅓ cup heavy whipping cream**
- **1 cup finely chopped pecans, toasted**

1. In a small bowl, combine raisins and figs. Add brandy; toss to combine. Let stand, covered, at room temperature until the brandy is absorbed, about 2 hours, stirring occasionally.
2. Preheat oven to 350°. Line bottoms of 3 greased 8-in. round cake pans with parchment; grease paper.
3. In a large bowl, mix flour, sugar, orange zest, baking powder, baking soda and salt until blended. Add buttermilk, butter and vanilla; beat on low speed just until the dry ingredients are moistened, about 30 seconds. Beat on medium for 2 minutes. Add egg whites; beat 2 minutes longer.
4. Transfer batter to prepared pans. Bake until a toothpick inserted in center comes out clean, 20-25 minutes. Cool in pans for 10 minutes before removing to wire racks to cool completely.
5. In a large bowl, cream butter until fluffy. Gradually beat in confectioners' sugar. Beat in vanilla and enough cream to reach desired consistency. For filling, remove 1 cup frosting to a small bowl; stir in pecans and raisin mixture.
6. Place 1 cake layer on a serving plate; spread with half the filling. Add another cake layer; top with remaining filling. Add remaining cake layer; spread remaining frosting over top and sides of cake.
NOTE: To toast nuts, bake in a shallow pan in a 350° oven for 5-10 minutes or cook in a skillet over low heat until lightly browned, stirring occasionally.
1 PIECE: *745 cal., 36g fat (20g sat. fat), 81mg chol., 373mg sod., 102g carb. (82g sugars, 2g fiber), 5g pro.*

BROWNIE KISS CUPCAKES

It's always fun to prepare individual brownie cupcakes with a chocolaty surprise inside. My goddaughter, Cara, asks me to make them for her birthday to share at school. This year, she requested 32. I later found out she only needed 27 for her class...wonder where the other five went!
—Pamela Lute, Mercersburg, PA

TAKES: 30 min. • **MAKES:** 9 servings

- **⅓ cup butter, softened**
- **1 cup sugar**
- **2 large eggs, room temperature**
- **1 tsp. vanilla extract**
- **¾ cup all-purpose flour**
- **½ cup baking cocoa**
- **¼ tsp. baking powder**
- **¼ tsp. salt**
- **9 milk chocolate kisses**

1. Preheat oven to 350°. In a large bowl, cream butter and sugar until light and fluffy, 5-7 minutes. Beat in eggs and vanilla. Combine the flour, cocoa, baking powder and salt; gradually add to the creamed mixture and mix well.
2. Fill paper- or foil-lined muffin cups two-thirds full. Place a chocolate kiss, tip end down, in the center of each.
3. Bake until top of brownie springs back when lightly touched, 20-25 minutes.
1 CUPCAKE: *239 cal., 10g fat (5g sat. fat), 66mg chol., 163mg sod., 36g carb. (24g sugars, 1g fiber), 4g pro.*

BROWNIE KISS CUPCAKES

PEANUT BUTTER SILK PIE

PEANUT BUTTER SILK PIE

My son wanted pies at his wedding, and this was one of his requests.
—Lee Steinmetz, Lansing, MI

PREP: 10 min. + chilling • **MAKES:** 8 servings

- ¾ **cup peanut butter**
- 4 **oz. cream cheese, softened**
- 1 **cup confectioners' sugar**
- 1 **carton (8 oz.) frozen whipped topping, thawed**
- 1 **graham cracker crust (9 in.)**
- **Salted chopped peanuts**
- **Optional: Additional whipped topping, chocolate sauce and peanut butter ice cream topping**

In a large bowl, beat the peanut butter, cream cheese and confectioners' sugar until smooth. Fold in whipped topping; pour into prepared crust. Refrigerate at least 2 hours before serving. Sprinkle with peanuts. If desired, top with additional whipped topping, chocolate sauce and peanut butter ice cream topping.

1 PIECE: *434 cal., 27g fat (11g sat. fat), 16mg chol., 276mg sod., 40g carb. (29g sugars, 2g fiber), 8g pro.*

PUMPKIN PIE TARTLETS WITH MAPLE PECAN CRUST

PUMPKIN PIE TARTLETS WITH MAPLE PECAN CRUST

I came up with this recipe after discovering I had multiple food sensitivities that were affecting my health. Learning to eat healthier has dramatically improved my health. It was important to me to still participate in family holidays and events where food was being served, so I began developing recipes that would be safe for me, but that others would enjoy, too. These mini pumpkin pie tarts are so delicious, you would never suspect that they're free of gluten, egg and dairy!
—Chantale Michaud, Guelph, ON

PREP: 45 min. + cooling
BAKE: 35 min+ cooling • **MAKES:** 1½ dozen

- 2 **cups old-fashioned oats**
- 4 **cups chopped pecans**
- ½ **cup maple syrup**
- 2 **tsp. ground cinnamon**
- 1 **tsp. sea salt**
- 1 **tsp. vanilla extract**
- ¼ **tsp. ground cloves**

FILLING

- ½ **cup maple syrup**
- 3 **Tbsp. cornstarch**
- 2¼ **cups canned pumpkin or homemade pumpkin puree**
- ¼ **cup cream of coconut, warmed**
- 2 **tsp. vanilla extract**
- 2 **tsp. ground cinnamon**
- ½ **tsp. sea salt**
- ½ **tsp. ground nutmeg**
- ¼ **tsp. ground ginger**
- ¼ **tsp. ground cloves**

TOPPING

- ½ **cup chopped pecans**
- 2 **tsp. maple syrup**
- **Dash sea salt**

1. Preheat oven to 350°. Process oats in a food processor until a fine powder forms. Add pecans; pulse until nuts are chopped. Add next 5 ingredients; pulse until mixture is moistened. Remove from processor.

2. Fill 18 greased muffin cups with ⅓ cup oat mixture each. Using a wet 1 Tbsp. measure, press mixture onto bottom and up sides of muffin cups. Bake until lightly browned, about 10 minutes. Cool on a wire rack.

3. For filling, whisk together maple syrup and cornstarch. In another bowl, mix remaining filling ingredients, then add maple syrup mixture. Spoon about 3 Tbsp. into each crust.

4. Combine topping ingredients; spoon about 1 tsp. onto each tartlet. Bake until dark golden and set, 35-40 minutes. Cool 10 minutes before removing the tartlets to a wire rack; cool 1 hour. If desired, refrigerate before serving.

1 TARTLET: *302 cal., 21g fat (2g sat. fat), 0 chol., 173mg sod., 28g carb. (16g sugars, 5g fiber), 4g pro.*

BANANA FUDGE PIE

This dessert, which is like a banana sundae, is both light and good. I make it often.
—Myra Innes, Auburn, KS

PREP: 20 min. • **BAKE:** 30 min. + chilling **MAKES:** 8 servings

- 1 **sheet refrigerated pie crust**
- ½ **cup miniature semisweet chocolate chips, melted**
- 3 **cups whipped topping, divided**
- 2 **large eggs**
- ¼ **cup sugar**
- 2 **to 3 bananas, sliced**
- **Additional miniature chocolate chips, optional**

1. Unroll crust into a 9-in. pie plate; flute edge. In a large bowl, combine melted chocolate, 1 cup whipped topping, eggs and sugar. Mix well. Pour into crust. Bake at 350° for 30 minutes. Cool 10 minutes, then refrigerate for 1 hour.
2. Layer sliced bananas over pie and top with remaining whipped topping. Sprinkle miniature chocolate chips on top if desired. Chill until serving.
1 PIECE: *317 cal., 16g fat (10g sat. fat), 58mg chol., 117mg sod., 39g carb. (22g sugars, 1g fiber), 3g pro.*

BANANA FUDGE PIE

HUCKLEBERRY CHEESE PIE

HUCKLEBERRY CHEESE PIE

To us Idahoans, huckleberries are a special treasure! We've enjoyed this recipe a lot, and serve it as a special treat whenever we have out-of-state guests.
—Pat Kuper, McCall, ID

PREP: 30 min. • **BAKE:** 20 min. + chilling **MAKES:** 10 servings

BUTTER CRUNCH CRUST
- 1 **cup all-purpose flour**
- ¼ **cup packed brown sugar**
- ½ **cup finely chopped nuts**
- ½ **cup cold butter**

CHEESE FILLING
- 1 **pkg. (8 oz.) cream cheese, softened**
- ¾ **cup confectioners' sugar**
- 1 **tsp. vanilla extract**
- 1 **cup whipped cream or 1 cup whipped topping**

FRUIT TOPPING
- ½ **cup sugar**
- 4½ **tsp. cornstarch**
- **Dash salt**
- ½ **cup water**
- 2 **cups fresh huckleberries or blueberries, divided**
- 1½ **tsp. butter**
- **Additional whipped cream, optional**

1. In a bowl, combine the flour, brown sugar and nuts. Cut in the butter until mixture resembles coarse crumbs. Spread on baking sheet; bake at 400° for 20 minutes, stirring occasionally.
2. Remove from oven. While mixture is still hot, press into a 9-in. pie plate, forming a pie shell. Cool completely.
3. For cheese filling, beat cream cheese, sugar and vanilla until smooth; gently fold in whipped cream. Pour or spoon filling into cooled crust; refrigerate.
4. For topping, combine sugar, cornstarch and salt in saucepan. Stir in water until smooth; add 1 cup berries. Bring to a boil. Cook and stir for 1-2 minutes or until thickened. Add butter and the remaining berries. Cool; pour over cheese filling. If desired, top with additional whipped cream.
1 PIECE: *379 cal., 23g fat (12g sat. fat), 56mg chol., 192mg sod., 41g carb. (28g sugars, 1g fiber), 5g pro.*

TRIPLE BERRY MINI PIES

I came up with these berry hand pies one summer day when I had an abundance of fresh blueberries, gooseberries and strawberries. The blend of flavors makes for a mouthwatering treat for breakfast, dessert or anytime in between! I typically make my crust from scratch. Raspberries can be substituted for the gooseberries.
—Brigette Kutschma, Lake Geneva, WI

PREP: 20 min. + cooling • **BAKE:** 15 min. **MAKES:** 8 servings

- **1½ cups fresh or frozen unsweetened blueberries, divided**
- **½ cup fresh raspberries or gooseberries**
- **⅓ cup sugar**
- **2 Tbsp. cornstarch**
- **1 cup sliced fresh strawberries or frozen unsweetened sliced strawberries**
- **2 Tbsp. butter**
- **2 sheets refrigerated pie crust**

1. In a small saucepan, combine ½ cup blueberries, raspberries, sugar and cornstarch. Cook and stir until mixture starts to thicken, about 5 minutes. Remove from heat; stir in strawberries, butter and remaining 1 cup blueberries. Transfer the berry mixture to a bowl; cool to room temperature.
2. Preheat oven to 425°. On a work surface, unroll crusts. Cut 8 circles with a 4-in. biscuit or cookie cutter. Press crusts onto bottom and up sides of ungreased muffin cups. Spoon berry mixture into muffin cups. Bake until filling is bubbly and crust golden brown, 12-15 minutes. Cool in pan 5 minutes; remove to wire racks to cool.
1 MINI PIE: *211 cal., 10g fat (5g sat. fat), 13mg chol., 123mg sod., 30g carb. (13g sugars, 2g fiber), 1g pro.*

TRIPLE BERRY MINI PIES

APRICOT UPSIDE-DOWN CAKE

APRICOT UPSIDE-DOWN CAKE

My Aunt Anne, who is a great cook, gave me a taste of this golden cake and I couldn't believe how delicious it was. Apricots give it a unique and attractive twist.
—Ruth Ann Stelfox, Raymond, AB

PREP: 30 min. • **BAKE:** 35 min. + cooling **MAKES:** 9 servings

- **2 large eggs, separated**
- **2 cans (15 oz. each) apricot halves**
- **¼ cup butter, cubed**
- **½ cup packed brown sugar**
- **⅔ cup cake flour**
- **¾ tsp. baking powder**
- **¼ tsp. salt**
- **⅔ cup sugar**

1. Place egg whites in a small bowl; let stand at room temperature 30 minutes. Preheat oven to 350°. Drain apricots, reserving 3 Tbsp. syrup (discard remaining syrup); set aside.
2. Place butter in a 9-in. square baking dish. Place in oven until butter is melted, 3-4 minutes; swirl carefully to coat evenly. Sprinkle with brown sugar. Arrange apricot halves in a single layer over brown sugar, cut side up.
3. In a small bowl, whisk flour, baking powder and salt. In a large bowl, beat egg yolks until slightly thickened. Gradually add sugar, beating on high speed until thick and lemon-colored. Beat in reserved apricot syrup. Fold in flour mixture.
4. With clean beaters, beat egg whites on medium speed until stiff peaks form. Fold into batter. Spoon over apricots. Bake until a toothpick inserted in center comes out clean, 35-40 minutes. Cool 10 minutes before inverting cake onto a serving plate. Serve warm.
1 PIECE: *272 cal., 6g fat (4g sat. fat), 55mg chol., 162mg sod., 53g carb. (44g sugars, 1g fiber), 3g pro.*

MAMA'S COCONUT PIE

My mama showed me how to make this buttermilk coconut pie about 40 years ago, and her mama showed her how to make it. I was 6 when Mawmaw passed away, but I can still remember her cooking in the kitchen in her beautiful cotton dresses dusted with flour. I am honored to teach my daughter how to make this pie.
—Lisa Allen, Joppa, AL

PREP: 20 min. • **BAKE:** 50 min.
MAKES: 8 servings

- **Dough for single-crust pie**
- **1 cup sugar**
- **3 large eggs, room temperature**
- **½ cup buttermilk**
- **½ cup unsalted butter, melted and cooled**
- **2 Tbsp. all-purpose flour**
- **1½ tsp. vanilla extract**
- **Dash salt**
- **1½ cups sweetened shredded coconut**

1. Preheat oven to 325°. On a lightly floured surface, roll dough to a ⅛-in.-thick circle; transfer to a 9-in. pie plate. Trim to ½ in. beyond rim of plate; flute edge. Place pie plate on a rimmed baking sheet.
2. In a large bowl, beat the sugar, eggs, buttermilk, melted butter, flour, vanilla and salt until blended. Stir in shredded coconut. Pour into crust. Bake until top is light golden brown and center is almost set, 50-60 minutes. Cool on a wire rack; serve or refrigerate within 2 hours.
1 PIECE: *550 cal., 35g fat (23g sat. fat), 142mg chol., 318mg sod., 54g carb. (34g sugars, 1g fiber), 6g pro.*

MAMA'S COCONUT PIE

TUSCAN SUN ORANGE CRANBERRY CAKE

This recipe came about through much trial and error. Growing up, my family used farina flour in desserts, and I thought it would lend a nice texture to this cake. It's an old-world Italian-style cake, delicious but not too sweet. The orange-cranberry combination is perfect!
—Ninette Holbrook, Orlando, FL

PREP: 25 min. • **BAKE:** 20 min. + cooling
MAKES: 8 servings

- **⅓ cup sugar**
- **⅓ cup canola oil**
- **2 large eggs, room temperature**
- **1 Tbsp. grated orange zest**
- **1 Tbsp. orange juice**
- **⅓ cup all-purpose flour**
- **⅓ cup cream of wheat or farina flour**
- **½ tsp. salt**
- **¼ tsp. baking powder**
- **⅓ cup dried cranberries, chopped**
- **¼ cup sliced almonds**

ORANGE GLAZE
- **¾ cup confectioners' sugar**
- **1 Tbsp. orange juice**
- **2 tsp. 2% milk**
- **Grated orange zest, optional**

1. Preheat oven to 350°. Grease an 8-in. round baking pan.
2. In a large bowl, beat sugar, oil, eggs, orange zest and juice until well blended. In another bowl, whisk flour, cream of wheat, salt and baking powder; gradually beat into oil mixture. Stir in cranberries.
3. Transfer to prepared pan; sprinkle with almonds. Bake until a toothpick inserted in center comes out clean, 20-25 minutes.
4. Combine glaze ingredients; pour over warm cake. Cool 10 minutes before serving. If desired, sprinkle with orange zest.
1 PIECE: *263 cal., 12g fat (1g sat. fat), 47mg chol., 182mg sod., 36g carb. (25g sugars, 1g fiber), 4g pro.*

TEST KITCHEN TIP

The outer peel of a citrus fruit has the best flavor. Be careful not to grate too deeply into the peel, as the light colored inner part, the pith, tastes bitter.

MAPLE-GLAZED APPLE PIE

Even though we've lived in Florida for three years, I still feel like a Vermonter. My parents send us a bushel of Vermont apples each fall, and we try to visit them in the spring to do some sugaring.
—Patricia Putnam, Lakeland, FL

PREP: 25 min. • **BAKE:** 55 min.
MAKES: 8 servings

Pastry for double-crust pie (9 in.)
- 6 **cups thinly sliced peeled apples, divided**
- ½ **cup sugar**
- ¼ **cup packed brown sugar**
- ½ **cup crushed gingersnaps**
- ½ **tsp. ground cinnamon**
- ½ **cup chopped walnuts or pecans**
- ¼ **cup butter, melted**
- ¼ **cup maple syrup**

1. Line a 9-in. pie pan with the bottom crust. Place half of the apples in the crust; set aside.
2. In a bowl, combine sugars, gingersnaps, cinnamon, nuts and butter; sprinkle half over apples in crust. Top with remaining apples and the sugar mixture. Roll out remaining pastry to fit top of pie. Cut a few slits in the top and place over apples; seal. Cover loosely with foil and bake at 375° for 35 minutes.
3. Meanwhile, bring syrup to a gentle boil in a small saucepan. Remove pie from oven; remove foil and brush hot syrup over pie and into vents. Return pie to oven and bake, uncovered, 20 minutes longer. Serve warm.
1 PIECE: *525 cal., 25g fat (10g sat. fat), 25mg chol., 325mg sod., 73g carb. (41g sugars, 2g fiber), 5g pro.*

MOCHA HAZELNUT TORTE

MOCHA HAZELNUT TORTE

I make this pretty cake on birthdays and other special occasions because it looks and tastes so amazing. The combination of mild hazelnut and coffee flavors is impossible to resist.
—Christina Pope, Speedway, IN

PREP: 35 min. • **BAKE:** 25 min. + cooling
MAKES: 16 servings

- ¾ **cup butter, softened**
- 1¼ **cups packed brown sugar**
- 1 **cup sugar**
- 3 **large eggs, room temperature**
- 3 **oz. unsweetened chocolate, melted and cooled slightly**
- 2 **tsp. vanilla extract**
- 2¼ **cups all-purpose flour**
- 1 **Tbsp. instant espresso powder**
- 1 **tsp. baking soda**
- ½ **tsp. baking powder**
- ¼ **tsp. salt**
- 1½ **cups 2% milk**

FROSTING
- 1 **cup butter, softened**
- 1 **cup Nutella**
- 4 **cups confectioners' sugar**
- 1 **tsp. vanilla extract**
- 3 **to 4 Tbsp. 2% milk**
- ½ **cup chopped hazelnuts, toasted**

1. Preheat oven to 350°. Line the bottoms of 2 greased 9-in. round baking pans with parchment; grease parchment.
2. In a large bowl, cream butter and sugars until light and fluffy, 5-7 minutes. Add eggs, 1 at a time, beating well after each addition. Beat in melted chocolate and vanilla. In another bowl, whisk the flour, espresso powder, baking soda, baking powder and salt; add to creamed mixture alternately with milk, beating well after each addition.
3. Transfer batter to prepared pans. Bake until a toothpick inserted in center comes out clean, 25-30 minutes. Cool in pans for 10 minutes before removing to wire racks; remove parchment. Cool completely.
4. For frosting, in a large bowl, beat butter and Nutella until blended. Gradually beat in confectioners' sugar, vanilla and enough milk to reach desired consistency.
5. Place 1 cake layer on a serving plate; spread with 1 cup frosting. Sprinkle with ¼ cup hazelnuts. Top with remaining cake layer. Frost top and sides with remaining frosting. Sprinkle with remaining hazelnuts.
NOTE: To toast nuts, bake in a shallow pan in a 350° oven for 5-10 minutes or cook in a skillet over low heat until lightly browned, stirring occasionally.
1 PIECE: *639 cal., 32g fat (16g sat. fat), 94mg chol., 311mg sod., 88g carb. (69g sugars, 2g fiber), 6g pro.*

PUMPKIN CRUNCH PARFAITS
PAGE 222

Just Desserts

It wouldn't be Taste of Home Annual Recipes *without a third dessert chapter—devoted to all things rich and creamy, crisp and frosty. Bring on more of the good stuff!*

CHECK OUT THESE SPECIALTIES

Fried Ice Cream Dessert Bars p. 211

Butter Pecan Cheesecake p. 212

Peach Bavarian p. 213

Almost It's-It Ice Cream Sandwiches p. 216

Rainbow Sherbet Angel Food Cake p. 219

JUST DESSERTS

5i

ROSE WATER RICE PUDDING

Rose water rice pudding is a popular Middle Eastern treat. Pomegranate seeds and chopped pistachios add a simple yet elegant touch to this floral Lebanese specialty.
—Michael & Mathil Chebat, Lake Ridge, VA

PREP: 10 min. • **COOK:** 45 min. + chilling • **MAKES:** 14 servings

- **4 cups water**
- **2 cups uncooked long grain rice**
- **4 cups half-and-half cream**
- **1½ cups sugar**
- **1 to 2 tsp. rose water**
- **Optional: Pomegranate seeds and chopped pistachios**

In a heavy saucepan, combine water and rice; bring to a boil over medium heat. Reduce heat; cover and simmer until the water is absorbed, about 15 minutes. Add cream and sugar; bring to a boil. Reduce heat; simmer, uncovered, until slightly thickened, 30-40 minutes. Stir in rose water. Refrigerate until chilled, at least 2 hours. Stir in additional cream to reach desired consistency. If desired, top with pomegranate seeds and pistachios.
½ CUP: *281 cal., 7g fat (5g sat. fat), 34mg chol., 35mg sod., 47g carb. (24g sugars, 0 fiber), 4g pro.*

ROSE WATER RICE PUDDING

PARISIAN SIPPING CHOCOLATE

PARISIAN SIPPING CHOCOLATE

One of my fondest memories of Paris was sipping a cup of thick, dark hot chocolate at one of their patisseries. Parisian hot chocolate is velvety smooth, rich and decadent, and almost the consistency of a molten chocolate bar. It is meant to be sipped slowly and savored. I bought Parisian espresso cups so we could enjoy this at home.
—Darlene Brenden, Salem, OR

TAKES: 15 min. • **MAKES:** 2 servings

- **⅔ cup 2% milk**
- **2 Tbsp. heavy whipping cream**
- **1 tsp. brown sugar**
- **½ tsp. confectioners' sugar**
- **⅛ tsp. instant espresso powder, optional**
- **2 oz. dark chocolate candy bar, chopped**
- **Whipped cream and chocolate shavings**

In a small saucepan, heat milk, cream, brown sugar, confectioners' sugar and, if desired, espresso powder over medium heat until bubbles form around sides of pan. Remove from heat; whisk in dark chocolate until melted. Serve in mugs with whipped cream and chocolate shavings.
½ CUP: *226 cal., 16g fat (10g sat. fat), 27mg chol., 43mg sod., 24g carb. (22g sugars, 2g fiber), 5g pro.*

TEST KITCHEN TIP

You can use instant coffee powder instead of espresso powder. You also could simply omit the espresso powder, but it intensifies the chocolate flavor.

FRIED ICE CREAM DESSERT BARS

Fried ice cream is such a delicious treat, but it can be a hassle to make the individual servings. This recipe gives you the same fabulous flavor in an easy and convenient bar form.
—Andrea Price, Grafton, WI

PREP: 25 min. + freezing
COOK: 5 min. + cooling • **MAKES:** 16 servings

- ½ **cup butter, cubed**
- 2 **cups crushed cornflakes**
- 1½ **tsp. ground cinnamon**
- 3 **Tbsp. sugar**
- 1¾ **cups heavy whipping cream**
- ¼ **cup evaporated milk**
- ⅛ **tsp. salt**
- 1 **can (14 oz.) sweetened condensed milk**
- 2 **tsp. vanilla extract**
- **Optional: Honey, whipped cream and maraschino cherries**

1. In a large skillet, melt the butter over medium heat. Add crushed cornflakes and cinnamon; cook and stir until golden brown, about 5 minutes. Remove from heat; stir in sugar. Cool completely.
2. In a large bowl, beat cream, evaporated milk and salt until it begins to thicken. Gradually beat in condensed milk and vanilla until thickened.
3. Sprinkle half of the cornflakes onto bottom of a greased 9-in. square baking pan. Pour filling over crust; sprinkle with remaining cornflakes. Cover and freeze overnight. Cut into bars. If desired, serve with honey, whipped cream and cherries.
1 BAR: *276 cal., 18g fat (11g sat. fat), 55mg chol., 187mg sod., 27g carb. (18g sugars, 0 fiber), 4g pro.*

HOLIDAY PRETZEL SALAD

I gave a classic summer salad a holiday twist by making green, white and red layers. The combination of salty, sweet, creamy and fruity is always a hit!
—Renee Conneally, Northville, MI

PREP: 35 min. + chilling • **BAKE:** 10 min.
MAKES: 15 servings

- ¾ **cup butter, melted**
- 3 **Tbsp. sugar**
- 2 **cups crushed pretzels**

LIME LAYER

- 1 **cup boiling water**
- 1 **pkg. (3 oz.) lime gelatin**
- 1 **pkg. (8 oz.) cream cheese, softened**
- 1 **carton (8 oz.) frozen whipped topping, thawed**
- 3 **to 5 drops green food coloring, optional**

CREAM CHEESE LAYER

- 1 **pkg. (8 oz.) cream cheese, softened**
- ½ **cup sugar**
- 1 **carton (8 oz.) frozen whipped topping, thawed**

STRAWBERRY LAYER

- 2 **cups boiling water**
- 2 **pkg. (3 oz. each) strawberry gelatin**
- 4 **cups sliced fresh strawberries**
- **Miniature pretzels, optional**

1. Preheat oven to 350°. Mix melted butter and sugar; stir in pretzels. Press onto bottom of an ungreased 13x9-in. baking dish. Bake 10 minutes. Cool completely on a wire rack.
2. Meanwhile, for lime layer, in a large bowl, add boiling water to lime gelatin; stir 2 minutes to completely dissolve. Refrigerate until partially set, about 1 hour. In a bowl, beat cream cheese until smooth. Add the cooled lime gelatin mixture; beat until smooth. Fold in whipped topping; if desired, add green food coloring. Spread over crust. Refrigerate until set but not firm, 25-30 minutes.
3. For cream cheese layer, in a bowl, beat cream cheese and sugar until smooth. Fold in whipped topping. Spread over lime layer. Refrigerate until set.
4. For strawberry layer, in a large bowl, add boiling water to strawberry gelatin; stir for 2 minutes to completely dissolve. Refrigerate until partially set, about 1 hour. Stir in strawberries. Gently spoon over cream cheese layer. Refrigerate, covered, until firm, 2-4 hours. To serve, cut into squares. If desired, top with additional whipped topping and miniature pretzels.
1 SERVING: *407 cal., 25g fat (17g sat. fat), 55mg chol., 368mg sod., 40g carb. (29g sugars, 1g fiber), 5g pro.*

HOLIDAY PRETZEL SALAD

BUTTER PECAN CHEESECAKE

Fall always makes me yearn for this pecan cheesecake, but it's delicious in any season. You'll want to put it on your list of favorite holiday desserts.
—Laura Sylvester, Mechanicsville, VA

PREP: 30 min. • **BAKE:** 70 min. + chilling
MAKES: 16 servings

- **1½ cups graham cracker crumbs**
- **½ cup finely chopped pecans**
- **⅓ cup sugar**
- **⅓ cup butter, melted**

FILLING

- **3 pkg. (8 oz. each) cream cheese, softened**
- **1½ cups sugar**
- **2 cups sour cream**
- **1 tsp. vanilla extract**
- **½ tsp. butter flavoring**
- **3 large eggs, room temperature, lightly beaten**
- **1 cup finely chopped pecans**

1. Preheat oven to 325°. In a large bowl, combine the graham cracker crumbs, pecans, sugar and butter; set aside ⅓ cup for topping. Press remaining crumb mixture onto the bottom and 1 in. up the sides of a greased 9-in. springform pan.

2. Place springform pan on a double thickness of heavy-duty foil (about 18 in. square). Securely wrap foil around pan.
3. In a large bowl, beat cream cheese and sugar until smooth. Beat in the sour cream, vanilla and butter flavoring. Add eggs; beat on low speed just until combined. Fold in the pecans. Pour into crust; sprinkle with reserved crumb mixture. Place springform pan in a large baking pan; add 1 in. of hot water to larger pan.
4. Bake until the center is almost set, 70-80 minutes. Remove springform pan from water bath. Cool on a wire rack for 10 minutes. Carefully run a knife around edge of pan to loosen; cool 1 hour longer. Refrigerate overnight, covering when completely cooled. Remove sides of pan.
1 PIECE: *456 cal., 33g fat (16g sat. fat), 116mg chol., 224mg sod., 33g carb. (27g sugars, 1g fiber), 7g pro.*

BUTTER PECAN CHEESECAKE

5i

JAZZY GELATIN

This colorful gelatin is loaded with mandarin oranges and crushed pineapple. It's so refreshing that guests won't be able to refrain from seconds.
—Taste of Home Test Kitchen

PREP: 10 min. + chilling • **MAKES:** 12 servings

- **1 pkg. (6 oz.) orange gelatin**
- **2 cups boiling water**
- **1 cup ice cubes**
- **1 can (15 oz.) mandarin oranges, drained**
- **1 can (8 oz.) unsweetened crushed pineapple, undrained**
- **1 can (6 oz.) frozen orange juice concentrate, thawed**
- **Optional: Green grapes and fresh mint**

1. In a large bowl, dissolve gelatin in boiling water. Add ice cubes, oranges, pineapple and orange juice concentrate. Pour into a 6-cup ring mold coated with cooking spray. Refrigerate overnight or until firm.
2. Just before serving, unmold onto a serving plate. Fill center with grapes and garnish with mint if desired.
1 PIECE: *107 cal., 0 fat (0 sat. fat), 0 chol., 35mg sod., 26g carb. (25g sugars, 1g fiber), 2g pro.*

CREAMY CORN CUSTARDS

CREAMY CORN CUSTARDS

I make this all summer long and when I serve it to guests, I try to make them guess what the secret ingredient is. Not many guess corn, so it's a fun surprise. Instead of blackberries, you can use raspberries instead.

—Margee Berry, White Salmon, WA

PREP: 30 min. • **COOK:** 10 min. + chilling • **MAKES:** 8 servings

- **2 cups heavy whipping cream**
- **¼ cup sugar**
- **1 Tbsp. light brown sugar**
- **2 medium ears sweet corn, husks removed**
- **1 envelope unflavored gelatin**
- **2 Tbsp. cold water**
- **1 cup whole milk**
- **16 fresh blackberries**
- **½ tsp. grated lemon zest**
- **2 tsp. lemon juice**
- **1 tsp. turbinado (washed raw) sugar**
- **Fresh mint leaves**

1. Place cream, sugar and brown sugar in a small saucepan. Cook and stir over medium heat until sugars are dissolved. Cut corn from cobs; add corn to saucepan. Cook and stir over low heat for 5 minutes, stirring occasionally. Remove from heat; cover and let stand 10 minutes. Transfer corn mixture to a blender; cover and process until pureed. Strain through a fine-mesh strainer into a small bowl; set aside.

2. In a large saucepan, sprinkle gelatin over cold water; let stand 1 minute. Heat and stir over low heat until gelatin is completely dissolved. Stir in milk and strained corn mixture. Pour into eight 4-oz. ramekins or custard cups. Refrigerate, covered, until set, 5 hours or overnight.

3. In a small bowl, combine berries, lemon zest and juice. Sprinkle custards with raw sugar; top with berries and mint.

1 SERVING: *289 cal., 23g fat (14g sat. fat), 71mg chol., 36mg sod., 18g carb. (14g sugars, 1g fiber), 5g pro.*

5i

PEACH BAVARIAN

Fruit molds are my specialty. This one, with its refreshing peach taste, makes a colorful salad or dessert.

—Adeline Piscitelli, Sayreville, NJ

PREP: 15 min. + chilling • **MAKES:** 8 servings

- **1 can (15¼ oz.) sliced peaches**
- **2 pkg. (3 oz. each) peach or apricot gelatin**
- **½ cup sugar**
- **2 cups boiling water**
- **1 tsp. almond extract**
- **1 carton (8 oz.) frozen whipped topping, thawed**
- **Additional sliced peaches, optional**

1. Drain peaches, reserving ⅔ cup juice. Chop peaches into small pieces; set aside.

2. In a large bowl, dissolve gelatin and sugar in boiling water. Stir in reserved juice. Chill until slightly thickened. Stir extract into whipped topping; gently fold in gelatin mixture. Fold in peaches.

3. Pour into an oiled 6-cup mold. Chill overnight. Unmold onto a serving platter; garnish with additional peaches if desired.

1 SLICE: *249 cal., 5g fat (5g sat. fat), 0 chol., 53mg sod., 47g carb. (47g sugars, 0 fiber), 2g pro.*

PEACH BAVARIAN

HAUTE CHOCOLATE

Warm up with a steamy mug of sippable cocoa dolled up with a sweet selection of stir-ins.

CHILI-ORANGE

In a saucepan, heat 4 cups half-and-half cream over medium heat until bubbles form around the sides of pan (do not boil). Remove from heat. Whisk in 2 bars (3 1/2 oz. each) chopped 70% cacao dark chocolate, 2 oz. chopped milk chocolate and a dash of salt. Stir in other ingredients and return to heat; cook and stir until heated through.

BISCOFF

Whisk in 1/3 cup **Biscoff creamy cookie spread** until smooth. Pour into mugs; top with **sweetened whipped cream** and a **Biscoff cookie** if desired.

CHAI

Steep 3 **chai tea bags** in simmering half-and-half for 5 minutes. Remove tea bags; whisk in **chocolates** and 1 tsp. **vanilla extract** until smooth. Pour into mugs; top with **sweetened whipped cream** and **cinnamon** if desired.

CHILI-ORANGE

Whisk in 2 tsp. **grated orange zest,** 1/4 tsp. **chili powder** and 1/8 tsp. **cayenne pepper** until smooth. Pour into mugs; top with **sweetened whipped cream, cayenne pepper** and an **orange peel twist** if desired.

CREAMY WHITE

Instead of the dark and milk chocolates, whisk in 1 1/2 cups **white baking chips** and 1 tsp. **vanilla extract** until smooth. If desired, dip rim of mugs in additional melted **white baking chips** and then in **sprinkles.** Fill mugs.

HAZELNUT MOCHA

Whisk in 1/2 cup **Nutella,** 1/4 cup **hazelnut liqueur** and 3 Tbsp. **espresso powder** until smooth. If desired, dip rim of the mugs in additional Nutella, then in chopped **hazelnuts.** Fill mugs.

HEAVENLY NUTMEG

Whisk in 1 tsp. **vanilla extract** and 1/4 tsp. **ground nutmeg** until smooth. Pour into mugs; top with **sweetened whipped cream** or **mini marshmallows** if desired.

PEPPERMINT RED VELVET

Instead of dark chocolate, whisk in 7 oz. chopped **white baking chocolate,** 1/4 tsp. **peppermint extract** and 1/4 tsp. **red food coloring** until smooth. Pour into mugs; top with **sweetened whipped cream** or **mini marshmallows** and a **candy cane** if desired.

PUMPKIN SPICE

Whisk in 3/4 cup **canned pumpkin** and 2 tsp. **pumpkin pie spice** until smooth. Pour into mugs; top with **sweetened whipped cream** if desired.

SALTED CARAMEL & BANANA

Whisk in 2 **pureed bananas** and 1/3 cup **salted caramel topping** until smooth. Pour into mugs; top with **sweetened whipped cream** if desired.

SNICKERDOODLE

Whisk in 1 tsp. **vanilla extract, 1 tsp. cinnamon,** 3/4 tsp. **ground ginger,** 1/2 tsp. **cardamom,** 1/4 tsp. **nutmeg** and 1/4 tsp. **allspice** until smooth. Pour into mugs; top with **sweetened whipped cream** if desired.

FRIED BANANA MILKSHAKES

I love bananas—candy, bread, muffins, smoothies, with peanut butter—everything banana. So why not add bananas, kicked up several notches, to a milkshake?
—Julie Tran Deily, Rockledge, FL

PREP: 5 min. • **COOK:** 10 min. + cooling
MAKES: 2 servings

- 3 **Tbsp. unsalted butter, cubed**
- 2 **ripe medium bananas, sliced**
- 2 **Tbsp. light brown sugar**
- 1 **cup vanilla ice cream**
- ½ **cup 2% milk**

In a small heavy skillet, melt butter over medium heat. Heat until golden brown, 3-4 minutes, stirring constantly. Add bananas and brown sugar; cook and stir until bananas are tender, 3-4 minutes. Remove from heat; cool completely. Using a slotted spoon, place bananas in a blender. Reserve cooking liquid for topping. Add milk and ice cream to blender; pulse until mixed. Pour into glasses; drizzle with the reserved butter mixture.

1 SERVING: *477 cal., 26g fat (16g sat. fat), 80mg chol., 89mg sod., 59g carb. (45g sugars, 4g fiber), 6g pro.*

NEW YORK CHEESECAKE WITH SHORTBREAD CRUST

NEW YORK CHEESECAKE WITH SHORTBREAD CRUST

Light, creamy and smooth, this traditional New York-style cheesecake will melt in your mouth. It is made with a shortbread crust and topped with a triple berry sauce of raspberries, blueberries and boysenberries. This recipe takes time but is not hard. It is well worth the effort.
—Karen Nielson, St. George, UT

PREP: 50 min. • **BAKE:** 1¼ hours + chilling
MAKES: 16 servings

- 1 **cup all-purpose flour**
- ¼ **cup sugar**
- 1 **tsp. grated lemon zest**
- ½ **cup cold butter, cubed**
- 2 **large egg yolks, room temperature**
- 1 **tsp. vanilla extract**

FILLING

- 5 **pkg. (8 oz. each) cream cheese, softened**
- 1¾ **cups sugar**
- ½ **cup heavy whipping cream**
- 3 **Tbsp. all-purpose flour**
- 2 **tsp. vanilla extract**
- 2 **tsp. lemon juice**
- 1½ **tsp. grated lemon zest**
- 5 **large eggs, room temperature, lightly beaten**
- 2 **large egg yolks, room temperature**

TRIPLE BERRY SAUCE

- 1¼ **cups sugar**
- ¼ **cup cornstarch**
- 2 **cups cranberry juice**
- 1 **tsp. lemon juice**
- 2 **cups fresh or frozen unsweetened raspberries, divided**
- 1 **Tbsp. butter**
- 1 **cup fresh or frozen blueberries**
- 1 **cup fresh or frozen blackberries or boysenberries**

1. Preheat oven to 325°. Place a greased 9-in. springform pan on a double thickness of heavy-duty foil (about 18 in. square). Wrap foil securely around pan. Place on a baking sheet.

2. In a small bowl, mix the flour, sugar and lemon zest; cut in butter until crumbly. Add egg yolks and vanilla, tossing with a fork until mixture pulls together.

3. Press onto bottom and 1½ in. up sides of prepared pan. Bake until lightly browned, 12-16 minutes. Cool on a wire rack.

4. Beat cream cheese and sugar until smooth. Beat in cream, flour, vanilla, lemon juice and zest. Add eggs and egg yolks; beat on low speed just until blended. Pour into crust. Place springform pan in a larger baking pan; add 1 in. of hot water to the larger pan.

5. Bake until center is just set and top appears dull, 1¼-1½ hours. Remove springform pan from water bath. Cool cheesecake on a wire rack 10 minutes. Loosen sides from pan with a knife; remove foil. Cool 1 hour longer. Refrigerate overnight, covering when completely cooled. Remove rim of pan. In a small saucepan, combine sugar and cornstarch. Gradually add cranberry and lemon juices. Stir in 1 cup raspberries. Bring to a boil; cook and stir until thickened, about 2 minutes. Remove from the heat; stir in the butter.

6. Strain sauce; discard seeds. Cool to room temperature. Stir in the blueberries, blackberries and remaining raspberries. Serve with cheesecake.

1 PIECE: *494 cal., 36g fat (21g sat. fat), 200mg chol., 295mg sod., 37g carb. (28g sugars, 0 fiber), 8g pro.*

ALMOST IT'S-IT ICE CREAM SANDWICHES

ALMOST IT'S-IT ICE CREAM SANDWICHES

You'll enjoy discovering why this treat is so popular in San Francisco. It's snack heaven... ice cream, delicious oatmeal cookies and a sweet touch of chocolate. Swap out the vanilla ice cream for your favorite flavor, such as chocolate, caramel or cherry.
—Jacyn Siebert, San Francisco, CA

PREP: 40 min. + freezing • **BAKE:** 15 min./batch + cooling • **MAKES:** 7 servings

- **½ cup butter, softened**
- **¾ cup packed brown sugar**
- **¼ cup sugar**
- **1 large egg, room temperature**
- **½ tsp. vanilla extract**
- **¾ cup all-purpose flour**
- **½ tsp. baking soda**
- **½ tsp. ground cinnamon**
- **¼ tsp. baking powder**
- **¼ tsp. salt**
- **1½ cups quick-cooking oats**
- **¼ cup chopped raisins, optional**

ASSEMBLY

- **3 cups vanilla ice cream**
- **1 bottle (7¼ oz.) chocolate hard-shell ice cream topping**

1. Preheat oven to 350°. In a large bowl, cream butter and sugars until light and fluffy, 5-7 minutes. Beat in egg and vanilla. In another bowl, whisk the flour, baking soda, cinnamon, baking powder and salt; gradually beat into creamed mixture. Stir in oats and, if desired, raisins.
2. Shape into fourteen 1¼-in. balls; place 2½ in. apart on ungreased baking sheets. Bake until golden brown, 11-13 minutes. Cool on pans 3 minutes. Remove to wire racks to cool completely.
3. To assemble ice cream sandwiches, place ⅓ cup ice cream on bottom of a cookie. Top with a second cookie, pressing gently to flatten ice cream; place on a baking sheet. Repeat with remaining cookies and ice cream. Freeze until firm.
4. Remove ice cream sandwiches from the freezer. Working over a small bowl, drizzle the chocolate topping over half of each sandwich, allowing excess to drip off.
5. Place dipped sandwiches on a waxed paper-lined baking sheet; freeze until serving. Wrap individually in waxed paper for longer storage.

1 ICE CREAM SANDWICH: *580 cal., 29g fat (16g sat. fat), 86mg chol., 364mg sod., 74g carb. (50g sugars, 3g fiber), 7g pro.*

MIXED BERRY TIRAMISU

Because I love tiramisu, I came up with this deliciously refreshing twist on the traditional coffee-flavored Italian dessert. Fresh softened berries star with crisp ladyfinger cookies and mascarpone cheese. Serve it from a glass bowl or in clear dishes to show off the luscious layers.
—Najmussahar Ahmed, Ypsilanti, MI

PREP: 35 min. + chilling • **MAKES:** 12 servings

- **3 cups fresh raspberries**
- **3 cups fresh blackberries**
- **2 cups fresh blueberries**
- **2 cups fresh strawberries, sliced**
- **1⅓ cups sugar, divided**
- **4 tsp. grated orange zest**
- **1 cup orange juice**
- **1 cup heavy whipping cream**
- **2 cartons (8 oz. each) mascarpone cheese**
- **1 tsp. vanilla extract**
- **2 pkg. (7 oz. each) crisp ladyfinger cookies**
- **Additional fresh berries, optional**

1. Place berries in a large bowl. Mix ⅓ cup sugar, orange zest and orange juice; toss gently with berries. Refrigerate, covered, 45 minutes.
2. Beat cream until soft peaks form. In another bowl, mix mascarpone cheese, vanilla and remaining sugar. Fold in whipped cream, a third at a time.
3. Drain the berries over a shallow bowl, reserving juices. Dip ladyfingers in reserved juices, allowing excess to drip off; arrange in a single layer on bottom of a 13x9-in. dish. Layer with half the berries and half the mascarpone mixture; repeat layers, starting with ladyfingers.
4. Refrigerate, covered, overnight. If desired, top with additional fresh berries before serving.

NOTE: This recipe was prepared with Alessi brand ladyfinger cookies.

1 PIECE: *501 cal., 26g fat (14g sat. fat), 105mg chol., 77mg sod., 63g carb. (45g sugars, 5g fiber), 8g pro.*

BISCUIT STRAWBERRY SHORTCAKE

This is a perfect finish to any meal. It's a great way to make the most of fresh strawberries.
—Stephanie Moon, Boise, ID

TAKES: 30 min. • **MAKES:** 8 servings

- **2 cups all-purpose flour**
- **3 Tbsp. sugar, divided**
- **1 Tbsp. baking powder**
- **½ tsp. salt**
- **¼ cup cold butter**
- **1 cup 2% milk**
- **2 pints strawberries, chopped**
- **1 Tbsp. orange juice**
- **1½ cups whipped topping**

1. In a large bowl, combine flour, 2 Tbsp. sugar, baking powder and salt. Cut in the butter until mixture resembles coarse crumbs. Gradually stir in milk until a soft dough forms.

2. Drop dough by heaping tablespoonfuls into 8 mounds on a lightly greased baking sheet. Bake at 425° until lightly browned, 12-15 minutes. Cool on a wire rack.

3. Meanwhile, place strawberries, orange juice and remaining 1 Tbsp. sugar in a bowl; toss gently. Split the shortcakes in half horizontally. Place bottom halves on serving plates; top with whipped topping and strawberries. Replace shortcake tops.

1 SERVING: *261 cal., 10g fat (6g sat. fat), 19mg chol., 372mg sod., 38g carb. (12g sugars, 2g fiber), 5g pro.*

BERRY SHORTCAKE: Substitute 1 pint of blueberries for 1 pint of the strawberries.

MIXED FRUIT SHORTCAKE: Substitute 2 cups mixed berries, 2 cups sliced peaches or nectarines, and 2 tsp. sugar for the strawberries and orange juice.

INDONESIAN BANANAS FOSTER

When I ate bananas Foster the first time, it reminded me of this dish. The concept is the same—sliced bananas with a very sweet sauce. However, the bananas used here are plantains, and instead of using rum in the sauce, this dessert uses creamy coconut milk.
—Loanne Chiu, Fort Worth, TX

PREP: 15 min. • **COOK:** 25 min.
MAKES: 6 servings

- **1 can (13.66 oz.) coconut milk**
- **1 cup packed brown sugar**
- **1 cup water**
- **¼ cup molasses**
- **1 tsp. vanilla extract**
- **¼ tsp. salt**
- **¼ tsp. apple pie spice**
- **¼ cup butter, cubed**
- **3 large ripe plantains, cut into ¾-in. slices**

1. Spoon 6 Tbsp. cream from top of coconut milk and set aside. Pour remaining coconut milk into a large saucepan. Stir in brown sugar, water, molasses, vanilla, salt and pie spice. Bring to a boil. Reduce heat; simmer, uncovered, until reduced by half, 25-30 minutes.

2. Meanwhile, in a large cast-iron or other skillet, melt butter over medium-low heat. Add plantains. Cook, stirring gently, until glazed and slightly softened, 3-5 minutes. Divide plantains among 6 bowls; drizzle with syrup. Top with reserved coconut milk cream.

1 SERVING: *460 cal., 18g fat (15g sat. fat), 20mg chol., 195mg sod., 76g carb. (60g sugars, 2g fiber), 2g pro.*

TEST KITCHEN TIPS

- If you use regular bananas instead of plantains, make sure they are still firm.
- Plantains are usually available in the Hispanic section of fresh produce, or next to the bananas.

INDONESIAN BANANAS FOSTER

BERRY PRETZEL FLUFF DESSERT

BERRY PRETZEL FLUFF DESSERT

If you're asked to bring dessert to a summer potluck, this is the perfect recipe. It can be made ahead and you don't have to heat up the oven. Don't plan on leftovers!
—Taste of Home *Test Kitchen*

PREP: 20 min. + chilling • **MAKES:** 16 servings

- 2 **cups crushed pretzels**
- ¾ **cup sugar**
- ¾ **cup butter, melted**
- 2 **pkg. (8 oz. each) cream cheese, softened**
- 1 **cup whole-milk ricotta cheese**
- 1½ **cups confectioners' sugar**
- 1 **tsp. vanilla extract**
- ½ **tsp. grated lemon zest**
- 1 **cup heavy whipping cream**
- 3 **cups quartered fresh strawberries**
- 1½ **cups fresh blueberries**
- 3 **Tbsp. apricot preserves, optional**
- **Additional whipped cream and miniature pretzels, optional**

1. In a large bowl, toss pretzels with sugar and melted butter. Press into an ungreased 13x9-in. dish. Refrigerate 30 minutes.
2. In a large bowl, beat cream cheese, ricotta, confectioners' sugar, vanilla and grated lemon zest until smooth. In another bowl, beat heavy cream until stiff peaks form; fold into cream cheese mixture.
3. Spread over pretzel layer. Refrigerate, covered, for at least 4 hours. Just before serving, toss berries with apricot preserves if desired; sprinkle over top of dessert. If desired, top each serving with additional whipped cream and miniature pretzels.
1 PIECE: *390 cal., 26g fat (16g sat. fat), 75mg chol., 344mg sod., 37g carb. (26g sugars, 1g fiber), 5g pro.*

COFFEE ICE CREAM

I combined two recipes—one for vanilla ice cream, the other for a special coffee sauce—to create this one. I serve it plain, just scooped into a dessert dish, so the mild, creamy coffee flavor can be enjoyed to the fullest.
—Theresa Hansen, Pensacola, FL

PREP: 30 min. + freezing • **MAKES:** 1½ qt.

- ¼ **cup sugar**
- 1 **Tbsp. cornstarch**
- 1 **Tbsp. instant coffee granules**
- 2 **Tbsp. butter, melted**
- 1 **cup whole milk**
- 1 **tsp. vanilla extract**
- 1 **can (14 oz.) sweetened condensed milk**
- 2 **cups heavy whipping cream**

1. In a large saucepan, combine the sugar, cornstarch, coffee and butter until blended. Stir in milk. Bring to a boil over medium heat; cook and stir until thickened, 2 minutes. Remove from heat; stir in vanilla. Cool completely. Stir in condensed milk.
2. In a large bowl, beat cream until stiff peaks form; fold into milk mixture. Pour into a 9-in. pan. Cover and freeze until firm, 6 hours.
½ CUP: *292 cal., 20g fat (13g sat. fat), 73mg chol., 87mg sod., 25g carb. (24g sugars, 0 fiber), 4g pro.*

COFFEE ICE CREAM

PEANUT BUTTER & JELLY CHEESECAKE

I wanted to create something based on my friend's love of peanut butter and jelly sandwiches. This recipe features decadent layers of peanut butter and a thick swirl of preserves—it truly feels as if you're biting into a sweet dessert version of your favorite childhood sandwich.
—Melinda Buchman, Rock Hill, NY

PREP: 35 min. + cooling
BAKE: 1¼ hours + chilling
MAKES: 16 servings

- 1 **cup graham cracker crumbs**
- 3 **Tbsp. sugar**
- 1 **tsp. ground cinnamon**
- 6 **Tbsp. butter, melted**
- 1 **tsp. cinnamon sugar**
- 1 **jar (16.3 oz.) creamy peanut butter**
- 2 **Tbsp. 2% milk**

FILLING

- 3 **pkg. (8 oz. each) cream cheese, softened**
- 1 **cup sugar**
- 2 **tsp. vanilla extract**
- 4 **large eggs, room temperature, lightly beaten**
- 1½ **cups seedless raspberry preserves**
- 1 **Tbsp. lemon juice**

1. Preheat oven to 350°. Place a greased 9-in. springform pan on a double thickness of heavy-duty foil (about 18 in. square). Wrap foil securely around pan. Place on a baking sheet. In a bowl, mix cracker crumbs, sugar and cinnamon; stir in butter. Press onto the bottom of prepared pan. Sprinkle with cinnamon sugar. Bake until crust starts to brown, 6-8 minutes. Cool on a wire rack. Reduce oven setting to 325°.
2. In a bowl, beat peanut butter and milk until combined. Spread over cooled crust; set aside. In another large bowl, beat cream cheese, sugar and vanilla until smooth. Add eggs; beat on low speed just until blended. Pour over crust. In a small saucepan, stir together preserves and lemon juice over medium heat until preserves have melted. Spoon mixture by tablespoonfuls over top. Cut through batter with a knife to swirl. Place springform pan in a larger baking pan; add 1 in. of hot water to larger pan.
3. Bake until center is just set and top appears dull, about 1¼ hours. (Center of cheesecake will jiggle when moved.) Cool cheesecake on a wire rack for 10 minutes. Loosen sides from the pan with a knife; remove foil. Cool 1 hour longer. Refrigerate overnight, covering when completely cooled. Remove rim from pan.

1 PIECE: *541 cal., 36g fat (15g sat. fat), 101mg chol., 338mg sod., 49g carb. (40g sugars, 2g fiber), 11g pro.*

RAINBOW SHERBET ANGEL FOOD CAKE

5i

RAINBOW SHERBET ANGEL FOOD CAKE

Talk about a dessert that pops off the plate! Sometimes I make this cake even more eye-catching by coloring the whipped cream, too. Use whatever sherbet flavor combination you like.
—Bonnie Hawkins, Elkhorn, WI

PREP: 25 min. + freezing • **MAKES:** 12 servings

- 1 **prepared angel food cake (8 to 10 oz.)**
- 3 **cups rainbow sherbet, softened if necessary**

WHIPPED CREAM

- 2 **cups heavy whipping cream**
- ⅓ **cup confectioners' sugar**
- 1 **tsp. vanilla extract**

1. Using a long serrated knife, cut cake horizontally into 4 layers. Place bottom layer on a freezer-safe serving plate; spread with 1 cup sherbet. Repeat twice with middle cake layers and remaining sherbet. Top with remaining cake layer. Freeze, covered, until sherbet is firm, about 1 hour.
2. In a large bowl, beat cream until it begins to thicken. Add confectioners' sugar and vanilla; beat until soft peaks form. Frost top and sides of cake. Freeze until firm.
3. Thaw in refrigerator 30 minutes before serving. Cut cake with a serrated knife.

1 PIECE: *253 cal., 16g fat (10g sat. fat), 54mg chol., 174mg sod., 27g carb. (12g sugars, 2g fiber), 2g pro.*

READER REVIEW

"I have been making this for years. Instead of the whipped cream, I use Cool Whip. This is my son's most requested birthday cake."
—PATELL, TASTEOFHOME.COM

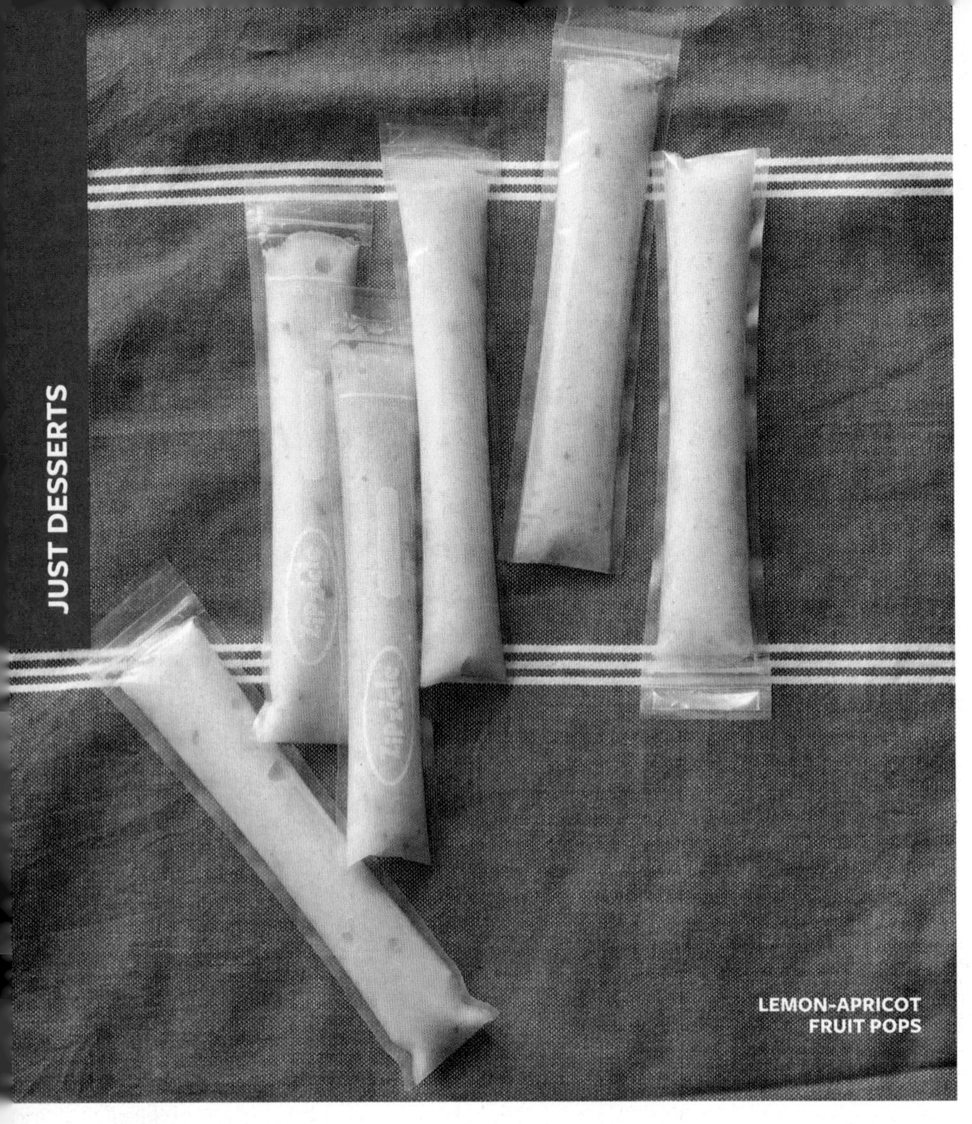
LEMON-APRICOT FRUIT POPS

LEMON-APRICOT FRUIT POPS

With just 31 calories, 4 teaspoons of sugar total and lots of vitamin C, this is one light and refreshing summer dessert everyone can find room for!
—Aysha Schurman, Ammon, ID

PREP: 15 min. + freezing • **MAKES:** 6 pops

- ¼ cup orange juice
- 1 tsp. grated lemon zest
- ¼ cup lemon juice
- 4 tsp. sugar
- 1 cup sliced fresh apricots (4-5 medium)
- ½ cup ice cubes
- 1 tsp. minced fresh mint, optional
- 6 freezer pop pouches, molds or 6 paper cups (3-oz. size) and wooden pop sticks

1. Place the first 6 ingredients in a blender; cover and process until blended. If desired, stir in mint.

2. Pour into pouches, molds or paper cups. Top molds with holders. If using cups, top with foil and insert sticks through foil. Freeze until firm.

1 POP: *31 cal., 0 fat (0 sat. fat), 0 chol., 0 sod., 8g carb. (6g sugars, 1g fiber), 0 pro.* **Diabetic exchanges:** *½ fruit.*

DOUBLE CHOCOLATE ESPRESSO CHEESECAKE

Every slice of this creamy cheesecake is a standout. The classic pairing of chocolate and coffee is sure to please partygoers.
—Cheryl Perry, Hertford, NC

PREP: 35 min. • **BAKE:** 1 hour + chilling
MAKES: 16 servings

- 1½ cups crushed vanilla wafers (about 45)
- ¼ cup butter, melted
- 2 Tbsp. sugar
- ¼ tsp. instant espresso powder

FILLING

- 4 pkg. (8 oz. each) cream cheese, softened
- 1½ cups sugar
- 1 cup sour cream
- 1 cup 60% cacao bittersweet chocolate baking chips, melted
- ½ cup baking cocoa
- ¼ cup half-and-half cream
- 1 Tbsp. all-purpose flour
- 5 large eggs, room temperature, lightly beaten
- 1½ tsp. instant espresso powder
- 1 tsp. vanilla extract

TOPPING

- 1 cup coffee liqueur
- 1 Tbsp. half-and-half cream
- 1 cup heavy whipping cream
- 2 Tbsp. confectioners' sugar
- ½ cup 60% cacao bittersweet chocolate baking chips, chopped
- 16 chocolate-covered coffee beans

1. Place a greased 9-in. springform pan on a double thickness of heavy-duty foil (about 18 in. square). Securely wrap foil around pan.

2. In a large bowl, combine the wafer crumbs, butter, sugar and espresso powder. Press onto the bottom and 1 in. up the sides of prepared pan.

3. In a large bowl, beat the cream cheese, sugar, sour cream, melted chocolate, cocoa, half-and-half and flour until smooth. Add the eggs; beat on low speed just until combined. Stir in the espresso powder and vanilla. Pour into crust. Place springform pan in a large baking pan; add 1 in. of hot water to larger pan.

4. Bake at 350° until center is just set and top appears dull, 60-70 minutes. Remove springform pan from water bath. Cool on a wire rack 10 minutes. Carefully run a knife around edge of pan to loosen; cool 1 hour longer. Refrigerate overnight. Remove sides of pan.

5. In a small saucepan, combine liqueur and half-and-half. Bring to a boil; cook until liquid is reduced by half. Meanwhile, in a large bowl, beat whipping cream until it begins to thicken. Add confectioners' sugar; beat until stiff peaks form.

6. Drizzle cheesecake with coffee syrup; garnish with whipped cream, chocolate chips and coffee beans.

1 PIECE: *610 cal., 40g fat (23g sat. fat), 170mg chol., 259mg sod., 52g carb. (41g sugars, 2g fiber), 9g pro.*

DOUBLE CHOCOLATE ESPRESSO CHEESECAKE

ROASTED GRAPE & SWEET CHEESE PHYLLO GALETTE

Faced with an abundant crop of grapes, I needed some creative ways to use them. This became a quick and easy way to make an impressive-looking dessert with phyllo dough, which is fun to work with and bakes up golden and flaky. A layer of orange-kissed cream cheese is topped with roasted grapes. I finish it off with a drizzle of honey and a sprinkle of coarse sugar. You can use berries instead of grapes for this.
—Kallee Krong-McCreery, Escondido, CA

PREP: 25 min. • **BAKE:** 35 min. + cooling
MAKES: 10 servings

- **1 pkg. (8 oz.) cream cheese, softened**
- **2 Tbsp. orange marmalade**
- **1 tsp. sugar**
- **8 sheets phyllo dough (14x9-in. size)**
- **4 Tbsp. butter, melted**
- **1 cup seedless grapes**
- **1 Tbsp. honey**
- **2 tsp. coarse sugar**

1. Preheat oven to 350°. In a large bowl, beat cream cheese, marmalade and sugar until smooth; set aside.
2. Place 1 sheet of phyllo on a parchment-lined baking sheet; brush with butter. Layer with remaining phyllo sheets, brushing each layer. (Keep remaining phyllo covered with a damp towel to prevent it from drying out.) Spread cream cheese mixture over phyllo to within 2 in. of edges. Arrange grapes over cream cheese.
3. Fold edges of phyllo over filling, leaving center uncovered. Brush folded phyllo with any remaining butter; drizzle with honey and sprinkle with coarse sugar. Bake until phyllo is golden brown, 35-40 minutes. Transfer to a wire rack to cool completely. Refrigerate leftovers.

1 PIECE: *177 cal., 13g fat (8g sat. fat), 35mg chol., 148mg sod., 15g carb. (9g sugars, 0 fiber), 2g pro.*

ROASTED GRAPE & SWEET CHEESE PHYLLO GALETTE

PUMPKIN CRUNCH PARFAITS

(SHOWN ON PAGE 208)

Have your little ones lend a hand with this dessert! It's a great treat for Thanksgiving or Halloween.
—Lorraine Darocha, Berkshire, MA

TAKES: 20 min. • **MAKES:** 6 servings

- **¾ cup cold 2% milk**
- **1 pkg. (3.4 oz.) instant vanilla pudding mix**
- **2 cups whipped topping**
- **1 cup canned pumpkin**
- **½ tsp. pumpkin pie spice**
- **1 cup chopped pecans**
- **32 gingersnap cookies, crushed (about 1½ cups)**
- **Optional: Additional whipped topping and chopped pecans**

1. In a large bowl, beat milk and pudding mix on low speed for 2 minutes. Stir in whipped topping, pumpkin and pie spice. Fold in pecans.
2. Spoon half the mixture into 6 parfait glasses; top with half of the gingersnap crumbs. Repeat layers. If desired, top with additional whipped topping and chopped pecans. Refrigerate leftovers.

1 PARFAIT: *447 cal., 23g fat (7g sat. fat), 4mg chol., 486mg sod., 55g carb. (31g sugars, 3g fiber), 5g pro.*

HOW-TO

Make Pumpkin Pie Spice

If you don't have pumpkin pie spice, you can make your own with a blend of 2 tsp. cinnamon, 1 tsp. ginger, and ½ tsp. each of ground nutmeg and cloves or allspice. Combine all ingredients. Store in a cool, dry place for up to 6 months.

MAPLE BLUEBERRY CRISP

APPLE HONEY TAPIOCA PUDDING

I'm glad that apple season is long, since my family requests this pudding quite often!
—Amy Kraemer, Glencoe, MN

TAKES: 25 min. • **MAKES:** 6 servings

- **4 cups sliced peeled tart apples, cut in eighths**
- **¾ cup honey**
- **3 Tbsp. butter**
- **1 Tbsp. lemon juice**
- **½ tsp. salt**
- **½ tsp. ground cinnamon**
- **2½ cups water**
- **⅓ cup quick-cooking tapioca**
- **Cream, ice cream or whipped cream**

1. In a Dutch oven, combine the first 6 ingredients. Cover and simmer just until apples are tender.
2. Using a slotted spoon, transfer apples to a bowl. Add water and tapioca to pan. Cook and stir until thickened and clear. Pour over apples. Serve warm with cream, ice cream or whipped cream.
1 CUP: *257 cal., 6g fat (4g sat. fat), 15mg chol., 256mg sod., 55g carb. (42g sugars, 2g fiber), 0 pro.*

APPLE HONEY TAPIOCA PUDDING

MAPLE BLUEBERRY CRISP

With sweet blueberries and a tender crumb topping, this yummy crisp makes a wonderful treat after brunch or an evening meal. I sometimes top servings with a scoop of vanilla ice cream.
—Mona Wright, Villa Rica, GA

PREP: 15 min. • **BAKE:** 35 min. • **MAKES:** 9 servings

- **4 cups fresh or frozen blueberries**
- **½ cup maple syrup**
- **2 Tbsp. cornstarch**
- **1 tsp. ground cinnamon**
- **1¼ cups all-purpose flour**
- **¾ cup packed brown sugar**
- **½ cup cold butter**
- **1 tsp. almond extract**
- **Vanilla ice cream, optional**

1. Preheat oven to 375°. In a large bowl, combine blueberries, syrup, cornstarch and cinnamon. Transfer to a greased 8-in. square baking dish. In a small bowl, combine flour and brown sugar. Cut in butter until mixture resembles coarse crumbs; stir in extract. Sprinkle over top.
2. Bake until the filling is bubbly and topping is golden brown, 35-40 minutes. If desired, serve with ice cream.
1 SERVING: *315 cal., 11g fat (6g sat. fat), 27mg chol., 82mg sod., 54g carb. (35g sugars, 2g fiber), 2g pro.*

PUMPKIN RUGELACH WITH
CREAM CHEESE ICING

PUMPKIN RUGELACH WITH CREAM CHEESE ICING

My twist on this classic pastry adds pumpkin to the filling and a rich cream cheese icing on top. Because you can make the dough ahead and refrigerate it, the recipe is ideal for the busy holiday season.
—Justine Duffy, Wooster, OH

PREP: 40 min. + chilling
BAKE: 20 min./batch + cooling
MAKES: 3 dozen

- **2 cups butter, softened**
- **12 oz. cream cheese, softened**
- **⅛ tsp. salt**
- **3¾ cups all-purpose flour**
- **1 can (15 oz.) pumpkin**
- **3 Tbsp. plus 1 cup sugar, divided**
- **3 Tbsp. honey**
- **1 tsp. vanilla extract**
- **4½ tsp. ground cinnamon**
- **1 large egg, room temperature**
- **1 Tbsp. 2% milk**

ICING
- **12 oz. cream cheese, softened**
- **1 cup confectioners' sugar**
- **⅔ cup 2% milk**
- **1 tsp. vanilla extract**

1. In a large bowl, cream butter, cream cheese and salt until blended. Gradually beat in flour. Divide dough into 3 portions. Shape each into a disk; wrap and refrigerate 1 hour.
2. Preheat oven to 350°. In a small bowl, combine pumpkin, 3 Tbsp. sugar, honey and vanilla. Mix cinnamon and remaining 1 cup sugar. On a lightly floured surface, roll each portion of dough into a 14-in. circle. Spread each with a third of the pumpkin mixture and sprinkle with ¼ cup sugar mixture.
3. Cut dough into 12 wedges. Roll up from wide ends; place 2 in. apart on parchment-lined baking sheets, point side down. Whisk together egg and milk; brush over pastries. Sprinkle with remaining sugar mixture.
4. Bake until bottoms are browned, 18-22 minutes. Remove from pans to wire racks to cool completely. In a small bowl, beat icing ingredients; drizzle over pastries. Let stand until set.
1 COOKIE: *258 cal., 17g fat (10g sat. fat), 52mg chol., 154mg sod., 24g carb. (13g sugars, 1g fiber), 3g pro.*

VEGAN CHOCOLATE MOUSSE

VEGAN CHOCOLATE MOUSSE

My son is allergic to dairy and eggs. I created this silky chocolate mousse so he could enjoy a treat that's delicious, chocolaty and also healthy! It's gluten-free and grain-free, too. If you're having company over, it can be prepared the night before and stored in the refrigerator.
—Sarah Meuser, New Milford, CT

PREP: 25 min. + chilling • **MAKES:** 6 servings

- **⅓ cup boiling water**
- **¾ cup dried Mission figs, stemmed and halved lengthwise**
- **1 cup dairy-free dark chocolate chips**
- **2 medium ripe avocados, peeled and pitted**
- **⅓ cup baking cocoa**
- **2 Tbsp. unsweetened almond milk**
- **1 Tbsp. maple syrup**
- **1 tsp. vanilla extract**
- **⅛ tsp. sea salt**
- **1 can (15 oz.) garbanzo beans or chickpeas, undrained**
- **¼ tsp. cream of tartar**
- **Fresh raspberries, optional**

1. Pour boiling water over figs in a small bowl; let stand 45 minutes. In a microwave, melt chocolate chips; stir until smooth. Cool to room temperature. Place figs and liquid in a food processor. Pulse until a paste forms. Add avocados, cooled chocolate, cocoa, almond milk, syrup, vanilla and sea salt; pulse until pureed. Transfer to a large bowl.
2. To make aquafaba, drain garbanzo beans, reserving liquid (save beans for another use). Add drained liquid and cream of tartar to bowl of a stand mixer. Beat on high speed until stiff peaks form, 2-3 minutes. Gently fold aquafaba into fig mixture. Spoon into dessert dishes. Refrigerate at least 2 hours or overnight before serving. If desired, serve with fresh raspberries.
⅔ CUP: *310 cal., 18g fat (7g sat. fat), 0 chol., 149mg sod., 41g carb. (26g sugars, 8g fiber), 5g pro.*

JUST DESSERTS

5i

BEST EVER VANILLA ICE CREAM

This ice cream is technically a custard since it contains eggs. I've found that eggs are the key to making a smooth and creamy treat that rivals what you can get at a premium ice cream shop.
—Peggy Woodward, Shullsburg, WI

PREP: 15 min. + chilling
PROCESS: 25 min./batch + freezing
MAKES: 45 cups

- **2 cups heavy whipping cream**
- **2 cups 2% milk**
- **¾ cup sugar**
- **⅛ tsp. salt**
- **1 vanilla bean**
- **6 large egg yolks**

1. In a large heavy saucepan, combine cream, milk, sugar and salt. Split vanilla bean in half lengthwise. With a sharp knife, scrape seeds into pan; add bean. Heat cream mixture over medium heat until bubbles form around sides of pan, stirring to dissolve sugar.
2. In a small bowl, whisk a small amount of the hot mixture into the egg yolks; return all to the pan, whisking constantly. Cook over low heat until mixture is just thick enough to coat a metal spoon and temperature reaches 180°, stirring constantly. Do not allow mixture to boil. Immediately transfer to a bowl.
3. Place bowl in a pan of ice water. Stir gently and occasionally for 2 minutes; discard vanilla bean. Press waxed paper onto surface of mixture. Refrigerate for several hours or overnight.
4. Fill cylinder of ice cream maker two-thirds full; freeze according to the manufacturer's directions. (Refrigerate remaining mixture until ready to freeze.) Transfer ice cream to a freezer container; freeze until firm, 4-6 hours. Repeat with remaining mixture.

NOTE: To prepare ice cream without an ice cream maker, chill the custard mixture overnight. Pour into a frozen 13x9-in. dish. Cover and freeze for 30 minutes. Beat with a hand mixer until smooth; return to the freezer. Repeat, beating every 30 minutes, until ice cream reaches desired consistency.

½ CUP: *310 cal., 23g fat (14g sat. fat), 188mg chol., 78mg sod., 21g carb. (21g sugars, 0 fiber), 5g pro.*

BEST EVER VANILLA ICE CREAM

COOKIES & CREAM ICE CREAM: After freezing in an ice cream freezer, layer 1 cup crushed Oreo cookies with ice cream in a freezer container; freeze until firm.

CHOCOLATE ICE CREAM: Melt 2 cups semisweet chocolate; cool to room temperature. Whisk melted chocolate into egg yolks before whisking a small amount of hot cream mixture into yolks. Proceed as directed.

STRAWBERRY ICE CREAM: In a small bowl, crush 2 cups sliced fresh strawberries with ¼ cup sugar. Stir into the cooked custard as it cools in a pan of ice water. Proceed as directed.

SUNNY CITRUS LAYERED CHEESECAKE

This beautiful layered cheesecake takes a bit longer to make, but the end result is so worth it! Citrus seems to be the perfect ending for an Easter meal, and the bright flavors really shine in this dessert.
—Sue Gronholz, Beaver Dam, WI

PREP: 35 min. + cooling
BAKE: 1 hour 25 min. + chilling
MAKES: 16 servings

- **1 cup all-purpose flour**
- **⅓ cup sugar**
- **1 tsp. grated lemon zest**
- **⅓ cup cold butter, cubed**

FILLING

- **4 pkg. (8 oz. each) cream cheese, softened**
- **1⅓ cups sugar**
- **2 Tbsp. all-purpose flour**
- **1 tsp. vanilla extract**
- **4 large eggs, room temperature, lightly beaten**
- **¼ cup lime juice**
- **1 Tbsp. grated lime zest**
- **3 drops green food coloring**
- **¼ cup lemon juice**
- **1 Tbsp. grated lemon zest**
- **6 drops yellow food coloring, divided**
- **¼ cup orange juice**
- **1 Tbsp. grated orange zest**
- **2 drops red food coloring**

TOPPING

- **¾ cup sour cream**
- **1 Tbsp. sugar**
- **¼ tsp. lemon extract**
- **Optional: Orange slices, lime slices and lemon slices**

SUNNY CITRUS LAYERED CHEESECAKE

1. Preheat oven to 325°. Place a greased 9-in. springform pan on a double thickness of heavy-duty foil (about 18 in. square). Wrap foil securely around pan. Place on a baking sheet.

2. In a small bowl, mix flour, sugar and zest; cut in the butter until crumbly. Press onto bottom of prepared pan. Bake until edges are lightly browned, 25-30 minutes. Cool on a wire rack.

3. In a large bowl, beat cream cheese and sugar until smooth. Beat in the flour and vanilla. Add eggs; beat on low speed just until blended. Divide batter into thirds. To 1 portion, add lime juice, lime zest and green food coloring. Pour batter over the crust.

4. Place springform pan in a larger baking pan; add 1 in. of hot water to larger pan. Bake until center is just set and top appears dull, about 25 minutes.

5. Meanwhile, to another portion of batter, add lemon juice, lemon zest and 3 drops yellow food coloring. Carefully remove pan from oven. Gently spoon over lime layer. Return to oven; bake until center is just set and top appears dull, about 25 minutes.

6. To remaining batter, add orange juice, orange zest, red food coloring and the remaining 3 drops yellow food coloring. Carefully remove pan from oven. Gently spoon over lemon layer.

7. Return to oven; bake until center is just set and top appears dull, 30-35 minutes. Carefully remove pan from oven.

8. In a small bowl, whisk the topping ingredients. Gently spoon over cheesecake in small dollops; spread carefully. Return to oven; bake 5 minutes.

9. Remove springform pan from water bath. Cool cheesecake on a wire rack for 10 minutes. Loosen sides from pan with a knife; remove foil. Cool 1 hour longer. Refrigerate overnight, covering when completely cooled. Remove rim from pan. If desired, top with orange, lime and lemon slices. Refrigerate leftovers.

1 PIECE: *394 cal., 27g fat (16g sat. fat), 117mg chol., 231mg sod., 33g carb. (25g sugars, 0 fiber), 6g pro.*

HOT ITALIAN PARTY
SANDWICHES, PAGE 230

Potluck Pleasers

Each recipe here serves eight or more with ease, making it perfect for large gatherings.

MOST-REQUESTED RECIPES

Rosemary Turkey Breast p. 231

Campfire Dessert Cones p. 232

Antipasto Picnic Salad p. 233

Jalapeno Sausage Quiche p. 236

Kiddie Crunch Mix p. 241

BARBECUED PARTY STARTERS

These sweet, tangy bites are sure to tide everyone over until dinner. At the buffet, set out some decorative toothpicks to make for easy nibbling.
—Anastasia Weiss, Punxsutawney, PA

PREP: 30 min. • **COOK:** 2¼ hours
MAKES: 16 servings

- **1 lb. ground beef**
- **¼ cup finely chopped onion**
- **1 pkg. (16 oz.) miniature hot dogs, drained**
- **1 jar (12 oz.) apricot preserves**
- **1 cup barbecue sauce**
- **1 can (20 oz.) pineapple chunks, drained**

1. In a large bowl, combine beef and onion, mixing lightly but thoroughly. Shape into 1-in. balls. In a large skillet over medium heat, cook meatballs in 2 batches until cooked through, turning occasionally.
2. Using a slotted spoon, transfer meatballs to a 3-qt. slow cooker. Add hot dogs; stir in preserves and barbecue sauce. Cook, covered, on high or until heated through, 2-3 hours.
3. Stir in pineapple; cook, covered, until heated through, 15-20 minutes longer.
⅓ CUP: *237 cal., 11g fat (4g sat. fat), 36mg chol., 491mg sod., 26g carb. (20g sugars, 0 fiber), 9g pro.*

BARBECUED PARTY STARTERS

HOT ITALIAN PARTY SANDWICHES

(SHOWN ON PAGE 228)

It doesn't get much easier or more delicious than these warm Italian sandwiches that are perfect for feeding a large crowd. Quick to prepare, they are wonderful as an appetizer for parties and other gatherings or to serve a hungry family.
—Joan Hallford, North Richland Hills, TX

PREP: 20 min. • **BAKE:** 15 min.
MAKES: 12 sandwiches

- **1 pkg. (12 oz.) Hawaiian sweet rolls**
- **½ cup mayonnaise**
- **2 Tbsp. prepared pesto**
- **6 slices part-skim mozzarella or provolone cheese**
- **6 thin slices deli ham**
- **9 thin slices hard salami**
- **6 thin slices deli pastrami**
- **1¼ cups giardiniera**
- **½ cup shredded Parmesan cheese**
- **1 cup fresh basil leaves**
- **½ cup sliced red onion**
- **¼ cup prepared zesty Italian salad dressing**
- **Pepperoncini**

1. Preheat oven to 350°. Cut rolls horizontally in half; place roll bottoms in a greased 11x7-in. baking dish. Mix mayonnaise and pesto until combined. Spread over cut sides of rolls. Layer bottoms with mozzarella cheese, ham, salami, pastrami, giardiniera, shredded Parmesan cheese, basil leaves and red onion. Place bun tops over filling and gently press to flatten.
2. Bake for 10 minutes. Remove from oven; brush with salad dressing. Bake until golden brown and cheese is melted, about 5 minutes longer. Cool slightly before cutting. Serve with pepperoncini and additional giardiniera if desired.
1 SANDWICH: *290 cal., 17g fat (6g sat. fat), 44mg chol., 1026mg sod., 20g carb. (7g sugars, 1g fiber), 15g pro.*

ROSEMARY TURKEY BREAST

CINNAMON TOASTED ALMONDS

Crunchy cinnamon almonds are a spectacular treat to take to a party or gathering. They taste just like the cinnamon-roasted almonds you get at the fair.
—Janice Thompson, Stacy, MN

PREP: 15 min. • **BAKE:** 25 min. + cooling • **MAKES:** about 4 cups

- **2 large egg whites**
- **6 tsp. vanilla extract**
- **4 cups unblanched almonds**
- **⅓ cup sugar**
- **⅓ cup packed brown sugar**
- **1 tsp. salt**
- **½ tsp. ground cinnamon**

1. In a large bowl, beat egg whites until frothy; beat in vanilla. Add almonds; stir gently to coat. Combine the sugars, salt and cinnamon; add to nut mixture and stir gently to coat.
2. Spread evenly in 2 greased 15x10x1-in. baking pans. Bake at 300° for 25-30 minutes or until almonds are crisp, stirring once. Cool. Store in an airtight container.
¼ CUP: *250 cal., 18g fat (1g sat. fat), 0 chol., 166mg sod., 16g carb. (10g sugars, 4g fiber), 8g pro.*

ROSEMARY TURKEY BREAST

I season turkey with a blend of rosemary, garlic and paprika. Because I rub that mixture directly on the meat under the skin, I can remove the skin before serving and not lose any of the flavor. The result is a lower-in-fat yet delicious entree that makes the perfect centerpiece for holiday meals.
—Dorothy Pritchett, Wills Point, TX

PREP: 10 min. • **BAKE:** 1½ hours + standing • **MAKES:** 15 servings

- **2 Tbsp. olive oil**
- **8 to 10 garlic cloves, peeled**
- **3 Tbsp. chopped fresh rosemary or 3 tsp. dried rosemary, crushed**
- **1 tsp. salt**
- **1 tsp. paprika**
- **½ tsp. coarsely ground pepper**
- **1 bone-in turkey breast (5 lbs.)**

1. In a food processor, combine the oil, garlic, rosemary, salt, paprika and pepper; cover and process until garlic is coarsely chopped.
2. With your fingers, carefully loosen the skin from both sides of turkey breast. Spread half the garlic mixture over the meat under the skin. Smooth skin over meat and secure to underside of breast with toothpicks. Spread remaining garlic mixture over turkey skin.
3. Place turkey breast on a rack in a shallow roasting pan. Bake, uncovered, at 325° until a thermometer reads 165°, 1½-2 hours. (Cover loosely with foil if turkey browns too quickly.) Let stand for 15 minutes before slicing. Discard toothpicks.
4 OZ. COOKED TURKEY: *148 cal., 3g fat (0 sat. fat), 78mg chol., 207mg sod., 1g carb. (0 sugars, 0 fiber), 29g pro.* **Diabetic exchanges:** *4 lean meat.*

CINNAMON TOASTED ALMONDS

PORK SANDWICHES WITH ROOT BEER BARBECUE SAUCE

CAMPFIRE DESSERT CONES

Kids love to make these! Set out the ingredients so they can mix and match for their own creations.
—Bonnie Hawkins, Elkhorn, WI

TAKES: 20 min. • **MAKES:** 8 servings

- **8 ice cream sugar cones**
- **½ cup milk chocolate M&M's**
- **½ cup miniature marshmallows**
- **½ cup salted peanuts**
- **½ cup white baking chips**

1. Prepare campfire or grill for medium heat. Fill cones with M&M's, marshmallows, peanuts and white chips. Fully wrap each cone with foil, sealing tightly.

2. Place packets over campfire or grill; cook until heated through, 7-10 minutes. Open foil carefully.

1 CONE: *217 cal., 11g fat (5g sat. fat), 4mg chol., 78mg sod., 26g carb. (18g sugars, 1g fiber), 5g pro.*

CAMPFIRE DESSERT CONES

PORK SANDWICHES WITH ROOT BEER BARBECUE SAUCE

My tasty recipe is sure to please a crowd! People say they love the subtle heat and hint of sweetness in these saucy sandwiches. Try serving them with coleslaw and pickles.
—Karen Currie, Kirkwood, MO

PREP: 30 min. • **COOK:** 9½ hours • **MAKES:** 8 servings

- **2 lbs. boneless pork sirloin roast**
- **1 medium onion, sliced**
- **2 Tbsp. dried minced garlic**
- **3 cups root beer, divided**
- **1 bottle (12 oz.) chili sauce**
- **⅛ tsp. hot pepper sauce**
- **8 kaiser rolls, split**

1. Place roast in a 3-qt. slow cooker. Add the onion, garlic and 1 cup root beer. Cover and cook on low for 9-10 hours or until meat is tender.

2. In a small saucepan, combine the chili sauce, hot pepper sauce and remaining 2 cups root beer. Bring to a boil. Reduce heat; simmer, uncovered, for 20-25 minutes or until thickened.

3. Remove meat from slow cooker; cool slightly. Discard cooking juices. Shred pork with 2 forks and return to slow cooker. Stir in barbecue sauce. Cover and cook on low for 30 minutes or until heated through. Serve on rolls.

1 SANDWICH: *424 cal., 9g fat (3g sat. fat), 68mg chol., 1066mg sod., 57g carb. (22g sugars, 2g fiber), 29g pro.*

ANTIPASTO PICNIC SALAD

With a tempting blend of meats, veggies and pasta for your picnic, how can you go wrong? The recipe comes together in no time, serves a crowd and tastes as good at room temperature as it does cold. If you're expecting a smaller group, simply halve the recipe to accommodate your number of guests.
—Michele Larson, Baden, PA

PREP: 30 min. • **COOK:** 15 min.
MAKES: 25 servings (1 cup each)

- **1 pkg. (16 oz.) medium pasta shells**
- **2 jars (16 oz. each) giardiniera**
- **1 lb. fresh broccoli florets**
- **½ lb. cubed part-skim mozzarella cheese**
- **½ lb. hard salami, cubed**
- **½ lb. deli ham, cubed**
- **2 pkg. (3½ oz. each) sliced pepperoni, halved**
- **1 large green pepper, cut into chunks**
- **1 can (6 oz.) pitted ripe olives, drained**

DRESSING

- **½ cup olive oil**
- **¼ cup red wine vinegar**
- **2 Tbsp. lemon juice**
- **1 tsp. Italian seasoning**
- **1 tsp. coarsely ground pepper**
- **½ tsp. salt**

1. Cook pasta according to package directions. Meanwhile, drain giardiniera, reserving ¾ cup liquid. In a large bowl, combine the giardiniera, broccoli, mozzarella, salami, ham, pepperoni, green pepper and olives. Drain pasta and rinse in cold water; stir into meat mixture.

2. For dressing, in a small bowl, whisk the oil, vinegar, lemon juice, Italian seasoning, pepper, salt and reserved giardiniera liquid. Pour dressing over salad and toss to coat. Refrigerate until serving.

1 CUP: *216 cal., 12g fat (4g sat. fat), 23mg chol., 527mg sod., 18g carb. (1g sugars, 1g fiber), 10g pro.*

CAULIFLOWER AU GRATIN

CAULIFLOWER AU GRATIN

This lower-carb side dish pairs well with pork, ham or beef. It's so creamy and delicious that even the kids will ask for seconds! If you like a little crunch, sprinkle buttered bread crumbs over the top after 30 minutes of baking.
—Mary Zinchiak, Boardman, OH

PREP: 25 min. • **BAKE:** 45 min.
MAKES: 8 servings

- **1 large head cauliflower, cut into florets**
- **2 Tbsp. olive oil**
- **1 tsp. salt, divided**
- **1 tsp. pepper, divided**
- **4 Tbsp. butter, cubed**
- **3 Tbsp. all-purpose flour**
- **2 cups 2% milk**
- **1 cup shredded Swiss cheese**
- **½ cup grated Parmesan cheese**
- **½ tsp. onion powder**
- **½ tsp. ground mustard**
- **½ tsp. Worcestershire sauce**
- **⅛ tsp. cayenne pepper**
- **Chopped fresh thyme, optional**

1. Preheat oven to 375°. Place cauliflower on a rimmed baking sheet. Drizzle with oil; sprinkle with ½ tsp. salt and ½ tsp. pepper. Toss to coat. Bake 8 minutes. Stir; bake until crisp-tender and lightly browned, 7-8 minutes longer.

2. In a large saucepan, melt butter over medium heat. Stir in flour until smooth; gradually whisk in milk. Bring to a simmer, stirring constantly; cook and stir until thickened, 2-3 minutes. Remove from heat. Stir in next 6 ingredients and remaining ½ tsp. salt and ½ tsp. pepper until smooth.

3. Pour ¾ cup cheese sauce into a greased 2-qt. baking dish. Top with cauliflower and the remaining cheese sauce. Bake, uncovered, until lightly browned and bubbly, 30-35 minutes. If desired, top with chopped fresh thyme.

¾ CUP: *196 cal., 14g fat (7g sat. fat), 34mg chol., 291mg sod., 11g carb. (5g sugars, 2g fiber), 9g pro.*

TEST KITCHEN TIP

Freshly shredded Parmesan cheese works best in this recipe. Canned grated Parmesan cheese will make the texture grainy.

READY, SET... *ROLL!*

Take cream cheese beyond the bagel with creative stir-ins and coatings! Just mix, shape and roll for easy apps that everyone will love.

+
Cucumbers add a cool, low-carb crunch.

+
Fill mini peppers for a grab-and-go snack.

Beat 8 oz. softened cream cheese until smooth. Fold in mix-ins. Cover; refrigerate for at least 2 hours. Roll the cheese mixture into 2 logs, each about 5 in. long. Roll logs in 1 cup of toppings. Serve with crackers, crostini and veggies.

Buffalo
Mix in 1 cup shredded **cheddar cheese,** ½ cup crumbled **blue cheese,** ¼ cup each minced **celery** and **carrot,** and 1 Tbsp. **hot sauce.** Roll the logs in 1 cup crushed **pretzels.**

Nacho
Mix in 1 cup shredded **sharp cheddar cheese,** 1 envelope **taco seasoning,** 2 Tbsp. minced **fresh cilantro** and 2 Tbsp. minced **jalapeno.** Roll the logs in 1 cup crushed **tortilla chips.**

+
Plain crackers let the flavors of the cheese logs shine.

+
Set out a basket of toasted crostini.

Pesto
Mix in 1 cup shredded **Parmesan cheese,** ¼ cup **prepared pesto** and 2 minced **garlic cloves.** Roll the logs in 1 cup toasted **pine nuts.**

Reuben
Mix in 1 cup shredded **Swiss cheese,** ½ cup chopped **pastrami,** ½ cup well-drained **sauerkraut,** 2 Tbsp. **Thousand Island dressing** and 1 tsp. **caraway seeds.** Roll logs in 1 cup chopped toasted **pecans.**

MORE LOGS TO LOVE!

Feta & Olive
Mix in 1 cup **feta cheese,** ½ cup **Kalamata olives,** 2 tsp. **Greek seasoning** and 1 tsp. **lemon zest.** Roll logs in crushed **pita chips.**

Curried Apricot
Mix in 1 cup **paneer cheese,** ½ cup diced **dried apricots,** ½ cup chopped **green onions,** 2 Tbsp. **mango chutney,** 2 tsp. **curry powder** and 1 chopped **serrano pepper.** Roll logs in finely chopped **cilantro.**

Smoked Salmon
Mix in 1 cup **goat cheese,** ¾ cup chopped **smoked salmon,** ¼ cup chopped **red onion** and 2 Tbsp. chopped **capers.** Roll logs in crushed **bagel chips.**

Chicken Noodle
Mix in 1 cup shredded **Gouda cheese,** ¼ cup each chopped **carrots, celery** and **onion,** and the **seasoning packet from 1 pkg. chicken-flavored ramen.** Crumble ramen; toast in a skillet until golden brown. Let cool. Roll logs in toasted ramen.

Pepperoni Pizza
Mix in 1 cup shredded **mozzarella,** 1 cup finely chopped **pepperoni,** 2 Tbsp. **pizza sauce** and 2 tsp. **Italian seasoning.** Combine ½ cup chopped **fresh basil** and ½ cup **panko bread crumbs.** Roll logs in basil mixture.

Blue Cheese
Mix in 1 cup shredded **sharp cheddar cheese** and ½ cup crumbled **blue cheese.** In a small skillet, saute 1½ tsp. **curry powder** in 1 Tbsp. **butter** for 1-2 minutes. Stir in ½ cup finely chopped **pecans;** cook and stir 1 minute. Stir in 2 Tbsp. minced **fresh parsley.** Cool slightly. Roll logs in pecan mixture.

JALAPENO SAUSAGE QUICHE

This is a fantastic recipe for an office potluck. You can prepare all the ingredients the night before, then mix together and pop the quiches into the oven the next morning. You may want to double the recipe because two is never enough.
—Pamela Williams, Meridian, MS

PREP: 30 min. + chilling
BAKE: 30 min. + standing
MAKES: 2 quiches (8 servings each)

- **Dough for double-crust pie**
- **1 lb. bulk pork sausage**
- **5 large eggs**
- **½ cup 2% milk**
- **⅓ cup mayonnaise**
- **1 tsp. salt**
- **1 tsp. pepper**
- **2 cups shredded sharp cheddar cheese**
- **1 can (4 oz.) diced jalapeno peppers, drained**
- **5 green onions, chopped**

1. Preheat oven to 400°. On a lightly floured surface, roll half the dough to a ⅛-in.-thick circle; transfer to a 9-in. pie plate. Trim to ½ in. beyond rim of plate; flute edge. Repeat with remaining dough. Refrigerate 30 minutes. Line unpricked crusts with a double thickness of heavy-duty foil. Bake for 10 minutes. Remove the foil; bake 5 minutes longer. Cool on wire racks.
2. Meanwhile, in a large skillet, cook pork over medium heat until no longer pink, 7-9 minutes; drain. In a large bowl, whisk eggs, milk, mayonnaise, salt and pepper. Stir in cheese, jalapenos, green onions and cooked sausage. Pour into crusts.
3. Bake until a knife inserted in center comes out clean, 30-35 minutes. Cover edges loosely with foil during the last 15 minutes if needed to prevent overbrowning. Remove foil. Let stand 10 minutes before cutting.
FREEZE OPTION: Cover and freeze unbaked quiches. To use, remove from freezer 30 minutes before baking (do not thaw). Preheat oven to 400°. Place quiches on baking sheets. Bake as directed, increasing time to 40-45 minutes. Cover edges loosely with foil during the last 15 minutes if needed to prevent overbrowning.
1 PIECE: *357 cal., 27g fat (13g sat. fat), 118mg chol., 636mg sod., 17g carb. (1g sugars, 1g fiber), 11g pro.*
DOUGH FOR DOUBLE-CRUST PIE (9 IN.) Combine 2½ cups all-purpose flour and ½ tsp. salt; cut in 1 cup cold butter until crumbly. Gradually add ⅓-⅔ cup ice water, tossing with a fork until dough holds together when pressed. Divide dough in half. Shape each into a disk; wrap tightly. Refrigerate 1 hour or overnight.

JALAPENO SAUSAGE QUICHE

GINGERSNAP DIP

I serve this dip in a pumpkin-shaped dish at all of our fall church gatherings. It's a nice way to dress up packaged gingersnaps.
—Tessie Hughes, Marion, VA

TAKES: 10 min. • **MAKES:** 3 cups

- **1 pkg. (8 oz.) cream cheese, softened**
- **1 cup confectioners' sugar**
- **2 tsp. pumpkin pie spice**
- **1 carton (8 oz.) frozen whipped topping, thawed**
- **Gingersnap cookies**

In a small bowl, beat the cream cheese, confectioners' sugar and pumpkin pie spice until fluffy. Beat in whipped topping until blended. Refrigerate until serving. Serve with gingersnaps.
2 TBSP.: *158 cal., 7g fat (4g sat. fat), 10mg chol., 152mg sod., 22g carb. (12g sugars, 0 fiber), 2g pro.*

SLOW-COOKER STRAWBERRY SODA CAKE

When you want a sweet cake without the heat of the oven, this slow-cooked strawberry spin on cola cake comes in handy. The topping smells divinely like chocolate-covered strawberries. (Remember this one for Valentine's Day!) It's delicious served with whipped cream or powdered sugar.
—Laura Herbage, Covington, LA

PREP: 30 min. • **COOK:** 2 hours
MAKES: 8 servings

- 1 **cup 1% chocolate milk**
- ½ **cup butter, melted and slightly cooled**
- 2 **tsp. vanilla extract**
- 2 **cups all-purpose flour**
- ½ **cup sugar**
- 2½ **tsp. baking powder**
- ½ **tsp. salt**
- ¼ **cup semisweet chocolate chips**

TOPPING

- 1 **cup strawberry soda**
- ¾ **cup packed brown sugar**
- ¼ **cup sugar**
- ¼ **cup dark chocolate chips**
- ¼ **cup seedless strawberry jam**
- ¼ **cup molasses**
- **Whipped cream and sliced fresh strawberries**

1. In a large bowl, mix chocolate milk, melted butter and vanilla until well blended. In another bowl, whisk flour, sugar, baking powder and salt; gradually mix into the chocolate milk mixture. Stir in chocolate chips. Spread into a greased 3- or 4-qt. slow cooker.
2. For topping, in a small saucepan, combine soda and sugars. Cook and stir over medium heat until sugar is dissolved; remove from heat. Stir in dark chocolate chips, jam and molasses; pour over batter.
3. Cook, covered, on high until a toothpick inserted in center comes out clean, 2-2½ hours. Serve with whipped cream and strawberries.

1 SERVING: *504 cal., 16g fat (10g sat. fat), 32mg chol., 423mg sod., 88g carb. (63g sugars, 2g fiber), 5g pro.*

TROPICAL SWEET POTATO BAKE

TROPICAL SWEET POTATO BAKE

Welcome fall with this simple side dish. It's a pleasant change of pace from the traditional casserole with marshmallows, and it's quite popular at potlucks.
—Joan Hallford, North Richland Hills, TX

PREP: 50 min. • **BAKE:** 35 min.
MAKES: 10 servings

- 5 **medium sweet potatoes (about 3 lbs.), peeled and cubed**
- ⅔ **cup packed brown sugar**
- 3 **Tbsp. butter**
- ¼ **tsp. salt**
- ¼ **tsp. ground cloves**
- ⅛ **tsp. pepper**
- 2 **tsp. grated orange zest**
- ⅓ **cup orange juice**
- ¼ **cup orange liqueur, optional**
- 3 **medium ripe bananas, mashed**
- 2 **large eggs, lightly beaten**

TOPPING

- ½ **cup granola cereal**
- ½ **cup chopped pecans, toasted**
- ¼ **cup sweetened shredded coconut, toasted**
- 2 **Tbsp. brown sugar**
- ¼ **cup butter, melted**

Preheat oven to 350°. Place sweet potatoes in a large Dutch oven; add water to cover. Bring to a boil. Reduce heat; cook, covered, just until tender, 12-15 minutes. Drain; cool slightly. Return to pan; mash with brown sugar, butter, salt, cloves and pepper until smooth. Stir in orange zest, orange juice and, if desired, liqueur. Add bananas and eggs; mix well. Transfer to a greased 2-qt. baking dish. For topping, mix granola, pecans, coconut and brown sugar; sprinkle over sweet potatoes. Drizzle with melted butter. Bake, uncovered, until heated through, 35-45 minutes.

¾ CUP: *355 cal., 15g fat (7g sat. fat), 59mg chol., 160mg sod., 54g carb. (33g sugars, 5g fiber), 5g pro.*

GRILLED JALAPENOS

SMOKED MACARONI & CHEESE

I found this recipe years ago in a magazine, and I kept adding and taking away ingredients until I found the perfect combination. You can make it in the oven, but grilling or smoking the dish is the best way to go.
—Stacey Dull, Gettysburg, OH

PREP: 40 min. • **GRILL:** 20 min. + standing
MAKES: 2 casseroles (8 servings each)

- **6 cups small pasta shells**
- **12 oz. Velveeta, cut into small cubes**
- **2 cups shredded smoked cheddar cheese, divided**
- **1 cup shredded cheddar cheese**
- **1 cup 2% milk**
- **4 large eggs, lightly beaten**
- **¾ cup heavy whipping cream**
- **⅔ cup half-and-half cream**
- **½ cup shredded provolone cheese**
- **½ cup shredded Colby-Monterey Jack cheese**
- **½ cup shredded pepper jack cheese**
- **1 tsp. salt**
- **½ tsp. pepper**
- **½ tsp. smoked paprika**
- **½ tsp. liquid smoke, optional**
- **Dash cayenne pepper, optional**
- **8 bacon strips, cooked and crumbled, optional**

1. Preheat grill or smoker to 350°. Cook pasta according to package directions for al dente. Drain and transfer to a large bowl. Stir in Velveeta, 1 cup smoked cheddar, cheddar cheese, milk, eggs, heavy cream, half-and-half, provolone, Colby-Monterey Jack, pepper jack, salt, pepper, smoked paprika and, if desired, liquid smoke and cayenne pepper.
2. Transfer to 2 greased 13x9-in. baking pans; sprinkle with remaining 1 cup smoked cheddar cheese. Place on grill or smoker rack. Grill or smoke, covered, until a thermometer reads at least 160°, 20-25 minutes, rotating pans partway through cooking. Do not overcook. Let stand for 10 minutes before serving; if desired, sprinkle with bacon.

1 CUP: *403 cal., 23g fat (13g sat. fat), 117mg chol., 670mg sod., 30g carb. (4g sugars, 1g fiber), 18g pro.*

GRILLED JALAPENOS

When barbecuing for friends at home, I also use the grill to serve up hot appetizers. These crowd-pleasing stuffed peppers have a bit of bite. They were concocted by my son.
—Catherine Hollie, Cleveland, TX

TAKES: 25 min. • **MAKES:** 2 dozen

- **24 fresh jalapeno peppers**
- **¾ lb. bulk pork sausage**
- **12 bacon strips, halved**

1. Wash peppers. Cut a slit along 1 side of each pepper. Remove seeds; rinse and dry peppers.
2. In a skillet, cook sausage over medium heat until no longer pink; drain. Stuff peppers with sausage and wrap with bacon; secure with soaked toothpicks.
3. Grill peppers, uncovered, turning frequently, over medium heat until tender and bacon is crisp, about 15 minutes.

NOTE: Wear disposable gloves when cutting hot peppers; the oils can burn skin. Avoid touching your face.

1 STUFFED PEPPER: *97 cal., 9g fat (3g sat. fat), 17mg chol., 179mg sod., 1g carb. (1g sugars, 0 fiber), 3g pro.*

SMOKED MACARONI & CHEESE

ALL-AMERICAN PIE

With apples, cherries and blueberries, this patriotic slab pie even tastes American. If the day doesn't call for stars and stripes, feel free to use any shaped cookie cutters you like for this awe-inspiring potluck dessert.
—James Schend, Pleasant Prairie, WI

PREP: 90 min. + cooling
BAKE: 30 min. + cooling • **MAKES:** 15 servings

- **5 cups all-purpose flour**
- **¼ cup sugar**
- **1 tsp. salt**
- **2 cups unsalted butter, cold**
- **⅔ to 1 cup ice water**

APPLE PIE FILLING

- **6 cups sliced peeled Golden Delicious apples**
- **⅔ cup plus 2 Tbsp. unsweetened apple juice, divided**
- **¾ cup sugar**
- **1 tsp. ground cinnamon**
- **½ tsp. apple pie spice**
- **3 Tbsp. cornstarch**
- **¼ tsp. vanilla extract**

CHERRY PIE FILLING

- **1¼ cups sugar**
- **⅓ cup cornstarch**
- **¾ cup cherry juice**
- **4 cups fresh or frozen pitted tart cherries, thawed**
- **½ tsp. ground cinnamon**
- **¼ tsp. ground nutmeg**
- **¼ tsp. almond extract**

BLUEBERRY PIE FILLING

- **4 cups fresh blueberries, divided**
- **¾ cup water**
- **1 Tbsp. butter**
- **¾ cup sugar**
- **3 Tbsp. cornstarch**
- **⅛ tsp. ground cinnamon**
- **Dash salt**
- **1 tsp. lemon juice**

1. Combine flour, sugar and salt in a food processor; pulse to combine. Add butter; pulse until crumbly. Transfer mixture to a large bowl. Gradually add ice water, tossing with a fork until dough holds together when pressed. Divide the dough in 2, making 1 portion slightly larger. Shape each into a rectangle; wrap and refrigerate 1 hour or overnight.

2. For apple pie filling, in a large saucepan, combine apples, ⅔ cup apple juice, sugar, cinnamon and apple pie spice; bring to a boil over medium heat. Cook and stir until apples soften, about 10 minutes. Combine cornstarch and remaining 2 Tbsp. apple juice; add to saucepan. Return to a boil, stirring constantly. Cook and stir until thickened, about 2 minutes. Remove from the heat. Stir in vanilla. Cool to room temperature, stirring occasionally.

3. For cherry pie filling, in a large saucepan, combine sugar and cornstarch; gradually stir in cherry juice until smooth. Bring to a boil; cook and stir until thickened, about 2 minutes. Remove from the heat. Add the cherries, cinnamon, nutmeg and almond extract. Cool to room temperature, stirring occasionally.

4. For blueberry pie filling, in a large saucepan, combine 1 cup blueberries, water and butter; simmer for 4 minutes. Combine the sugar, cornstarch, cinnamon and salt; add to saucepan. Bring to a boil over medium heat, stirring constantly. Cook and stir for 2 minutes. Stir in lemon juice and remaining 3 cups blueberries. Cool to room temperature, stirring occasionally.

5. Preheat oven to 425°. For crust, on a lightly floured surface roll out the larger portion of dough to a 17x12-in. rectangle. Transfer to a 15x10x1-in. baking pan. Press onto the bottom and up the sides of pan. Line crust with a double thickness of foil. Fill with pie weights, dried beans or uncooked rice. Bake on a lower oven rack until edges are golden brown, about 20 minutes. Remove foil and weights; bake 6-8 minutes longer or until bottom is golden brown. Cool on a wire rack.

6. Meanwhile, roll out remaining dough to a 15x10-in. rectangle. Using a pastry wheel and star cutouts of varying sizes, cut out stars and stripes for decorative topping of flag pie. Arrange pieces 1 in. apart on an ungreased baking sheet. Bake at 400° until golden brown, about 15 minutes for stripes and 8 minutes for stars. Cool on a wire rack.

7. To assemble, place blueberry filling in ⅓ of crust; fill remaining portion of crust with stripes of cherry and apple fillings. Top pie with star and stripe cutouts.

1 SERVING: *632 cal., 26g fat (16g sat. fat), 67mg chol., 24mg sod., 97g carb. (55g sugars, 4g fiber), 5g pro.*

ALL-AMERICAN PIE

COCONUT-MACADAMIA SHEET-PAN PANCAKES

COCONUT-MACADAMIA SHEET-PAN PANCAKES

These are great for brunch when you want to serve a group without standing over the stove. The various flavors give this dish a tropical flair. Pineapple-flavored ice cream topping is an apt swap for the usual maple syrup.
—Trisha Kruse, Eagle, ID

PREP: 15 min. + standing • **BAKE:** 15 min. • **MAKES:** 10 servings

3½ cups complete buttermilk pancake mix
½ cup sweetened shredded coconut
2 cups 2% milk
1 Tbsp. coconut oil or butter, softened
½ cup macadamia nuts, coarsely chopped
2 medium bananas, sliced
Butter and maple syrup

1. Preheat oven to 425°. In a large bowl, combine pancake mix and coconut. Stir in milk just until dry ingredients are moistened; let stand 10 minutes. Meanwhile, line a 15x10x1-in. baking pan with parchment; grease parchment with coconut oil.
2. Spread batter into prepared pan; sprinkle with macadamia nuts. Bake until puffy and golden brown, 15-20 minutes. Cool in pan on a wire rack 5 minutes. Lifting with parchment, remove from pan. Top with bananas; serve with butter and syrup.
1 PIECE: *288 cal., 11g fat (4g sat. fat), 4mg chol., 642mg sod., 44g carb. (13g sugars, 2g fiber), 7g pro.*

KIDDIE CRUNCH MIX

This no-bake snack mix is a delightful treat for kids, and you can easily increase the amount to fit your needs. Place in individual bags, or pour some into colored ice cream cones for a fun presentation.
—Kara de la Vega, Santa Rosa, CA

TAKES: 10 min. • **MAKES:** 6 cups

1 cup plain or frosted animal crackers
1 cup bear-shaped crackers
1 cup miniature pretzels
1 cup salted peanuts
1 cup M&M's
1 cup yogurt- or chocolate-covered raisins

In a bowl, combine all ingredients. Store in an airtight container.
½ CUP: *266 cal., 14g fat (5g sat. fat), 4mg chol., 159mg sod., 33g carb. (23g sugars, 3g fiber), 6g pro.*

KIDDIE CRUNCH MIX

SAGE TURKEY SAUSAGE PATTIES

SAGE TURKEY SAUSAGE PATTIES

Turkey sausage is a good option when you want to cut salt and saturated fat. You'll love the aroma of this recipe when it's sizzling in the pan.
—Sharman Schubert, Seattle, WA

TAKES: 30 min. • **MAKES:** 12 servings

- **¼ cup grated Parmesan cheese**
- **3 Tbsp. minced fresh parsley or 1 Tbsp. dried parsley flakes**
- **2 Tbsp. fresh sage or 2 tsp. dried sage leaves**
- **2 garlic cloves, minced**
- **1 tsp. fennel seed, crushed**
- **¾ tsp. salt**
- **½ tsp. pepper**
- **1½ lbs. lean ground turkey**
- **1 Tbsp. olive oil**

In a large bowl, combine the first 7 ingredients. Crumble turkey over mixture and mix well. Shape into twelve 3-in. patties. In a large skillet, cook patties in oil in batches over medium heat until meat is no longer pink, 3-5 minutes on each side. Drain on paper towels if necessary.

FREEZE OPTION: Place cooled, cooked patties on a waxed paper-lined baking sheet; cover and freeze until firm. Remove from pan and transfer to a resealable freezer container. To use, place patties on a baking sheet coated with cooking spray. Bake in a preheated 350° oven 15 minutes on each side or until heated through.

1 PATTY: *104 cal., 6g fat (2g sat. fat), 46mg chol., 227mg sod., 0 carb. (0 sugars, 0 fiber), 11g pro.* **Diabetic exchanges:** *1 lean meat, 1 fat.*

SWISS POTATO PUFFS

Encourage guests to mingle by serving these cute little morsels. They're transportable, mess-free and easy to eat in a few bites.
—Myra Innes, Auburn, KS

PREP: 20 min. • **BAKE:** 20 min. • **MAKES:** about 3 dozen

- **1⅓ cups water**
- **¼ cup butter, cubed**
- **½ tsp. salt**
- **¾ cup all-purpose flour**
- **¼ cup mashed potato flakes**
- **3 large eggs**
- **1 cup shredded Gruyere or Swiss cheese**

1. In a large saucepan, bring the water, butter and salt to a boil. Remove from heat.
2. Combine the flour and potato flakes; slowly stir into pan. Cook and stir over medium heat until a smooth ball forms. Remove from heat. Add eggs, 1 at a time, beating well after each addition. Continue beating until mixture is smooth and shiny. Stir in cheese.
3. Drop by tablespoonfuls 2 in. apart onto greased baking sheets. Bake at 375° for 18-22 minutes or until golden brown.

1 POTATO PUFF: *37 cal., 2g fat (1g sat. fat), 22mg chol., 53mg sod., 2g carb. (0 sugars, 0 fiber), 2g pro.*

SWISS POTATO PUFFS

BEEF TENDERLOIN WITH ROASTED VEGETABLES

I appreciate this recipe because it includes a side dish of roasted potatoes, Brussels sprouts and carrots. I prepare it for celebrations throughout the year.
—Janet Singleton, Bellevue, OH

PREP: 20 min. + marinating
BAKE: 1 hour + standing • **MAKES:** 10 servings

- **1 beef tenderloin roast (3 lbs.)**
- **¾ cup dry white wine or beef broth**
- **¾ cup reduced-sodium soy sauce**
- **4 tsp. minced fresh rosemary**
- **4 tsp. Dijon mustard**
- **1½ tsp. ground mustard**
- **3 garlic cloves, peeled and sliced**
- **1 lb. Yukon Gold potatoes, cut into 1-in. wedges**
- **1 lb. Brussels sprouts, halved**
- **1 lb. fresh baby carrots**

1. Place tenderloin in a large shallow dish. Combine the wine, soy sauce, rosemary, Dijon mustard, ground mustard and garlic. Pour half of the marinade over tenderloin and turn to coat. Cover and refrigerate 4-12 hours, turning several times. Cover and refrigerate remaining marinade.
2. Place the potatoes, Brussels sprouts and carrots in a greased 13x9-in. baking dish; add reserved marinade and toss to coat. Cover and bake at 425° for 20 minutes; stir.
3. Drain tenderloin, discarding marinade; if desired, tie tenderloin with baker's twine. Place tenderloin over vegetables. Bake, uncovered, for 40-50 minutes or until meat reaches desired doneness (for medium-rare, a thermometer should read 135°; medium, 140°; medium-well, 145°).
4. Remove the beef and let stand for 15 minutes. Check vegetables for doneness. If additional roasting is needed, cover with foil and bake for 10-15 minutes or until tender. Slice beef; serve with vegetables.

1 SERVING: *283 cal., 8g fat (3g sat. fat), 60mg chol., 627mg sod., 16g carb. (4g sugars, 3g fiber), 33g pro.* **Diabetic exchanges:** *4 lean meat, 1 vegetable, ½ starch.*

POLPETTE DI MAMMA

POLPETTE DI MAMMA

When you think of Italian food, spaghetti with meatballs is probably one of the first dishes that comes to mind. Every Italian mother and grandmother has their signature meatball recipe, and their children will always boast that their meatballs are the best.
—Taste of Home *Test Kitchen*

PREP: 45 min. • **COOK:** 45 min.
MAKES: 8 servings

- **½ cup extra virgin olive oil**
- **4 to 5 fresh basil leaves**
- **2 garlic cloves, peeled and smashed**
- **8 cups crushed tomatoes**
- **2 cups water**
- **2 Tbsp. tomato paste**
- **1 Tbsp. kosher salt**
- **1 Tbsp. chopped fresh basil**
- **1 tsp. freshly ground pepper**

POLPETTE (MEATBALLS)

- **½ lb. ground pork**
- **½ lb. ground veal or pork**
- **½ lb. ground beef (85% lean)**
- **1 Tbsp. chopped fresh parsley**
- **1 Tbsp. kosher salt**
- **1 tsp. freshly ground pepper**
- **2 large eggs, beaten**
- **1 cup grated Pecorino Romano cheese**
- **1 cup Italian seasoned bread crumbs**
- **½ cup 2% milk**

1. In a small saucepan, combine olive oil, basil leaves and garlic over very low heat until mixture is very fragrant and garlic turns golden brown, 10-15 minutes. Strain mixture, discarding basil and garlic; set the oil aside.
2. In a Dutch oven, combine crushed tomatoes, water, tomato paste, salt, chopped basil, pepper and reserved olive oil. Bring to a boil; remove ½ cup and set aside. Reduce heat and simmer, covered, while preparing polpette.
3. Meanwhile, to make polpette, in a large bowl, combine all polpette ingredients and reserved ½ cup tomato mixture. Gently mix until combined (mixture will be loose). With wet hands, roll ¼ cupfuls of mixture into balls. Place on a baking sheet or plate. Add raw meatballs to simmering sauce, gently shaking pan to allow for more space. Bring to a simmer; cook, covered, at least 45 minutes or up to 2 hours.

1 SERVING: *453 cal., 27g fat (7g sat. fat), 110mg chol., 2352mg sod., 31g carb. (13g sugars, 5g fiber), 26g pro.*

MAPLE-SAGE BRINED TURKEY, PAGE 283

Holiday & Seasonal Celebrations

No matter what the season, you'll find a delicious way to celebrate it in this festive chapter.

DISHES WE LOVE

Bacon Hash Brown Bake p. 256
Pineapple Salsa p. 265
Chewy Soft Pretzels p. 275
Hot Cider p. 280
Flavorful Mashed Potatoes p. 285
Corn Pudding p. 285
Maple-Gingerroot Vegetables p. 292
Truffle Topiary p. 299

POTATO BAR

LINE YOUR BUFFET WITH AWESOME TOPPINGS, SLOW-COOKED SAUCES AND STEAMY SPUDS, THEN DIG IN!

Slow-cook the potatoes in heavy-duty foil, then serve them as is. The foil shell keeps 'em warm.

Serve warm toppings straight from the crock so they remain at the just-right temp for chowing down.
French's
Crispy Fried ONIONS
ORIGINAL
HOT SURFACE
Proctor Silex
HOT CHILI CHEESE DIP
STONEWALL KITCHEN
Bourbon Bacon Jam
Marzetti
Simply DRESSED
CUCUMBER RANCH
Cacique
Ballpark food trays are the perfect size for a solo spud. Plus, cleanup is so easy!

WHISKEY BARBECUE PORK

(SHOWN ON PAGE 246)

Once the tangy-sweet sauce is mixed, the slow cooker does the rest of the work to make the most flavorful, tender pork ever! The liquid smoke gives the barbecue its authentic taste. I typically make this for sandwiches, but it's also tasty atop baked potatoes, pizza, nachos and more.
—Rebecca Horvath, Johnson City, TN

PREP: 15 min. • **COOK:** 6 hours
MAKES: 8 servings

- **½ to ¾ cup packed brown sugar**
- **1 can (6 oz.) tomato paste**
- **⅓ cup barbecue sauce**
- **¼ cup whiskey**
- **2 Tbsp. liquid smoke**
- **2 Tbsp. Worcestershire sauce**
- **3 garlic cloves, minced**
- **½ tsp. chili powder**
- **½ tsp. salt**
- **½ tsp. pepper**
- **½ tsp. hot pepper sauce**
- **¼ tsp. ground cumin**
- **1 boneless pork shoulder butt roast (3 to 4 lbs.)**
- **1 medium onion, quartered**
- **8 hamburger buns, split**

1. In a bowl, mix first 12 ingredients. Place pork roast and onion in a 5-qt. slow cooker. Add the sauce mixture. Cook, covered, on low until pork is tender, 6-8 hours.
2. Remove roast and onion. Cool the pork slightly; discard the onion. Meanwhile, skim fat from sauce. If desired, transfer sauce to a small saucepan; bring to a boil and cook to thicken slightly.
3. Shred pork. Return pork and sauce to slow cooker; heat through. Serve on buns or baked potatoes.

1 SANDWICH: *505 cal., 19g fat (7g sat. fat), 101mg chol., 618mg sod., 43g carb. (21g sugars, 2g fiber), 35g pro.*

HOT CHILI CHEESE DIP

(SHOWN ON PAGE 247)

To simplify party preparation, I use my slow cooker to create this thick, cheesy dip. Your guests won't be able to stop themselves!
—Jeanie Carrigan, Madera, CA

PREP: 20 min. • **COOK:** 4 hours
MAKES: 6 cups

- **1 medium onion, finely chopped**
- **2 tsp. canola oil**
- **2 garlic cloves, minced**
- **2 cans (15 oz. each) chili without beans**
- **2 cups salsa**
- **6 oz. cream cheese, cubed**
- **2 cans (2¼ oz. each) sliced ripe olives, drained**
- **Tortilla chips**

1. In a small skillet, saute onion in oil until tender. Add garlic; cook 1 minute longer.
2. Transfer to a 3-qt. slow cooker. Stir in the chili, salsa, cream cheese and olives. Cover and cook on low until heated through, stirring occasionally, about 4 hours. Stir dip before serving it with tortilla chips.

2 TBSP.: *38 cal., 2g fat (1g sat. fat), 7mg chol., 144mg sod., 3g carb. (1g sugars, 0 fiber), 1g pro.*

CHIVE BUTTER BALLS

Bring 1 cup **butter** to room temperature. Once butter is softened, mix with ¼ cup freshly cut **chives.** Using a melon baller, scoop butter into individual portions. Top potatoes with butter as desired.

SLOW-COOKER BAKED POTATOES

(SHOWN ON PAGE 246)

Scrub 6 medium **russet potatoes;** pierce each several times with a fork. In a small bowl, mix 3 Tbsp. **butter** and 3 minced **garlic cloves.** Rub potatoes with butter mixture. Wrap each tightly with a piece of foil. Pour 1 cup **water** into a 6-qt. slow cooker; add potatoes. Cook, covered, on low until tender, 8-10 hours. Season and top as desired.
Makes 6 potatoes.
—Teresa Emrick, Tipp City, OH

SLOW-COOKED SALSA

(SHOWN ON PAGE 246)

I love the fresh taste of homemade salsa, but as a working mother, I don't have much time to make it. So I came up with this easy version that practically makes itself. Yep, it uses only five ingredients!
—Toni Menard, Lompoc, CA

PREP: 15 min. • **COOK:** 2½ hours + cooling
MAKES: about 2 cups

- **10 plum tomatoes**
- **2 garlic cloves**
- **1 small onion, cut into wedges**
- **2 jalapeno peppers**
- **¼ cup cilantro leaves**
- **½ tsp. salt, optional**

1. Core tomatoes. Cut a small slit in 2 tomatoes; insert a garlic clove into each slit. Place tomatoes and onion in a 3-qt. slow cooker.
2. Cut stems off jalapenos; remove the seeds if a milder salsa is desired. Place jalapenos in the slow cooker.
3. Cover and cook on high until the vegetables are softened (some vegetables may brown slightly), 2½-3 hours; cool.
4. In a blender, combine the tomato mixture, cilantro and, if desired, salt; cover and process salsa until blended. Refrigerate leftovers.

¼ CUP: *20 cal., 0 fat (0 sat. fat), 0 chol., 5mg sod., 4g carb. (3g sugars, 1g fiber), 1g pro.*
Diabetic exchanges: *1 free food.*

Inspired Spuds

SOUR CREAM AND SHREDDED CHEDDAR ARE CLASSICS, SURE. BUT WHY STOP THERE?

THE CANDIED EARTH APPLE
Sweet potato
+ crumbled bacon
+ brown sugar
+ maple syrup
+ Chive Butter Balls

TRY YOUR OWN CREATIVE COMBO!

TEX-MEX TATER
Russet potato
+ Hot Chili Cheese Dip
+ sliced jalapenos
+ black beans
+ tortilla chips
+ fresh cilantro

LOADED MEAT LOVER'S
Russet potato
+ Whiskey Barbecue Pork
+ crumbled bacon
+ barbecue sauce
+ bourbon bacon jam
+ green onions

QUICK AMBROSIA FRUIT SALAD

Morning, Y'all!

Start your day the southern way by savoring these springy brunch faves.

HOMEMADE BISCUITS & MAPLE SAUSAGE GRAVY
GRITS & SAUSAGE CASSEROLE
SWEET TEA CONCENTRATE
COLLARDS QUICHE

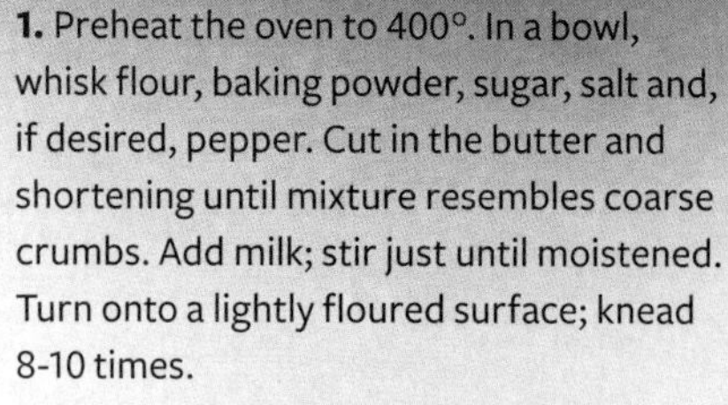

HOMEMADE BISCUITS & MAPLE SAUSAGE GRAVY

I remember digging in to flaky, gravy-smothered biscuits on special occasions when I was a child.
-Jenn Tidwell, Fair Oaks, CA

PREP: 30 min. • **BAKE:** 15 min.
MAKES: 8 servings

- **2 cups all-purpose flour**
- **3 tsp. baking powder**
- **1 Tbsp. sugar**
- **1 tsp. salt**
- **¼ tsp. pepper, optional**
- **3 Tbsp. cold butter, cubed**
- **1 Tbsp. shortening**
- **¾ cup 2% milk**

SAUSAGE GRAVY

- **1 lb. bulk maple pork sausage**
- **¼ cup all-purpose flour**
- **3 cups 2% milk**
- **2 Tbsp. maple syrup**
- **½ tsp. salt**
- **¼ tsp. ground sage**
- **¼ tsp. coarsely ground pepper**

1. Preheat the oven to 400°. In a bowl, whisk flour, baking powder, sugar, salt and, if desired, pepper. Cut in the butter and shortening until mixture resembles coarse crumbs. Add milk; stir just until moistened. Turn onto a lightly floured surface; knead 8-10 times.

2. Pat or roll dough to 1-in. thickness; cut with a floured 2-in. biscuit cutter. Place 1 in. apart on an ungreased baking sheet. Bake until golden brown, 15-17 minutes.

3. Meanwhile, in a large skillet, cook the sausage over medium heat until no longer pink, 6-8 minutes, breaking into crumbles. Stir in flour until blended; gradually stir in milk. Bring to a boil, stirring constantly; cook and stir until the gravy is thickened, 4-6 minutes. Stir in all of the remaining ingredients. Serve gravy with biscuits.

1 BISCUIT WITH ½ CUP GRAVY: *371 cal., 19g fat (8g sat. fat), 41mg chol., 915mg sod., 38g carb. (11g sugars, 1g fiber), 11g pro.*

Best Biscuits

Be sure not to twist the biscuit cutter as you insert it into the dough. Twisting prevents the fluffy treats from baking evenly on top and rising properly. Simply press straight down and hard enough to cut all the way through the dough to the work surface.

COLLARDS QUICHE

I love quiche and wanted to make something that incorporates my southern roots, so I came up with this version. With eggs, cheese, ham and nutritious collard greens in a flaky crust, it's a complete meal.
—Billie Williams-Henderson, Bowie, MD

PREP: 20 min.
BAKE: 35 min. + standing
MAKES: 6 servings

- **1 sheet refrigerated pie crust**
- **2 Tbsp. olive oil**
- **1 cup frozen chopped collard greens, thawed and drained**
- **1 small onion, chopped**
- **1 garlic clove, minced**
- **¼ tsp. salt**
- **¼ tsp. pepper**
- **2 cups shredded Colby-Monterey Jack cheese**
- **¾ cup cubed fully cooked ham**
- **6 large eggs**
- **1 cup 2% milk**

1. Preheat oven to 375°. Unroll crust into a 9-in. pie plate; flute edge. Chill while preparing filling.

2. In a large skillet, heat olive oil over medium-high heat. Add collard greens and onion; cook and stir until onion is tender, 5-7 minutes. Add garlic; cook 1 minute longer. Stir in salt and pepper. Cool slightly; stir in cheese and ham. Spoon into crust.

3. In a large bowl, whisk the eggs and milk until blended. Pour over the top. Bake on lower oven rack until a knife inserted in the center comes out clean, 35-40 minutes. Cover edge loosely with foil during the last 15 minutes if needed to prevent overbrowning. Remove foil. Let stand for 10 minutes before cutting.

FREEZE OPTION: Cover and freeze unbaked quiche. To use, remove from the freezer 30 minutes before baking (do not thaw). Preheat oven to 375°. Place the quiche on a baking sheet. Bake as directed, increasing the time to 50-60 minutes.

1 PIECE: *457 cal., 31g fat (15g sat. fat), 240mg chol., 766mg sod., 23g carb. (4g sugars, 1g fiber), 21g pro.*

The Upper Crust

To make this scalloped crust edge, press a floured spoon into the dough near the inner rim. Repeat all the way around, then press into the dough again, just below the first indents.

Fun with Flavor

For a boost of flavor, simmer the quick-cooking grits in broth or stock rather than water.

GRITS & SAUSAGE CASSEROLE

You could call this dish the "so good" casserole—that's what people say when they try it. You can assemble it a day ahead. Just remove it from the fridge for 30 minutes, then bake as directed.
—Marie Poppenhager, Old Town, FL

PREP: 30 min. • **BAKE:** 1¼ hours
MAKES: 12 servings

- **3 cups water**
- **1 cup quick-cooking grits**
- **¾ tsp. salt, divided**
- **2 lbs. bulk pork sausage, cooked and drained**
- **2 cups shredded cheddar cheese, divided**
- **3 large eggs**
- **1½ cups whole milk**
- **2 Tbsp. butter, melted**
- **Pepper to taste**

1. In a saucepan, bring water to a boil. Slowly whisk in the grits and ½ tsp. salt. Reduce the heat; cover and simmer for 5 minutes, stirring occasionally.
2. In a large bowl, combine grits, sausage and 1½ cups cheese. Beat together the eggs and milk; stir into grits mixture. Add butter, pepper and remaining ¼ tsp. salt.
3. Transfer to a greased 13x9-in. baking dish. Bake, uncovered, at 350° until a knife inserted in the center comes out clean, about 1 hour. Sprinkle with the remaining ½ cup cheese; bake 15 minutes longer or until cheese is melted. Let stand for 5 minutes before serving.

1 CUP: *316 cal., 24g fat (11g sat. fat), 110mg chol., 621mg sod., 13g carb. (3g sugars, 1g fiber), 13g pro.*

BEST STRAWBERRY SHORTCAKE

For a dazzling summer dessert, you can't beat juicy strawberries and fresh whipped cream atop homemade shortcake. My father added even more indulgence to this recipe by buttering the cake.
—Shirley Joan Helfenbein, Lapeer, MI

PREP: 15 min. • **BAKE:** 15 min. + cooling
MAKES: 4 servings

- **1 cup all-purpose flour**
- **1 Tbsp. sugar**
- **1½ tsp. baking powder**
- **¼ tsp. salt**
- **¼ cup plus 2 tsp. cold butter, divided**
- **1 large egg, room temperature**
- **⅓ cup half-and-half cream**
- **½ cup heavy whipping cream**
- **1 Tbsp. confectioners' sugar**
- **⅛ tsp. vanilla extract**
- **2 cups fresh strawberries, sliced**

1. Preheat the oven to 450°. In a small bowl, combine the flour, sugar, baking powder and salt. Cut in ¼ cup butter until mixture resembles coarse crumbs. In a bowl, combine egg and half-and-half; stir into crumb mixture just until moistened.

2. Spread batter into a 6-in. round baking pan coated with cooking spray, slightly building up the edges. Bake until golden, 13-15 minutes. Cool for 10 minutes, then remove shortcake from pan to a wire rack.

3. In a bowl, beat whipping cream, confectioners' sugar and vanilla until soft peaks form. Cut the cake horizontally in half. Soften remaining 2 tsp. butter. Place bottom layer on a serving plate; spread with butter. Top with half the strawberries and half the cream mixture. Repeat layers of cake, berries and cream.

1 PIECE: *420 cal., 28g fat (17g sat. fat), 140mg chol., 471mg sod., 36g carb. (10g sugars, 2g fiber), 7g pro.*

BACON HASH BROWN BAKE

This tasty side dish is simple to make, with wonderful from-scratch flavor that's so comforting at brunch. It's very popular with guests at my bed-and-breakfast.
—Mark Clark, Twin Mountain, NH

PREP: 10 min.
BAKE: 35 min.
MAKES: 8 servings

- **4 cups frozen hash brown potatoes, thawed**
- **12 bacon strips, cooked and crumbled**
- **½ cup 2% milk**
- **⅓ cup chopped onion**
- **½ tsp. salt**
- **¼ tsp. pepper**
- **¼ tsp. garlic powder**
- **1 Tbsp. butter, melted**
- **½ tsp. paprika**

In a large bowl, combine the first 7 ingredients. Transfer mixture to a greased 9-in. pie plate. Drizzle with butter; sprinkle with paprika. Bake at 350° until lightly browned, 35-45 minutes.

½ CUP: *159 cal., 7g fat (3g sat. fat), 14mg chol., 372mg sod., 19g carb. (1g sugars, 2g fiber), 6g pro.*

SWEET TEA CONCENTRATE

Sweet iced tea is a southern classic. This is a fabulous recipe for tea lovers or a party.
—Natalie Bremson, Plantation, FL

PREP: 30 min. + cooling
MAKES: 20 servings (5 cups concentrate)

- 2 **medium lemons**
- 4 **cups sugar**
- 4 **cups water**
- 1½ **cups English breakfast tea leaves or 20 black tea bags**

EACH SERVING:

- 1 **cup cold water**
- **Ice cubes**

1. Remove peels from the lemons; squeeze fruit, reserving ⅓ cup juice. Save remaining juice for another use.
2. In a large saucepan, combine sugar and water. Bring to a boil over medium heat. Reduce heat; simmer, uncovered, until the sugar is dissolved, 3-5 minutes, stirring occasionally. Remove from the heat; add tea leaves and lemon peels. Cover and steep for 15 minutes. Strain tea, discarding tea leaves and lemon peels; stir in reserved ⅓ cup lemon juice. Cool to room temperature.
3. Transfer to a container with a tight-fitting lid. Store in the refrigerator for up to 2 weeks.
4. To prepare tea: In a tall glass, combine water with ¼ cup concentrate; add ice.
¼ CUP CONCENTRATE: *165 cal., 0 fat (0 sat. fat), 0 chol., 27mg sod., 43g carb. (40g sugars, 0 fiber), 0 pro.*

QUICK AMBROSIA FRUIT SALAD

In a large bowl, combine 1 can (8¼ oz.) drained **fruit cocktail,** 1 can (8 oz.) drained unsweetened **pineapple chunks,** 1 cup **green grapes,** 1 cup **seedless red grapes,** 1 cup **mini marshmallows,** 1 sliced medium **banana,** ¾ cup **vanilla yogurt** and ½ cup **sweetened shredded coconut.** Chill until serving. **Serves 6.**
—Trisha Kruse, Eagle, ID

Fireside Chats

The sun's gone, but the fun is on! Get cozy with your crew, some can't-miss snacks and a crackling bonfire for a roasty, toasty good time.

FAVORITE HOT CHOCOLATE

Hershey's bars aren't the only chocolates fit for a bonfire! Load up your s'mores, cupcakes and even cocoa with other favorites, like Reese's cups, Crunch bars and Butterfingers.

S'MORES CUPCAKES

Along with fresh veggies, include star-shaped crackers on your platter of dippers to match the twinkly night sky above you.
Want to avoid having fire around little fingers? Use flameless tea lights on your spread of food for the same cozy effect.
CHEESE & PIMIENTO SPREAD
WATERMELON & CUCUMBER SALSA

CHEESE & PIMIENTO SPREAD

My mother made delicious pimiento cheese. This is a spicy, modern version of her recipe. Serve it with celery or crackers, or spread it on a sandwich or slices of toasted baguette.
—Elizabeth Hester, Elizabethtown, NC

TAKES: 15 min. • **MAKES:** 2¾ cups

- 12 **oz. sharp white cheddar cheese**
- 8 **oz. reduced-fat cream cheese, softened**
- 2 **tsp. Worcestershire sauce**
- 2 **tsp. white vinegar**
- ¼ **tsp. white pepper**
- ¼ **tsp. garlic powder**
- ¼ **tsp. cayenne pepper**
- 1 **jar (4 oz.) diced pimientos, undrained**
- **Assorted crackers and vegetables**

Shred the cheddar cheese; transfer to a bowl. Add cream cheese, Worcestershire sauce, vinegar, pepper, garlic powder and cayenne; beat on low speed until blended. Drain pimientos, reserving 2 Tbsp. juice. Stir in pimientos and reserved juice. Serve with crackers and vegetables.

2 TBSP.: *90 cal., 7g fat (4g sat. fat), 23mg chol., 150mg sod., 1g carb. (1g sugars, 0 fiber), 5g pro.*

CHEESE & PIMIENTO SPREAD

FAVORITE HOT CHOCOLATE

(SHOWN ON PAGE 258)

You need just a few ingredients to stir up this yummy sipper. It makes for a cozy night.
—Flo Snodderly, North Vernon, IN

TAKES: 15 min. • **MAKES:** 8 servings

- 1 **can (14 oz.) sweetened condensed milk**
- ½ **cup baking cocoa**
- 6½ **cups water**
- 2 **tsp. vanilla extract**
- **Optional: Whipped cream, marshmallows, chocolate syrup and Pirouette cookies**

1. Place milk and cocoa in a saucepan; cook and stir over medium heat until blended. Gradually stir in water; heat through, stirring occasionally.

2. Remove from heat; stir in vanilla. If desired, top with whipped cream and other toppings.

1 CUP: *177 cal., 5g fat (3g sat. fat), 17mg chol., 63mg sod., 30g carb. (27g sugars, 1g fiber), 5g pro.*

WATERMELON & CUCUMBER SALSA

(SHOWN ON PAGE 259)

The combo of watermelon and cucumber may sound unusual, but it tastes great. Serve the salsa as a hot dog topper or eat it with chips or on chicken tacos.
—Suzanne Curletto, Walnut Creek, CA

TAKES: 15 min. • **MAKES:** 3 cups

- 1½ **cups seeded chopped watermelon**
- ¾ **cup finely chopped cucumber**
- ½ **cup finely chopped sweet onion**
- ¼ **cup minced fresh cilantro**
- 1 **jalapeno pepper, seeded and minced**
- 2 **Tbsp. lime juice**
- ¼ **tsp. salt**

In a small bowl, combine all ingredients; refrigerate until serving.

NOTE: Wear disposable gloves when cutting hot peppers; the oils can burn skin. Avoid touching your face.

¼ CUP: *10 cal., 0 fat (0 sat. fat), 0 chol., 50mg sod., 3g carb. (2g sugars, 0 fiber), 0 pro.*
Diabetic exchanges: *1 free food.*

PEANUT BUTTER GRANOLA PINWHEELS

I came across this easy, tasty snack while searching online for healthy munchies for kids. It's quick to make and filling enough to hold the kids until dinner.
—Mary Haluch, Ludlow, MA

TAKES: 10 min. • **MAKES:** 16 pinwheels

- 4 **Tbsp. creamy peanut butter**
- 2 **flour tortillas (8 in.)**
- 2 **tsp. honey**
- ½ **cup granola without raisins**

Spread peanut butter over each tortilla; drizzle with honey and sprinkle with granola. Roll up; cut into slices.

1 PINWHEEL: *60 cal., 3g fat (1g sat. fat), 0 chol., 48mg sod., 7g carb. (2g sugars, 1g fiber), 2g pro.*

S'MORES CUPCAKES

The marshmallow frosting puts these cupcakes over the top. Feel free to garnish however you'd like with chocolate and graham crackers to make them scream "s'mores!"
—Erin Rachwal, Hartland, WI

PREP: 30 min. • **BAKE:** 20 min. + cooling
MAKES: 2 dozen

- ¾ **cup water**
- ¾ **cup buttermilk**
- 2 **large eggs, room temperature**
- 3 **Tbsp. canola oil**
- 1 **tsp. vanilla extract**
- 1½ **cups all-purpose flour**
- 1½ **cups sugar**
- ¾ **cup baking cocoa**
- 1½ **tsp. baking soda**
- ¾ **tsp. salt**
- ¾ **tsp. baking powder**

FROSTING

- 1½ **cups butter, softened**
- 2 **cups confectioners' sugar**
- ½ **tsp. vanilla extract**
- 2 **jars (7 oz. each) marshmallow creme**
- 2 **Tbsp. graham cracker crumbs**
- 2 **milk chocolate candy bars (1.55 oz. each)**
- **Optional: Toasted marshmallows and graham cracker pieces**

S'MORES CUPCAKES

1. Preheat oven to 350°. In a bowl, beat water, buttermilk, eggs, oil and vanilla until well blended. Combine flour, sugar, cocoa, baking soda, salt and baking powder; gradually beat into buttermilk mixture until blended.
2. Fill paper-lined muffin cups half full. Bake until a toothpick comes out clean, 16-20 minutes. Cool in pans for 10 minutes before removing from pans to wire racks to cool completely.
3. For frosting, in a bowl, beat butter until fluffy; beat in confectioners' sugar and vanilla until smooth. Add marshmallow creme; beat until light and fluffy. Spread or pipe over the cupcakes. Sprinkle with the cracker crumbs. Break each candy bar into 12 pieces; garnish the cupcakes. If desired, top with marshmallows and graham cracker pieces.

1 CUPCAKE: *330 cal., 15g fat (8g sat. fat), 47mg chol., 298mg sod., 43g carb. (35g sugars, 1g fiber), 3g pro.*

TEST KITCHEN TIP

No need to toast the 'mallows in advance! Show up to your soiree with the cupcakes simply iced. Then plunk on the rest of the s'mores goodies as the fire is roaring.

HOLIDAY IN PARADISE

Bask in tropical treats, sunny decor and warm memories with your squad.

SHAKE IT UP

Because this beverage isn't a big-batch recipe, be sure to set out a cocktail shaker, the makings and lots of extra ice so partygoers can play bartender when they need a refill.

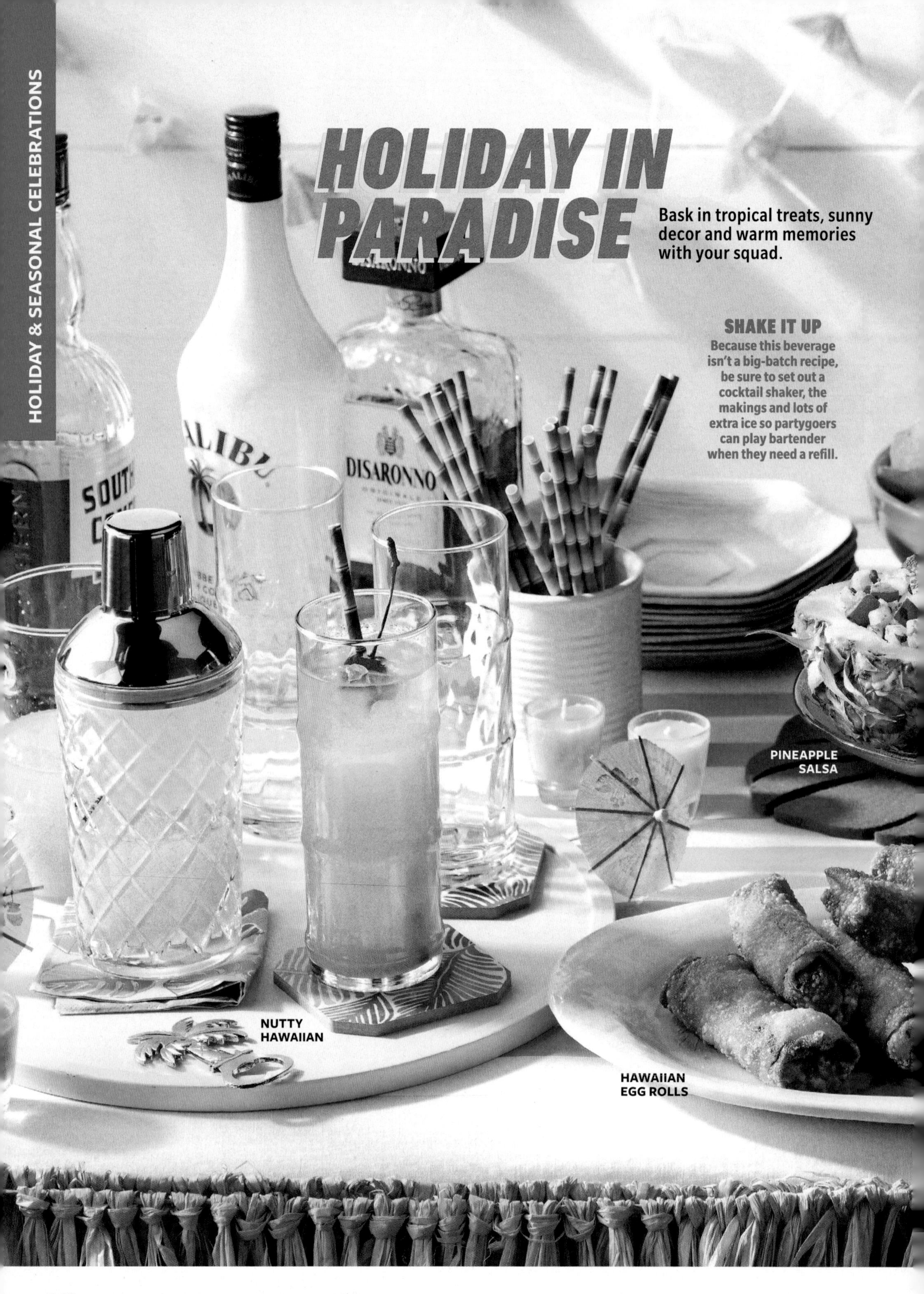
DISARONNO
PINEAPPLE SALSA
NUTTY HAWAIIAN
HAWAIIAN EGG ROLLS

ABSOLUTELY SUB-LIME
This chips-and-dip combo is already bursting with flavor, but to take it to the next level, fill the bowl with lime tortilla chips.
GO GREEN
Help keep plastic away from our beloved oceans and beaches with eco-friendly utensils and straws—such as these biodegradable paper bamboo-themed ones.
A NEW LEAF
Monstera leaves are all the rage. You've seen them on clothes, artwork and more. Here, serve up the stylish pattern on napkins and trivets for island vibes all around.
EASY COCONUT SHRIMP

EASY COCONUT SHRIMP

NUTTY HAWAIIAN

I came up with this tropical-tasting cocktail on a whim one day. Later, when my husband and I went to Key West, Florida, I asked the bartender at an open bar to make it. He loved it so much he asked if he could use it, and of course I said yes!
—Tracy Davidheiser, Reading, PA

TAKES: 5 min. • **MAKES:** 2 servings

- **Ice cubes**
- **2 oz. Southern Comfort**
- **2 oz. coconut rum**
- **1½ oz. amaretto**
- **2 cans (6 oz. each) unsweetened pineapple juice**
- **Maraschino cherries**

Fill a shaker three-fourths full with ice. Add Southern Comfort, rum, amaretto and juice. Cover and shake for 10-15 seconds or until condensation forms on outside of shaker. Strain into chilled glasses filled with ice. Top with cherries.

1 CUP: *299 cal., 0 fat (0 sat. fat), 0 chol., 6mg sod., 30g carb. (25g sugars, 0 fiber), 1g pro.*

NUTTY HAWAIIAN

EASY COCONUT SHRIMP

Guests are always impressed when I serve these restaurant-quality shrimp. A selection of sauces alongside for dipping adds the perfect touch.
—Tacy Holliday, Germantown, MD

TAKES: 25 min. • **MAKES:** about 2 dozen

- **1¼ cups all-purpose flour**
- **¼ tsp. seafood seasoning**
- **1 large egg, beaten**
- **¾ cup pineapple juice**
- **1 pkg. (14 oz.) sweetened shredded coconut**
- **1 lb. large shrimp, peeled and deveined**
- **Oil for deep-fat frying**
- **Optional: Apricot preserves, sweet-and-sour sauce, plum sauce or Dijon mustard**

1. In a bowl, combine the flour, seasoning, egg and pineapple juice until smooth. Place coconut in a shallow bowl. Dip shrimp into batter, then coat with coconut.

2. In an electric skillet or deep-fat fryer, heat oil to 375°. Fry shrimp, a few at a time, until golden brown, about 1½ minutes, turning occasionally. Drain on paper towels. Serve with dipping sauce or mustard if desired.

1 SHRIMP: *171 cal., 11g fat (6g sat. fat), 31mg chol., 76mg sod., 14g carb. (8g sugars, 1g fiber), 5g pro.*

HAWAIIAN EGG ROLLS

PINEAPPLE SALSA

This mouthwatering salsa features fresh pineapple and cilantro. Besides serving it with chips, you can spoon it over grilled chicken or fish to jazz up a meal.
—Suzi LaPar, Wahiawa, HI

TAKES: 20 min. • **MAKES:** 3½ cups

- **2 cups diced fresh pineapple**
- **2 medium tomatoes, seeded and chopped**
- **¾ cup chopped sweet onion**
- **¼ cup minced fresh cilantro**
- **1 jalapeno pepper, seeded and chopped**
- **1 Tbsp. olive oil**
- **1 tsp. ground coriander**
- **¾ tsp. ground cumin**
- **½ tsp. salt**
- **½ tsp. minced garlic**
- **Tortilla chips**

In a large bowl, combine the first 10 ingredients. Cover and refrigerate until serving. Serve with tortilla chips.

NOTE: Wear disposable gloves when cutting hot peppers; the oils can burn skin. Avoid touching your face.

¼ CUP: *29 cal., 1g fat (0 sat. fat), 0 chol., 87mg sod., 5g carb. (4g sugars, 1g fiber), 0 pro.*

PINEAPPLE SALSA

HAWAIIAN EGG ROLLS

An avid cook, I am constantly trying to come up with recipes for leftovers. This one gives a whole new twist to extra ham. My two children think these egg rolls are great, and they freeze well. I thaw as many as needed and bake them.
—Terri Wheeler, Vadnais Heights, MN

TAKES: 25 min. • **MAKES:** 7 egg rolls

- **10 fresh spinach leaves, julienned**
- **½ tsp. ground ginger**
- **2 Tbsp. olive oil**
- **½ lb. fully cooked ham, coarsely ground (about 2 cups)**
- **4 water chestnuts, chopped**
- **¼ cup crushed pineapple, undrained**
- **2 Tbsp. chopped green onion**
- **1 Tbsp. soy sauce**
- **7 egg roll wrappers**
- **Canola oil for frying**
- **Sweet-and-sour sauce**

1. In a large saucepan, saute spinach and ginger in olive oil for 1-2 minutes. In a large bowl, combine the ham, water chestnuts, pineapple, green onion and soy sauce. Stir in the spinach mixture.
2. Place 3 Tbsp. ham mixture in the center of each egg roll wrapper. Fold bottom corner over filling; fold sides over filling toward center. Moisten remaining corner with water; roll up tightly to seal.
3. In an electric skillet, heat 1 in. of canola oil to 375°. Fry egg rolls until golden brown, about 2 minutes on each side. Drain on paper towels. Serve with sweet-sour sauce.

1 EGG ROLL: *311 cal., 20g fat (4g sat. fat), 21mg chol., 743mg sod., 22g carb. (2g sugars, 1g fiber), 10g pro.*

No Work & All Play

WE'RE NOT BLUFFING WHEN WE SAY THIS IS THE BEST WAY TO SPEND A SATURDAY NIGHT. GET YOUR GAME FACE ON—IT'S TIME TO SNACK, THEN ATTACK!

Keep the table (and, maybe more importantly, the game pieces!) clean and dry with fun and functional drink coasters.

Cranberry Cherry Punch

Mini Corn Dogs
These small bites are all dunkable. No utensils needed! Now have some fun mixing and matching with dip flavors.
Lake Charles Dip
Serve up easy-to-grab snacks on a Lazy Susan. This way, everyone can reach, even as they're strategizing.

CRANBERRY CHERRY PUNCH

This crimson-colored beverage is wonderful for Christmas. It looks festive in a glass punch bowl.
—Lori Daniels, Beverly, WV

PREP: 15 min. + freezing • **MAKES:** 3½ qt.

- **⅓ cup fresh or frozen cranberries**
- **2 lemon slices, cut into 6 wedges**
- **1 pkg. (3 oz.) cherry gelatin**
- **1 cup boiling water**
- **3 cups cold water**
- **6 cups cranberry juice, chilled**
- **¾ cup thawed lemonade concentrate**
- **1 liter ginger ale, chilled**

1. Place several cranberries and a piece of lemon in each compartment of an ice cube tray; fill with water and freeze.
2. In a punch bowl or large container, dissolve gelatin in boiling water. Stir in the cold water, cranberry juice and lemonade concentrate. Just before serving, stir in ginger ale. Serve over cranberry-lemon ice cubes.
¾ CUP: *99 cal., 0 fat (0 sat. fat), 0 chol., 17mg sod., 25g carb. (24g sugars, 0 fiber), 1g pro.* **Diabetic exchanges:** *1 starch, ½ fruit.*

CRANBERRY CHERRY PUNCH

CHOCOLATE CARAMEL COOKIES

CHOCOLATE CARAMEL COOKIES

This is my favorite recipe for bake sales and bazaars. Each delightfully sweet chocolate cookie has a fun caramel surprise in the middle, thanks to Rolo candy. Dipped in pecans before baking, they look so nice that they sell in a hurry.
—Melissa Vannoy, Childress, TX

PREP:25 min. • **BAKE:** 10 min./batch + cooling • **MAKES:** 5 dozen

- **1 cup butter, softened**
- **1 cup plus 1 Tbsp. sugar, divided**
- **1 cup packed brown sugar**
- **2 large eggs, room temperature**
- **2 tsp. vanilla extract**
- **2½ cups all-purpose flour**
- **¾ cup baking cocoa**
- **1 tsp. baking soda**
- **1 cup chopped pecans, divided**
- **1 pkg. (13 oz.) Rolo candies**

1. In a large bowl, cream butter, 1 cup sugar and brown sugar. Beat in eggs and vanilla. Combine flour, cocoa and baking soda; gradually add to creamed mixture just until combined. Stir in ½ cup pecans.
2. Shape dough by tablespoonfuls around each candy. In a small bowl, combine remaining pecans and sugar; dip each cookie halfway.
3. Place with nut side up on ungreased baking sheets. Bake at 375° until top is slightly cracked, 7-10 minutes. Cool for 3 minutes; remove to wire racks to cool completely.
1 COOKIE: *121 cal., 6g fat (3g sat. fat), 15mg chol., 60mg sod., 16g carb. (11g sugars, 1g fiber), 1g pro.*

LAKE CHARLES DIP

Italian salad dressing mix gives this simply delicious dip its marvelous flavor. Serve it with fresh veggies or crackers for an easy appetizer.
—Shannon Copley, Upper Arlington, OH

PREP: 15 min. + chilling • **MAKES:** 1½ cups

- **1 cup sour cream**
- **2 Tbsp. reduced-fat mayonnaise**
- **1 Tbsp. Italian salad dressing mix**
- **⅓ cup finely chopped avocado**
- **1 tsp. lemon juice**
- **½ cup finely chopped seeded tomato**
- **Optional: Assorted crackers, cucumber slices, julienned sweet red pepper and carrot sticks**

In a small bowl, combine the sour cream, mayonnaise and dressing mix. Toss avocado with lemon juice; stir into sour cream mixture. Stir in tomato. Cover and refrigerate for at least 1 hour. Serve with desired crackers and assorted vegetables.

¼ CUP: *111 cal., 9g fat (5g sat. fat), 27mg chol., 216mg sod., 3g carb. (2g sugars, 1g fiber), 2g pro.*

LAKE CHARLES DIP

MINI CORN DOGS

MINI CORN DOGS

Bring a county fair favorite into your home with these bite-sized corn dogs! I make my own by wrapping cornmeal dough around mini hot dogs. Kids and the young at heart love them.
—Geralyn Harrington, Floral Park, NY

TAKES: 30 min. • **MAKES:** 2 dozen

- **1⅔ cups all-purpose flour**
- **⅓ cup cornmeal**
- **3 tsp. baking powder**
- **1 tsp. salt**
- **3 Tbsp. cold butter**
- **1 Tbsp. shortening**
- **1 large egg, room temperature**
- **¾ cup 2% milk**
- **24 miniature hot dogs**

HONEY MUSTARD SAUCE

- **⅓ cup honey**
- **⅓ cup prepared mustard**
- **1 Tbsp. molasses**

1. In a large bowl, combine the first 4 ingredients. Cut in butter and shortening until mixture resembles coarse crumbs. Beat egg and milk; stir into dry ingredients until a soft dough forms; dough will be sticky.

2. Turn onto a generously floured surface; knead 6-8 times or until smooth, adding additional flour as needed. Roll out to ¼-in. thickness. Cut with a 2¼-in. biscuit cutter. Fold each dough circle over a hot dog and press edges to seal. Place on greased baking sheets.

3. Bake at 450° until golden brown, 10-12 minutes. In a small bowl, combine the sauce ingredients. Serve with corn dogs.

1 CORN DOG: *109 cal., 5g fat (2g sat. fat), 18mg chol., 306mg sod., 14g carb. (5g sugars, 0 fiber), 3g pro.*

Galactic Gala

Gather your squad of extraterrestrials for an unforgettable get-together filled with intergalactic goodies that will take you to a galaxy far, far away.

ROBOT CAKE

CHEWY COOKIES

These adorable cutouts will be a fan favorite at any kind of Star Wars *party.*
—Taste of Home *Test Kitchen*

PREP: 45 min. + chilling
BAKE: 10 min./batch + cooling
MAKES: About 1½ dozen

- ⅓ **cup butter, softened**
- ¾ **cup packed dark brown sugar**
- ½ **cup molasses**
- 1 **large egg, room temperature**
- 2 **tsp. vanilla extract**
- 3 **cups all-purpose flour**
- 3 **tsp. ground ginger**
- 1½ **tsp. baking powder**
- 1¼ **tsp. ground cinnamon**
- ¾ **tsp. baking soda**
- ¼ **tsp. salt**
- ¼ **tsp. ground cloves**
- 1 **cup semisweet chocolate chips, melted**
- 1 **cup white baking chips, melted**

1. In a large bowl, beat butter and brown sugar until light and fluffy, 5-7 minutes. Beat in molasses, egg and vanilla. In another bowl, whisk flour, ginger, baking powder, cinnamon, baking soda, salt and cloves; gradually beat into creamed mixture. Divide dough in half. Shape each into a disk. Cover and refrigerate until easy to handle, about 1 hour.
2. Preheat oven to 350°. On a lightly floured surface, roll out each portion to ¼-in. thickness. Cut out shapes with a floured 3-in. gingerbread man cookie cutter.
3. Place 2 in. apart on greased baking sheets. Create lines in each cutout with tines of a fork to look like fur. Bake until edges are firm, 7-9 minutes. Remove from pans to wire racks to cool completely.
4. To decorate, pipe melted semisweet chocolate for eyes, nose and utility belt, then pipe melted white chocolate for mouth and bullets. Let stand until set.
1 COOKIE: *202 cal., 6g fat (4g sat. fat), 19mg chol., 154mg sod., 34g carb. (19g sugars, 1g fiber), 3g pro.*

YODA SODA

It takes only three ingredients to create this jazzed-up party punch. Instead of vanilla ice cream, try it with lime sherbet for a tropical twist.
—Taste of Home *Test Kitchen*

TAKES: 5 min. • **MAKES:** 36 servings

- **1 gallon Hawaiian Punch Green Berry Rush, chilled**
- **1 bottle (2 liters) lemon-lime soda, chilled**
- **2 pints vanilla ice cream**
- **Optional: Fresh blueberries and lime wedges**

In a punch bowl, combine Hawaiian Punch and soda. Top with scoops of ice cream. If desired, garnish each serving glass with fresh blueberries and lime wedges.

¾ CUP: *82 cal., 2g fat (1g sat. fat), 6mg chol., 64mg sod., 16g carb. (15g sugars, 0 fiber), 1g pro.*

ROBOT CAKE

(*SHOWN ON PAGE 270*)

This 3-D droid cake is easy to assemble and decorate. Using a cake mix gives you a jump-start so you can spend more time arranging the decorations.
—Taste of Home *Test Kitchen*

PREP: 40 min. • **BAKE:** 1 hour + cooling
MAKES: 40 servings

- **2 pkg. (16 oz. each) pound cake mix**
- **1 cup shortening**
- **1 cup butter, softened**
- **8 cups confectioners' sugar**
- **2 tsp. vanilla extract**
- **4 to 6 Tbsp. 2% milk**
- **2 cups orange and 1 single brown Reese's Pieces**
- **Silver nonpareils**
- **1 mini Oreo cookie**
- **2 pretzel sticks**

1. Preheat oven to 350°. Prepare cake mixes according to package directions. Pour batter into 2 greased 1.5-qt. ovenproof bowls and 2 greased 10-oz. custard cups, filling custard cups three-fourths full and evenly dividing rest of batter between the bowls.

2. Bake until a toothpick inserted in the center of each cake comes out clean, 40-45 minutes for custard cups and 60-65 minutes for bowls. Cool in pans for 5 minutes before removing to wire racks to cool completely.

3. For frosting, beat shortening and butter in a bowl. Beat in confectioners' sugar, vanilla and enough milk to reach spreading consistency.

4. Use a serrated knife to level the cakes. Place 1 large cake flat side up on an 8-in. serving plate. Frost top of cake. Place remaining large cake on top with flat side down and edges even. Frost top and sides.

5. For the head, place 1 custard-cup cake with flat side up on serving plate. Frost top of the cake. Place remaining custard-cup cake on top with the flat side down and edges even. Frost top and side. Trim 1 side of assembled head so it is flat, then place head above the body, using extra frosting to adhere.

6. To decorate the cake, use orange Reese's Pieces to create four 3-in. circles randomly placed on the body. Arrange silver nonpareils and additional orange Reese's Pieces in decorative patterns inside each circle. Use additional orange Reese's Pieces and nonpareils to form parallel lines at the top and bottom of the head. Place 1 mini Oreo and 1 brown Reese's Pieces candy outlined with nonpareils in between the parallel lines to make the cameras. Insert pretzels sticks into head for antenna, leaving 1 longer than the other.

1 PIECE: *318 cal., 13g fat (6g sat. fat), 22mg chol., 140mg sod., 49g carb. (39g sugars, 1g fiber), 2g pro.*

YODA SODA

LIGHTSABER PRETZELS

(SHOWN ON PAGE 271)

Candy-coated pretzels take on a fun Star Wars theme with these sweet and salty treats.
—Taste of Home *Test Kitchen*

PREP: 1 hour + standing • **MAKES:** 2½ dozen

- 8 **oz. each blue, green and red candy coating disks**
- 30 **pretzel rods**
- **Blue, green and red colored sugar**
- 6 **oz. each white and black candy coating disks**
- 30 **M&M's minis**

1. Place each color of candy melts in separate microwave-safe bowls. Working with 1 color at a time, heat in microwave, stirring every 30 seconds until smooth. Dip 10 pretzel rods in each blue, green and red melted candy coating, stopping 2 in. from end; allow excess to drip off. Immediately roll in matching colored sugar. Let stand on a parchment-lined pan until set. Reheat candy coating as needed.
2. Adding 1 tsp. at a time, stir melted black candy coating into the white until desired shade of gray is achieved; reserve the remaining melted black candy coating. Dip the uncoated end of the pretzel rods into melted gray candy coating for handle; allow excess to drip off. Return pretzels to parchment-lined pan until set.
3. Place reserved melted black candy coating in a piping bag fitted with a small round tip; pipe 3 lines onto handle. For power buttons, secure M&M's minis to handles with melted black candy coating. Allow to set completely before serving. Store at room temperature in an airtight container between layers of waxed paper.

1 PRETZEL ROD: *223 cal., 11g fat (9g sat. fat), 1mg chol., 244mg sod., 31g carb. (24g sugars, 0 fiber), 1g pro.*

GALAXY BITES

GALAXY BITES

These perky gelatin cubes are fun to serve and to eat! I vary the colors to match the occasion—pink and blue for a baby shower, school colors for a graduation party, etc. Kids of all ages snap them up.
—Deanna Pietrowicz, Bridgeport, CT

PREP: 30 min. + chilling • **MAKES:** 9 dozen

- 4 **pkg. (3 oz. each) assorted flavored gelatin, divided**
- 6 **envelopes unflavored gelatin, divided**
- 5¾ **cups boiling water, divided**
- 1 **can (14 oz.) sweetened condensed milk**
- ¼ **cup cold water**

1. In a small bowl, combine 1 package flavored gelatin and 1 envelope unflavored gelatin. Stir in 1 cup boiling water until dissolved. Pour into a 13x9-in. dish coated with cooking spray; refrigerate until set but not firm, about 20 minutes.
2. In small bowl, combine the condensed milk and 1 cup boiling water. In another bowl, sprinkle 2 envelopes unflavored gelatin over cold water; let stand for 1 minute. Stir in ¾ cup boiling water. Add to milk mixture. Spoon 1 cup creamy gelatin mixture over the first flavored gelatin layer. Refrigerate until set but not firm, about 25 minutes.
3. Repeat from beginning of recipe twice, alternating flavored gelatin with creamy gelatin layers. Chill each layer until set but not firm before spooning next layer on top. Make final flavored gelatin layer; spoon over top. Refrigerate at least 1 hour after completing last layer before cutting into 1-in. squares.

1 PIECE: *25 cal., 0 fat (0 sat. fat), 1mg chol., 13mg sod., 5g carb. (5g sugars, 0 fiber), 1g pro.*

Oktoberfest

Munich may be thousands of miles away, but the fun is well within reach. Re-create the German celebration at home with soft pretzels, Bavarian brews and fun party games.

CURRYWURST

I lived in Berlin, Germany, many years ago, and one of my favorite things to eat was currywurst and pommes frites. When I came back to the States, I created my own version, which is a pretty close second.
—Julie Merriman, Seattle, WA

PREP: 15 min. • **COOK:** 40 min.
MAKES: 4 servings

- **1 lb. uncooked bratwurst links**
- **3 Tbsp. water**
- **1 Tbsp. olive oil**
- **1 medium onion, finely chopped**
- **2 cups ketchup**
- **½ cup chicken broth**
- **¼ cup packed brown sugar**
- **4 Tbsp. red wine vinegar**
- **2 Tbsp. curry powder**
- **2 Tbsp. smoked paprika**
- **Hot cooked french fries**

1. Place bratwurst and water in a skillet, cover and cook over medium heat for 10 minutes. Uncover; turn bratwurst and cook until browned and centers are no longer pink, 13-17 minutes longer. Remove and cool slightly. Cut into ½-in.-thick slices.
2. In the same skillet, heat oil over medium heat. Add onion; cook and stir until tender, 5-7 minutes. Add ketchup, broth, brown sugar, vinegar, curry powder and paprika. Bring to a boil; reduce heat. Simmer, uncovered, until slightly thickened, 8-10 minutes, stirring occasionally. Add sliced bratwurst; heat through.
3. Serve sausage mixture with french fries; sprinkle with additional curry powder.
1 SERVING: *612 cal., 37g fat (12g sat. fat), 85mg chol., 2611mg sod., 56g carb. (47g sugars, 3g fiber), 17g pro.*

OBATZDA (GERMAN BEER CHEESE DIP)

This dip is so delicious and creamy. It's the perfect dip to make the night before a get-together.
—Beate Trinkl, Einsbach, Germany

TAKES: 15 min. • **MAKES:** 3½ cups

- **2 rounds (8 oz. each) Camembert cheese, rind on, sliced**
- **1 pkg. (8 oz.) cream cheese, softened**
- **1 medium onion, finely chopped**
- **1 tsp. paprika**
- **½ tsp. caraway seeds**
- **¼ tsp. salt**
- **⅛ tsp. pepper**

In a small bowl, mash Camembert cheese with a fork to desired consistency. Beat in cream cheese, onion and seasonings. If desired, sprinkle with additional caraway seeds.
2 TBSP.: *79 cal., 7g fat (4g sat. fat), 20mg chol., 183mg sod., 1g carb. (1g sugars, 0 fiber), 4g pro.*

CHEWY SOFT PRETZELS

These homemade pretzels never last long around our house. My kids love to make them and eat them. I serve them to company with a variety of dips, such as pizza sauce, ranch dressing, spinach dip or hot mustard.
—Elvira Martens, Aldergrove, BC

PREP: 1 hour + rising • **BAKE:** 15 min.
MAKES: 1 dozen

- **1 pkg. (¼ oz.) active dry yeast**
- **1½ cups warm water (110° to 115°)**
- **1 Tbsp. sugar**
- **2 tsp. salt**
- **4 to 4¼ cups all-purpose flour**
- **8 cups water**
- **½ cup baking soda**
- **1 large egg, lightly beaten**
- **Optional toppings: Kosher salt, sesame seeds, poppy seeds and grated Parmesan cheese**

1. Dissolve yeast in warm water. In a large bowl, combine sugar, salt, yeast mixture and 2 cups flour; beat on medium speed until smooth. Stir in enough remaining flour to form a stiff dough.
2. Turn dough onto a floured surface; knead until smooth and elastic, about 5 minutes. Place in a greased bowl, turning once to grease the top. Cover and let rise in a warm place until doubled, about 1 hour.
3. Punch down dough; divide and shape into 12 balls. Roll each into a 22-in. rope; shape into a pretzel.
4. Preheat oven to 425°. Place water and baking soda in a large saucepan; bring to a boil. Place pretzels, 1 at a time, in boiling water for 30 seconds. Remove; drain on paper towels that have been lightly coated with cooking spray.
5. Place pretzels on greased baking sheets. Brush with egg; top as desired. Bake until golden brown, 12-14 minutes. Remove from pans to wire racks; serve warm.
1 PRETZEL: *164 cal., 1g fat (0 sat. fat), 16mg chol., 400mg sod., 33g carb. (1g sugars, 1g fiber), 5g pro.*
TO MAKE LARGE PRETZELS: Divide dough into 4 pieces. Roll each into a 40-in. rope. Proceed as directed, increasing bake time to 16-20 minutes.

TEST KITCHEN TIP

Don't add too much flour when mixing or kneading the dough. You want the dough fairly sticky. Otherwise, the pretzels will be harder to roll out and won't hold their shape as well. If you knead while wearing gloves, the dough won't stick to your hands. You'll find the as you knead it, the flour with hydrate and the dough will firm up so you won't need the extra flour.

Boo-rrific Halloween

No need to be frightened—this devilishly decadent haunted house is a scream to decorate. Start with a fudgy brownie base and trick out your treat with your favorite candies.

BROWNIE HAUNTED HOUSE

BROWNIE HAUNTED HOUSE

Don't worry about getting this sweet showstopper to stand upright. The fudgy brownies are the perfect foundation for building a tasty haunted house. Trick-or-treaters beware!
—Sarah Farmer, Waukesha, WI

PREP: 20 min. • **BAKE:** 30 min. + cooling
MAKES: 16 servings

- **1 cup sugar**
- **½ cup packed brown sugar**
- **⅔ cup butter, cubed**
- **¼ cup water**
- **2 tsp. instant coffee granules, optional**
- **1¾ cups semisweet chocolate chips**
- **4 large eggs, room temperature**
- **2 tsp. vanilla extract**
- **1½ cups all-purpose flour**
- **½ tsp. baking soda**
- **½ tsp. salt**
- **Vanilla frosting**
- **Chocolate frosting**
- **Paste food coloring**
- **Assorted sprinkles**
- **Assorted candies**

1. Preheat oven to 325°. Line a 13x9-in. baking pan with foil, letting ends extend up sides. In a large heavy saucepan, combine sugars, butter, water and, if desired, coffee granules; bring to a boil, stirring constantly. Remove from heat; add chocolate chips and stir until melted. Cool slightly.
2. Whisk the eggs until foamy, about 3 minutes. Add vanilla; gradually whisk in chocolate mixture. In another bowl, whisk the flour, baking soda and salt; stir into chocolate mixture.
3. Pour into prepared pan. Bake on a lower oven rack until a toothpick inserted in center comes out with moist crumbs (do not overbake), 30-40 minutes. Cool in pan on a wire rack.
4. Lifting with foil, remove brownies from pan; let cool completely. Discard foil. Cut off corners of brownie to resemble a house. If desired, cut scraps into pumpkins and ghosts using cookie cutters. Tint vanilla frosting as desired with paste food coloring. Decorate brownie house with frosting and candies.
1 PIECE: *293 cal., 15g fat (9g sat. fat), 67mg chol., 196mg sod., 40g carb. (29g sugars, 1g fiber), 4g pro.*

BONES & BLOOD

BONES & BLOOD

Like a zombie, you'll be desperate for more of these bone-shaped cookies and dip. Fight nicely over them—no biting!
—Taste of Home Test Kitchen

PREP: 45 min. • **BAKE:** 25 min./batch + cooling
MAKES: 40 cookies (2 cups sauce)

- **5 large egg whites**
- **½ cup cake flour**
- **½ cup ground almonds**
- **¼ tsp. ground cinnamon**
- **⅛ tsp. ground cloves**
- **⅛ tsp. ground nutmeg**
- **1 tsp. vanilla extract**
- **¼ tsp. cream of tartar**
- **Dash salt**
- **4 drops yellow food coloring, optional**
- **¾ cup plus 2 Tbsp. sugar**

SAUCE

- **1¼ cups heavy whipping cream**
- **½ cup semisweet chocolate chips**
- **½ cup strawberry jelly**
- **Red food coloring, optional**

1. Place egg whites in a large bowl; let stand at room temperature for 30 minutes. Meanwhile, combine the flour, almonds, cinnamon, cloves and nutmeg.
2. Add the vanilla, cream of tartar, salt and, if desired, food coloring to the egg whites. Beat on medium speed until soft peaks form. Gradually add sugar, 1 Tbsp. at a time, beating on high until stiff glossy peaks form and sugar is dissolved. Fold in flour mixture.
3. Cut a ½-in. hole in the corner of a pastry or plastic bag. Fill bag with egg white mixture. Pipe 4-in. logs onto parchment-lined baking sheets. Pipe two ½-in. balls at both ends of each log. Bake at 300° 25-30 minutes or until firm to the touch. Remove to wire racks. Store in an airtight container.
4. In a small microwave-safe bowl, combine the cream, chocolate chips and jelly. Microwave on high in 30-second intervals until melted; stir until smooth. Tint red if desired. Cool to room temperature and serve with bones. Refrigerate any leftover sauce.
1 COOKIE WITH 2 TSP. SAUCE: *78 cal., 4g fat (2g sat. fat), 10mg chol., 14mg sod., 10g carb. (8g sugars, 0 fiber), 1g pro.*

PUMPKIN CHEESE BALL

No one will guess this make-ahead spread contains pumpkin. The subtle ingredient lends harvest color and extra nutrition.
—Linnea Rein, Topeka, KS

PREP: 20 min. + chilling • **MAKES:** 3 cups

- **1 pkg. (8 oz.) cream cheese, softened**
- **½ cup canned pumpkin**
- **1 can (8 oz.) crushed pineapple, well drained**
- **2 cups shredded sharp cheddar cheese**
- **1 pkg. (2½ oz.) dried beef, finely chopped**
- **1 Tbsp. finely chopped onion**
- **Green pepper stem**
- **Crackers or assorted fresh vegetables**

In a bowl, beat cream cheese, pumpkin and pineapple. Stir in cheddar cheese, beef and onion. Shape into a ball; wrap in plastic wrap. Wrap cheese ball in 4 pieces of string or 4 rubber bands, creating indentions to resemble a pumpkin. Chill for 1 hour. Add green pepper stem for pumpkin stem. Serve with crackers.
2 TBSP.: *85 cal., 6g fat (4g sat. fat), 21mg chol., 174mg sod., 3g carb. (2g sugars, 0 fiber), 4g pro.*

PUMPKIN CHEESE BALL

EYES ON YOU

EYES ON YOU

Look out! This crazy cupcake only has eyes for you. Don't worry though, he's delicious!
—Karen Tack, Riverside, CT

TAKES: 30 min. • **MAKES:** 6 cupcakes

- **1 can (16 oz.) vanilla frosting**
- **Neon green food coloring**
- **6 prepared vanilla or chocolate cupcakes, baked in liners**
- **¼ cup purple sprinkles**
- **1 tube (4.25 oz.) brown decorating frosting**
- **8 to 10 large marshmallows**
- **25 miniature marshmallows**
- **35 M&M's minis**

1. Tint vanilla frosting with neon green food coloring. Spread a generous mound of frosting on each cupcake. Before frosting dries, top with purple sprinkles.
2. Pipe a small dot of brown decorating frosting onto a marshmallow. Lightly press an M&M mini into frosting dot to resemble an eye. Repeat with remaining marshmallows; let dry.
3. Pierce marshmallow eyes with toothpicks; insert opposite ends of toothpicks into cupcakes in any pattern desired.
1 CUPCAKE: *787 cal., 29g fat (12g sat. fat), 47mg chol., 465mg sod., 126g carb. (67g sugars, 1g fiber), 5g pro.*

HOT DOG MUMMIES WITH HONEY MUSTARD DIP

These flaky mummy sandwiches are instant party hits! The accompanying mustard dip adds just the right kick.
—Jessie Sarrazin, Livingston, MT

PREP: 25 min. • **BAKE:** 10 min.
MAKES: 20 appetizers (about 1 cup dip)

- 1 **tube (8 oz.) refrigerated crescent rolls**
- 20 **miniature hot dogs**
- 1 **large egg**
- 2 **tsp. water**
- **Dijon mustard**

DIP

- ½ **cup mayonnaise**
- 3 **Tbsp. Dijon mustard**
- 3 **Tbsp. honey**
- 1 **Tbsp. cider vinegar**
- **Dash hot pepper sauce**

1. Separate crescent roll dough into 2 rectangles; seal seams and perforations. Cut each rectangle horizontally into 10 strips. Wrap 1 strip around each hot dog.
2. Place 1 in. apart on an ungreased baking sheet. In a small bowl, whisk egg and water; brush over tops. Bake at 375° until golden brown, 10-15 minutes. Using mustard, add eyes. In a small bowl, combine the dip ingredients; serve with mummies.
1 APPETIZER WITH 2 TSP. DIP: *128 cal., 10g fat (2g sat. fat), 18mg chol., 287mg sod., 8g carb. (4g sugars, 0 fiber), 2g pro.*

HOT DOG MUMMIES WITH HONEY MUSTARD DIP

WARM SPICED NUTS

WARM SPICED NUTS

I like to set out bowls of spiced nuts when hosting holiday parties. Sometimes I stir in M&M's for a sweet and salty snack.
—Jill Matson, Zimmerman, MN

PREP: 5 min. • **BAKE:** 30 min. • **MAKES:** 3 cups

- 1 **cup pecan halves**
- 1 **cup unblanched almonds**
- 1 **cup unsalted dry-roasted peanuts**
- 3 **Tbsp. butter, melted**
- 4½ **tsp. Worcestershire sauce**
- 1 **tsp. chili powder**
- ½ **tsp. garlic salt**
- ¼ **tsp. cayenne pepper**

1. In a large bowl, combine the pecans, almonds and peanuts. Combine butter and Worcestershire sauce; pour over nuts and toss to coat.
2. Spread in a single layer in an ungreased 15x10x1-in. baking pan. Bake at 300° until browned, about 30 minutes, stirring occasionally.
3. Transfer warm nuts to a bowl. Combine the chili powder, garlic salt and cayenne; sprinkle over nuts and stir to coat. Serve warm, or allow to cool before storing in an airtight container.
¼ CUP: *231 cal., 22g fat (4g sat. fat), 8mg chol., 123mg sod., 7g carb. (2g sugars, 3g fiber), 6g pro.*

HOT CIDER

I dress up traditional apple cider using lemonade, orange juice, honey and spices. It's a new version of a classic fall beverage.
—Glenna Tooman, Boise, ID

PREP: 5 min. • **COOK:** 45 min.
MAKES: 18 servings (4½ qt.)

- **4 cups water**
- **2 tsp. ground allspice**
- **1 cinnamon stick (3 in.)**
- **Dash ground cloves**
- **1 gallon apple cider or unsweetened apple juice**
- **1 can (12 oz.) frozen lemonade concentrate, thawed**
- **¾ cup orange juice**
- **⅓ cup honey**
- **1 tea bag**

1. In a stockpot, combine the water, allspice, cinnamon stick and cloves. Bring to a boil. Reduce heat; simmer, uncovered, 30 minutes.
2. Add the remaining ingredients. Return just to a boil. Discard cinnamon stick and tea bag. Stir and serve warm.
1 CUP: *168 cal., 0 fat (0 sat. fat), 0 chol., 24mg sod., 42g carb. (38g sugars, 0 fiber), 0 pro.*

HOT CIDER

TOMBSTONE TREATS

My brother loves Rice Krispies squares, and my mom loves sugar cookies. I came up with a cute treat they would both like.
—Jill Wright, Dixon, IL

PREP: 45 min. • **BAKE:** 10 min. + cooling
MAKES: 16 treats

- **3 Tbsp. butter**
- **4 cups miniature marshmallows**
- **7½ cups crisp rice cereal**
- **1 tube (16½ oz.) refrigerated sugar cookie dough**
- **⅔ cup all-purpose flour**
- **1 tsp. water**
- **4 drops green food coloring**
- **1½ cups sweetened shredded coconut**
- **Black paste food coloring**
- **Vanilla frosting**
- **Brown decorating icing**
- **1 cup semisweet chocolate chips, melted**
- **Candy pumpkins**

1. In a large saucepan over low heat, melt butter. Stir in marshmallows until melted. Remove from heat. Stir in cereal until well coated. With a buttered spatula, press into a greased 13x9-in. pan. Cool.
2. Beat cookie dough and flour until combined. On a lightly floured surface, roll out dough to ¼-in. thickness. With a 2-in. tombstone-shaped cookie cutter, cut out 16 tombstones from the dough. Place 2 in. apart on ungreased baking sheets.
3. Along bottom edge of each cookie, insert 2 toothpicks halfway into dough. Bake at 350° until edges are golden brown, 8-10 minutes. Remove to wire racks to cool.
4. Place water and green food coloring in a bowl. Add coconut; cover and shake or toss to coat. Toast coconut in a shallow pan in a 350° oven for 5-10 minutes or cook in a skillet over low heat until golden brown, stirring occasionally. Using black paste food coloring, tint frosting gray. Frost cookies and decorate with brown decorating icing.
5. Cut cereal bars into 3x2-in. rectangles; spread with melted chocolate chips. Using toothpicks, insert cookies into cereal bars. Decorate with coconut and candies as desired.
1 TREAT: *358 cal., 15g fat (8g sat. fat), 15mg chol., 306mg sod., 55g carb. (25g sugars, 1g fiber), 4g pro.*

Izzy
Next

Traditional Thanksgiving

If you dream of a holiday that could have inspired a Norman Rockwell painting, then this traditional Thanksgiving dinner is for you.

MAPLE-SAGE BRINED TURKEY

MAPLE-SAGE BRINED TURKEY

When the leaves start turning, it's turkey time at our house. We use a maple-sage brine to help brown the bird and make the meat incredibly juicy.
—Kimberly Forni, Laconia, NH

PREP: 40 min. + brining
BAKE: 2½ hours + standing
MAKES: 20 servings

- **4 qt. water**
- **1½ cups packed brown sugar**
- **1 cup sea salt**
- **1 cup maple syrup**
- **1 cup cider vinegar**
- **24 fresh sage leaves**
- **6 bay leaves**
- **2 Tbsp. yellow prepared mustard**
- **2 Tbsp. coarsely ground pepper**
- **1 tsp. ground cloves**
- **4 qt. ice water**
- **2 turkey-size oven roasting bags**
- **1 turkey (14 to 16 lbs.)**

TURKEY

- **2 Tbsp. olive oil**
- **½ tsp. pepper**
- **½ tsp. salt, optional**

1. In a large stockpot, combine the first 10 ingredients; bring to a boil. Cook and stir until sugar and salt are dissolved. Remove from heat. Add 4 qt. ice water to cool the brine to room temperature.
2. Put 1 turkey-size oven roasting bag inside the other; place in a large stockpot. Place turkey in inner bag; pour in cooled brine. Seal bags, pressing out as much air as possible. Refrigerate 18-24 hours.
3. Preheat oven to 350°. Remove turkey from brine; rinse and pat dry. Discard brine. Place turkey on a rack in a shallow roasting pan, breast side up. Tuck wings under turkey; tie drumsticks together. Rub oil over outside of turkey; sprinkle with pepper and, if desired, salt.
4. Roast, uncovered, until a thermometer inserted in thickest part of thigh reads 170°-175°, 2½-3 hours. (Cover loosely with foil if turkey browns too quickly.)
5. Remove turkey from oven; tent with foil. Let stand 20 minutes before carving.
7 OZ. COOKED TURKEY WITH SKIN: *384 cal., 18g fat (5g sat. fat), 172mg chol., 168mg sod., 0 carb. (0 sugars, 0 fiber), 51g pro.*

TRADITIONAL HOLIDAY STUFFING

Sausage and sage add gourmet flavors to this stuffing, which gets added zest from mayonnaise and mustard. The recipe is sized perfectly for large family gatherings.
—Lorraine Brauckhoff, Zolfo Springs, FL

PREP: 35 min. • **BAKE:** 45 min.
MAKES: 24 servings

- **1 pkg. (12 oz.) reduced-fat bulk pork sausage or breakfast turkey sausage links, casings removed**
- **3 celery ribs, chopped**
- **1 large onion, chopped**
- **2 Tbsp. reduced-fat mayonnaise**
- **2 Tbsp. prepared mustard**
- **4 tsp. rubbed sage**
- **1 Tbsp. poultry seasoning**
- **2 loaves (16 oz. each) day-old white bread, cubed**
- **1 loaf (16 oz.) day-old whole wheat bread, cubed**
- **3 large eggs, lightly beaten**
- **2 cans (14½ oz. each) reduced-sodium chicken broth**
- **Chopped fresh parsley, optional**

1. Preheat oven to 350°. In a large nonstick skillet, cook sausage, celery and onion over medium heat until meat is no longer pink, breaking up sausage into crumbles; drain. Remove from heat; stir in mayonnaise, mustard, sage and poultry seasoning.
2. Place bread cubes in a large bowl; add sausage mixture and toss. In a small bowl, whisk eggs and broth; pour over bread cubes and stir gently to combine. Transfer to two 3-qt. baking dishes coated with cooking spray.
3. Bake, covered, 30 minutes. Uncover and bake until lightly browned and a thermometer reads 165°, 12-18 minutes longer. If desired, top with chopped parsley.
¾ CUP: *202 cal., 6g fat (2g sat. fat), 37mg chol., 572mg sod., 28g carb. (3g sugars, 2g fiber), 9g pro.* **Diabetic exchanges:** *2 starch, 1 fat.*

ELEGANT GREEN BEANS

ELEGANT GREEN BEANS

Mushrooms and water chestnuts give new life to ordinary green bean casserole. Every time I make it for friends, I'm asked to share the recipe.
—Linda Poe, Sandstone, MN

PREP: 20 min. • **BAKE:** 50 min.
MAKES: 8 servings

- **1 can (8 oz.) sliced water chestnuts, drained**
- **1 small onion, chopped**
- **1 jar (4½ oz.) sliced mushrooms, drained**
- **6 Tbsp. butter, divided**
- **¼ cup all-purpose flour**
- **1 cup 2% milk**
- **½ cup chicken broth**
- **1 tsp. reduced-sodium soy sauce**
- **⅛ tsp. hot pepper sauce**
- **Dash salt**
- **1 pkg. (16 oz.) frozen french-style green beans, thawed**
- **½ cup shredded cheddar cheese**
- **1 cup crushed french-fried onions**

1. Preheat oven to 350°. In a small skillet, saute water chestnuts, onion and mushrooms in 2 Tbsp. butter until onion is crisp-tender, 4-5 minutes.
2. In large skillet, melt remaining 4 Tbsp. butter; stir in flour until smooth. Stir in milk, broth, soy sauce, pepper sauce and salt. Bring to a boil; cook and stir until thickened, about 2 minutes. Remove from the heat; stir in green beans and cheese.
3. Spoon half of the bean mixture into a greased 1½-qt. baking dish. Layer with water chestnut mixture and remaining bean mixture.
4. Bake, uncovered, 45 minutes. Top with french-fried onions. Bake until heated through, about 5 minutes longer.
¾ CUP: *218 cal., 15g fat (8g sat. fat), 35mg chol., 392mg sod., 17g carb. (5g sugars, 3g fiber), 5g pro.*

FLAVORFUL MASHED POTATOES

Earthy herbs bring a full chorus of flavor to creamy red potatoes, making this side dish anything but ordinary. Save it for special occasions or serve as a dressy accompaniment to a weeknight meal.
—Mary Relyea, Canastota, NY

PREP: 20 min. • **COOK:** 15 min. • **MAKES:** 12 servings

- **4 lbs. red potatoes (about 12 medium), quartered**
- **6 garlic cloves, peeled and thinly sliced**
- **½ cup fat-free milk**
- **½ cup reduced-fat sour cream**
- **2 Tbsp. butter, melted**
- **2 Tbsp. minced fresh parsley**
- **1 to 2 Tbsp. minced fresh thyme**
- **2 to 3 tsp. minced fresh rosemary**
- **1¼ tsp. salt**

1. Place potatoes and garlic in a Dutch oven; add water to cover. Bring to a boil. Reduce heat; cook, uncovered, 15-20 minutes or until potatoes are tender.
2. Drain; return to pan. Mash potatoes, gradually adding remaining ingredients.
¾ CUP: *146 cal., 3g fat (2g sat. fat), 9mg chol., 280mg sod., 26g carb. (3g sugars, 3g fiber), 4g pro.* **Diabetic exchanges:** *2 starch, ½ fat.*

FLAVORFUL MASHED POTATOES

CORN PUDDING

CORN PUDDING

The pleasing flavor of this golden side dish makes it real comfort food. And because the recipe calls for a packaged cornbread mix, it's easy to prepare.
—P. Lauren Fay-Neri, Syracuse, NY

PREP: 20 min. • **BAKE:** 45 min. • **MAKES:** 8 servings

- **½ cup butter, softened**
- **½ cup sugar**
- **2 large eggs, room temperature**
- **1 cup sour cream**
- **1 pkg. (8½ oz.) cornbread/muffin mix**
- **½ cup 2% milk**
- **1 can (15¼ oz.) whole kernel corn, drained**
- **1 can (14¾ oz.) cream-style corn**

1. Preheat oven to 325°. In a large bowl, cream butter and sugar until light and fluffy, 5-7 minutes. Add eggs, 1 at a time, beating well after each addition. Beat in sour cream. Gradually add muffin mix alternately with milk. Fold in corn.
2. Pour into a greased 3-qt. baking dish or 13x9-in. baking pan. Bake, uncovered, until set and lightly browned, 45-50 minutes.
¾ CUP: *435 cal., 22g fat (12g sat. fat), 112mg chol., 700mg sod., 52g carb. (24g sugars, 2g fiber), 7g pro.*

HOT SPICED CRANBERRY DRINK

I serve this rosy spiced beverage at parties and family gatherings during the winter. Friends like the tangy twist it gets from Red Hots. It's a nice change from the usual hot chocolate.
—Laura Burgess, Ballwin, MO

PREP: 10 min. • **COOK:** 2 hours
MAKES: 14 servings (3½ qt.)

- **8 cups hot water**
- **1½ cups sugar**
- **4 cups cranberry juice**
- **¾ cup orange juice**
- **¼ cup lemon juice**
- **12 whole cloves, optional**
- **½ cup Red Hot candies**

In a 5-qt. slow cooker, combine water, sugar and juices; stir until sugar is dissolved. If desired, place cloves in a double thickness of cheesecloth; bring up corners of cloth and tie with string to form a bag. Add spice bag and Red Hots to slow cooker. Cover and cook on low until heated through, 2-3 hours. Before serving, discard spice bag and stir punch.

1 CUP: *155 cal., 0 fat (0 sat. fat), 0 chol., 2mg sod., 40g carb. (37g sugars, 0 fiber), 0 pro.*

HOT SPICED CRANBERRY DRINK

AUTUMN HARVEST PUMPKIN PIE

This is the best holiday pie I've ever tasted. Use canned pumpkin if you don't have fresh pumpkins or to save time.
—Stan Strom, Gilbert, AZ

PREP: 30 min. + chilling
BAKE: 55 min. + cooling • **MAKES:** 8 servings

- **2 cups all-purpose flour**
- **1 cup cake flour**
- **2 Tbsp. sugar**
- **½ tsp. salt**
- **½ cup cold unsalted butter, cubed**
- **½ cup butter-flavored shortening**
- **1 large egg**
- **⅓ cup cold water**
- **1 Tbsp. cider vinegar**

FILLING

- **2½ cups canned pumpkin (about 19 oz.)**
- **1¼ cups packed light brown sugar**
- **¾ cup half-and-half cream**
- **2 large eggs**
- **¼ cup apple butter**
- **2 Tbsp. orange juice**
- **2 Tbsp. maple syrup**
- **2 tsp. ground cinnamon**
- **2 tsp. pumpkin pie spice**
- **¼ tsp. salt**

1. In a large bowl, mix first 4 ingredients; cut in butter and shortening until crumbly. Whisk egg, water and vinegar; gradually add to flour mixture, tossing with a fork until dough holds together when pressed. Divide dough in half so that 1 portion is slightly larger than the other; shape into 2 disks. Wrap; refrigerate at least 1 hour.
2. Preheat oven to 425°. On a lightly floured surface, roll larger portion to a ⅛-in.-thick circle; transfer to a 9-in. deep-dish pie plate. Trim crust to ½ in. beyond edge of pie plate. Refrigerate until ready to fill.
3. Roll smaller portion of dough to ⅛-in. thickness. Cut with a small floured pumpkin-shaped cookie cutter; place some cutouts 1 in. apart on a baking sheet, reserving unbaked cutouts for decorative edge if desired. Bake until golden brown, 8-10 minutes.
4. Meanwhile, beat together all filling ingredients until blended; transfer to crust. Flute or decorate edge with unbaked cutouts, brushing off flour before pressing lightly onto edge. Bake on a lower oven rack 10 minutes. Cover edge loosely with foil. Reduce oven setting to 350°. Bake until a knife inserted near the center comes out clean, 45-50 minutes.
5. Cool on a wire rack; serve or refrigerate within 2 hours. Top with baked pumpkin cutouts before serving.

NOTE: This recipe was tested with commercially prepared apple butter.

1 PIECE: *647 cal., 28g fat (12g sat. fat), 112mg chol., 277mg sod., 89g carb. (47g sugars, 4g fiber), 9g pro.*

AUTUMN HARVEST PUMPKIN PIE

Ham for the Holidays

Savor a classic Christmas ham dinner with all the trimmings: green bean casserole, fluffy potatoes, and a kiss of tangy winter fruit.

SPIRAL HAM WITH CRANBERRY GLAZE

SPIRAL HAM WITH CRANBERRY GLAZE

Baked ham with cranberry glaze has been a tradition in my family for as long as I can remember. You can dice up any leftovers and mix with your favorite dip recipe for an appetizer the next night.
—Pattie Prescott, Manchester, NH

PREP: 15 min. • **BAKE:** 3 hours
MAKES: 16 servings

- **1 bone-in fully cooked spiral-sliced ham (8 lbs.)**
- **1 can (14 oz.) whole-berry cranberry sauce**
- **1 pkg. (12 oz.) fresh or frozen cranberries**
- **1 jar (12 oz.) red currant jelly**
- **1 cup light corn syrup**
- **½ tsp. ground ginger**

1. Place ham on a rack in a shallow roasting pan. Cover and bake at 325° for 2½ hours.
2. Meanwhile, for glaze, combine the remaining ingredients in a saucepan. Bring to a boil. Reduce heat; simmer, uncovered, until cranberries pop, stirring occasionally. Remove from the heat.
3. Uncover ham; bake until a thermometer reads 140°, about 30 minutes longer, basting twice with 1½ cups glaze. Serve remaining glaze with ham.

6 OZ. HAM: *439 cal., 5g fat (2g sat. fat), 50mg chol., 2072mg sod., 59g carb. (32g sugars, 1g fiber), 41g pro.*

MOMMA'S GREEN BEANS

Momma made these green beans only at Thanksgiving because, at the time, the ingredients were out of her everyday budget. Her original recipe had five stars drawn on it. I would have to agree!
—Marcia Shires, San Antonio, TX

PREP: 45 min. • **BAKE:** 10 min.
MAKES: 16 servings (¾ cup each)

- **2 cups sour cream**
- **2 tsp. sugar**
- **1 tsp. salt**
- **½ tsp. dill weed**
- **1 lb. bacon strips, cut into 1-in. pieces**
- **2 lbs. fresh green beans, cut into 1½-in. pieces (6 cups)**
- **1 lb. medium fresh mushrooms, quartered**
- **6 green onions, chopped**
- **1 cup slivered almonds, optional**
- **4 garlic cloves, minced**
- **2 cups onion and garlic salad croutons**
- **1½ cups shredded Monterey Jack cheese**

1. Preheat oven to 350°. In a small bowl, combine sour cream, sugar, salt and dill weed. In a 6-qt. stockpot, cook the bacon over medium heat until crisp, stirring occasionally.
2. Meanwhile, in a large saucepan, bring 6 cups water to a boil. Add beans in batches; cook, uncovered, just until crisp-tender, 2-3 minutes. Drain.
3. Remove bacon from stockpot with a slotted spoon; drain on paper towels. Discard drippings, reserving 6 Tbsp. in pan. Add mushrooms, onions and, if desired, almonds to drippings; cook and stir over medium heat until mushrooms are tender, 4-6 minutes. Add garlic; cook and stir 1 minute longer. Remove from heat; stir in beans, bacon and croutons. Stir in sour cream mixture. Transfer to an ungreased 13x9-in. baking dish. Sprinkle with cheese. Bake until cheese is melted, 10-15 minutes.
¾ CUP: *246 cal., 19g fat (9g sat. fat), 32mg chol., 468mg sod., 11g carb. (3g sugars, 2g fiber), 9g pro.*

TRIPLE-CHEESE BROCCOLI PUFF

TRIPLE-CHEESE BROCCOLI PUFF

This rich-tasting side dish is a must for our Christmas morning menu. Like any puffy souffle, it will settle a bit after you remove it from the oven, but the pretty golden top is very attractive. I often toss in some cubed ham.
—Maryellen Hays, Wolcottville, IN

PREP: 15 min. • **BAKE:** 50 min. + standing
MAKES: 8 servings

- **1 cup sliced fresh mushrooms**
- **1 Tbsp. butter**
- **3 oz. cream cheese, softened**
- **6 large eggs, room temperature**
- **1 cup 2% milk**
- **¾ cup biscuit/baking mix**
- **3 cups frozen chopped broccoli, thawed**
- **2 cups shredded Monterey Jack cheese**
- **1 cup 4% cottage cheese**
- **¼ tsp. salt**

1. In a small skillet, saute mushrooms in butter until tender. In a large bowl, beat the cream cheese, eggs, milk and biscuit mix just until combined. Stir in the broccoli, cheeses, salt and mushrooms.
2. Pour into a greased 2½-qt. baking dish. Bake, uncovered, at 350° until a thermometer reads 160°, 50-60 minutes. Let stand for 10 minutes before serving.
1 SERVING: *315 cal., 21g fat (12g sat. fat), 210mg chol., 578mg sod., 13g carb. (4g sugars, 1g fiber), 19g pro.*

BRIE CHERRY PASTRY CUPS

Golden brown and flaky, these bite-sized puff pastries with creamy Brie and sweet cherry preserves could easily double as a scrumptious dessert.
—Marilyn McSween, Mentor, OH

TAKES: 30 min. • **MAKES:** 3 dozen

- **1 sheet frozen puff pastry, thawed**
- **½ cup cherry preserves**
- **4 oz. Brie cheese, cut into ½-in. cubes**
- **¼ cup chopped pecans or walnuts**
- **2 Tbsp. minced chives**

1. Unfold puff pastry; cut into 36 squares. Gently press squares onto the bottoms of 36 greased miniature muffin cups.
2. Bake at 375° for 10 minutes. Using the end of a wooden spoon handle, make a ½-in.-deep indentation in the center of each. Bake until golden brown, 6-8 minutes longer. With spoon handle, press squares down again.
3. Spoon ½ rounded tsp. of preserves into each cup. Top with cheese; sprinkle with nuts and chives. Bake until cheese is melted, 3-5 minutes.
1 APPETIZER: *61 cal., 3g fat (1g sat. fat), 3mg chol., 42mg sod., 7g carb. (3g sugars, 1g fiber), 1g pro.*

BRIE CHERRY PASTRY CUPS

CITRUS FENNEL SALAD

CITRUS FENNEL SALAD

I guarantee guests will love the taste of this unusual salad. The pleasant orange flavor pairs well with the tender fennel.
—Marion Karlin, Waterloo, IA

TAKES: 20 min. • **MAKES:** 8 servings

- **2 large fennel bulbs**
- **2 Tbsp. olive oil**
- **1 Tbsp. butter**
- **6 Tbsp. orange juice**
- **3 Tbsp. lemon juice**
- **1 tsp. salt**
- **½ tsp. coarsely ground pepper**
- **2 large navel oranges, peeled and sliced**
- **Salad greens**

1. Remove fronds from fennel bulbs; set aside for garnish. Cut bulbs into thin slices. In a large skillet, saute fennel slices in oil and butter until crisp-tender.
2. Stir in the juices, salt and pepper. Bring to a boil; reduce heat to medium. Cook and stir until fennel is tender, 5-6 minutes.
3. Remove from the heat; stir in orange segments. Cool slightly. Serve over salad greens; top with reserved fennel fronds.
½ CUP: *89 cal., 5g fat (1g sat. fat), 4mg chol., 336mg sod., 11g carb. (6g sugars, 3g fiber), 1g pro.* **Diabetic exchanges:** *1 vegetable, 1 fat, ½ fruit.*

PUMPKIN EGG BRAID

I developed this bread to celebrate our two favorite holidays, Thanksgiving and Hanukkah. Try it with flavored butters, and use leftovers for French toast or sandwiches.
—Sara Mellas, Hartford, CT

PREP: 30 min. + rising • **BAKE:** 20 min.
MAKES: 1 loaf (12 slices)

- 1 pkg. (¼ oz.) active dry yeast
- 3 Tbsp. warm water (110° to 115°)
- ½ cup canned pumpkin
- 1 large egg, room temperature
- 2 Tbsp. light brown sugar
- 2 Tbsp. butter, softened
- 1 tsp. pumpkin pie spice
- ½ tsp. salt
- 2 to 2½ cups bread flour

EGG WASH
- 1 large egg
- 1 Tbsp. water

1. In a small bowl, dissolve yeast in warm water. In a large bowl, combine pumpkin, egg, brown sugar, butter, pie spice, salt, yeast mixture and 1 cup flour; beat on medium speed until smooth. Stir in enough remaining flour to form a soft dough (dough will be sticky).
2. Turn dough onto a floured surface; knead until smooth and elastic, 6-8 minutes. Place in a greased bowl, turning once to grease the top. Cover and let rise in a warm place until doubled, about 1 hour.
3. Punch down dough. Turn onto a lightly floured surface; divide into thirds. Roll each into a 16-in. rope. Place ropes on a greased baking sheet and braid. Pinch ends to seal; tuck under.
4. Cover with a kitchen towel; let rise in a warm place until almost doubled, about 45 minutes. Preheat oven to 350°.
5. For egg wash, in a small bowl, whisk egg and water until blended; brush over loaf. Bake until golden brown, 20-25 minutes. Remove from pan to a wire rack to cool.
1 PIECE: *126 cal., 3g fat (2g sat. fat), 36mg chol., 129mg sod., 20g carb. (3g sugars, 1g fiber), 4g pro.* **Diabetic exchanges:** *1 starch, ½ fat.*

PUMPKIN EGG BRAID

MAPLE-GINGERROOT VEGETABLES

MAPLE-GINGERROOT VEGETABLES

My family loves the drizzling of golden maple syrup on these roasted vegetables. I prefer to use dark maple syrup. Either way, it's an easy way to get kids (and adults) to eat their veggies.
—Kelli Ritz, Innisfail, AB

PREP: 35 min. • **BAKE:** 45 min.
MAKES: 24 servings

- 5 **medium parsnips, peeled and sliced**
- 5 **small carrots, sliced**
- 3 **medium turnips, peeled and cubed**
- 1 **large sweet potato, peeled and cubed**
- 1 **small rutabaga, peeled and cubed**
- 1 **large sweet onion, cut into wedges**
- 1 **small red onion, cut into wedges**
- 2 **Tbsp. olive oil**
- 1 **Tbsp. minced fresh gingerroot**
- 1 **tsp. salt**
- ½ **tsp. pepper**
- 1 **cup maple syrup**

1. Place the first 7 ingredients in a large bowl; add the oil, ginger, salt and pepper. Toss to coat. Arrange vegetables in a single layer in two 15x10x1-in. baking pans coated with cooking spray.
2. Bake, uncovered, at 425° for 25 minutes, stirring once. Drizzle with syrup. Bake until vegetables are tender, 20-25 minutes longer, stirring once more.
¾ CUP: *92 cal., 1g fat (0 sat. fat), 0 chol., 119mg sod., 20g carb. (13g sugars, 2g fiber), 1g pro.* **Diabetic exchanges:** *1 starch.*

DUO TATER BAKE

Cut down on holiday prep time with this creamy potato dish that combines sweet potatoes with regular spuds. I served this for Thanksgiving, and it was a winner with my family.
—Joan McCulloch, Abbotsford, BC

PREP: 40 min. • **BAKE:** 20 min.
MAKES: 2 casseroles (10 servings each)

- 4 **lbs. russet or Yukon Gold potatoes, peeled and cubed**
- 3 **lbs. sweet potatoes, peeled and cubed**
- 2 **cartons (8 oz. each) spreadable chive and onion cream cheese**
- 1 **cup sour cream**
- ¼ **cup shredded Colby-Monterey Jack cheese**
- ⅓ **cup 2% milk**
- ¼ **cup shredded Parmesan cheese**
- ½ **tsp. salt**
- ½ **tsp. pepper**

TOPPING
- 1 **cup shredded Colby-Monterey Jack cheese**
- ½ **cup chopped green onions**
- ¼ **cup shredded Parmesan cheese**

1. Place russet potatoes in a Dutch oven and cover with water. Bring to a boil. Reduce heat; cover and cook until tender, 10-15 minutes.
2. Meanwhile, place sweet potatoes in a large saucepan; cover with water. Bring to a boil. Reduce heat; cover and cook until tender, 10-15 minutes. Drain; mash with half of the cream cheese and sour cream and all of the Colby cheese.
3. Drain russet potatoes; mash with the remaining cream cheese and sour cream. Stir in the milk, Parmesan cheese, salt and pepper.
4. Spread 1⅓ cups russet potato mixture into each of 2 greased 11x7-in. baking dishes. Layer each with 2 cups sweet potato mixture. Repeat layers. Spread with remaining russet potato mixture.
5. Bake, uncovered, at 350° until heated through, about 15 minutes. Combine topping ingredients; sprinkle over casseroles. Bake until cheese is melted, 2-3 minutes longer.
¾ CUP: *236 cal., 12g fat (8g sat. fat), 38mg chol., 246mg sod., 25g carb. (7g sugars, 2g fiber), 5g pro.*

DUO TATER BAKE

Christmas Sweets & Treats

This year, make it magical—with sprinkle-kissed sweets, shimmering treats, swirly delights and jolly bites.

CRISPY CHRISTMAS TREES

CRISPY CHRISTMAS TREES

These holiday novelties will draw admiring comments wherever you serve them. A sprinkle of sugar supplies a yuletide touch to each fanciful hand-shaped creation.
—Taste of Home *Test Kitchen*

TAKES: 15 min. • **MAKES:** about 1½ dozen

- **2 Tbsp. butter**
- **2 cups pastel miniature marshmallows**
- **3 cups crisp rice cereal**
- **¼ cup finely chopped pecans**
- **Green decorator's sugar**
- **Assorted sprinkles, optional**
- **Confectioners' sugar**

1. In a heavy saucepan, melt butter. Stir in marshmallows; cook and stir over low heat until melted. Remove from the heat; stir in cereal and pecans. Let cool just enough to handle.

2. With greased hands, shape into trees. (Work quickly, as the cereal hardens quickly and becomes difficult to form.) Roll in green sugar. If desired, decorate with sprinkles. Place on a serving tray; dust with confectioners' sugar.

1 TREE: *57 cal., 3g fat (1g sat. fat), 3mg chol., 58mg sod., 9g carb. (4g sugars, 0 fiber), 1g pro.*

CREAM CHEESE RED VELVET THUMBPRINT COOKIES

These festive sugar-coated thumbprint cookies are perfect for Christmas. They're just as delicious as they are beautiful.
—Colleen Delawder, Herndon, VA

PREP: 25 min. • **BAKE:** 20 min./batch + cooling • **MAKES:** 2 dozen

- **1 cup unsalted butter, softened**
- **½ cup sugar**
- **1 large egg yolk, room temperature**
- **1 tsp. vanilla extract**
- **½ tsp. red paste food coloring**
- **2 cups all-purpose flour**
- **2 Tbsp. baking cocoa**
- **½ cup coarse sugar**

FILLING

- **4 oz. cream cheese, softened**
- **¼ cup sugar**
- **1 large egg white, room temperature**
- **½ tsp. vanilla extract**
- **¼ tsp. kosher salt**

1. Preheat oven to 300°. In a large bowl, cream together butter and sugar until light and fluffy, 5-7 minutes. Beat in egg yolk, vanilla and food coloring. In another bowl, whisk flour and cocoa; gradually beat into creamed mixture. Roll into 1-in. balls; roll in coarse sugar. Place 2 in. apart on parchment-lined baking sheets. Press a deep indentation in center of each with the back of a ½-tsp. measure.

2. Bake 10 minutes. Meanwhile, for filling, beat cream cheese, sugar, egg white, vanilla and salt until blended. Reshape indentations in par-baked cookies as needed. Fill each with 1 tsp. filling. Bake until filling is set, 10-12 minutes longer. Remove to wire racks to cool completely.

1 COOKIE: *166 cal., 10g fat (6g sat. fat), 33mg chol., 39mg sod., 19g carb. (10g sugars, 0 fiber), 2g pro.*

5i

PEPPERMINT POPCORN

Crisp and minty, this simple snack is a hit with all 10 of our children. For variety, try substituting other flavors of candy instead of peppermint.
—Shirley Mars, Kent, OH

PREP: 10 min. • **MAKES:** 24 servings

- **1 lb. white candy coating, coarsely chopped**
- **24 cups popped popcorn**
- **½ to ¾ cup finely crushed peppermint candy (4 to 6 candy canes)**
- **Red nonpareils, optional**

In a microwave, melt candy coating; stir until smooth. In a large bowl, combine the popcorn and crushed candy. Pour candy coating over top; toss to coat. Pour onto a waxed paper-lined baking sheet. If desired, sprinkle with nonpareils. When hardened, break apart. Store in an airtight container.

1 CUP: *163 cal., 8g fat (5g sat. fat), 0 chol., 98mg sod., 22g carb. (14g sugars, 1g fiber), 1g pro.*

MINTY COOKIES & CREAM CHOCOLATE FUDGE

MINTY COOKIES & CREAM CHOCOLATE FUDGE

I altered a plain chocolate fudge recipe to create this festive mint Oreo fudge. Mint Oreo cookies can be used instead of plain for even more minty flavor.
—Dawn Lowenstein, Huntingdon Vy, PA

PREP: 20 minutes + chilling
MAKES: 2½ pounds (64 pieces)

- 6 **Tbsp. butter, divided**
- 1 **pkg. (11½ oz.) milk chocolate chips**
- 2 **oz. unsweetened chocolate, chopped**
- 1 **can (14 oz.) sweetened condensed milk**
- ¼ **cup crushed candy canes (about 3 regular)**
- 1 **tsp. mint extract**
- 16 **Oreo cookies**
- 1½ **cups miniature marshmallows**

1. Line an 8-in. square baking pan with foil, letting ends extend up sides; grease foil with 2 Tbsp. butter. In a metal bowl over simmering water, melt chocolate chips, unsweetened chocolate and remaining 4 Tbsp. butter; stir until smooth. Add milk, crushed candy canes and extract; stir until blended.
2. Pour half the chocolate mixture into prepared pan. Arrange cookies over chocolate, cutting to fit as needed. Stir marshmallows into remaining chocolate mixture; spread over cookies. If desired, top with additional crushed candy canes. Refrigerate until firm, about 1 hour. Using foil, lift fudge out of pan. Remove foil; cut fudge into 1-in. squares. Store between layers of waxed paper in an airtight container.

1 PIECE: *82 cal., 4g fat (2g sat. fat), 6mg chol., 33mg sod., 10g carb. (8g sugars, 0 fiber), 1g pro.*

PEANUT BUTTER CINNAMON SNAP COOKIES

These cookies are perfect for bake sales, potlucks or holiday gift baskets. Use fun cookie cutters for any occasion you are celebrating. The cookie glaze dries shiny, so they look professional.
—Kallee Krong-McCreery, Escondido, CA

PREP: 30 min. + chilling
BAKE: 10 min./batch + cooling
MAKES: 5 dozen

- ½ **cup butter, softened**
- ½ **cup creamy peanut butter**
- ½ **cup sugar**
- 1 **large egg, room temperature**
- ½ **cup molasses**
- 2 **Tbsp. thawed orange juice concentrate**
- 3½ **cups all-purpose flour**
- 2 **tsp. ground cinnamon**
- ½ **tsp. baking soda**

GLAZE

- 2½ **cups confectioners' sugar**
- 2 **to 4 Tbsp. water**
- 1 **Tbsp. butter, softened**
- 1 **Tbsp. light corn syrup**
- ½ **tsp. vanilla or orange extract**

1. In a large bowl, cream butter, peanut butter and sugar until light and fluffy, 5-7 minutes. Beat in egg, molasses and orange juice. In another bowl, whisk flour, cinnamon and baking soda; gradually beat into creamed mixture.
2. Divide dough into 3 portions. Shape each into a disk; wrap tightly. Refrigerate 30 minutes or until firm enough to roll.
3. Preheat oven to 350°. On a lightly floured surface, roll each portion of dough to ⅛-in. thickness. Cut with a floured 3¼-in. star-shaped cookie cutter. Place 2 in. apart on parchment-lined baking sheets. Bake until edges are firm and edges begin to brown, 8-10 minutes. Remove from pans to wire racks to cool completely.
4. Combine glaze ingredients; drizzle over cookies. Let stand until set. Store cookies between pieces of waxed paper in airtight containers.

1 COOKIE: *86 cal., 3g fat (1g sat. fat), 7mg chol., 34mg sod., 14g carb. (9g sugars, 0 fiber), 1g pro.*

PEANUT BUTTER CINNAMON SNAP COOKIES

MINCEMEAT-FILLED BRAID

Mincemeat has gotten such a bad rap over the years. Raisins, currants and other dried fruit, richly spiced and soaked in brandy... what's wrong with that? My family and I love it tucked inside this gorgeous-looking bread. It's perfect for breakfast or with dinner.
—Loraine Steinfort, Shelbyville, IN

PREP: 35 min. + rising • **BAKE:** 20 min.
MAKES: 1 loaf (16 slices)

- **1 pkg. (¼ oz.) active dry yeast**
- **1 cup warm water (110° to 115°)**
- **1 large egg, room temperature**
- **¼ cup butter, softened**
- **¼ cup sugar**
- **3 Tbsp. buttermilk blend powder**
- **1 tsp. salt**
- **¼ tsp. baking soda**
- **3 to 3½ cups bread flour**

FILLING
- **1 pkg. (9 oz.) condensed mincemeat**
- **1 cup water**

ICING
- **⅓ cup confectioners' sugar**
- **2 tsp. water**
- **⅛ tsp. almond extract**

1. Dissolve yeast in warm water. In a large bowl, combine next 6 ingredients, yeast mixture and 1½ cups flour; beat on medium speed 2 minutes. Stir in enough remaining flour to form a soft dough (dough will be sticky).

2. Turn onto a floured surface; knead until smooth and elastic, 6-8 minutes. Place in a greased bowl, turning once to grease the top. Cover and let rise in a warm place until doubled, about 1 hour.

3. Meanwhile, for filling, crumble mincemeat in a small saucepan; add water. Bring to a boil. Reduce heat; cook over medium-low heat until thickened, 20-25 minutes. Set aside to cool.

4. Punch down dough. Turn onto a lightly floured surface; divide into thirds. Roll each into a 14x4-in. rectangle. Spread a third of the filling down the center of each strip; bring the sides of each strip together over filling. Pinch seams to seal. Place strips, seam side down, on a greased baking sheet and braid. Pinch ends to seal; tuck under. Cover and let rise in a warm place until doubled, about 1 hour.

5. Preheat oven to 350°. Bake until golden brown, 20-25 minutes. Remove from pan to a wire rack to cool.

6. Combine icing ingredients; drizzle over braid.

NOTE: We tested this recipe with a 9-oz. package of None Such Classic Original Condensed Mincemeat, which we ordered online.

1 PIECE: *206 cal., 4g fat (2g sat. fat), 20mg chol., 287mg sod., 38g carb. (18g sugars, 1g fiber), 4g pro.*

MINCEMEAT-FILLED BRAID

CHOCOLATE-COVERED CHERRIES

Not only is this my family's favorite festive dessert, it also makes a delicious gift. Best of all, you can (and should) prepare these ahead. The candy gets better as it's stored, with the centers becoming even juicier.
—Linda Hammerich, Bonanza, OR

PREP: 25 min. + chilling • **MAKES:** 3 dozen

- **2½ cups confectioners' sugar**
- **¼ cup butter, softened**
- **1 Tbsp. 2% milk**
- **½ tsp. almond extract**
- **2 jars (8 oz. each) maraschino cherries with stems, well drained**
- **2 cups semisweet chocolate chips**
- **2 Tbsp. shortening**

1. In a small bowl, combine the sugar, butter, milk and extract. Knead until smooth and pliable. Shape into 1-in. balls and flatten each into a 2-in. circle.
2. Wrap 1 circle around each cherry and lightly roll in hands. Place with stems up on waxed paper-lined baking sheet. Cover loosely and refrigerate 4 hours or overnight.
3. In a microwave, melt chocolate and shortening; stir until smooth. Holding on to the stems, dip cherries into chocolate; allow excess to drip off. Place on waxed paper until set. Store in a covered container. Refrigerate 1-2 weeks before serving.
2 CANDIES: *206 cal., 10g fat (5g sat. fat), 7mg chol., 28mg sod., 33g carb. (31g sugars, 1g fiber), 1g pro.*

TRUFFLE TOPIARY

TRUFFLE TOPIARY

I wanted to give family and friends something they would remember, so I whipped up piles of these sweets for everyone. Set them out in a pretty pattern on a cookie tray or turn them into a stunning centerpiece.
—Elisa Schmidt, Bethel Park, PA

PREP: 1 hour + standing
COOK: 15 min. + chilling • **MAKES:** 11 dozen

- **3 pkg. (12 oz. each) semisweet chocolate chips, divided**
- **2¼ cups sweetened condensed milk, divided**
- **½ tsp. orange extract**
- **½ to 1 tsp. peppermint extract**
- **½ tsp. almond extract**
- **¾ lb. white candy coating, coarsely chopped**
- **¾ lb. dark chocolate candy coating, coarsely chopped**
- **½ cup ground almonds**
- **1 each 6- and 8-in. Styrofoam cones or a single 12-in. cone**

1. In a microwave-safe bowl, melt 1 pkg. of chocolate chips. Add ¾ cup condensed milk; mix well. Stir in the orange extract. Cover and chill until firm enough to shape, about 45 minutes. Repeat 2 more times with remaining chips and milk, adding peppermint extract to 1 portion and almond extract to the other.
2. Shaping truffles: Shape chilled mixture into 1-in. balls; place on 3 separate waxed paper-lined baking sheets. Chill 1-2 hours or until firm.
3. Melt white candy coating in a microwave-safe bowl. Dip orange-flavored balls in coating and return to waxed paper to harden. Melt remaining white candy coating again and dip balls once more to thoroughly cover. Let harden.
4. Melt chocolate candy coating in a microwave-safe bowl. Dip peppermint-flavored balls in coating and return to waxed paper to harden.
5. Roll the almond-flavored truffles in ground almonds.
6. Making the tree: Brush the Styrofoam cones with remaining chocolate if desired. Using toothpicks, stick 1 end into each truffle and the other end into the cone, covering entire cone with truffles.
1 TRUFFLE: *83 cal., 4g fat (3g sat. fat), 2mg chol., 7mg sod., 11g carb. (10g sugars, 1g fiber), 1g pro.*

PEPPERMINT CHEESECAKE ON A STICK

PEPPERMINT CHEESECAKE ON A STICK

Surprise guests with a fun holiday treat: dipped cheesecake wedges you can eat without a fork. Whenever my son has one, he jokes that he wants to quit his job so he can sell these!
—Maria Morelli, West Kelowna, BC

PREP: 1¼ hours + freezing
BAKE: 1 hour + chilling • **MAKES:** 1 dozen

- **1¼ cups graham cracker crumbs**
- **¼ cup sugar**
- **¼ cup butter, melted**

CHEESECAKE
- **4 pkg. (8 oz. each) cream cheese, softened**
- **¾ cup sugar**
- **⅓ cup sour cream**
- **¼ cup eggnog or half-and-half cream**
- **2 Tbsp. cornstarch**
- **1 tsp. vanilla extract**
- **3 large eggs, room temperature, lightly beaten**
- **1 cup crushed peppermint candies (about 35 candies)**

ASSEMBLY
- **12 wooden pop sticks**
- **28 oz. semisweet chocolate, chopped**
- **3 Tbsp. shortening**
- **½ cup green candy coating disks, melted**
- **¼ cup red candy coating disks, melted**

1. Preheat oven to 325°. Place a greased 9-in. springform pan on a double thickness of heavy-duty foil (about 18 in. square). Wrap foil securely around pan. Place on a baking sheet.
2. In a small bowl, mix cracker crumbs and sugar; stir in butter. Press onto bottom of prepared pan. Bake until lightly browned, 10-12 minutes. Cool on a wire rack.
3. In a large bowl, beat cream cheese and sugar until smooth. Beat in sour cream, eggnog, cornstarch and vanilla. Add eggs; beat on low speed just until blended. Fold in peppermint candies. Pour over crust. Place springform pan in a larger baking pan; add 1 in. of hot water to larger pan.
4. Bake until center is just set and top appears dull, 60-65 minutes. Remove springform pan from water bath. Cool cheesecake on a wire rack 10 minutes. Loosen sides from pan with a knife; remove foil. Cool 1 hour longer. Refrigerate overnight, covering when completely cooled.
5. Remove rim from pan. Cut cheesecake into 12 slices; gently insert a wooden stick into the wide end of each. Place on a waxed paper-lined 15x10x1-in. baking pan; freeze until firm.
6. In a microwave, melt chocolate and shortening; stir until smooth. Spoon chocolate mixture over each slice until all sides are coated; allow excess to drip off. (Keep remaining slices in freezer until ready to dip.) Place on a waxed paper-lined baking pan. Seal any gaps by drizzling with melted chocolate, reheating chocolate if necessary. Refrigerate 10 minutes or until set.
7. Decorate with melted candy coating as desired. Refrigerate until serving.

NOTE: This recipe was tested with commercially prepared eggnog.

1 PIECE: *951 cal., 64g fat (37g sat. fat), 138mg chol., 356mg sod., 61g carb. (48g sugars, 2g fiber), 12g pro.*

FRUITCAKE COOKIES

These old-fashioned goodies are fun, colorful and chewy without being sticky.
—Dorcas Wright, Guelph, ON

PREP: 15 min. • **BAKE:** 15 min./batch
MAKES: 5 dozen

- **½ cup butter, softened**
- **½ cup shortening**
- **½ cup sugar**
- **½ cup packed brown sugar**
- **1 large egg, room temperature**
- **1 tsp. vanilla extract**
- **1 cup all-purpose flour**
- **½ tsp. baking soda**
- **½ tsp. salt**
- **2 cups old-fashioned oats**
- **1 cup sweetened shredded coconut**
- **½ cup chopped dates**
- **½ cup each chopped red and green candied cherries**
- **½ cup chopped candied pineapple**

1. In a bowl, cream butter, shortening and sugars. Add egg and vanilla; mix well. Combine flour, baking soda, salt and oats; add to creamed mixture and mix well. Stir in the coconut, dates, cherries and pineapple.
2. Shape into 1-in. balls; place on greased baking sheets. Bake at 325° until lightly browned, about 15 minutes. Cool on wire racks.

1 COOKIE: *84 cal., 4g fat (2g sat. fat), 7mg chol., 53mg sod., 12g carb. (7g sugars, 1g fiber), 1g pro.*

CHRISTMAS STAR TWISTED BREAD

BRANDY ALEXANDER FUDGE

At Christmastime, we love to indulge in this marbled fudge inspired by the popular brandy drink. My sister-in-law won first place with this recipe at the county fair.
—Debbie Neubauer, Pine City, MN

PREP: 30 min. **COOK:** 15 min. + chilling
MAKES: about 3 lbs. (64 pieces)

- **1 tsp. plus ¾ cup butter, divided**
- **3 cups sugar**
- **1 can (5 oz.) evaporated milk**
- **1 jar (7 oz.) marshmallow creme**
- **1 cup semisweet chocolate chips**
- **2 Tbsp. brandy**
- **1 cup white baking chips**
- **2 Tbsp. creme de cacao or Kahlua (coffee liqueur)**

1. Line an 8-in. square pan with foil and grease the foil with 1 tsp. butter. In a large heavy saucepan, combine the sugar, milk and remaining ¾ cup butter. Bring to a full boil over medium heat, stirring constantly; cook and stir for 4 minutes. Remove from the heat.
2. Divide marshmallow creme between 2 small heat-resistant bowls. Pour half of the sugar mixture into each bowl. To 1 bowl, stir in semisweet chips until melted, then stir in brandy. Into the remaining bowl, stir in white chips until melted; stir in creme de cacao.
3. Spread chocolate mixture into prepared pan. Top with white mixture; cut through with a knife to swirl. Cool to room temperature. Chill until set completely.
4. Using foil, lift fudge out of pan. Discard foil; cut fudge into 1-in. squares. Store in an airtight container in the refrigerator.
1 PIECE: *85 cal., 3g fat (2g sat. fat), 7mg chol., 22mg sod., 13g carb. (13g sugars, 0 fiber), 0 pro.*

CHRISTMAS STAR TWISTED BREAD

This gorgeous sweet bread swirled with jam may look tricky, but it's not. The best part is opening the oven to find this star-shaped beauty in all its glory.
—Darlene Brenden, Salem, OR

PREP: 45 min. + rising
BAKE: 20 min. + cooling • **MAKES:** 16 servings

- **1 pkg. (¼ oz.) active dry yeast**
- **¼ cup warm water (110° to 115°)**
- **¾ cup warm 2% milk (110° to 115°)**
- **1 large egg, room temperature**
- **¼ cup butter, softened**
- **¼ cup sugar**
- **1 tsp. salt**
- **3¼ to 3¾ cups all-purpose flour**
- **¾ cup seedless raspberry jam**
- **2 Tbsp. butter, melted**
- **Confectioners' sugar**

1. Dissolve yeast in warm water until foamy. In another bowl, combine milk, egg, butter, sugar and salt; add yeast mixture and 3 cups flour. Beat on medium speed until smooth, about 1 minute. Stir in enough remaining flour to form a soft dough.
2. Turn onto a floured surface; knead until smooth and elastic, 6-8 minutes. Place in a greased bowl, turning once to grease top. Cover and let rise in a warm place until doubled, about 1 hour.
3. Punch down dough. Turn onto a lightly floured surface; divide into 4 portions. Roll 1 portion into a 12-in. circle. Place on a greased 14-in. pizza pan. Spread with one-third of the jam to within ½ in. of edge. Repeat twice, layering dough and jam, and ending with final portion of dough.
4. Place a 2½-in. round cutter on top of the dough in center of circle (do not press down). With a sharp knife, make 16 evenly spaced cuts from round cutter to edge of dough, forming a starburst. Remove cutter; grasp 2 adjacent strips and rotate twice outward. Pinch ends together. Repeat with remaining strips.
5. Cover and let rise until almost doubled, about 30 minutes. Preheat oven to 375°. Bake until golden brown, 18-22 minutes. (Watch during final 5 minutes for any dripping.) Remove from oven; brush with melted butter, avoiding areas where jam is visible. Cool completely on a wire rack. Dust with confectioners' sugar.
1 PIECE: *193 cal., 5g fat (3g sat. fat), 24mg chol., 192mg sod., 33g carb. (13g sugars, 1g fiber), 4g pro.*

5i

GOODY-GOODY GUMDROPS

My jewel-toned squares are softer than store-bought gumdrops, and their terrific taste has a true old-fashioned quality that people love. You can't eat just one!
—Richard Bunt, Painted Post, NY

PREP: 10 min. + standing
COOK: 10 min. + chilling
MAKES: about 1 lb. (about 20 dozen pieces)

- 3 **envelopes unflavored gelatin**
- 1¼ **cups water, divided**
- 1½ **cups sugar**
- ¼ **to ½ tsp. peppermint extract**
- 4 **drops each red and green food coloring**
- **Additional sugar**

1. In a small bowl, sprinkle gelatin over ½ cup water; let stand 5 minutes. In a small saucepan, bring sugar and remaining ¾ cup water to a boil over medium heat, stirring constantly. Add gelatin mixture; simmer and stir over low heat until gelatin is completely dissolved, about 5 minutes. Remove from heat; stir in extract.
2. Divide mixture between 2 bowls; tint 1 red and the other green with food coloring. Transfer each to a greased 8x4-in. loaf pan; cool completely. Refrigerate, covered, until firm, about 3 hours.
3. Loosen sides from pan with a knife; turn onto a sugared cutting board. Cut into ½-in. cubes; roll in additional sugar.
4. Let candy stand, uncovered, at room temperature until all sides are dry, 3-4 hours, turning every hour.

1 PIECE (NOT CALCULATED WITH ADDITIONAL SUGAR): *23 cal., 0 fat (0 sat. fat), 0 chol., 3mg sod., 5g carb. (5g sugars, 0 fiber), 1g pro.*

GOODY-GOODY GUMDROPS

Substitutions & Equivalents

EQUIVALENT MEASURES

3 TEASPOONS	= 1 tablespoon	16 TABLESPOONS	= 1 cup
4 TABLESPOONS	= ¼ cup	2 CUPS	= 1 pint
5⅓ TABLESPOONS	= ⅓ cup	4 CUPS	= 1 quart
8 TABLESPOONS	= ½ cup	4 QUARTS	= 1 gallon

FOOD EQUIVALENTS

EGG NOODLES	4 ounces (3 cups) uncooked	= 4 cups cooked
MACARONI	4 ounces (1 cup) uncooked	= 2½ cups cooked
POPCORN	⅓ to ½ cup unpopped	= 8 cups popped
RICE, LONG GRAIN	1 cup uncooked	= 3 cups cooked
RICE, QUICK-COOKING	1 cup uncooked	= 2 cups cooked
SPAGHETTI	2 ounces uncooked	= 1 cup cooked
BREAD	1 slice	= ¾ cup soft crumbs, ¼ cup fine dry crumbs
GRAHAM CRACKERS	7 squares	= ½ cup finely crushed
BUTTERY ROUND CRACKERS	12 crackers	= ½ cup finely crushed
SALTINE CRACKERS	14 crackers	= ½ cup finely crushed
BANANA	1 medium	= ⅓ cup mashed
LEMON	1 medium	= 3 tablespoons juice, 2 teaspoons grated zest
LIME	1 medium	= 2 tablespoons juice, 1½ teaspoons grated zest
ORANGE	1 medium	= ¼-⅓ cup juice, 4 teaspoons grated zest

CABBAGE	1 head = 5 cups shredded	GREEN PEPPER	1 large = 1 cup chopped
CARROTS	1 pound = 3 cups shredded	MUSHROOMS	½ pound = 3 cups sliced
CELERY	1 rib = ½ cup chopped	ONION	1 medium = ½ cup chopped
CORN	1 ear fresh = ⅔ cup kernels	POTATOES	3 medium = 2 cups cubed
ALMONDS	1 pound = 3 cups chopped	PECANS	1 pound = 3¾ cups chopped
GROUND NUTS	3¾ ounces = 1 cup	WALNUTS	1 pound = 4½ cups chopped

EASY SUBSTITUTIONS

WHEN YOU NEED...		USE...
BAKING POWDER	1 teaspoon	½ teaspoon cream of tartar + ¼ teaspoon baking soda
BUTTERMILK	1 cup	1 tablespoon lemon juice or vinegar + enough milk to measure 1 cup (let stand 5 minutes before using)
CORNSTARCH	1 tablespoon	2 tablespoons all-purpose flour
HONEY	1 cup	1¼ cups sugar + ¼ cup water
HALF-AND-HALF CREAM	1 cup	1 tablespoon melted butter + enough whole milk to measure 1 cup
ONION	1 small, chopped (⅓ cup)	1 teaspoon onion powder or 1 tablespoon dried minced onion
TOMATO JUICE	1 cup	½ cup tomato sauce + ½ cup water
TOMATO SAUCE	2 cups	¾ cup tomato paste + 1 cup water
UNSWEETENED CHOCOLATE	1 square (1 ounce)	3 tablespoons baking cocoa + 1 tablespoon shortening or oil
WHOLE MILK	1 cup	½ cup evaporated milk + ½ cup water

Cooking Terms

AL DENTE An Italian term meaning "to the tooth." Used to describe pasta that is cooked but still firm.

BASTE To moisten food with melted butter, pan drippings, marinade or other liquid to add flavor and juiciness.

BEAT To mix rapidly with a spoon, fork, wire whisk or electric mixer.

BLEND To combine ingredients until just mixed.

BOIL To heat liquids until bubbles that cannot be stirred down are formed. In the case of water, the temperature will reach 212° at sea level.

BONE To remove all bones from meat, poultry or fish.

BROIL To cook food 4 to 6 inches from a direct, radiant heat source.

CREAM To blend ingredients to a smooth consistency by beating; frequently done with butter and sugar for baking.

CUT IN To break down and distribute cold butter, margarine or shortening into a flour mixture with a pastry blender or two knives.

DASH A measurement less than ⅛ teaspoon that is used for herbs, spices and hot pepper sauce. This is not a precise measurement.

DREDGE To coat foods with flour or other dry ingredients. Most often done with pot roasts and stew meat before browning.

FLUTE To make a V shape or scalloped edge on pie crust with your thumb and fingers.

FOLD To blend dissimilar ingredients by careful and gentle turning with a spatula. Used most commonly to incorporate whipped cream, beaten egg whites, fruit, candy or nuts into a thick, heavy batter.

JULIENNE To cut foods into long thin strips much like matchsticks. Used often for salads and stir-fries.

KNEAD To work dough by using a pressing and folding action to make it smooth and elastic.

MARINATE To tenderize and/or flavor foods, usually vegetables or uncooked meat, by placing them in a mixture that may contain oil, vinegar, wine, lime or lemon juice, and herbs and spices.

MINCE To cut into very fine pieces. Often used for garlic, hot peppers and fresh herbs.

PARBOIL To boil foods, such as vegetables, until partially cooked. Most often used when vegetables are to be finished using another cooking method or chilled for marinated salads or dips.

PINCH A measurement less than ⅛ teaspoon that is easily held between the thumb and index finger. This is not a precise measurement.

PULSE To process foods in a food processor or blender with short bursts of power.

PUREE To mash solid foods into a smooth mixture with a food processor, mill, blender or sieve.

SAUTE To fry quickly in a small amount of fat, stirring almost constantly. Most often done with onions, mushrooms and other chopped vegetables.

SCORE To cut slits partway through the outer surface of foods. Often required for ham or flank steak.

SIMMER To cook liquids, or a combination of ingredients with liquid, at just under the boiling point (180-200°). The surface of the liquid will have some movement and there may be small bubbles around the sides of the pan.

STEAM To cook foods covered on a rack or in a steamer basket over a small amount of boiling water. Most often used for vegetables.

STIR-FRY To cook meats, grains and/or vegetables with a constant stirring motion, in a small amount of oil, in a wok or skillet over high heat.

General Index

✓ Indicates an Eat Smart recipe

AIR-FRYER RECIPES
✓Air-Fryer Almond Chicken, 58
Air-Fryer Nashville Hot Chicken, 73
Air-Fryer Spicy Ginger Beef Skewers, 81
General Tso's Chicken Sandwich with Broccoli Slaw, 42
Samosas, 17

APPETIZERS
(also see Salsa)
Cold Appetizers
Best Deviled Eggs, 15
✓Peanut Butter Granola Pinwheels, 261
Smashed Olives, 19
Dips
Apple & White Onion Guacamole, 103
Bacon & Cotija Cheese Guacamole, 103
Black Bean & Corn Guacamole, 103
Blue Cheese & Toasted Almond Guacamole, 103
Cajun Shrimp & Red Pepper Guacamole, 102
Chili Queso Dip, 18
Gingersnap Dip, 236
Grilled Chicken & Cherry Tomato Guacamole, 102
Hot Chili Cheese Dip, 248
Hot Shrimp Dip, 13
Jicama & Pineapple Guacamole, 103
Lake Charles Dip, 269
Mango & Habanero Guacamole, 103
Obatzda (German Beer Cheese Dip), 275
✓Peachy Jalapeno Guacamole, 100
Radish & Mandarin Orange Guacamole, 102
Red Lentil Hummus with Brussels Sprout Hash, 16
✓The Best Hummus, 7
Warm Strawberry Fondue, 17
Hot Appetizers
Barbecued Party Starters, 230
BLT Bruschetta, 99
Blue-Ribbon Beef Nachos, 7
Brie Cherry Pastry Cups, 290
Easy Coconut Shrimp, 264
Garlic Mozzarella Bread Bites, 18
Grilled Jalapenos, 238
Hawaiian Egg Rolls, 265
Hot Dog Mummies with Honey Mustard Dip, 279
Hot Italian Party Sandwiches, 230
Mini Corn Dogs, 269
Peachy-Keen Halloumi Fritters, 13
Pepper Jelly Hogs in a Blanket, 9
Philly Cheesesteak Egg Rolls, 8
Potato Latke Funnel Cakes, 6
Roasted Brussels Sprouts with Sriracha Aioli, 9
Samosas, 17
Spinach Puffs, 14
Swiss Potato Puffs, 242
Tomato Galette with Basil Pesto & Feta, 12
✓Zucchini Pizza Fritters, 6
Nuts & Snacks
Cinnamon Toasted Almonds, 231
Kiddie Crunch Mix, 241
Lightsaber Pretzels, 273
Peppermint Popcorn, 295
✓Warm Spiced Nuts, 279
Spreads
Blue Cheese Logs, 235
Buffalo Cheese Logs, 235
Cheese & Pimiento Spread, 260
Chicken Noodle Cheese Logs, 235
Curried Apricot Cheese Logs, 235
Feta & Olive Cheese Logs, 235
Nacho Cheese Logs, 235
Pepperoni Pizza Cheese Logs, 235
Pesto Cheese Logs, 235
Pumpkin Cheese Ball, 278
Reuben Cheese Logs, 235
Smoked Salmon Cheese Logs, 235

APPLES, APPLE CIDER & APPLESAUCE
All-American Pie, 240
Apple & White Onion Guacamole, 103
Apple Balsamic Chicken, 119
Apple Cider Biscuits, 154
Apple Honey Tapioca Pudding, 223
✓Apple Matchstick Salad, 32
Caramel Apple Krispies Treats, 181
✓Carrot Zucchini Bread, 146
✓Cran-Apple Praline Gingerbread, 200
Grandma's Apple Cake, 200
Granny's Apple Scalloped Potatoes, 134
Hot Cider, 280
Maple-Glazed Apple Pie, 207
Sausage & Pancake Bake, 171

APRICOTS
Apricot Bars, 184
✓Apricot Upside-Down Cake, 205
Curried Apricot Cheese Logs, 235
✓Fruit & Almond Bites, 184
✓Lemon-Apricot Fruit Pops, 220

AVOCADOS
Apple & White Onion Guacamole, 103
Bacon & Cotija Cheese Guacamole, 103
Black Bean & Corn Guacamole, 103
Blue Cheese & Toasted Almond Guacamole, 103
Brown Sugar Bacon BLT Sandwiches, 38
Cajun Shrimp & Red Pepper Guacamole, 102
✓Cherry Tomato Pasta with Avocado Sauce, 129
Grilled Chicken & Cherry Tomato Guacamole, 102
✓Healthy Avocado Pineapple Muffins, 150
Jicama & Pineapple Guacamole, 103
Mango & Habanero Guacamole, 103
✓Peachy Jalapeno Guacamole, 100
✓Quick & Easy Chicken Poke Bowl, 76
Radish & Mandarin Orange Guacamole, 102
✓Shrimp Tostadas with Avocado Salsa, 53
Vegan Chocolate Mousse, 225

BACON
Bacon & Cotija Cheese Guacamole, 103
Bacon Breakfast Cookies, 161
Bacon Hash Brown Bake, 256
Bacon Mac & Cheese Cornbread Skillet, 137
Beer & Bacon Macaroni & Cheese, 89
BLT Bruschetta, 99
Breakfast BLT Waffles, 166
Brown Sugar Bacon BLT Sandwiches, 38
Chicken with Pumpkin Alfredo, 64
Easy Cheesy Cauliflower Breakfast Casserole, 169
Granny's Apple Scalloped Potatoes, 134
Green Bean Bundles, 135
Grilled Jalapenos, 238
Grilled Pimiento Cheese Sandwiches, 44
Irish Beef Stew, 47
Maple-Bacon Krispies Treats, 181
✓Maple Bacon Walnut Coffee Cake, 170
Mexican Street Corn Chowder, 42
Mint Lamb Stew, 73
Momma's Green Beans, 289
Potato Soup, 120
Pumpkin Clam Chowder, 45
Pumpkin French Toast with Bacon Maple Syrup, 163
Spaghetti with Bacon, 71

Swiss Potato Soup, 40
The Best Quiche Lorraine, 170

BANANAS
Banana Fudge Pie, 204
Coconut-Macadamia Sheet-Pan Pancakes, 241
Fried Banana Milkshakes, 215
Funky Monkey Krispies Treats, 181
Salted Caramel & Banana Drinking Chocolate, 214
Tropical Sweet Potato Bake, 237

BARS & BROWNIES
Apricot Bars, 184
Brownie Haunted House, 277
Brownie Kiss Cupcakes, 201
Caramel Apple Krispies Treats, 181
Caramel Heavenlies, 186
Chocolate-Raspberry Krispies Treats, 181
Classic Lemon Bars, 178
Crumb-Topped Date Bars, 106
Funky Monkey Krispies Treats, 181
Gluten-Free Brownie Bars, 182
Maple-Bacon Krispies Treats, 181
Morning Buzz Krispies Treats, 181
Oatmeal Breakfast Bars, 162
Oreo Krispies Treats, 181
Rocky Road Krispies Treats, 181
Salted Caramel Pretzel Krispies Treats, 181
Sparkly Princess Krispies Treats, 181
Tombstone Treats, 280
Two-Tone Caramel Brownies, 187
Watermelon Krispies Treats, 181

BEANS
Black Bean & Corn Guacamole, 103
Black Bean Rice Burgers, 40
Blue-Ribbon Beef Nachos, 7
✓Chickpea & Potato Curry, 122
Frijoles y Chorizo, 133
✓Lora's Red Beans & Rice, 112
Middle Eastern Macaroni Salad, 24
✓Salsa Black Bean Burgers, 101
✓Shrimp Tostadas with Avocado Salsa, 53
✓Tex-Mex Grain Bowl, 172
✓The Best Hummus, 7
Truly Texan Chili, 36
✓Turkey Chili, 118

BEEF
(also see Ground Beef)
Air-Fryer Spicy Ginger Beef Skewers, 81
Beef Short Ribs Vindaloo, 113
✓Beef Tenderloin with Roasted Vegetables, 243
Chicken-Fried Steaks, 60
✓Easy Marinated Grilled Flank Steak, 94
Home-Style Roast Beef, 78
Irish Beef Stew, 47
Mandarin Steak Salad, 95
Mexican Steak Fajitas, 60
Philly Cheesesteak Egg Rolls, 8
Pumpkin Cheese Ball, 278
Reuben Cheese Logs, 235
Slow-Cooker Asian Short Ribs, 64
Slow-Cooker Beef Brisket, 87
Steak Sandwiches with Crispy Onions, 46
Steak Tortillas, 95
Steakhouse Pizza, 79
The Best Grilled Sirloin Tip Roast, 82

BEETS
✓Minted Beet Salad, 33
Spicy Beet Relish, 135
✓Spinach Salad with Goat Cheese & Beets, 22

BELL PEPPERS
Chicken Taco Macaroni Salad, 25
✓Garden Chicken Cacciatore, 121
Mexican Street Corn Chowder, 42
Polynesian Macaroni Salad, 25

BEVERAGES
Amaretto Margarita, 10
Biscoff Drinking Chocolate, 214
Blackberry Shrub, 12
Blueberry-Mint Frozen Margarita, 11
Caribbean Margarita, 10
Chai Drinking Chocolate, 214
Chili-Orange Drinking Chocolate, 214
Classic Margarita, 10
Cranberry Cherry Punch, 268
Creamy White Drinking Chocolate, 214
Favorite Hot Chocolate, 260
Fried Banana Milkshakes, 215
Frozen Coconut Margarita, 11
Grapefruit Sunset Margarita, 10
Hazelnut Mocha Drinking Chocolate, 214
Heavenly Nutmeg Drinking Chocolate, 214
Hot Cider, 280
Hot Spiced Cranberry Drink, 286
Lemon, Ginger & Turmeric Infused Water, 8
Melon Margarita, 10
Mulled Wine Margaritas, 15
Nutty Hawaiian, 264
Parisian Sipping Chocolate, 210
Peppermint Red Velvet Drinking Chocolate, 214
Pumpkin Spice Drinking Chocolate, 214
Raspberry-Ginger Frozen Margarita, 11
Salted Caramel & Banana Drinking Chocolate, 214
Salty Dog Sangria, 16
Snickerdoodle Drinking Chocolate, 214
Sriracha-Mango Frozen Margarita, 11
Strawberry-Basil Frozen Margarita, 11
Sweet Tea Concentrate, 257
Tajin Limeade, 14
Yoda Soda, 272

BISCUITS & BISCUIT MIX
Apple Cider Biscuits, 154
Chicken Biscuit Skillet, 52
Garden Herb Drop Biscuits, 152
Homemade Biscuits & Maple Sausage Gravy, 252
Sausage & Pancake Bake, 171
Triple-Cheese Broccoli Puff, 289
Waffle-Iron Pizzas, 53

BLACKBERRIES
Blackberry Shrub, 12
Mixed Berry Tiramisu, 216
New York Cheesecake with Shortbread Crust, 215

BLUEBERRIES
All-American Pie, 240
Berry Pretzel Fluff Dessert, 218
Blueberry-Mint Frozen Margarita, 11
Cinnamon Blueberry Jam, 129
Five-Minute Blueberry Pie, 194
Maple Blueberry Crisp, 223
Mixed Berry Tiramisu, 216
New York Cheesecake with Shortbread Crust, 215
Triple Berry Mini Pies, 205

BREADS, ROLLS & MUFFINS
(also see Cornbread & Cornmeal)
Apple Cider Biscuits, 154
Boston Brown Bread, 156
Caraway Puffs, 149
✓Carrot Zucchini Bread, 146
Cherry-Go-Round, 155
Chewy Soft Pretzels, 275
Chocolate Chip Muffins, 154
Chocolate Yeast Bread, 148
Christmas Star Twisted Bread, 302
Conchas (Seashells), 157
Cristen's Giant Cinnamon Rolls, 153
Double Chocolate Scones, 147
Garden Herb Drop Biscuits, 152
Garlic Rosemary Pull-Apart Bread, 149
✓Gluten-Free Spiced Sweet Potato Muffins, 148
Green Onion Rolls, 147
Grilled Elote Flatbread, 130
✓Healthy Avocado Pineapple Muffins, 150
Heavenly Cheese Danish, 155

BREADS, ROLLS & MUFFINS (*continued*)
Mincemeat-Filled Braid, 298
Peaches & Cream Whiskey Loaf, 156
Pepper Jack Muffins, 157
Pumpkin Egg Braid, 291
Raisin Rye Muffins, 153
Snickerdoodle Pumpkin Bread, 150
Sweet Potato Spice Bread, 152
Wonderful English Muffins, 146

BREAKFAST & BRUNCH
Breads
Chocolate-Hazelnut Espresso Cinnamon Rolls, 173
✓Maple Bacon Walnut Coffee Cake, 170
✓Vegan Lemon Poppy Seed Doughnuts, 173
Egg Dishes
Caramelized Mushroom & Onion Frittata, 164
Collards Quiche, 253
Easy Cheesy Cauliflower Breakfast Casserole, 169
Finnish Cheese Pie, 164
Freezer Breakfast Sandwiches, 165
Jalapeno Sausage Quiche, 236
✓Muffin-Tin Scrambled Eggs, 168
Spinach Chicken Frittata, 93
The Best Quiche Lorraine, 170
French Toast, Pancakes & Waffles
Coconut-Macadamia Sheet-Pan Pancakes, 241
✓Crispy French Toast, 168
✓High-Octane Pancakes, 165
✓Peachy Danish Pancake Balls (Aebleskiver), 166
Pumpkin French Toast with Bacon Maple Syrup, 163
The Best French Toast, 162
Grains
Grits & Sausage Casserole, 254
Oatmeal Breakfast Bars, 162
✓Pear Quinoa Breakfast Bake, 163
✓Strawberry Overnight Oats, 171
✓Tex-Mex Grain Bowl, 172
Other
Bacon Breakfast Cookies, 161
Bacon Hash Brown Bake, 256
Breakfast BLT Waffles, 166
Chiles Rellenos Croque-Madame, 160
Homemade Biscuits & Maple Sausage Gravy, 252
✓Mean Green Smoothie Bowls, 160
✓Pumpkin & Chicken Sausage Hash, 161
✓Sage Turkey Sausage Patties, 242
Salmon Croquette Breakfast Sandwich, 169
Sausage & Pancake Bake, 171
✓Spicy Hash Brown Waffles with Fried Eggs, 101
✓Warm Grapefruit with Ginger-Sugar, 172

BROCCOLI & BROCCOLI COLESLAW MIX
Antipasto Picnic Salad, 233
Broccoli Turkey Casserole, 68
Caribbean Shrimp Bowl, 57
General Tso's Chicken Sandwich with Broccoli Slaw, 42
Triple-Cheese Broccoli Puff, 289

BRUSSELS SPROUTS
✓Red Lentil Hummus with Brussels Sprout Hash, 16
Roasted Brussels Sprouts with Sriracha Aioli, 9

CABBAGE
✓Beefy Cabbage Bean Stew, 123
Lebanese Stuffed Cabbages, 68

CAKE MIX
Birthday Cake Fudge, 179
Eggnog Tres Leches Cake, 192
✓Pineapple Poke Cake, 198
Red Velvet Cake in a Jar, 195
Robot Cake, 272
Two-Tone Caramel Brownies, 187

CAKES & CUPCAKES
✓Apricot Upside-Down Cake, 205
Brownie Haunted House, 277
Brownie Kiss Cupcakes, 201
Eggnog Tres Leches Cake, 192
Eyes On You, 278
Grandma's Apple Cake, 200
Lady Baltimore Cake, 201
Mocha Hazelnut Torte, 207
✓Pineapple Poke Cake, 198
Rainbow Sherbet Angel Food Cake, 219
Red Velvet Cake in a Jar, 195
Robot Cake, 272
Slow-Cooker Strawberry Soda Cake, 237
S'mores Cupcakes, 261
Southern Lane Cake, 196
Summer Squash Pound Cake, 194
Swedish Flop, 193
Tuscan Sun Orange Cranberry Cake, 206
Vanilla Bean Cupcakes, 198

CANDIES
Birthday Cake Fudge, 179
Brandy Alexander Fudge, 302
Candy Bar Fudge, 176
Chocolate Caramels, 188
Chocolate-Covered Cherries, 299
Coconut Egg Nests, 189
✓Fruit & Almond Bites, 184
Goody-Goody Gumdrops, 303
Minty Cookies & Cream Chocolate Fudge, 296
Orange Gumdrops, 189
Pacoca (Brazilian Peanut Candy), 185
Salted Peanut Squares, 186
Truffle Topiary, 299

CARAMEL
Caramel Apple Krispies Treats, 181
Caramel Heavenlies, 186
Chocolate Caramel Cookies, 268
Chocolate Caramels, 188
Indonesian Bananas Foster, 217
Salted Caramel & Banana Drinking Chocolate, 214
Salted Caramel Pretzel Krispies Treats, 181
Two-Tone Caramel Brownies, 187

CARROTS
✓Carrot Zucchini Bread, 146
Glazed Carrots with Green Grapes, 142

CAULIFLOWER
Caribbean Shrimp Bowl, 57
Cauliflower au Gratin, 233
Creamy Cauliflower Rice, 142
Easy Cheesy Cauliflower Breakfast Casserole, 169
✓Gobi Aloo, 139
Mashed Cauliflower with Parmesan, 128
Vegan Butter Cauliflower, 76

CHEESE
(also see Cream Cheese; Goat Cheese)
Appetizers
Blue Cheese & Toasted Almond Guacamole, 103
Blue Cheese Logs, 235
Brie Cherry Pastry Cups, 290
Buffalo Cheese Logs, 235
Cheese & Pimiento Spread, 260
Chili Queso Dip, 18
Feta & Olive Cheese Logs, 235
Hot Italian Party Sandwiches, 230
Nacho Cheese Logs, 235
Obatzda (German Beer Cheese Dip), 275
Peachy-Keen Halloumi Fritters, 13
Pepperoni Pizza Cheese Logs, 235
Pesto Cheese Logs, 235
Pumpkin Cheese Ball, 278
Reuben Cheese Logs, 235
Spinach Puffs, 14
Swiss Potato Puffs, 242

Tomato Galette with Basil Pesto & Feta, 12
✓Zucchini Pizza Fritters, 6
Breads
Garden Herb Drop Biscuits, 152
Garlic Mozzarella Bread Bites, 18
Garlic Rosemary Pull-Apart Bread, 149
Pepper Jack Muffins, 157
Breakfast & Brunch
Caramelized Mushroom & Onion Frittata, 164
Collards Quiche, 253
Easy Cheesy Cauliflower Breakfast Casserole, 169
Finnish Cheese Pie, 164
The Best Quiche Lorraine, 170
Condiments
Alfredo Sauce, 97
Classic Pesto, 99
Main Dishes
Baked Pasta Puttanesca, 66
Catfish Parmesan, 70
Feta-Stuffed Kibbeh with Harissa, 66
Fettuccine Alfredo, 97
Greek Tilapia, 82
Malai Kofta, 75
Mexican Lasagna, 87
Polpette di Mamma, 243
Ravioli Casserole, 84
Salads
Caprese Macaroni Salad, 24
Slow-Cooker Buffalo Chicken Salad, 23
✓Spinach Salad with Goat Cheese & Beets, 22
Side Dishes
Beer & Bacon Macaroni & Cheese, 89
Mashed Cauliflower with Parmesan, 128
Smoked Macaroni & Cheese, 238
Triple-Cheese Broccoli Puff, 289
Soups
Potato Soup, 120
Swiss Potato Soup, 40

CHERRIES
All-American Pie, 240
Cherry-Go-Round, 155
Cherry Plum Slab Pie with Walnut Streusel, 196
Cherry Surprise Cookies, 106
Chocolate-Covered Cherries, 299
✓Fruit & Almond Bites, 184
Southern Lane Cake, 196

CHICKEN
Appetizers
Bacon & Cotija Cheese Guacamole, 103
Grilled Chicken & Cherry Tomato Guacamole, 102
Breakfast & Brunch
Spinach Chicken Frittata, 93
Main Dishes
✓Air-Fryer Almond Chicken, 58
Air-Fryer Nashville Hot Chicken, 73
Apple Balsamic Chicken, 119
Baked Chicken & Zucchini, 69
Chicken Biscuit Skillet, 52
✓Chicken Breasts with Melon Relish, 50
Chicken Scampi, 56
✓Chicken Tikka Masala, 111
Chicken with Pumpkin Alfredo, 64
✓Chipotle Pumpkin Chicken Pizza, 71
Coconut Chicken Nuggets with Creamy Caribbean Salsa, 81
Dad's Lemony Grilled Chicken, 86
✓Garden Chicken Cacciatore, 121
Hearty Chicken Enchiladas, 74
Italian Chicken Stew, 98
Poppy Seed Chicken, 93
✓Quick & Easy Chicken Poke Bowl, 76
✓Ramen Noodle Stir-Fry, 51
✓Saucy Indian-Style Chicken & Vegetables, 116
Savory Roasted Chicken, 92
✓Simple Salsa Chicken, 83
Salads
Chicken Caesar Macaroni Salad, 24
Chicken Strawberry Spinach Salad, 29
Chicken Taco Macaroni Salad, 25
Slow-Cooker Buffalo Chicken Salad, 23
Toasted Chicken Salad Sandwiches, 47
Sandwiches & Wraps
Chicken Alfredo Sandwiches, 97
General Tso's Chicken Sandwich with Broccoli Slaw, 42
Hoisin Chicken Wraps, 45
Soups
Ceylon Chicken Curry & Rice Noodle Soup, 39
✓Hearty Homemade Chicken Noodle Soup, 41

CHOCOLATE & COCOA
(*also see White Chocolate*)
Beverages
Biscoff Drinking Chocolate, 214
Chai Drinking Chocolate, 214
Chili-Orange Drinking Chocolate, 214
Favorite Hot Chocolate, 260
Hazelnut Mocha Drinking Chocolate, 214
Heavenly Nutmeg Drinking Chocolate, 214
Parisian Sipping Chocolate, 210
Pumpkin Spice Drinking Chocolate, 214
Salted Caramel & Banana Drinking Chocolate, 214
Snickerdoodle Drinking Chocolate, 214
Breads
Chocolate Chip Muffins, 154
Chocolate Yeast Bread, 148
Double Chocolate Scones, 147
Desserts
Banana Fudge Pie, 204
Bones & Blood, 277
Brandy Alexander Fudge, 302
Brownie Haunted House, 277
Brownie Kiss Cupcakes, 201
Candy Bar Fudge, 176
Cherry Surprise Cookies, 106
Chocolate Caramel Cookies, 268
Chocolate Caramels, 188
Chocolate-Covered Cherries, 299
Chocolate-Raspberry Krispies Treats, 181
Chocolate Zucchini Cookies, 177
Double Chocolate Espresso Cheesecake, 220
Ganache-Topped Pumpkin Tart, 192
Gluten-Free Brownie Bars, 182
Minty Cookies & Cream Chocolate Fudge, 296
Mocha Hazelnut Torte, 207
Morning Buzz Krispies Treats, 181
Peppermint Cheesecake on a Stick, 301
Popcorn Cookies, 187
Red Velvet Cake in a Jar, 195
Rocky Road Krispies Treats, 181
S'mores Cupcakes, 261
Salted Caramel Pretzel Krispies Treats, 181
Slow-Cooker Strawberry Soda Cake, 237
Tombstone Treats, 280
Truffle Topiary, 299
Two-Tone Caramel Brownies, 187
Vegan Chocolate Mousse, 225

COCONUT & COCONUT MILK
Caramel Heavenlies, 186
Ceylon Chicken Curry & Rice Noodle Soup, 39
Coconut Chicken Nuggets with Creamy Caribbean Salsa, 81
Coconut Egg Nests, 189
Coconut-Macadamia Sheet-Pan Pancakes, 241
Easy Coconut Shrimp, 264
Frozen Coconut Margarita, 11
Indonesian Bananas Foster, 217
Mama's Coconut Pie, 206
Oatmeal Breakfast Bars, 162
Southern Lane Cake, 196
Vegan Butter Cauliflower, 76

COFFEE
Coffee Ice Cream, 218
Double Chocolate Espresso Cheesecake, 220
French Toast Spirals, 183
Hazelnut Macarons, 188
Hazelnut Mocha Drinking Chocolate, 214
Mocha Hazelnut Torte, 207
✓Mocha-Walnut Macarons, 179
Morning Buzz Krispies Treats, 181
Parisian Sipping Chocolate, 210

CONDIMENTS, PICKLES & SAUCES
Alabama White BBQ Sauce, 143
Alfredo Sauce, 97
Ash's Sweet & Spicy Enchilada Sauce, 132
✓Best Ever Cashew Cheese Sauce, 126
Chive Butter Balls, 248
Citrus Cantaloupe Butter, 130
Classic Pesto, 99
Homemade Marinara Sauce, 98
Homemade Taco Seasoning Mix, 128
✓Mint Chutney, 132
Pumpkin Butter, 141
Quick Pickled Radishes, 127
✓Quick Roasted Red Pepper Spread, 140
✓Romesco Sauce, 136
Spicy Beet Relish, 135
Strawberry Butter, 143
Winter Fruit Compote, 117
Zucchini Pickles, 133

COOKIES
Bacon Breakfast Cookies, 161
Basic Cookie Dough, 104
Bones & Blood, 277
Butter Brickle Biscotti, 176
Cherry Surprise Cookies, 106
✓Chewy Cookies, 271
Chocolate Caramel Cookies, 268
Chocolate Mallow Cookies, 105
Chocolate Zucchini Cookies, 177
Classic Sugar Cookies, 107
Cranberry Nutella Sandwich Cookies, 183
Cranberry Pecan Cookies, 185
Cream Cheese Red Velvet Thumbprint Cookies, 295
French Toast Spirals, 183
Fruitcake Cookies, 301
Gumdrop Cookies, 182
Hazelnut Macarons, 188
Jelly Sandwich Cookies, 105
✓Mocha-Walnut Macarons, 179
Peanut Butter Cinnamon Snap Cookies, 296
Popcorn Cookies, 187
Rolled Butter Almond Cookies, 177
Spicy Oatmeal Cookie Mix, 178

CORN
Black Bean & Corn Guacamole, 103
Corn Pudding, 285
Creamy Corn Custards, 213
Fiesta Corn, 141
Grilled Elote Flatbread, 130
Mexican Street Corn Chowder, 42
Rustic Fish Chowder, 38
✓Salmon Sweet Potato Soup, 44

CORNBREAD MIX & CORNMEAL
Bacon Mac & Cheese Cornbread Skillet, 137
Corn Pudding, 285
Mini Corn Dogs, 269

CRANBERRIES & CRANBERRY JUICE
✓Cran-Apple Praline Gingerbread, 200
Cranberry Ambrosia Salad, 23
Cranberry Cherry Punch, 268
Cranberry Nutella Sandwich Cookies, 183
Cranberry Pecan Cookies, 185
Hot Spiced Cranberry Drink, 286
Spiral Ham with Cranberry Glaze, 288
Tuscan Sun Orange Cranberry Cake, 206
Winter Fruit Compote, 117

CREAM CHEESE
Appetizers
Blue Cheese Logs, 235
Buffalo Cheese Logs, 235
Chicken Noodle Cheese Logs, 235
Curried Apricot Cheese Logs, 235
Feta & Olive Cheese Logs, 235
Gingersnap Dip, 236
Hot Chili Cheese Dip, 248
Hot Shrimp Dip, 13
Nacho Cheese Logs, 235
Pepperoni Pizza Cheese Logs, 235
Pesto Cheese Logs, 235
Reuben Cheese Logs, 235
Smoked Salmon Cheese Logs, 235
Desserts
Berry Pretzel Fluff Dessert, 218
Butter Pecan Cheesecake, 212
Cream Cheese Red Velvet Thumbprint Cookies, 295
Double Chocolate Espresso Cheesecake, 220
Huckleberry Cheese Pie, 204
New York Cheesecake with Shortbread Crust, 215
Peanut Butter & Jelly Cheesecake, 219
Peanut Butter Silk Pie, 203
Peppermint Cheesecake on a Stick, 301
Pumpkin Rugelach with Cream Cheese Icing, 225
Red Velvet Cake in a Jar, 195
Roasted Grape & Sweet Cheese Phyllo Galette, 222
Sunny Citrus Layered Cheesecake, 227
Vanilla Bean Cupcakes, 198
Other
Duo Tater Bake, 292
Heavenly Cheese Danish, 155
Holiday Pretzel Salad, 211
Salmon Croquette Breakfast Sandwich, 169
Strawberry Butter, 143

CUCUMBERS
Grilled Romaine Salad, 26
✓Mean Green Smoothie Bowls, 160
Shrimp & Crab Macaroni Salad, 25
✓Watermelon & Cucumber Salsa, 260

DESSERTS
(also see Bars & Brownies; Beverages; Cakes & Cupcakes; Candies; Pies & Tarts)
Cheesecakes
Butter Pecan Cheesecake, 212
Double Chocolate Espresso Cheesecake, 220
New York Cheesecake with Shortbread Crust, 215
Peanut Butter & Jelly Cheesecake, 219
Peppermint Cheesecake on a Stick, 301
Sunny Citrus Layered Cheesecake, 227
Gelatin
Galaxy Bites, 273
Holiday Pretzel Salad, 211
Jazzy Gelatin, 212
Peach Bavarian, 213

Ice Cream & Frozen Desserts
Almost It's-It Ice Cream Sandwiches, 216
Best Ever Vanilla Ice Cream, 226
Coffee Ice Cream, 218
Fried Banana Milkshakes, 215
Fried Ice Cream Dessert Bars, 211
✓Lemon-Apricot Fruit Pops, 220
Rainbow Sherbet Angel Food Cake, 219
Other
Apple Honey Tapioca Pudding, 223
Berry Pretzel Fluff Dessert, 218
Best Strawberry Shortcake, 255
Biscuit Strawberry Shortcake, 217
Bones & Blood, 277
Campfire Dessert Cones, 232
Creamy Corn Custards, 213
Crispy Christmas Trees, 294
Gingersnap Dip, 236

Indonesian Bananas Foster, 217
Maple Blueberry Crisp, 223
Mixed Berry Tiramisu, 216
Pumpkin Crunch Parfaits, 222
Pumpkin Rugelach with Cream Cheese Icing, 225
Roasted Grape & Sweet Cheese Phyllo Galette, 222
Rose Water Rice Pudding, 210
Tombstone Treats, 280
Vegan Chocolate Mousse, 225

EGGS
Bacon Mac & Cheese Cornbread Skillet, 137
Barbecue Macaroni Salad, 25
Best Deviled Eggs, 15
Best Ever Vanilla Ice Cream, 226
Breakfast BLT Waffles, 166
Caramelized Mushroom & Onion Frittata, 164
Chiles Rellenos Croque-Madame, 160
Collards Quiche, 253
Easy Cheesy Cauliflower Breakfast Casserole, 169
Freezer Breakfast Sandwiches, 165
✓Grandma's Classic Potato Salad, 30
✓Grandma's French Tuna Salad Wraps, 39
Hazelnut Macarons, 188
Heavenly Cheese Danish, 155
Jalapeno Sausage Quiche, 236
Madras Curried Eggs with Rice, 79
✓Muffin-Tin Scrambled Eggs, 168
✓Spicy Hash Brown Waffles with Fried Eggs, 101
Spinach Chicken Frittata, 93
Swiss Potato Puffs, 242
The Best Quiche Lorraine, 170

FISH
Catfish Parmesan, 70
✓Crumb-Topped Sole, 51
Finnish Cheese Pie, 164
✓Grandma's French Tuna Salad Wraps, 39
Greek Tilapia, 82
Grilled Tuna Salad, 32
Rustic Fish Chowder, 38
Salmon Croquette Breakfast Sandwich, 169
Salmon Grilled in Foil, 58
✓Salmon Sweet Potato Soup, 44
Smoked Salmon Cheese Logs, 235
✓Tarragon Tuna Salad, 28
Tasty Tuna Casserole, 78

FRUIT
(also see specific kinds)
Cherry Plum Slab Pie with Walnut Streusel, 196
✓Chicken Breasts with Melon Relish, 50
Citrus Cantaloupe Butter, 130
Crumb-Topped Date Bars, 106
Fruitcake Cookies, 301
Huckleberry Cheese Pie, 204
Indonesian Bananas Foster, 217
Mandarin Steak Salad, 95
✓Pear Quinoa Breakfast Bake, 163
✓Pork Chops with Nectarine Salsa, 59
Quick Ambrosia Fruit Salad, 257
Special Fruit Salad, 27
Sunny Citrus Layered Cheesecake, 227
Tajin Limeade, 14
Vegan Chocolate Mousse, 225
Winter Fruit Compote, 117

GELATIN
Cranberry Cherry Punch, 268
Galaxy Bites, 273
Holiday Pretzel Salad, 211
Jazzy Gelatin, 212
Peach Bavarian, 213

GOAT CHEESE
Mandarin Steak Salad, 95
Smoked Salmon Cheese Logs, 235

GRAINS
(also see Oats; Rice)
Farro Salad with Charred Shishito Peppers & Corn, 30
Feta-Stuffed Kibbeh with Harissa, 66
Grits & Sausage Casserole, 254
✓Pear Quinoa Breakfast Bake, 163
✓Tabbouleh, 26

GRAPEFRUIT & GRAPEFRUIT JUICE
Grapefruit Sunset Margarita, 10
Salty Dog Sangria, 16
✓Warm Grapefruit with Ginger-Sugar, 172

GRAPES
Glazed Carrots with Green Grapes, 142
Quick Ambrosia Fruit Salad, 257
Roasted Grape & Sweet Cheese Phyllo Galette, 222

GREEN BEANS
Elegant Green Beans, 284
Green Bean Bundles, 135
Italian Chicken Stew, 98
✓Jalapeno Green Beans, 127
Momma's Green Beans, 289

GRILLED RECIPES
Campfire Dessert Cones, 232
Chicken Strawberry Spinach Salad, 29
Crunchy Burger Quesadillas, 54
Dad's Lemony Grilled Chicken, 86
✓Easy Marinated Grilled Flank Steak, 94
Grilled Elote Flatbread, 130
Grilled Jalapenos, 238
Grilled Romaine Salad, 26
Grilled Shrimp with Cilantro Dipping Sauce, 65
Grilled Tuna Salad, 32
Lebanese Street Sandwiches, 41
My Juicy Lucy, 37
Salmon Grilled in Foil, 58
Shrimp & Scallops Tropical Salad, 22
Skewered Lamb with Blackberry-Balsamic Glaze, 70
Smoked Macaroni & Cheese, 238
Steak Sandwiches with Crispy Onions, 46
The Best Grilled Sirloin Tip Roast, 82

GROUND BEEF
Baked Pasta Puttanesca, 66
Barbecued Party Starters, 230
✓Beefy Cabbage Bean Stew, 123
Blue-Ribbon Beef Nachos, 7
Chili Queso Dip, 18
Crunchy Burger Quesadillas, 54
Ground Beef Wellingtons, 65
Hamburger Noodle Casserole, 86
Hamburger Stroganoff, 52
Indian-Spiced Beefy Lettuce Wraps, 56
Lebanese Street Sandwiches, 41
Lebanese Stuffed Cabbages, 68
Meatball Subs, 98
Mexican Lasagna, 87
My Juicy Lucy, 37
One-Skillet Lasagna, 50
Pesto Hamburgers, 99
Polpette di Mamma, 243
Truly Texan Chili, 36

HAM & PROSCIUTTO
Antipasto Picnic Salad, 233
Chiles Rellenos Croque-Madame, 160
Cubano Macaroni Salad, 25
Hawaiian Egg Rolls, 265
Hot Italian Party Sandwiches, 230
Kilbourn Sandwich, 36
Peachy-Keen Halloumi Fritters, 13
Polynesian Macaroni Salad, 25
Spiral Ham with Cranberry Glaze, 288

HONEY
Apple Honey Tapioca Pudding, 223
✓Gluten-Free Spiced Sweet Potato Muffins, 148
Hot Cider, 280

HONEY
(continued)
Hot Dog Mummies with Honey Mustard Dip, 279
Mini Corn Dogs, 269
Sweet Potato Spice Bread, 152

HOT PEPPERS
Chiles Rellenos Croque-Madame, 160
Chili Queso Dip, 18
Chimichangas, 59
Curried Apricot Cheese Logs, 235
Fiesta Corn, 141
Frijoles y Chorizo, 133
Grilled Jalapenos, 238
✓Jalapeno Green Beans, 127
Jalapeno Sausage Quiche, 236
Mango & Habanero Guacamole, 103
Nacho Cheese Logs, 235
✓Peachy Jalapeno Guacamole, 100
✓Salsa Black Bean Burgers, 101
✓Slow-Cooked Salsa, 248
✓ Southwestern Pork & Squash Soup, 110
✓Spicy Hash Brown Waffles with Fried Eggs, 101
✓Watermelon & Cucumber Salsa, 260

JAM, JELLY, MARMALADE & PRESERVES
Barbecued Party Starters, 230
Bones & Blood, 277
Brie Cherry Pastry Cups, 290
Christmas Star Twisted Bread, 302
Cinnamon Blueberry Jam, 129
Glazed Carrots with Green Grapes, 142
Grilled Pimiento Cheese Sandwiches, 44
Jelly Sandwich Cookies, 105
Kilbourn Sandwich, 36
Oatmeal Breakfast Bars, 162
Peanut Butter & Jelly Cheesecake, 219
Pepper Jelly Hogs in a Blanket, 9
Roasted Grape & Sweet Cheese Phyllo Galette, 222
Skewered Lamb with Blackberry-Balsamic Glaze, 70
Slow-Cooker Strawberry Soda Cake, 237
Spiral Ham with Cranberry Glaze, 288
Swedish Flop, 193
Violet Jelly, 134

LAMB
Feta-Stuffed Kibbeh with Harissa, 66
Middle Eastern Macaroni Salad, 24
Mint Lamb Stew, 73
✓New England Lamb Bake, 89
Skewered Lamb with Blackberry-Balsamic Glaze, 70

LASAGNA
Mexican Lasagna, 87
One-Skillet Lasagna, 50

LEMON
Classic Lemon Bars, 178
Cranberry Cherry Punch, 268
Dad's Lemony Grilled Chicken, 86
Grecian Macaroni Salad, 24
✓Italian Dressing, 27
✓Lemon-Apricot Fruit Pops, 220
Lemon, Ginger & Turmeric Infused Water, 8
✓Lemon Red Potatoes, 114
Sweet Tea Concentrate, 257
✓Vegan Lemon Poppy Seed Doughnuts, 173

LENTILS
✓Lentil Pumpkin Soup, 115
✓Red Lentil Hummus with Brussels Sprout Hash, 16

LETTUCE
BLT Bruschetta, 99
✓Citrus Fennel Salad, 290
Grilled Romaine Salad, 26
Indian-Spiced Beefy Lettuce Wraps, 56
Mandarin Steak Salad, 95
✓Shrimp & Scallops Tropical Salad, 22
Slow-Cooker Buffalo Chicken Salad, 23

MANGOES
Mango & Habanero Guacamole, 103
Sriracha-Mango Frozen Margarita, 11

MAPLE
French Toast Spirals, 183
Homemade Biscuits & Maple Sausage Gravy, 252
Maple-Bacon Krispies Treats, 181
✓Maple Bacon Walnut Coffee Cake, 170
Maple Blueberry Crisp, 223
✓Maple-Gingerroot Vegetables, 292
Maple-Glazed Apple Pie, 207
Maple Pecan Pie, 199
Maple-Sage Brined Turkey, 283
Pumpkin French Toast with Bacon Maple Syrup, 163
Pumpkin Pie Tartlets with Maple Pecan Crust, 203

MARSHMALLOWS & MARSHMALLOW CREME
Brandy Alexander Fudge, 302
Campfire Dessert Cones, 232
Caramel Apple Krispies Treats, 181
Caramel Heavenlies, 186
Chocolate Mallow Cookies, 105
Chocolate-Raspberry Krispies Treats, 181
Cranberry Ambrosia Salad, 23
Crispy Christmas Trees, 294
Eyes On You, 278
Funky Monkey Krispies Treats, 181
Maple-Bacon Krispies Treats, 181
Minty Cookies & Cream Chocolate Fudge, 296
Morning Buzz Krispies Treats, 181
Oreo Krispies Treats, 181
Quick Ambrosia Fruit Salad, 257
Rocky Road Krispies Treats, 181
Salted Caramel Pretzel Krispies Treats, 181
Salted Peanut Squares, 186
S'mores Cupcakes, 261
Sparkly Princess Krispies Treats, 181
Tombstone Treats, 280
Watermelon Krispies Treats, 181

MEATBALLS & MEAT LOAVES
Barbecued Party Starters, 230
Meatball Subs, 98
Polpette di Mamma, 243

MOLASSES
Boston Brown Bread, 156
✓Chewy Cookies, 271
✓Cran-Apple Praline Gingerbread, 200
Slow-Cooker Strawberry Soda Cake, 237

MUSHROOMS
Caramelized Mushroom & Onion Frittata, 164
Mushroom Pork Ragout, 83
Spicy Bratwurst Supper, 98

NOODLES
Ceylon Chicken Curry & Rice Noodle Soup, 39
Chicken Noodle Cheese Logs, 235
Hamburger Noodle Casserole, 86
Mushroom Pork Ragout, 83
✓Ramen Noodle Stir-Fry, 51
Spicy Thai-Inspired Noodle Watermelon Salad, 29

NUTELLA
Chocolate-Hazelnut Espresso Cinnamon Rolls, 173
Cranberry Nutella Sandwich Cookies, 183
Hazelnut Mocha Drinking Chocolate, 214
Mocha Hazelnut Torte, 207

NUTS
(also see Peanuts & Peanut Butter)
✓Air-Fryer Almond Chicken, 58
✓Best Ever Cashew Cheese Sauce, 126

Blue Cheese & Toasted Almond Guacamole, 103
Butter Pecan Cheesecake, 212
Caramel Heavenlies, 186
Cinnamon Toasted Almonds, 231
Coconut-Macadamia Sheet-Pan Pancakes, 241
Cranberry Pecan Cookies, 185
✓Fruit & Almond Bites, 184
Gluten-Free Brownie Bars, 182
Grandma's Apple Cake, 200
Hazelnut Macarons, 188
Lady Baltimore Cake, 201
✓Maple Bacon Walnut Coffee Cake, 170
Maple Pecan Pie, 199
✓Mocha-Walnut Macarons, 179
Momma's Green Beans, 289
Oatmeal Breakfast Bars, 162
✓Pear Quinoa Breakfast Bake, 163
Pumpkin Pie Tartlets with Maple Pecan Crust, 203
Reuben Cheese Logs, 235
Rocky Road Krispies Treats, 181
Rolled Butter Almond Cookies, 177
✓Romesco Sauce, 136
Salted Caramel Pretzel Krispies Treats, 181
Sweet Potato Spice Bread, 152
✓Warm Spiced Nuts, 279

OATS

Fruitcake Cookies, 301
Oatmeal Breakfast Bars, 162
Spicy Oatmeal Cookie Mix, 178
✓Strawberry Overnight Oats, 171
✓Tex-Mex Grain Bowl, 172

OLIVES

Baked Pasta Puttanesca, 66
Blue-Ribbon Beef Nachos, 7
Feta & Olive Cheese Logs, 235
Greek Tilapia, 82
Hot Chili Cheese Dip, 248
Smashed Olives, 19

ONIONS

Apple & White Onion Guacamole, 103
Caramelized Mushroom & Onion Frittata, 164
✓Gobi Aloo, 139
Green Onion Rolls, 147
Lebanese Street Sandwiches, 41
The Best Quiche Lorraine, 170

ORANGE

Chili-Orange Drinking Chocolate, 214
Citrus Cantaloupe Butter, 130
✓Citrus Fennel Salad, 290
Jazzy Gelatin, 212
Orange Gumdrops, 189
✓Portuguese Shrimp, 61
Radish & Mandarin Orange Guacamole, 102
Southern Lane Cake, 196
Tropical Sweet Potato Bake, 237
Tuscan Sun Orange Cranberry Cake, 206

PARSLEY

Blue Cheese Logs, 235
Lebanese Street Sandwiches, 41
Lebanese Stuffed Cabbages, 68
✓Lemon Red Potatoes, 114
✓Mean Green Smoothie Bowls, 160
✓Pumpkin & Chicken Sausage Hash, 161
✓Romesco Sauce, 136
✓Sage Turkey Sausage Patties, 242
Steak Sandwiches with Crispy Onions, 46
✓Tabbouleh, 26

PASTA
(also see Noodles)

Angel Hair Pasta with Sausage & Spinach, 57
Antipasto Picnic Salad, 233
Bacon Mac & Cheese Cornbread Skillet, 137
Baked Pasta Puttanesca, 66
Barbecue Macaroni Salad, 25
Beer & Bacon Macaroni & Cheese, 89
Caprese Macaroni Salad, 24
✓Cherry Tomato Pasta with Avocado Sauce, 129
Chicken Caesar Macaroni Salad, 24
Chicken Scampi, 56
Chicken Taco Macaroni Salad, 25
Chicken with Pumpkin Alfredo, 64
Cubano Macaroni Salad, 25
Fettuccine Alfredo, 97
Grecian Macaroni Salad, 24
✓Hearty Homemade Chicken Noodle Soup, 41
Mexican Lasagna, 87
Middle Eastern Macaroni Salad, 24
One-Skillet Lasagna, 50
Polynesian Macaroni Salad, 25
Ravioli Casserole, 84
Scandinavian Macaroni Salad, 24
Seafood Alfredo, 97
Shrimp & Crab Macaroni Salad, 25
Smoked Macaroni & Cheese, 238
Spaghetti with Bacon, 71
✓Summer Zucchini Pasta, 136
Tasty Tuna Casserole, 78

PEACHES

Peach Bavarian, 213
Peaches & Cream Whiskey Loaf, 156
✓Peachy Danish Pancake Balls (Aebleskiver), 166
✓Peachy Jalapeno Guacamole, 100
Peachy-Keen Halloumi Fritters, 13

PEANUTS & PEANUT BUTTER

Campfire Dessert Cones, 232
Candy Bar Fudge, 176
Funky Monkey Krispies Treats, 181
Kiddie Crunch Mix, 241
Pacoca (Brazilian Peanut Candy), 185
Peanut Butter & Jelly Cheesecake, 219
Peanut Butter Cinnamon Snap Cookies, 296
✓Peanut Butter Granola Pinwheels, 261
Peanut Butter Silk Pie, 203
Salted Peanut Squares, 186
Spicy Thai-Inspired Noodle Watermelon Salad, 29
✓Strawberry Overnight Oats, 171
✓Warm Spiced Nuts, 279

PEPPERS
(see Bell Peppers; Hot Peppers)

PESTO

BLT Bruschetta, 99
Easy Pesto Pizza, 99
Pesto Cheese Logs, 235
Pesto Hamburgers, 99

PIES & TARTS

All-American Pie, 240
Banana Fudge Pie, 204
Cherry Plum Slab Pie with Walnut Streusel, 196
Classic Butter Pie Pastry, 199
✓Cran-Apple Praline Gingerbread, 200
Five-Minute Blueberry Pie, 194
Ganache-Topped Pumpkin Tart, 192
Huckleberry Cheese Pie, 204
Mama's Coconut Pie, 206
Maple-Glazed Apple Pie, 207
Maple Pecan Pie, 199
Peanut Butter Silk Pie, 203
Pumpkin Pie Tartlets with Maple Pecan Crust, 203
The Best Sweet Potato Pie, 195
Triple Berry Mini Pies, 205

PINEAPPLE & PINEAPPLE JUICE

Barbecued Party Starters, 230
Cranberry Ambrosia Salad, 23
Hawaiian Egg Rolls, 265
✓Healthy Avocado Pineapple Muffins, 150
Jicama & Pineapple Guacamole, 103
Nutty Hawaiian, 264
✓Pineapple Poke Cake, 198

PINEAPPLE & PINEAPPLE JUICE (*continued*)
Pineapple Salsa, 265
Pineapple Sweet Potato Casserole with Marshmallows, 140
Pumpkin Cheese Ball, 278

PIZZAS
✓Chipotle Pumpkin Chicken Pizza, 71
Easy Pesto Pizza, 99
Steakhouse Pizza, 79
Waffle-Iron Pizzas, 53

POPCORN
Peppermint Popcorn, 295
Popcorn Cookies, 187

PORK
Cubano Macaroni Salad, 25
Mom's Oven-Barbecued Ribs, 75
Mushroom Pork Ragout, 83
Polpette di Mamma, 243
✓Pork Chops with Nectarine Salsa, 59
Pork Sandwiches with Root Beer Barbecue Sauce, 232
✓ Southwestern Pork & Squash Soup, 110
Whiskey Barbecue Pork, 248

POTATOES
Bacon Hash Brown Bake, 256
✓Chickpea & Potato Curry, 122
Duo Tater Bake, 292
Flavorful Mashed Potatoes, 285
Fried Mashed Potato Balls, 139
✓Grandma's Classic Potato Salad, 30
Granny's Apple Scalloped Potatoes, 134
Irish Beef Stew, 47
Italian Chicken Stew, 98
✓Lemon Red Potatoes, 114
✓Lentil Pumpkin Soup, 115
Malai Kofta, 75
✓New England Lamb Bake, 89
Potato Latke Funnel Cakes, 6
Potato Soup, 120
Rustic Fish Chowder, 38
Samosas, 17
Sausage Potato Skillet, 54
Slow-Cooker Baked Potatoes, 248
✓Spicy Hash Brown Waffles with Fried Eggs, 101
Swiss Potato Puffs, 242
Swiss Potato Soup, 40

PRESSURE-COOKER RECIPES
✓Gobi Aloo, 139
Lora's Pressure-Cooker Red Beans & Rice, 112
Malai Kofta, 75
Pressure-Cooker Apple Balsamic Chicken, 119
Pressure-Cooker Beef Short Ribs Vindaloo, 113
Pressure-Cooker Beefy Cabbage Bean Stew, 123
Pressure-Cooker Chicken Tikka Masala, 111
Pressure-Cooker Chickpea & Potato Curry, 122
Pressure-Cooker Garden Chicken Cacciatore, 121
Pressure-Cooker Lemon Red Potatoes, 114
Pressure-Cooker Lentil Pumpkin Soup, 115
Pressure-Cooker Potato Soup, 120
Pressure-Cooker Saucy Indian-Style Chicken & Vegetables, 116
Pressure-Cooker Southwestern Pork & Squash Soup, 110
Pressure-Cooker Turkey Chili, 118
Pressure-Cooker Winter Fruit Compote, 117

PUMPKIN
Autumn Harvest Pumpkin Pie, 286
Chicken with Pumpkin Alfredo, 64
✓Chipotle Pumpkin Chicken Pizza, 71
Ganache-Topped Pumpkin Tart, 192
✓Lentil Pumpkin Soup, 115
✓Pumpkin & Chicken Sausage Hash, 161
Pumpkin Butter, 141
Pumpkin Cheese Ball, 278
Pumpkin Clam Chowder, 45
Pumpkin Crunch Parfaits, 222
Pumpkin Egg Braid, 291
Pumpkin French Toast with Bacon Maple Syrup, 163
Pumpkin Pie Tartlets with Maple Pecan Crust, 203
Pumpkin Rugelach with Cream Cheese Icing, 225
Pumpkin Spice Drinking Chocolate, 214
Snickerdoodle Pumpkin Bread, 150

RADISHES
Quick Pickled Radishes, 127
Radish & Mandarin Orange Guacamole, 102

RAISINS
Bacon Breakfast Cookies, 161
Kiddie Crunch Mix, 241
Lady Baltimore Cake, 201
Raisin Rye Muffins, 153
Southern Lane Cake, 196

RASPBERRIES
Chocolate-Raspberry Krispies Treats, 181
Mixed Berry Tiramisu, 216
New York Cheesecake with Shortbread Crust, 215
Raspberry-Ginger Frozen Margarita, 11
Triple Berry Mini Pies, 205

RICE
Black Bean Rice Burgers, 40
Creamy Cauliflower Rice, 142
Hot Chili Cheese Dip, 248
✓Lora's Red Beans & Rice, 112
Madras Curried Eggs with Rice, 79
Poppy Seed Chicken, 93
✓Portuguese Shrimp, 61
✓Quick & Easy Chicken Poke Bowl, 76
Rose Water Rice Pudding, 210
✓Simple Salsa Chicken, 83
✓Tex-Mex Grain Bowl, 172

SALADS & DRESSINGS
Dressings
French Dressing, 28
✓Italian Dressing, 27
Fruit Salads
✓Apple Matchstick Salad, 32
Cranberry Ambrosia Salad, 23
Quick Ambrosia Fruit Salad, 257
Special Fruit Salad, 27
Green Salads
Grilled Romaine Salad, 26
✓Spinach Salad with Goat Cheese & Beets, 22
Main-Dish Salads
Chicken Strawberry Spinach Salad, 29
Grilled Tuna Salad, 32
Mandarin Steak Salad, 95
✓Shrimp & Scallops Tropical Salad, 22
Slow-Cooker Buffalo Chicken Salad, 23
✓Tarragon Tuna Salad, 28
Other Salads
✓Citrus Fennel Salad, 290
Farro Salad with Charred Shishito Peppers & Corn, 30
✓Grandma's Classic Potato Salad, 30
✓Minted Beet Salad, 33
✓Tabbouleh, 26
✓Watermelon "Pizza", 33
Pasta Salads
Antipasto Picnic Salad, 233
Barbecue Macaroni Salad, 25
Caprese Macaroni Salad, 24
Chicken Caesar Macaroni Salad, 24
Chicken Taco Macaroni Salad, 25
Cubano Macaroni Salad, 25
Grecian Macaroni Salad, 24
Middle Eastern Macaroni Salad, 24
Polynesian Macaroni Salad, 25

Scandinavian Macaroni Salad, 24
Shrimp & Crab Macaroni Salad, 25
Spicy Thai-Inspired Noodle Watermelon Salad, 29

SALSA

Coconut Chicken Nuggets with Creamy Caribbean Salsa, 81
✓Green Tomato Salsa, 19
Hot Chili Cheese Dip, 248
Pineapple Salsa, 265
✓Pork Chops with Nectarine Salsa, 59
✓Shrimp Tostadas with Avocado Salsa, 53
✓Simple Salsa Chicken, 83
✓Slow-Cooked Salsa, 248
✓Tex-Mex Grain Bowl, 172
✓Watermelon & Cucumber Salsa, 260

SANDWICHES & WRAPS

Black Bean Rice Burgers, 40
Brown Sugar Bacon BLT Sandwiches, 38
Chicken Alfredo Sandwiches, 97
Chiles Rellenos Croque-Madame, 160
Freezer Breakfast Sandwiches, 165
General Tso's Chicken Sandwich with Broccoli Slaw, 42
✓Grandma's French Tuna Salad Wraps, 39
Grilled Pimiento Cheese Sandwiches, 44
Hoisin Chicken Wraps, 45
Hot Italian Party Sandwiches, 230
Kilbourn Sandwich, 36
Lebanese Street Sandwiches, 41
Meatball Subs, 98
My Juicy Lucy, 37
Pesto Hamburgers, 99
Pork Sandwiches with Root Beer Barbecue Sauce, 232
Salmon Croquette Breakfast Sandwich, 169
✓Salsa Black Bean Burgers, 101
Steak Sandwiches with Crispy Onions, 46
Toasted Chicken Salad Sandwiches, 47
Turkey Ranch Wraps, 46
Whiskey Barbecue Pork, 248

SAUSAGE

Angel Hair Pasta with Sausage & Spinach, 57
Antipasto Picnic Salad, 233
Barbecued Party Starters, 230
Chili Queso Dip, 18
Currywurst, 275
Frijoles y Chorizo, 133
Grilled Jalapenos, 238
Grits & Sausage Casserole, 254
Homemade Biscuits & Maple Sausage Gravy, 252
Hot Dog Mummies with Honey Mustard Dip, 279
Hot Italian Party Sandwiches, 230
Jalapeno Sausage Quiche, 236
✓Lora's Red Beans & Rice, 112
Mini Corn Dogs, 269
Pepper Jelly Hogs in a Blanket, 9
Pepperoni Pizza Cheese Logs, 235
✓Pumpkin & Chicken Sausage Hash, 161
Sausage & Pancake Bake, 171
Sausage Potato Skillet, 54
Sheet-Pan Jambalaya with Cauliflower Rice, 69
Spicy Bratwurst Supper, 98
✓Traditional Holiday Stuffing, 283
Waffle-Iron Pizzas, 53

SEAFOOD
(also see Fish)

Cajun Shrimp & Red Pepper Guacamole, 102
Caribbean Shrimp Bowl, 57
Easy Coconut Shrimp, 264
Grilled Shrimp with Cilantro Dipping Sauce, 65
Hot Shrimp Dip, 13
✓Portuguese Shrimp, 61
Pumpkin Clam Chowder, 45
Scandinavian Macaroni Salad, 24
Seafood Alfredo, 97
Sheet-Pan Jambalaya with Cauliflower Rice, 69
Shrimp & Crab Macaroni Salad, 25
✓Shrimp & Scallops Tropical Salad, 22
✓Shrimp Tostadas with Avocado Salsa, 53
✓Stir-Fried Scallops, 61

SIDE DISHES

Bacon Mac & Cheese Cornbread Skillet, 137
Cauliflower au Gratin, 233
✓Cherry Tomato Pasta with Avocado Sauce, 129
Corn Pudding, 285
Creamy Cauliflower Rice, 142
Duo Tater Bake, 292
Elegant Green Beans, 284
Fiesta Corn, 141
Flavorful Mashed Potatoes, 285
Fried Mashed Potato Balls, 139
Frijoles y Chorizo, 133
Glazed Carrots with Green Grapes, 142
✓Gobi Aloo, 139
Granny's Apple Scalloped Potatoes, 134
Green Bean Bundles, 135
Grilled Elote Flatbread, 130
✓Jalapeno Green Beans, 127
✓Lemon Red Potatoes, 114
✓Maple-Gingerroot Vegetables, 292
Mashed Cauliflower with Parmesan, 128
Momma's Green Beans, 289
Pineapple Sweet Potato Casserole with Marshmallows, 140
Slow-Cooker Baked Potatoes, 248
Smoked Macaroni & Cheese, 238
Stir-Fried Zucchini, 137
✓Succotash, 126
✓Summer Zucchini Pasta, 136
✓Traditional Holiday Stuffing, 283
Triple-Cheese Broccoli Puff, 289
Tropical Sweet Potato Bake, 237

SLOW-COOKER RECIPES

Appetizers

Barbecued Party Starters, 230
Hot Chili Cheese Dip, 248
✓Slow-Cooked Salsa, 248

Main Dishes

Hearty Chicken Enchiladas, 74
Lora's Slow-Cooker Red Beans & Rice, 112
Mint Lamb Stew, 73
Mushroom Pork Ragout, 83
Slow-Cooker Apple Balsamic Chicken, 119
Slow-Cooker Asian Short Ribs, 64
Slow-Cooker Beef Brisket, 87
Slow-Cooker Beef Short Ribs Vindaloo, 113
Slow-Cooker Beefy Cabbage Bean Stew, 123
Slow-Cooker Buffalo Chicken Salad, 23
Slow-Cooker Chicken Tikka Masala, 111
Slow-Cooker Chickpea & Potato Curry, 122
Slow-Cooker Garden Chicken Cacciatore, 121
Slow-Cooker Saucy Indian-Style Chicken & Vegetables, 116

Other

Hot Spiced Cranberry Drink, 286
Slow-Cooker Strawberry Soda Cake, 237
Slow-Cooker Winter Fruit Compote, 117

Sandwiches

Pork Sandwiches with Root Beer Barbecue Sauce, 232
Whiskey Barbecue Pork, 248

Side Dishes

Glazed Carrots with Green Grapes, 142
Slow-Cooker Baked Potatoes, 248
Slow-Cooker Lemon Red Potatoes, 114

Soups

✓Hearty Homemade Chicken Noodle Soup, 41

SLOW-COOKER RECIPES (*continued*)

Soups

Mexican Street Corn Chowder, 42
✓Salmon Sweet Potato Soup, 44
Slow-Cooker Lentil Pumpkin Soup, 115
Slow-Cooker Potato Soup, 120
Slow-Cooker Southwestern Pork & Squash Soup, 110
Slow-Cooker Turkey Chili, 118

SOUPS

Ceylon Chicken Curry & Rice Noodle Soup, 39
✓Hearty Homemade Chicken Noodle Soup, 41
Irish Beef Stew, 47
✓Lentil Pumpkin Soup, 115
Mexican Street Corn Chowder, 42
Potato Soup, 120
Pumpkin Clam Chowder, 45
Quick Tomato Soup, 37
Rustic Fish Chowder, 38
✓Salmon Sweet Potato Soup, 44
✓Southwestern Pork & Squash Soup, 110
Swiss Potato Soup, 40
Truly Texan Chili, 36
✓Turkey Chili, 118

SPINACH

Angel Hair Pasta with Sausage & Spinach, 57
Chicken Strawberry Spinach Salad, 29
Grilled Tuna Salad, 32
Spinach Chicken Frittata, 93
Spinach Puffs, 14
✓Spinach Salad with Goat Cheese & Beets, 22

STRAWBERRIES

Berry Pretzel Fluff Dessert, 218
Best Strawberry Shortcake, 255
Biscuit Strawberry Shortcake, 217
Chicken Strawberry Spinach Salad, 29
Mixed Berry Tiramisu, 216
Strawberry-Basil Frozen Margarita, 11
Strawberry Butter, 143
✓Strawberry Overnight Oats, 171
Triple Berry Mini Pies, 205
Warm Strawberry Fondue, 17

SWEET POTATOES

Duo Tater Bake, 292
✓Gluten-Free Spiced Sweet Potato Muffins, 148
Pineapple Sweet Potato Casserole with Marshmallows, 140
✓Salmon Sweet Potato Soup, 44
Sweet Potato Spice Bread, 152
The Best Sweet Potato Pie, 195
Tropical Sweet Potato Bake, 237

TOMATOES

Baked Chicken & Zucchini, 69
BLT Bruschetta, 99
Breakfast BLT Waffles, 166
Brown Sugar Bacon BLT Sandwiches, 38
Caprese Macaroni Salad, 24
✓Cherry Tomato Pasta with Avocado Sauce, 129
Fiesta Corn, 141
✓Gobi Aloo, 139
✓Green Tomato Salsa, 19
Grilled Chicken & Cherry Tomato Guacamole, 102
Grilled Romaine Salad, 26
Homemade Marinara Sauce, 98
Madras Curried Eggs with Rice, 79
Polpette di Mamma, 243
Salmon Croquette Breakfast Sandwich, 169
Salmon Grilled in Foil, 58
Sheet-Pan Jambalaya with Cauliflower Rice, 69
✓Slow-Cooked Salsa, 248
Spaghetti with Bacon, 71
✓Stir-Fried Scallops, 61
✓Summer Zucchini Pasta, 136
✓Tabbouleh, 26
Tomato Galette with Basil Pesto & Feta, 12

TORTILLAS

Chimichangas, 59
Crunchy Burger Quesadillas, 54
✓Grandma's French Tuna Salad Wraps, 39
Hearty Chicken Enchiladas, 74
Hoisin Chicken Wraps, 45
Mexican Steak Fajitas, 60
✓Peanut Butter Granola Pinwheels, 261
Steak Tortillas, 95
Turkey Ranch Wraps, 46

TURKEY

Broccoli Turkey Casserole, 68
✓Herbed Roast Turkey Breast, 84
Kilbourn Sandwich, 36
✓Rosemary Turkey Breast, 231
✓Sage Turkey Sausage Patties, 242
✓Turkey Chili, 118
Turkey Ranch Wraps, 46

VEGETABLES (*also see specific kinds*)

✓Beef Tenderloin with Roasted Vegetables, 243
✓Beefy Cabbage Bean Stew, 123
Breakfast BLT Waffles, 166
Chicken Caesar Macaroni Salad, 24
✓Citrus Fennel Salad, 290
Collards Quiche, 253
Farro Salad with Charred Shishito Peppers & Corn, 30
✓Hearty Homemade Chicken Noodle Soup, 41
Hoisin Chicken Wraps, 45
✓Maple-Gingerroot Vegetables, 292
✓Mean Green Smoothie Bowls, 160
Mint Lamb Stew, 73
✓Saucy Indian-Style Chicken & Vegetables, 116
✓ Southwestern Pork & Squash Soup, 110
✓Succotash, 126
✓Tarragon Tuna Salad, 28

VEGETARIAN/MEATLESS

Appetizers

Apple & White Onion Guacamole, 103
Basil & Toasted Pine Nut Guacamole, 22
Best Deviled Eggs, 15
Black Bean & Corn Guacamole, 103
Blue Cheese & Toasted Almond Guacamole, 103
Blue Cheese Logs, 235
Buffalo Cheese Logs, 235
Curried Apricot Cheese Logs, 235
Feta & Olive Cheese Logs, 235
✓Green Tomato Salsa, 19
Hot Chili Cheese Dip, 248
Jicama & Pineapple Guacamole, 103
Lake Charles Dip, 269
Mango & Habanero Guacamole, 103
Nacho Cheese Logs, 235
Obatzda (German Beer Cheese Dip), 275
Pesto Cheese Logs, 235
Pineapple Salsa, 265
Radish & Mandarin Orange Guacamole, 102
✓Red Lentil Hummus with Brussels Sprout Hash, 16
Samosas, 17
✓Slow-Cooked Salsa, 248
Smashed Olives, 19
Tomato Galette with Basil Pesto & Feta, 12
Warm Strawberry Fondue, 17
✓Watermelon & Cucumber Salsa, 260
✓Zucchini Pizza Fritters, 6

Breakfast & Brunch

Caramelized Mushroom & Onion Frittata, 164
✓Crispy French Toast, 168

✓High-Octane Pancakes, 165
✓Pear Quinoa Breakfast Bake, 163
Spicy Hash Brown Waffles with Fried Eggs, 101
✓Strawberry Overnight Oats, 171
✓Tex-Mex Grain Bowl, 172
Main Dishes
✓Chickpea & Potato Curry, 122
Easy Pesto Pizza, 99
Fettuccine Alfredo, 97
Madras Curried Eggs with Rice, 79
Malai Kofta, 75
Ravioli Casserole, 84
Sandwiches
Black Bean Rice Burgers, 40
✓Salsa Black Bean Burgers, 101
Soups
✓Lentil Pumpkin Soup, 115
Mexican Street Corn Chowder, 42
Quick Tomato Soup, 37

WATERMELON
Spicy Thai-Inspired Noodle Watermelon Salad, 29
✓Watermelon & Cucumber Salsa, 260
✓Watermelon "Pizza", 33

WHITE CHOCOLATE
Birthday Cake Fudge, 179
Brandy Alexander Fudge, 302
Campfire Dessert Cones, 232
Cranberry Pecan Cookies, 185
Creamy White Drinking Chocolate, 214
Oreo Krispies Treats, 181
Peppermint Red Velvet Drinking Chocolate, 214
Sparkly Princess Krispies Treats, 181

ZUCCHINI & SUMMER SQUASH
Baked Chicken & Zucchini, 69
✓Carrot Zucchini Bread, 146
Chocolate Zucchini Cookies, 177
Stir-Fried Zucchini, 137
Summer Squash Pound Cake, 194
✓Summer Zucchini Pasta, 136
Zucchini Pickles, 133
✓Zucchini Pizza Fritters, 6

Alphabetical Index

✓ Indicates an Eat Smart recipe

A
✓Air-Fryer Almond Chicken, 58
Air-Fryer Nashville Hot Chicken, 73
Air-Fryer Spicy Ginger Beef Skewers, 81
Alabama White BBQ Sauce, 143
Alfredo Sauce, 97
All-American Pie, 240
Almost It's-It Ice Cream Sandwiches, 216
Amaretto Margarita, 10
Angel Hair Pasta with Sausage & Spinach, 57
Antipasto Picnic Salad, 233
Apple & White Onion Guacamole, 103
Apple Balsamic Chicken, 119
Apple Cider Biscuits, 154
Apple Honey Tapioca Pudding, 223
✓Apple Matchstick Salad, 32
Apricot Bars, 184
✓Apricot Upside-Down Cake, 205
Ash's Sweet & Spicy Enchilada Sauce, 132

B
Bacon & Cotija Cheese Guacamole, 103
Bacon Breakfast Cookies, 161
Bacon Hash Brown Bake, 256
Bacon Mac & Cheese Cornbread Skillet, 137
Baked Chicken & Zucchini, 69
Baked Pasta Puttanesca, 66
Banana Fudge Pie, 204
Barbecue Macaroni Salad, 25
Barbecued Party Starters, 230
Basic Cookie Dough, 104
Beef Short Ribs Vindaloo, 113
✓Beef Tenderloin with Roasted Vegetables, 243
✓Beefy Cabbage Bean Stew, 123
Beer & Bacon Macaroni & Cheese, 89
Berry Pretzel Fluff Dessert, 218
Best Deviled Eggs, 15
✓Best Ever Cashew Cheese Sauce, 126
Best Ever Vanilla Ice Cream, 226
Best Strawberry Shortcake, 255
Birthday Cake Fudge, 179
Biscoff Drinking Chocolate, 214
Biscuit Strawberry Shortcake, 217
Black Bean & Corn Guacamole, 103
Black Bean Rice Burgers, 40
Blackberry Shrub, 12
BLT Bruschetta, 99
Blue Cheese & Toasted Almond Guacamole, 103
Blue Cheese Logs, 235
Blue-Ribbon Beef Nachos, 7
Blueberry-Mint Frozen Margarita, 11
Bones & Blood, 277
Boston Brown Bread, 156
Brandy Alexander Fudge, 302
Breakfast BLT Waffles, 166
Brie Cherry Pastry Cups, 290
Broccoli Turkey Casserole, 68
Brown Sugar Bacon BLT Sandwiches, 38
Brownie Haunted House, 277
Brownie Kiss Cupcakes, 201
Buffalo Cheese Logs, 235
Butter Brickle Biscotti, 176
Butter Pecan Cheesecake, 212

C
Cajun Shrimp & Red Pepper Guacamole, 102
Campfire Dessert Cones, 232
Candy Bar Fudge, 176
Caprese Macaroni Salad, 24
Caramel Apple Krispies Treats, 181
Caramel Heavenlies, 186
Caramelized Mushroom & Onion Frittata, 164
Caraway Puffs, 149
Caribbean Margarita, 10
Caribbean Shrimp Bowl, 57
✓Carrot Zucchini Bread, 146
Catfish Parmesan, 70
Cauliflower au Gratin, 233
Ceylon Chicken Curry & Rice Noodle Soup, 39
Chai Drinking Chocolate, 214
Cheese & Pimiento Spread, 260
Cherry-Go-Round, 155
Cherry Plum Slab Pie with Walnut Streusel, 196
Cherry Surprise Cookies, 106
✓Cherry Tomato Pasta with Avocado Sauce, 129
✓Chewy Cookies, 271
Chewy Soft Pretzels, 275
Chicken Alfredo Sandwiches, 97
Chicken Biscuit Skillet, 52
✓Chicken Breasts with Melon Relish, 50
Chicken Caesar Macaroni Salad, 24
Chicken-Fried Steaks, 60
Chicken Noodle Cheese Logs, 235
Chicken Scampi, 56
Chicken Strawberry Spinach Salad, 29
Chicken Taco Macaroni Salad, 25
✓Chicken Tikka Masala, 111
Chicken with Pumpkin Alfredo, 64
✓Chickpea & Potato Curry, 122
Chiles Rellenos Croque-Madame, 160
Chili Queso Dip, 18

Chili-Orange Drinking Chocolate, 214
Chimichangas, 59
✓Chipotle Pumpkin Chicken Pizza, 71
Chive Butter Balls, 248
Chocolate Caramel Cookies, 268
Chocolate Caramels, 188
Chocolate Chip Muffins, 154
Chocolate-Covered Cherries, 299
Chocolate-Hazelnut Espresso Cinnamon Rolls, 173
Chocolate Mallow Cookies, 105
Chocolate-Raspberry Krispies Treats, 181
Chocolate Yeast Bread, 148
Chocolate Zucchini Cookies, 177
Christmas Star Twisted Bread, 302
Cinnamon Blueberry Jam, 129
Cinnamon Toasted Almonds, 231
Citrus Cantaloupe Butter, 130
✓Citrus Fennel Salad, 290
Classic Butter Pie Pastry, 199
Classic Lemon Bars, 178
Classic Margarita, 10
Classic Pesto, 99
Classic Sugar Cookies, 107
Coconut Chicken Nuggets with Creamy Caribbean Salsa, 81
Coconut Egg Nests, 189
Coconut-Macadamia Sheet-Pan Pancakes, 241
Coffee Ice Cream, 218
Collards Quiche, 253
Conchas (Seashells), 157
Corn Pudding, 285
✓Cran-Apple Praline Gingerbread, 200
Cranberry Ambrosia Salad, 23
Cranberry Cherry Punch, 268
Cranberry Nutella Sandwich Cookies, 183
Cranberry Pecan Cookies, 185
Cream Cheese Red Velvet Thumbprint Cookies, 295
Creamy Cauliflower Rice, 142
Creamy Corn Custards, 213
Creamy White Drinking Chocolate, 214
Crispy Christmas Trees, 294
✓Crispy French Toast, 168
Cristen's Giant Cinnamon Rolls, 153
Crumb-Topped Date Bars, 106
✓Crumb-Topped Sole, 51
Crunchy Burger Quesadillas, 54
Cubano Macaroni Salad, 25
Curried Apricot Cheese Logs, 235
Currywurst, 275

D

Dad's Lemony Grilled Chicken, 86
Double Chocolate Espresso Cheesecake, 220
Double Chocolate Scones, 147
Duo Tater Bake, 292

E

Easy Cheesy Cauliflower Breakfast Casserole, 169
Easy Coconut Shrimp, 264
✓Easy Marinated Grilled Flank Steak, 94
Easy Pesto Pizza, 99
Eggnog Tres Leches Cake, 192
Elegant Green Beans, 284
Eyes On You, 278

F

Farro Salad with Charred Shishito Peppers & Corn, 30
Favorite Hot Chocolate, 260
Feta & Olive Cheese Logs, 235
Feta-Stuffed Kibbeh with Harissa, 66
Fettuccine Alfredo, 97
Fiesta Corn, 141
Finnish Cheese Pie, 164
Five-Minute Blueberry Pie, 194
Flavorful Mashed Potatoes, 285
Freezer Breakfast Sandwiches, 165
French Dressing, 28
French Toast Spirals, 183
Fried Banana Milkshakes, 215
Fried Ice Cream Dessert Bars, 211
Fried Mashed Potato Balls, 139
Frijoles y Chorizo, 133
Frozen Coconut Margarita, 11
✓Fruit & Almond Bites, 184
Fruitcake Cookies, 301
Funky Monkey Krispies Treats, 181

G

Galaxy Bites, 273
Ganache-Topped Pumpkin Tart, 192
✓Garden Chicken Cacciatore, 121
Garden Herb Drop Biscuits, 152
Garlic Mozzarella Bread Bites, 18
Garlic Rosemary Pull-Apart Bread, 149
General Tso's Chicken Sandwich with Broccoli Slaw, 42
Gingersnap Dip, 236
Glazed Carrots with Green Grapes, 142
Gluten-Free Brownie Bars, 182
✓Gluten-Free Spiced Sweet Potato Muffins, 148
✓Gobi Aloo, 139
Goody-Goody Gumdrops, 303
Grandma's Apple Cake, 200
✓Grandma's Classic Potato Salad, 30
✓Grandma's French Tuna Salad Wraps, 39
Granny's Apple Scalloped Potatoes, 134
Grapefruit Sunset Margarita, 10
Grecian Macaroni Salad, 24
Greek Tilapia, 82
Green Bean Bundles, 135
Green Onion Rolls, 147
✓Green Tomato Salsa, 19
Grilled Chicken & Cherry Tomato Guacamole, 102
Grilled Elote Flatbread, 130
Grilled Jalapenos, 238
Grilled Pimiento Cheese Sandwiches, 44
Grilled Romaine Salad, 26
Grilled Shrimp with Cilantro Dipping Sauce, 65
Grilled Tuna Salad, 32
Grits & Sausage Casserole, 254
Ground Beef Wellingtons, 65
Gumdrop Cookies, 182

H

Hamburger Noodle Casserole, 86
Hamburger Stroganoff, 52
Hawaiian Egg Rolls, 265
Hazelnut Macarons, 188
Hazelnut Mocha Drinking Chocolate, 214
✓Healthy Avocado Pineapple Muffins, 150
Hearty Chicken Enchiladas, 74
✓Hearty Homemade Chicken Noodle Soup, 41
Heavenly Cheese Danish, 155
Heavenly Nutmeg Drinking Chocolate, 214
✓Herbed Roast Turkey Breast, 84
✓High-Octane Pancakes, 165
Hoisin Chicken Wraps, 45
Holiday Pretzel Salad, 211
Home-Style Roast Beef, 78
Homemade Biscuits & Maple Sausage Gravy, 252
Homemade Marinara Sauce, 98
Homemade Taco Seasoning Mix, 128
Hot Chili Cheese Dip, 248
Hot Cider, 280
Hot Dog Mummies with Honey Mustard Dip, 279
Hot Italian Party Sandwiches, 230
Hot Shrimp Dip, 13
Hot Spiced Cranberry Drink, 286
Huckleberry Cheese Pie, 204

I

Indian-Spiced Beefy Lettuce Wraps, 56
Indonesian Bananas Foster, 217
Irish Beef Stew, 47
Italian Chicken Stew, 98
✓Italian Dressing, 27

J

✓Jalapeno Green Beans, 127
Jalapeno Sausage Quiche, 236
Jazzy Gelatin, 212

Jelly Sandwich Cookies, 105
Jicama & Pineapple Guacamole, 103

K
Kiddie Crunch Mix, 241
Kilbourn Sandwich, 36

L
Lady Baltimore Cake, 201
Lake Charles Dip, 269
Lebanese Street Sandwiches, 41
Lebanese Stuffed Cabbages, 68
✓Lemon-Apricot Fruit Pops, 220
Lemon, Ginger & Turmeric Infused Water, 8
✓Lemon Red Potatoes, 114
✓Lentil Pumpkin Soup, 115
Lightsaber Pretzels, 273
✓Lora's Red Beans & Rice, 112

M
Madras Curried Eggs with Rice, 79
Malai Kofta, 75
Mama's Coconut Pie, 206
Mandarin Steak Salad, 95
Mango & Habanero Guacamole, 103
Maple-Bacon Krispies Treats, 181
✓Maple Bacon Walnut Coffee Cake, 170
Maple Blueberry Crisp, 223
✓Maple-Gingerroot Vegetables, 292
Maple-Glazed Apple Pie, 207
Maple Pecan Pie, 199
Maple-Sage Brined Turkey, 283
Mashed Cauliflower with Parmesan, 128
✓Mean Green Smoothie Bowls, 160
Meatball Subs, 98
Melon Margarita, 10
Mexican Lasagna, 87
Mexican Steak Fajitas, 60
Mexican Street Corn Chowder, 42
Middle Eastern Macaroni Salad, 24
Mincemeat-Filled Braid, 298
Mini Corn Dogs, 269
✓Mint Chutney, 132
Mint Lamb Stew, 73
✓Minted Beet Salad, 33
Minty Cookies & Cream Chocolate Fudge, 296
Mixed Berry Tiramisu, 216
Mocha Hazelnut Torte, 207
✓Mocha-Walnut Macarons, 179
Mom's Oven-Barbecued Ribs, 75
Momma's Green Beans, 289
Morning Buzz Krispies Treats, 181
✓Muffin-Tin Scrambled Eggs, 168
Mulled Wine Margaritas, 15
Mushroom Pork Ragout, 83
My Juicy Lucy, 37

N
Nacho Cheese Logs, 235
✓New England Lamb Bake, 89
New York Cheesecake with Shortbread Crust, 215
Nutty Hawaiian, 264

O
Oatmeal Breakfast Bars, 162
Obatzda (German Beer Cheese Dip), 275
One-Skillet Lasagna, 50
Orange Gumdrops, 189
Oreo Krispies Treats, 181

P
Pacoca (Brazilian Peanut Candy), 185
Parisian Sipping Chocolate, 210
Peach Bavarian, 213
Peaches & Cream Whiskey Loaf, 156
✓Peachy Danish Pancake Balls (Aebleskiver), 166
✓Peachy Jalapeno Guacamole, 100
Peachy-Keen Halloumi Fritters, 13
Peanut Butter & Jelly Cheesecake, 219
Peanut Butter Cinnamon Snap Cookies, 296
✓Peanut Butter Granola Pinwheels, 261
Peanut Butter Silk Pie, 203
✓Pear Quinoa Breakfast Bake, 163
Pepper Jack Muffins, 157
Pepper Jelly Hogs in a Blanket, 9
Peppermint Cheesecake on a Stick, 301
Peppermint Popcorn, 295
Peppermint Red Velvet Drinking Chocolate, 214
Pepperoni Pizza Cheese Logs, 235
Pesto Cheese Logs, 235
Pesto Hamburgers, 99
Philly Cheesesteak Egg Rolls, 8
✓Pineapple Poke Cake, 198
Pineapple Salsa, 265
Pineapple Sweet Potato Casserole with Marshmallows, 140
Polpette di Mamma, 243
Polynesian Macaroni Salad, 25
Popcorn Cookies, 187
Poppy Seed Chicken, 93
✓Pork Chops with Nectarine Salsa, 59
Pork Sandwiches with Root Beer Barbecue Sauce, 232
✓Portuguese Shrimp, 61
Potato Latke Funnel Cakes, 6
Potato Soup, 120
✓Pumpkin & Chicken Sausage Hash, 161
Pumpkin Butter, 141
Pumpkin Cheese Ball, 278
Pumpkin Clam Chowder, 45
Pumpkin Crunch Parfaits, 222
Pumpkin Egg Braid, 291
Pumpkin French Toast with Bacon Maple Syrup, 163
Pumpkin Pie Tartlets with Maple Pecan Crust, 203
Pumpkin Rugelach with Cream Cheese Icing, 225
Pumpkin Spice Drinking Chocolate, 214

Q
✓Quick & Easy Chicken Poke Bowl, 76
Quick Ambrosia Fruit Salad, 257
Quick Pickled Radishes, 127
✓Quick Roasted Red Pepper Spread, 140
Quick Tomato Soup, 37

R
Radish & Mandarin Orange Guacamole, 102
Rainbow Sherbet Angel Food Cake, 219
Raisin Rye Muffins, 153
✓Ramen Noodle Stir-Fry, 51
Raspberry-Ginger Frozen Margarita, 11
Ravioli Casserole, 84
✓Red Lentil Hummus with Brussels Sprout Hash, 16
Red Velvet Cake in a Jar, 195
Reuben Cheese Logs, 235
Roasted Brussels Sprouts with Sriracha Aioli, 9
Roasted Grape & Sweet Cheese Phyllo Galette, 222
Robot Cake, 272
Rocky Road Krispies Treats, 181
Rolled Butter Almond Cookies, 177
✓Romesco Sauce, 136
Rose Water Rice Pudding, 210
✓Rosemary Turkey Breast, 231
Rustic Fish Chowder, 38

S
✓Sage Turkey Sausage Patties, 242
Salmon Croquette Breakfast Sandwich, 169
Salmon Grilled in Foil, 58
✓Salmon Sweet Potato Soup, 44
✓Salsa Black Bean Burgers, 101
Salted Caramel & Banana Drinking Chocolate, 214
Salted Caramel Pretzel Krispies Treats, 181
Salted Peanut Squares, 186
Salty Dog Sangria, 16
Samosas, 17
✓Saucy Indian-Style Chicken & Vegetables, 116
Sausage & Pancake Bake, 171
Sausage Potato Skillet, 54
Savory Roasted Chicken, 92

Scandinavian Macaroni Salad, 24
Seafood Alfredo, 97
Sheet-Pan Jambalaya with Cauliflower Rice, 69
Shrimp & Crab Macaroni Salad, 25
✓Shrimp & Scallops Tropical Salad, 22
✓Shrimp Tostadas with Avocado Salsa, 53
✓Simple Salsa Chicken, 83
Skewered Lamb with Blackberry-Balsamic Glaze, 70
✓Slow-Cooked Salsa, 248
Slow-Cooker Asian Short Ribs, 64
Slow-Cooker Baked Potatoes, 248
Slow-Cooker Beef Brisket, 87
Slow-Cooker Buffalo Chicken Salad, 23
Slow-Cooker Strawberry Soda Cake, 237
Smashed Olives, 19
Smoked Macaroni & Cheese, 238
Smoked Salmon Cheese Logs, 235
S'mores Cupcakes, 261
Snickerdoodle Drinking Chocolate, 214
Snickerdoodle Pumpkin Bread, 150
Southern Lane Cake, 196
Southwestern Pork & Squash Soup, 110
Spaghetti with Bacon, 71
Sparkly Princess Krispies Treats, 181
Special Fruit Salad, 27
Spicy Beet Relish, 135
Spicy Bratwurst Supper, 98
✓Spicy Hash Brown Waffles with Fried Eggs, 101
Spicy Oatmeal Cookie Mix, 178
Spicy Thai-Inspired Noodle Watermelon Salad, 29
Spinach Chicken Frittata, 93
Spinach Puffs, 14
✓Spinach Salad with Goat Cheese & Beets, 22
Spiral Ham with Cranberry Glaze, 288
Sriracha-Mango Frozen Margarita, 11
Steak Sandwiches with Crispy Onions, 46
Steak Tortillas, 95
Steakhouse Pizza, 79
✓Stir-Fried Scallops, 61
Stir-Fried Zucchini, 137
Strawberry-Basil Frozen Margarita, 11
Strawberry Butter, 143
✓Strawberry Overnight Oats, 171
✓Succotash, 126
Summer Squash Pound Cake, 194
✓Summer Zucchini Pasta, 136
Sunny Citrus Layered Cheesecake, 227
Swedish Flop, 193
Sweet Potato Spice Bread, 152
Sweet Tea Concentrate, 257
Swiss Potato Puffs, 242
Swiss Potato Soup, 40

T

✓Tabbouleh, 26
Tajin Limeade, 14
✓Tarragon Tuna Salad, 28
Tasty Tuna Casserole, 78
✓Tex-Mex Grain Bowl, 172
The Best French Toast, 162
The Best Grilled Sirloin Tip Roast, 82
✓The Best Hummus, 7
The Best Quiche Lorraine, 170
The Best Sweet Potato Pie, 195
Toasted Chicken Salad Sandwiches, 47
Tomato Galette with Basil Pesto & Feta, 12
Tombstone Treats, 280
✓Traditional Holiday Stuffing, 283
Triple Berry Mini Pies, 205
Triple-Cheese Broccoli Puff, 289
Tropical Sweet Potato Bake, 237
Truffle Topiary, 299
Truly Texan Chili, 36
✓Turkey Chili, 118
Turkey Ranch Wraps, 46
Tuscan Sun Orange Cranberry Cake, 206
Two-Tone Caramel Brownies, 187

V

Vanilla Bean Cupcakes, 198
Vegan Butter Cauliflower, 76
Vegan Chocolate Mousse, 225
✓Vegan Lemon Poppy Seed Doughnuts, 173
Violet Jelly, 134

W

Waffle-Iron Pizzas, 53
✓Warm Grapefruit with Ginger-Sugar, 172
✓Warm Spiced Nuts, 279
Warm Strawberry Fondue, 17
✓Watermelon & Cucumber Salsa, 260
Watermelon Krispies Treats, 181
✓Watermelon "Pizza", 33
Whiskey Barbecue Pork, 248
Winter Fruit Compote, 117
Wonderful English Muffins, 146

Y

Yoda Soda, 272

Z

Zucchini Pickles, 133
✓Zucchini Pizza Fritters, 6